In the Garden with Blue Butterflies

by

Thomas Wang

Mission Blue Butterfly Project

IN THE GARDEN WITH BLUE BUTTERFLIES

Copyright © 2010 by Thomas Y. Wang.

The book author and artist retains sole copyright to this book. No part of this book may be used or reproduced in any manner whatsoever without written permission.

ISBN 978-0-9840505-5-0
First edition: July 2010
Second edition: July 2012
Third edition: July 2014

Published by:
Mission Blue Project
San Francisco, California, USA

The **Mission Blue Butterfly Project** is working to
help butterflies and their friends,
engage people in the study of plants,
bridge the mythological and scientific worlds
in stories and pictures, and
transform our relationship within nature.

This book is dedicated to my wife
Dolores Gamez
and children,
Maria Teresa and Sebastian David

Your love and support
creates the world of blue butterflies
Thank you family

Table of Contents

Introduction

Plant world	6
Air and wind	7-19
Water and rain	20-39
Earth and soil	40-69
Fire and light	70-74
From roots to spores	75
Roots	76-87
Stems	88-105
Wood	106-117
Leaves	118-129
Growth and repair	130-150
Flowers	151-164
Pollination	165-177
Fertilization	178-183
Fruit	184-204
Seed	205-220
Spore	221-225
Amongst friends and decomposers	226
Plant parasites	227-229
Birds	230-234
Mammals	235-240
Reptiles and amphibians	241-244
Arthropods	245-256
Fungi	257-265
Worms	266-269
Snails and slugs	270-273
Bacteria and relatives	274-283
Viruses	284-288

Families and teachers	289
Cone or no cone	290-295
Botany versus horticulture	296-310
Two groups of flowering plants	311-315
Vascular systems	316-319
Leafy diversity	320-335
Folk and butterfly classification	336-340
Transformation	341
Atoms and molecules	342-350
Elements and compounds	351-358
Ions	359-366
Plant nutrients	367-371
Oxygen	372-377
Hydrogen	378-386
Carbon	387-395
Nitrogen	396-405
Phosphorus & Potassium	406-410
Calcium & Sulfur	411-416
Magnesium	417-419
Zinc	420-422
Iron	423-425
Copper & Sodium	426-430
Silicon	431-434
Chromium & Cobalt	435
Iodine	436
Places to go	437
Nature concepts	438-441

Plant world

This is the story of ancient beings that create our material universe. A group of creatures that make the atmosphere of air that we breathe; capture the rays of the sun and become the food that we eat; absorb and filter the water that we drink; hold and churn the soils of the land; and in death, form the fossil fuels that are burned to drive machines and build cities.

Happiness is a watermelon; awe is a tree; roots are strength; a flower is beauty. The smell of paradise drifts out of an orange blossom. We owe plants gratitude and respect for the existence of life and culture. Hopefully, this book can serve as a guide while you explore and work in the garden.

Air and wind

Air is the stuff we breathe in and out, in and out. The giant air bubble of gases around the earth protects us from scorching heat and freezing cold. Floating around in the air are plant pollen, seeds and spores, metal and rock dusts, and burnt specks of stuff.

Winds start where hot and cool temperatures meet. Where sea meets rock, where plains touch the mountains, high and low pressures wrestle. Streams of air swirl and collide - hurtling ocean swells towards distant sandbars. It gathers force, sips water, and spins into tornadoes or shakes typhoons.

In the Garden

Let's go to the pond

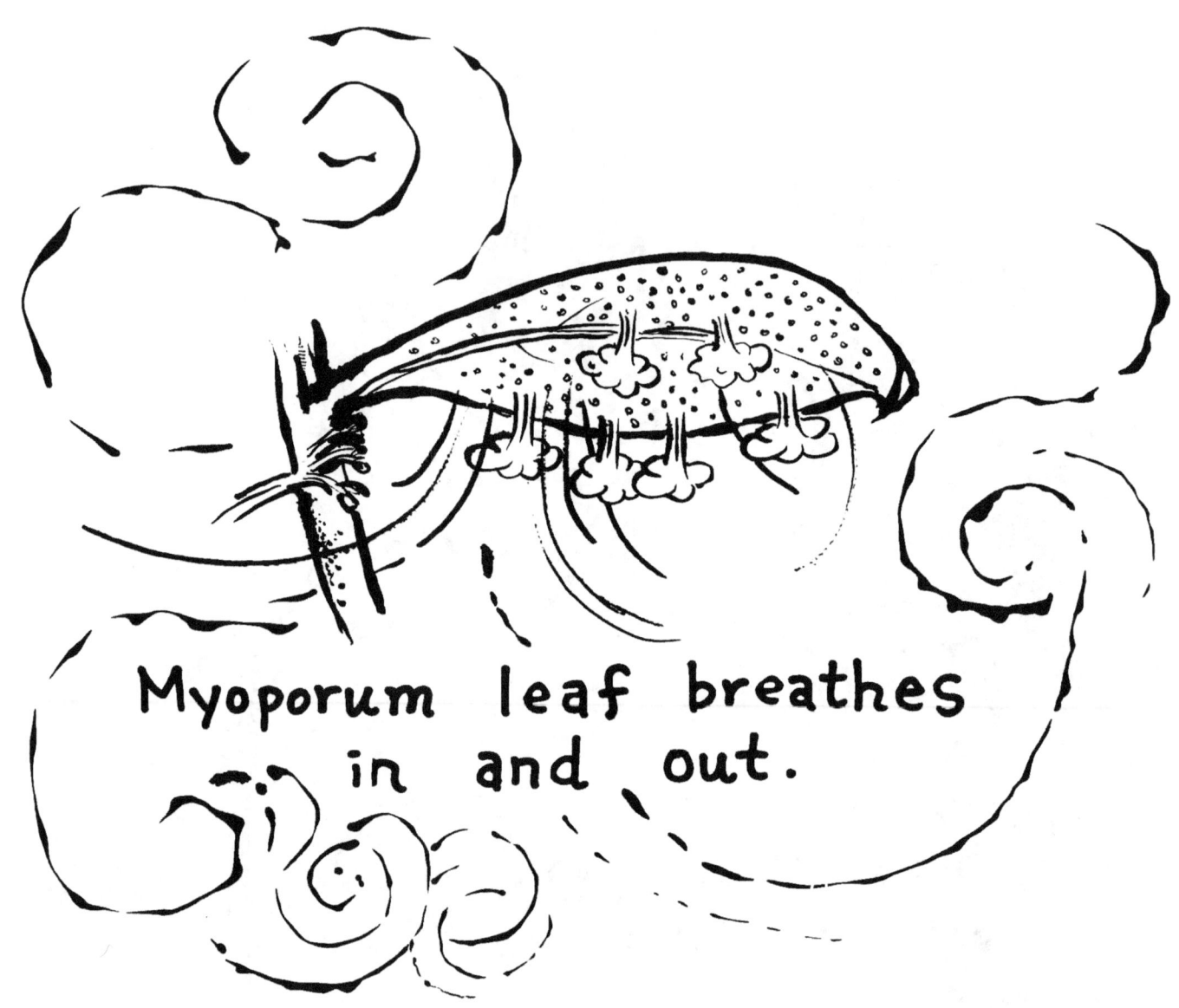

Little holes on the trunk of the birch tree inhale and exhale.

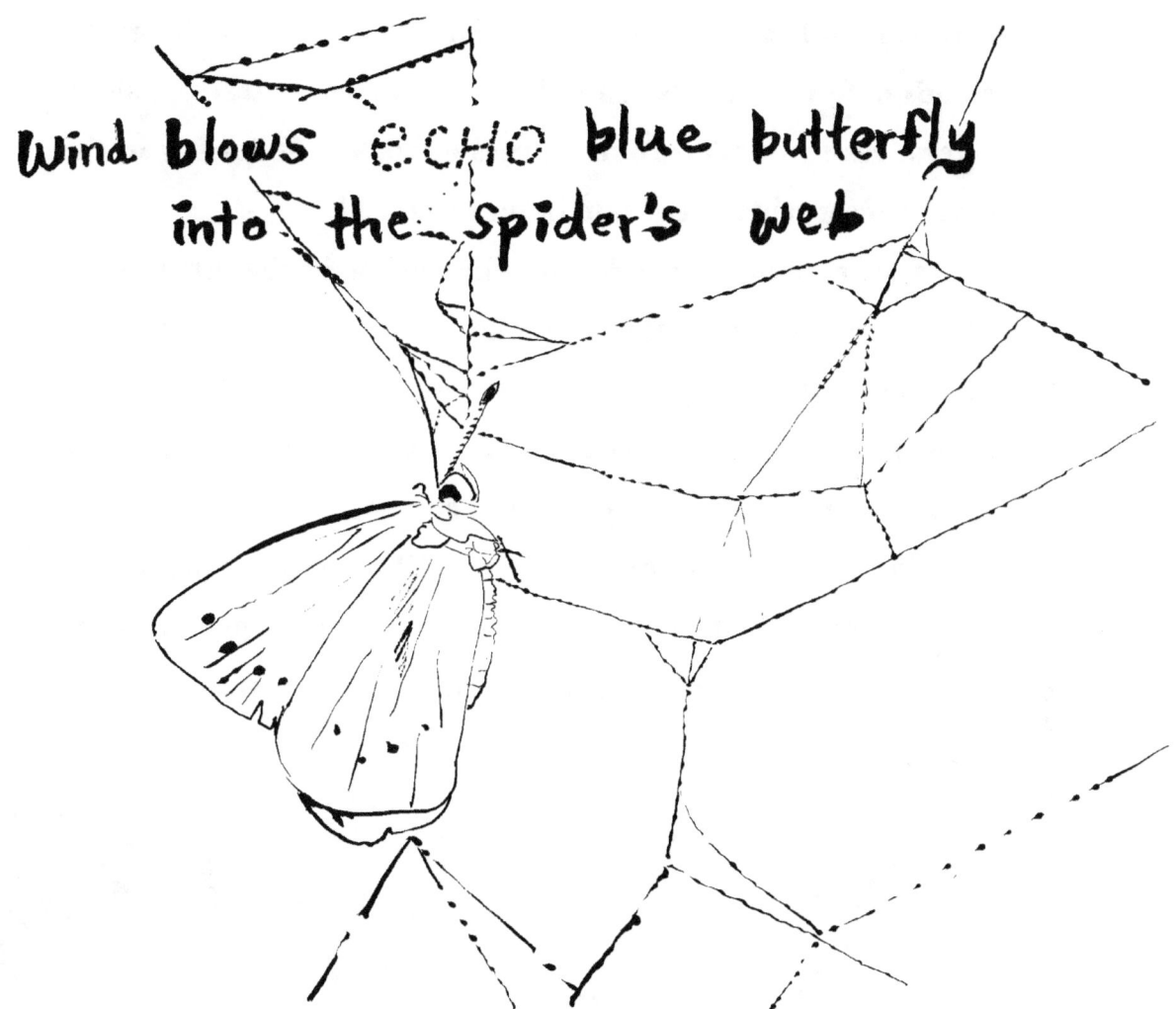

Water and rain

Water is the liquid juice of the heavens, the lifeblood of all cultures, and the essence of our planet. Water falls from the clouds onto the earth as rain, hail, and snow. It feeds gushing rivers; rests in underground layers of rocks. Following in the tracks of serpents, it ends up in the ocean.

As water moves, it picks up whatever is in the air and the earth. Water cuts through and dissolves the hardest of materials. It carries stuff downstream, leaving debris on the sides of rivers, inside cracks of caves, or in the sea. Its cargo includes sand and soot, crystals and corpses.

When cold, water turns into ice. The strange solid floats. By the actions of the sun and the wind, water evaporates back up into the sky, as mountains of cottony white crystals.

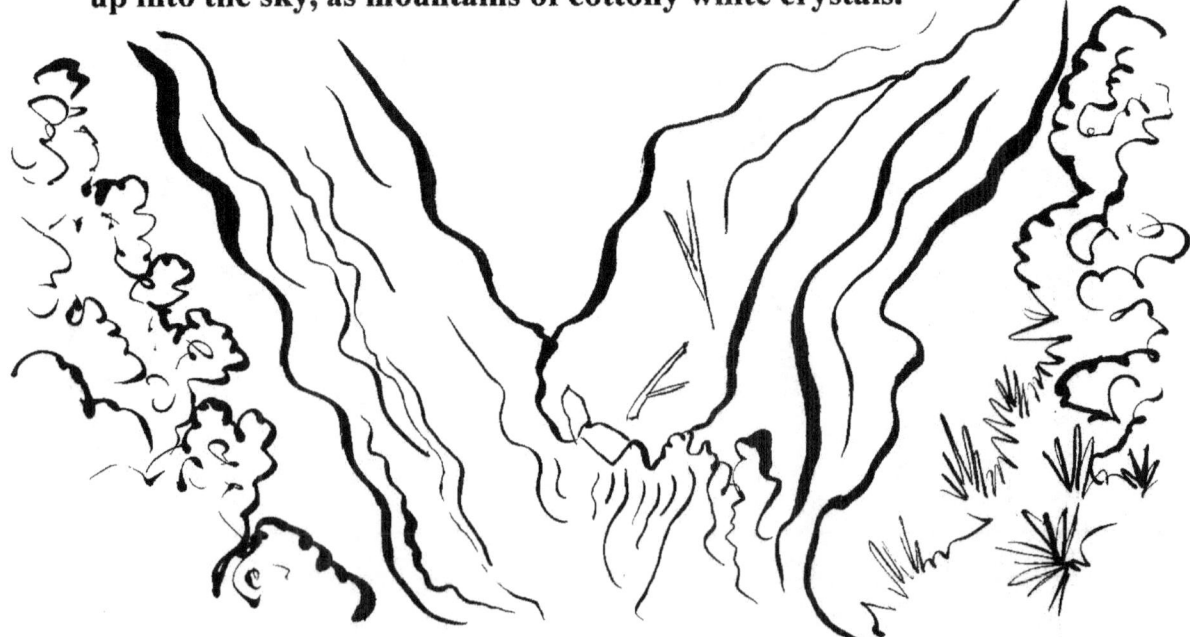

Water gathers around specks of dust,
spores and pollen
clouds of crystals floating in the sky

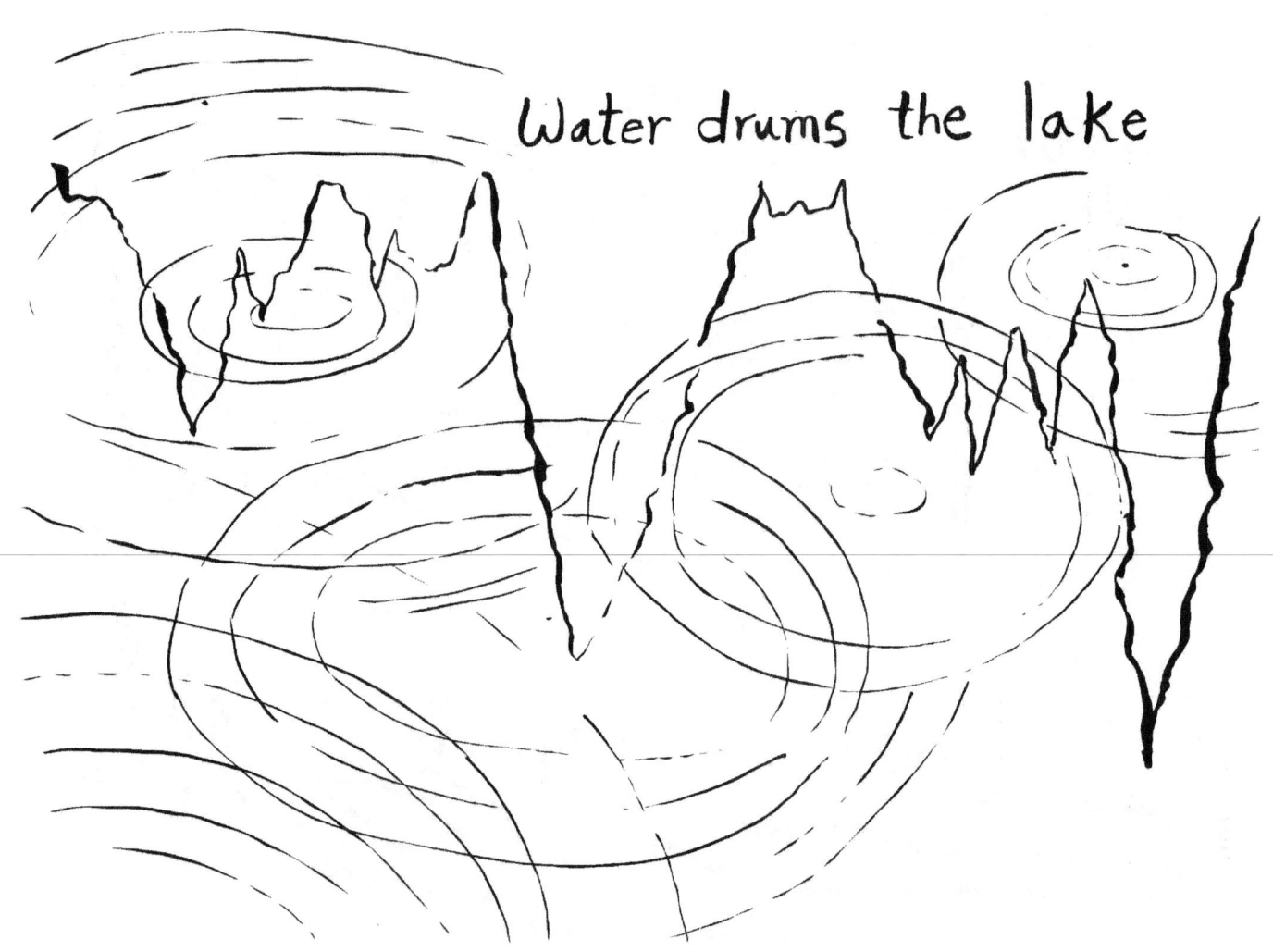

Water stopped holding up Gerbera Daisy's leaves and flowers

Echo blue butterflies
sip water by the
lake shore

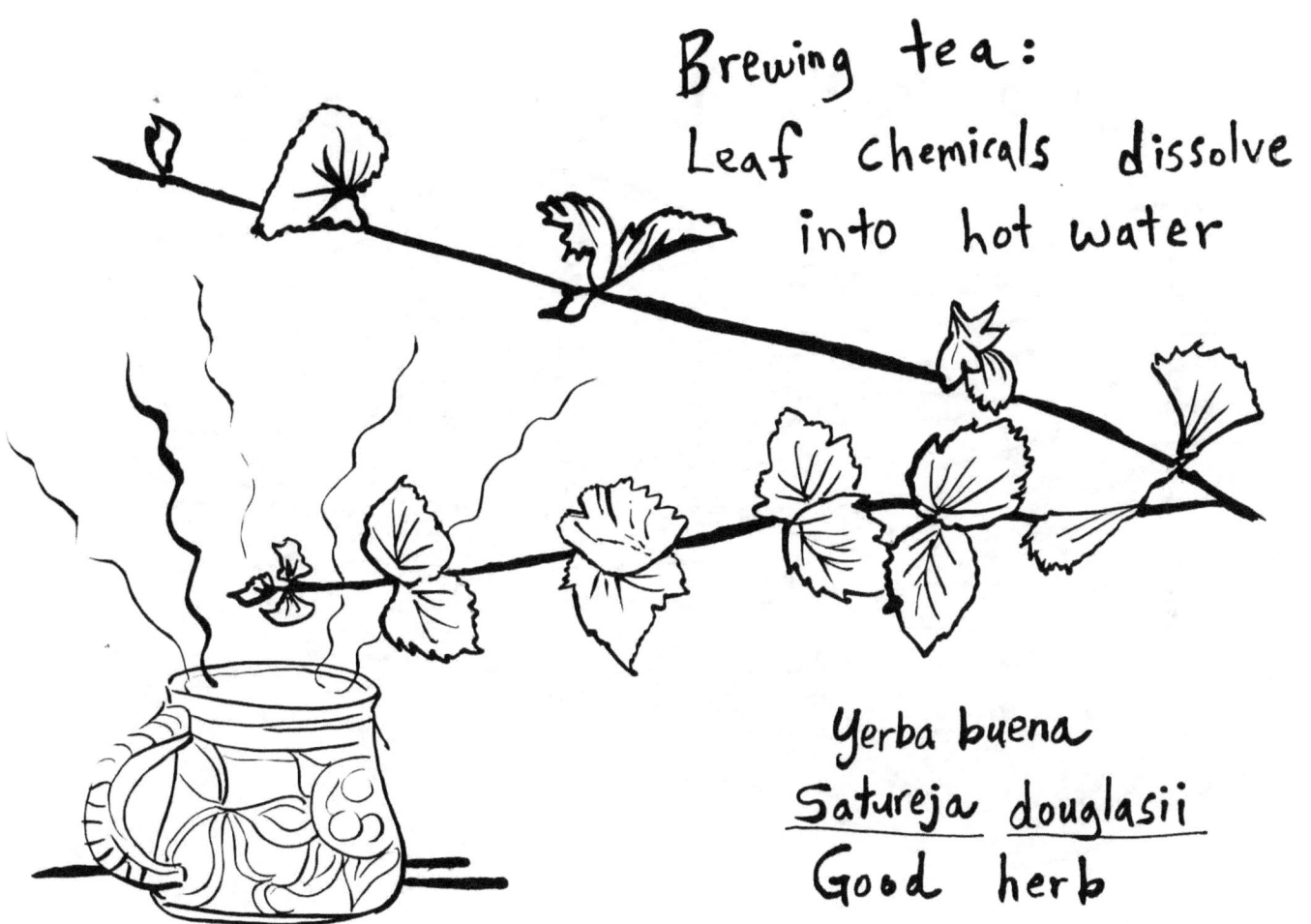

Brewing tea:
Leaf chemicals dissolve
into hot water

Yerba buena
<u>Satureja</u> <u>douglasii</u>
Good herb

who is the best carver?

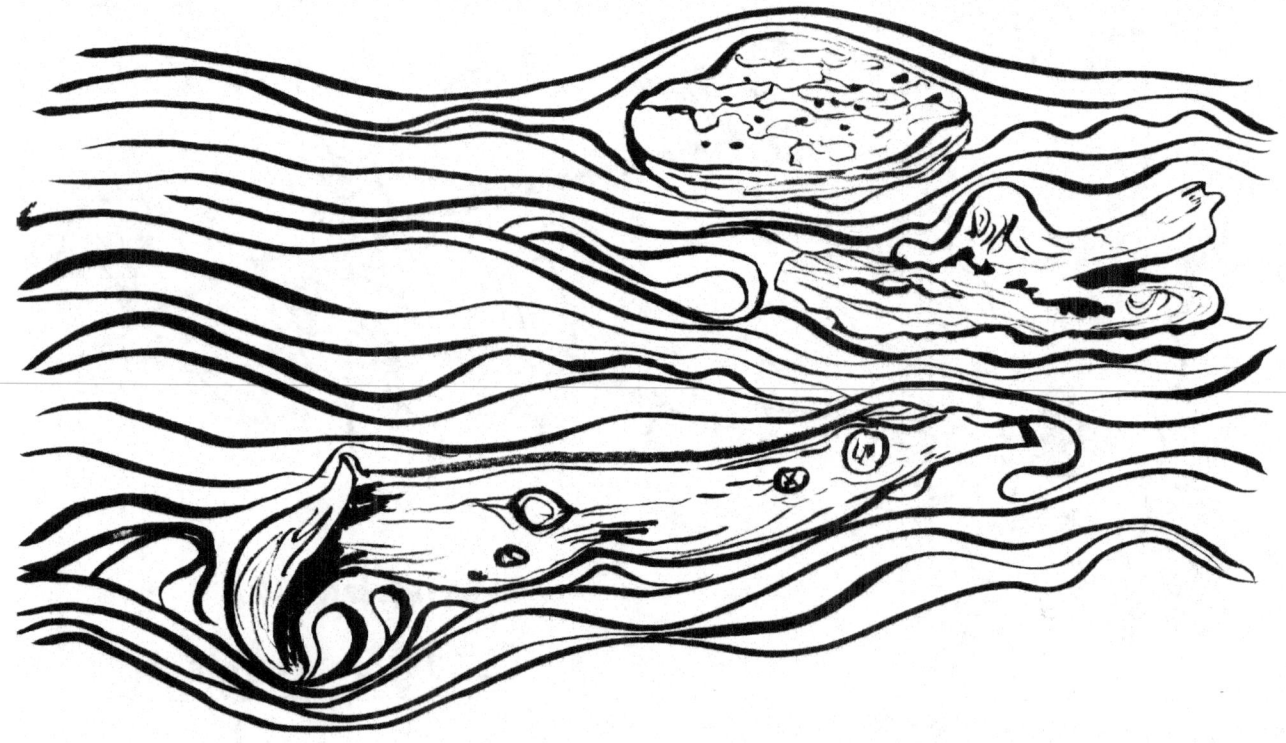

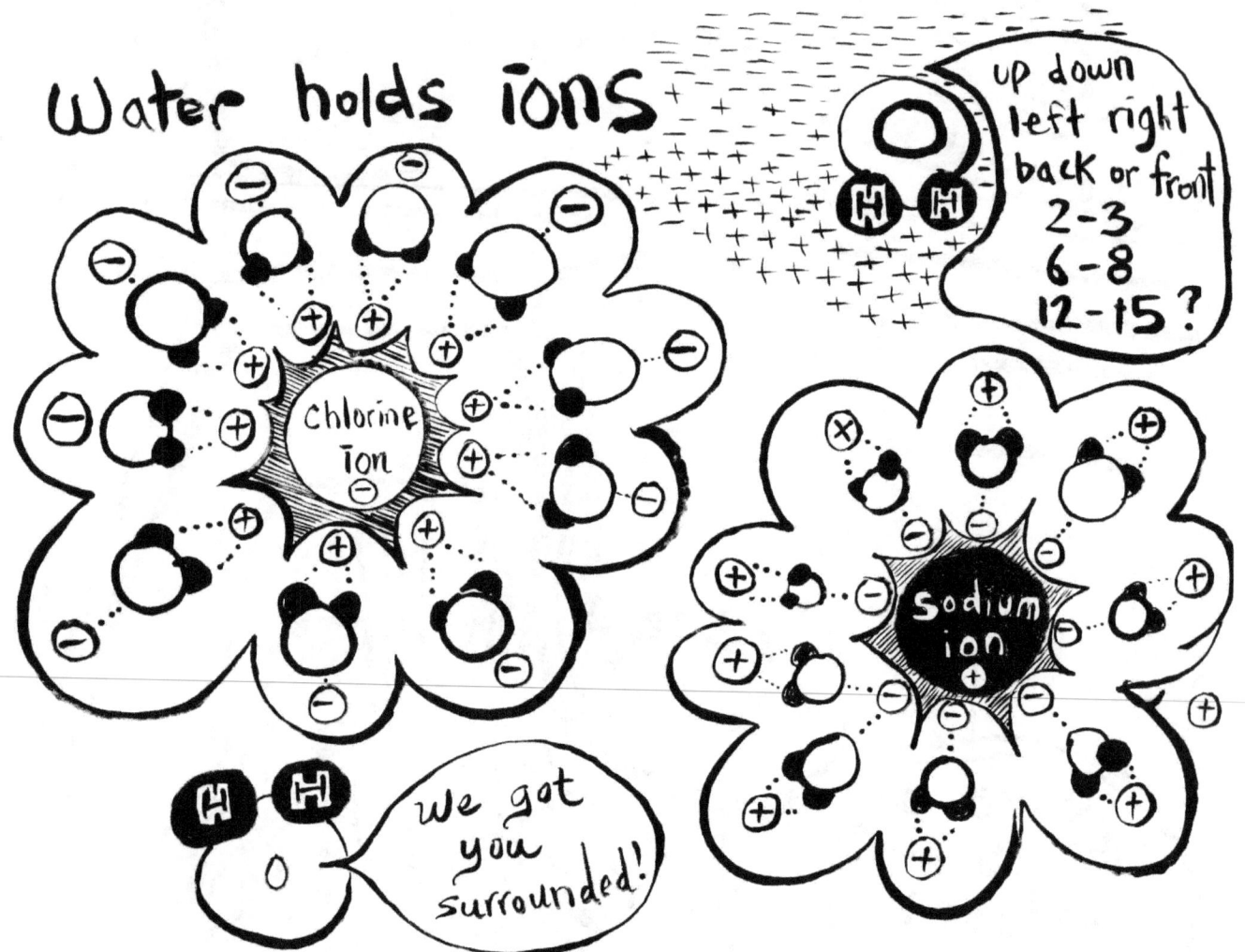

Pull tight together
Form a skin against air
Hold onto each other

Surface tension
can you feel it?

Earth and soil

Earth is a round chunk of spinning rock, metal, and fire. The sun and night heat and cool it. Moving plates of land push each other into mountains, grind out earthquakes, and dive beneath one another into the waves.

Some stones are laid down gently, grain by grain, bit by bit; sticky glues hold all the pieces together. Other chunks are squeezed and pressed, pressed then pulled, pulled then pummeled, pummeled then pounded into other forms and shapes. Rocks gurgle out of earth's fire filled belly, and cool down in the salty sea.

Rocks become smaller as they are beaten down by the wind, tumbled in the sea, cracked by roots, and swallowed by birds. After a lot of grinding and polishing, jagged rocks become smooth. Little rocks are crushed into sand, sand breaks up into finer silt, and the tiniest mineral pieces join together as clay.

Graywacke rock crumbles at the edge of the sea

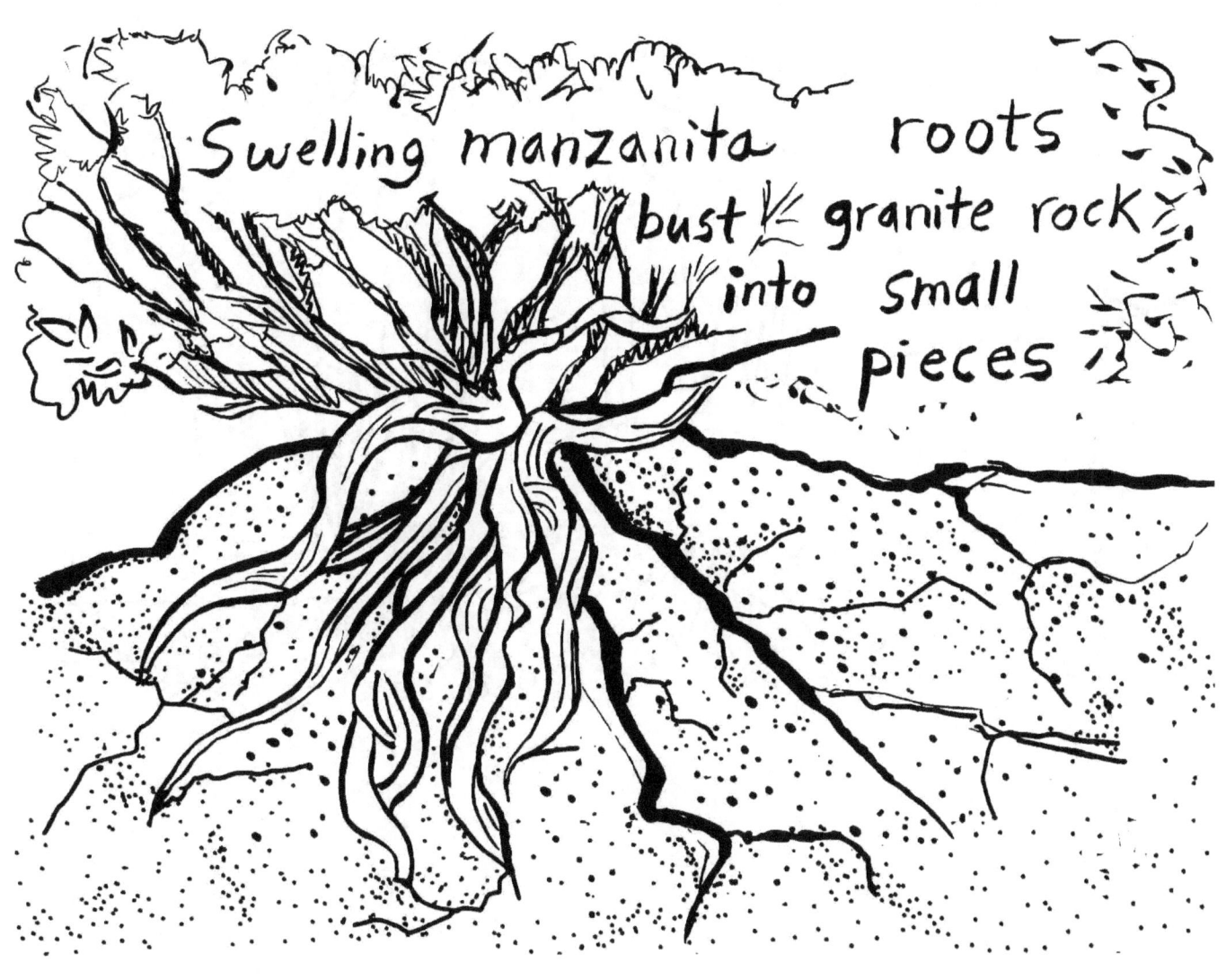

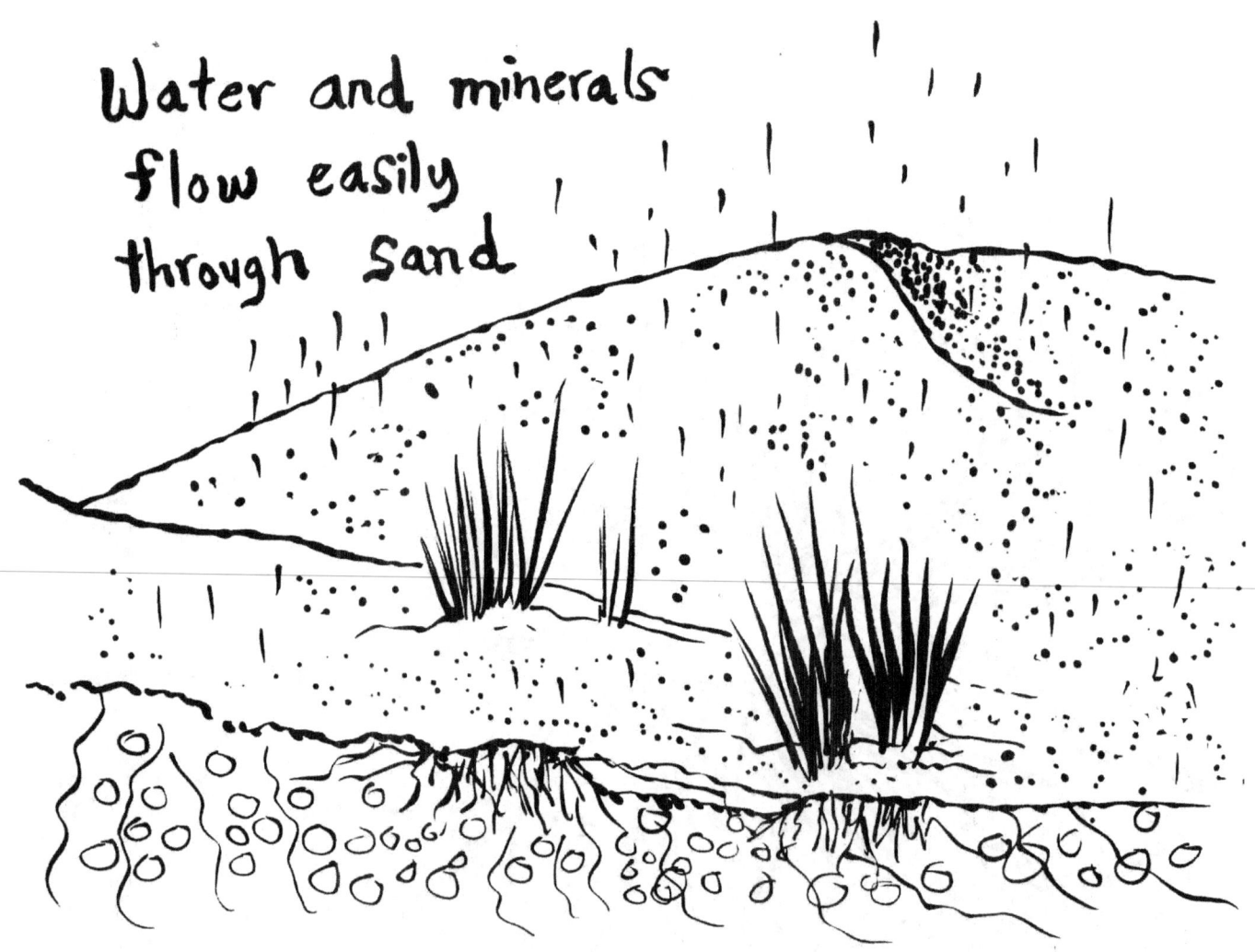

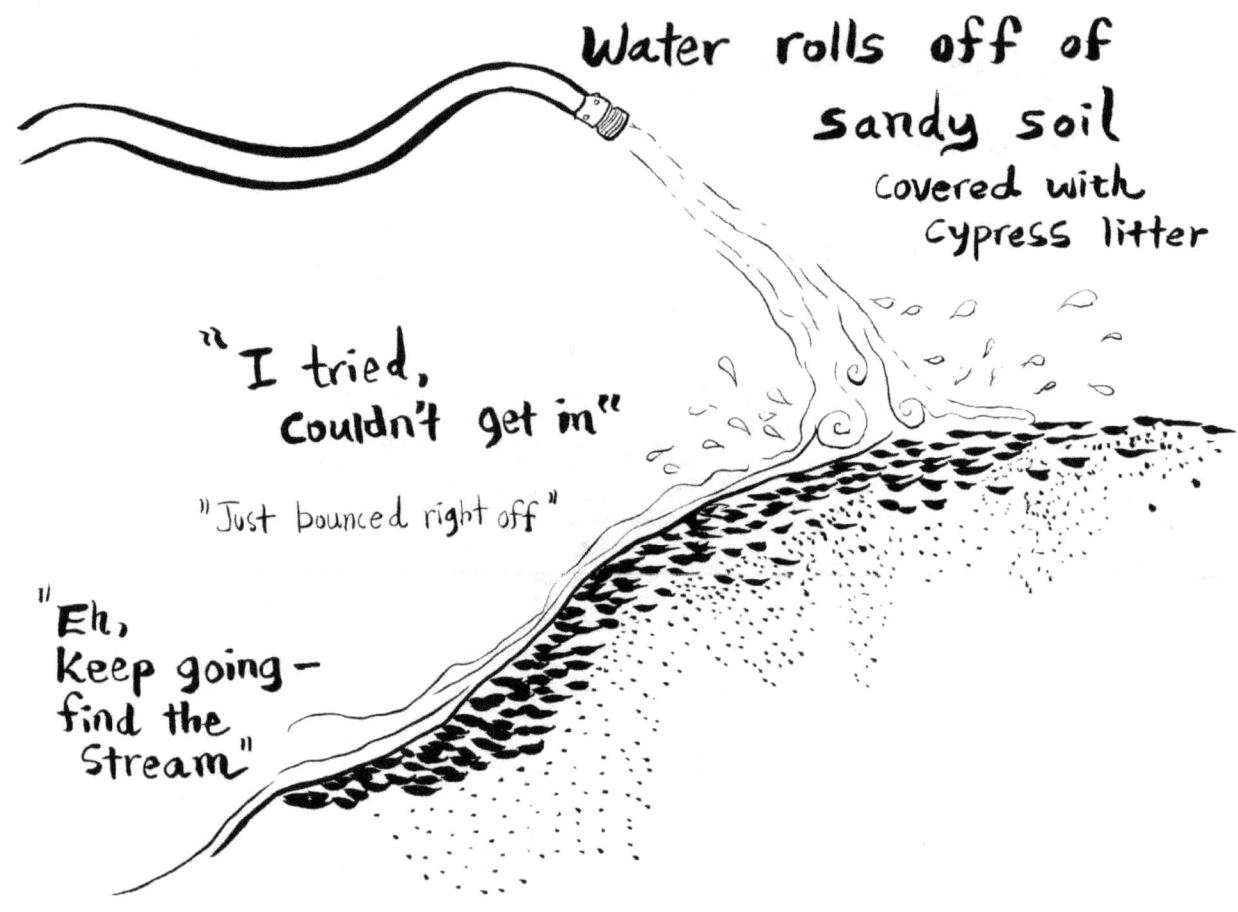

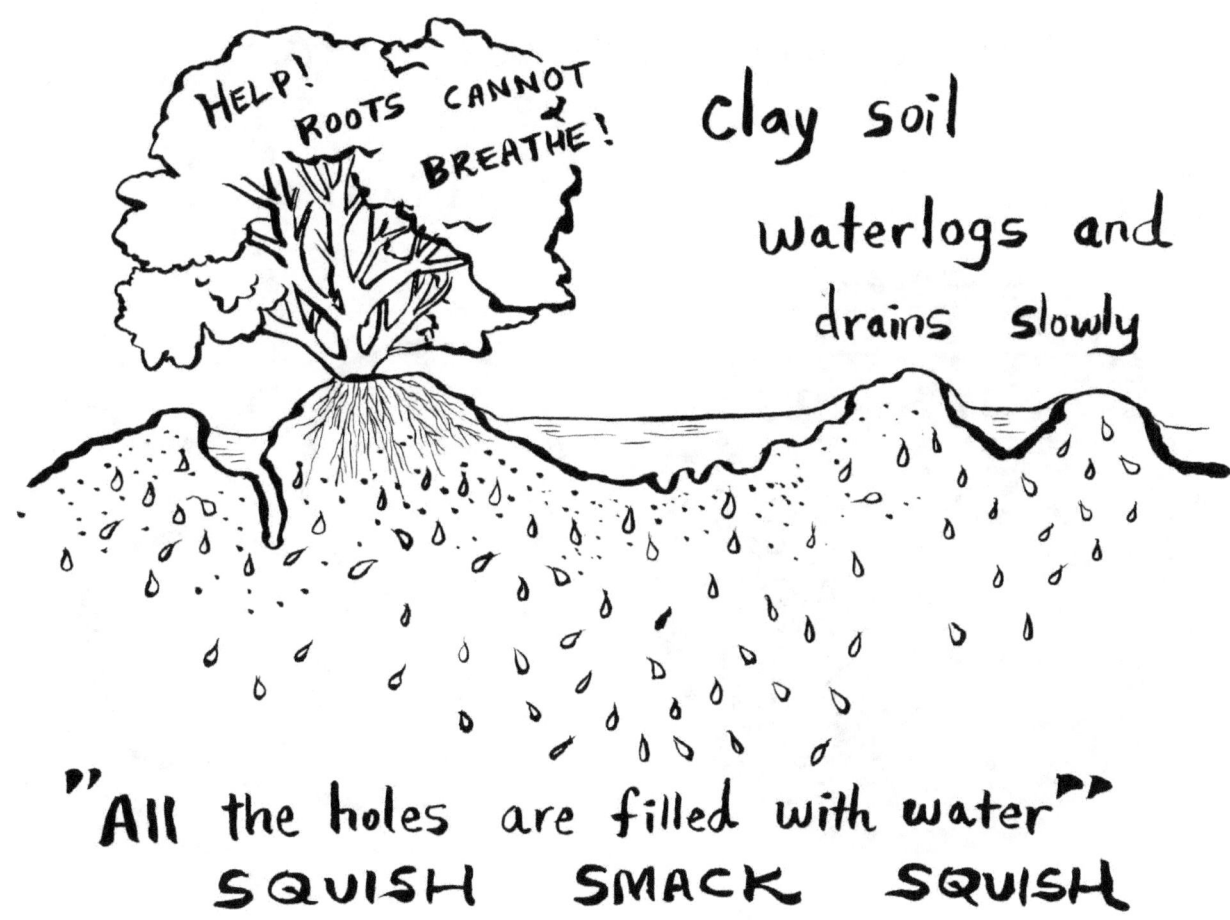

Who has greater surface area —

☐ clay? ☐ sand?

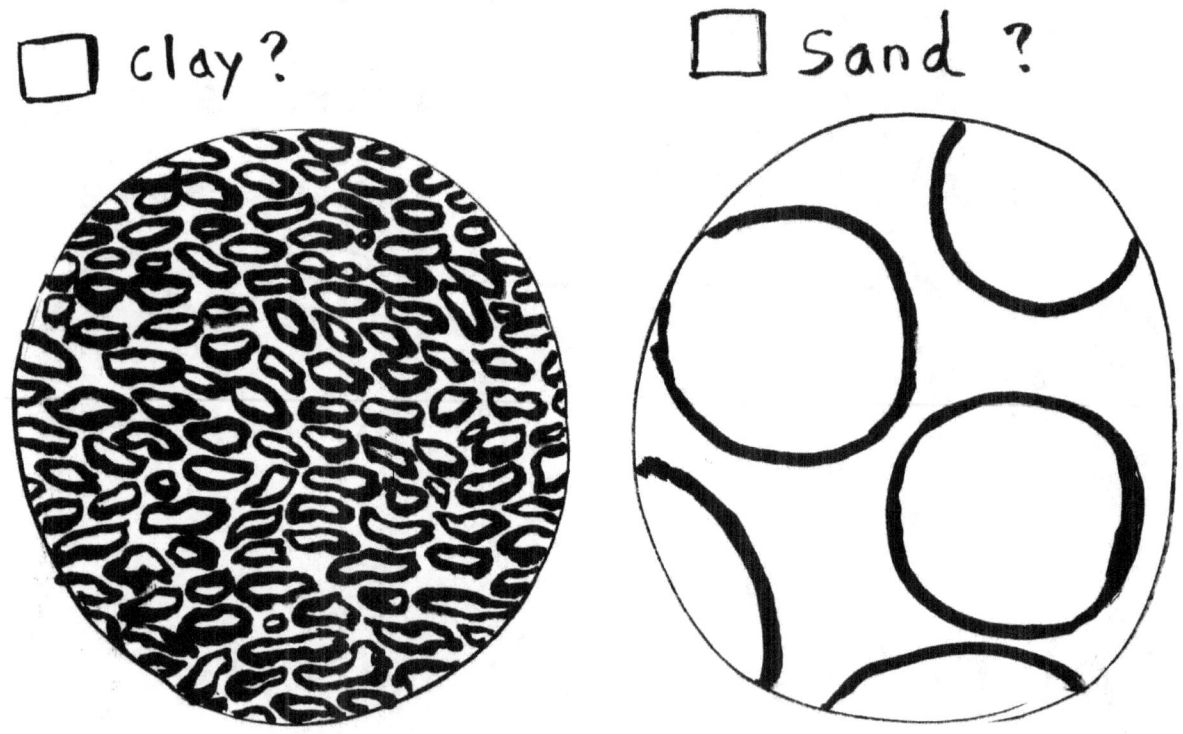

Water is held:
  on the surface, and
     between, particles of
         sand, silt and clay.

The mystery dwells in the PORES

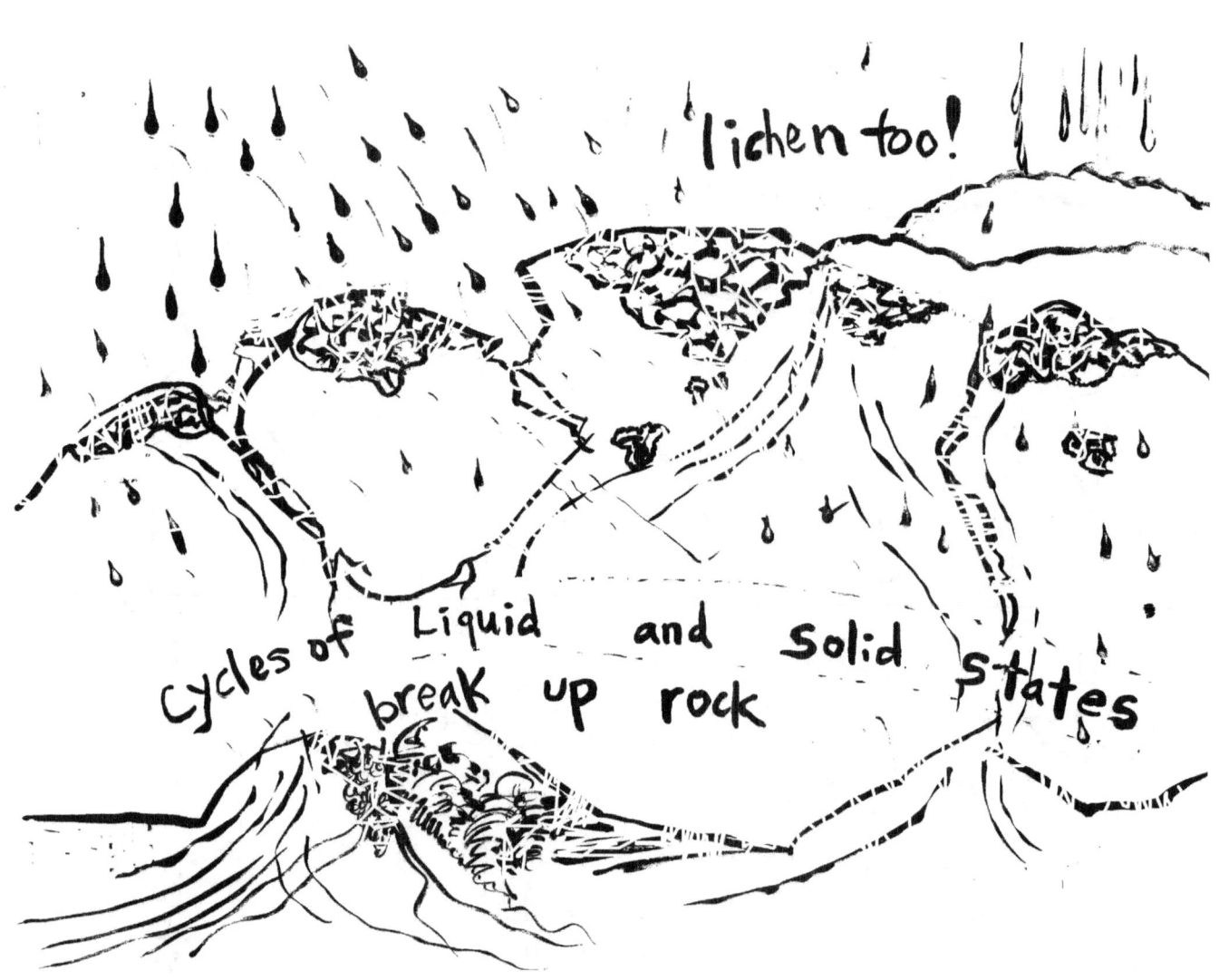

On top of the rocks is a layer of soil. It is made up of different sized minerals, living and dead creatures, air, and water. Our food grows out of the soil.

Heavy storms flood winding channels with water and debris. Next to these riverbanks, the soil grows deep, nourished by mud and life. In an old forest, the soil is spongy and thick. It is built up of many years of fallen leaves and twigs, and miles and miles of fungi. Around cities, the soil is squashed and compacted, or has been moved and washed away.

The soil is home to creatures feeding on each other and reproducing. They transform big chunks into smaller and smaller pieces. With time, the soil becomes sticky sweet smelling humus. A twig, a log, a leaf, a turd - are all food for *somebody*. Warmth, wetness, and oxygen make stuff break down quickly. Decomposition without oxygen, in the bottom of a swampy lake for example, is slow and stinky. Eventually, the tiny pieces dissolve in water, and can be taken up by the plants' roots.

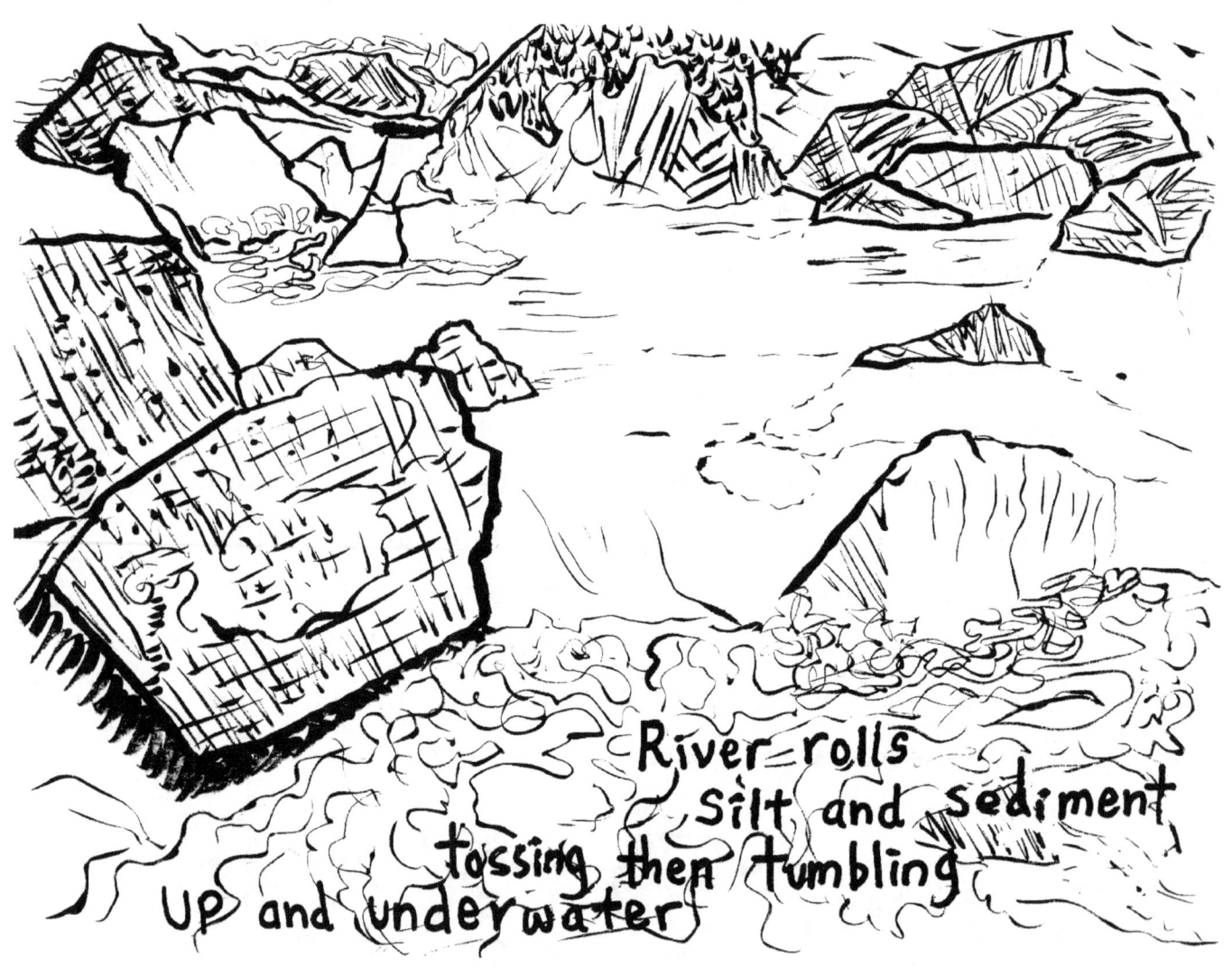

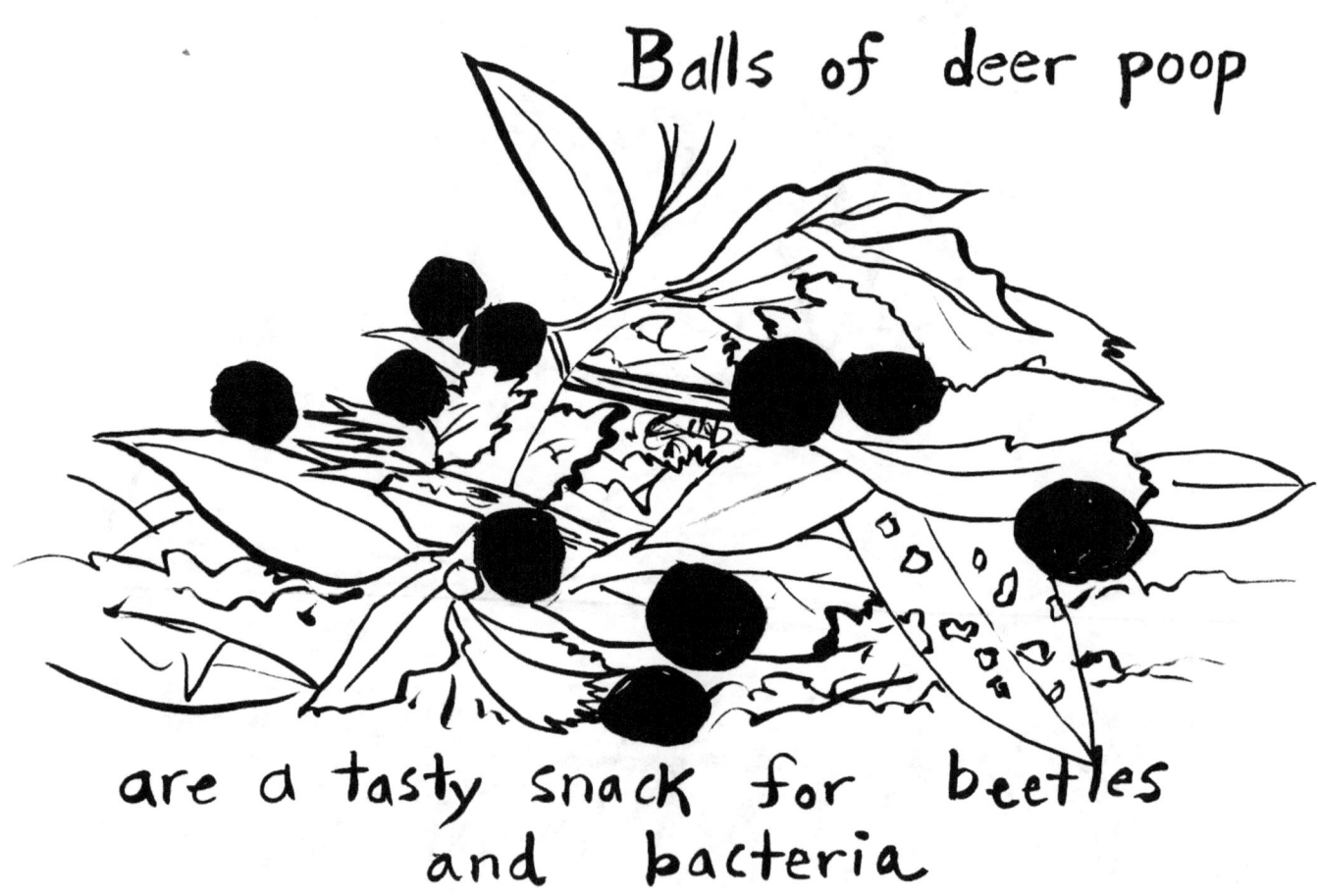

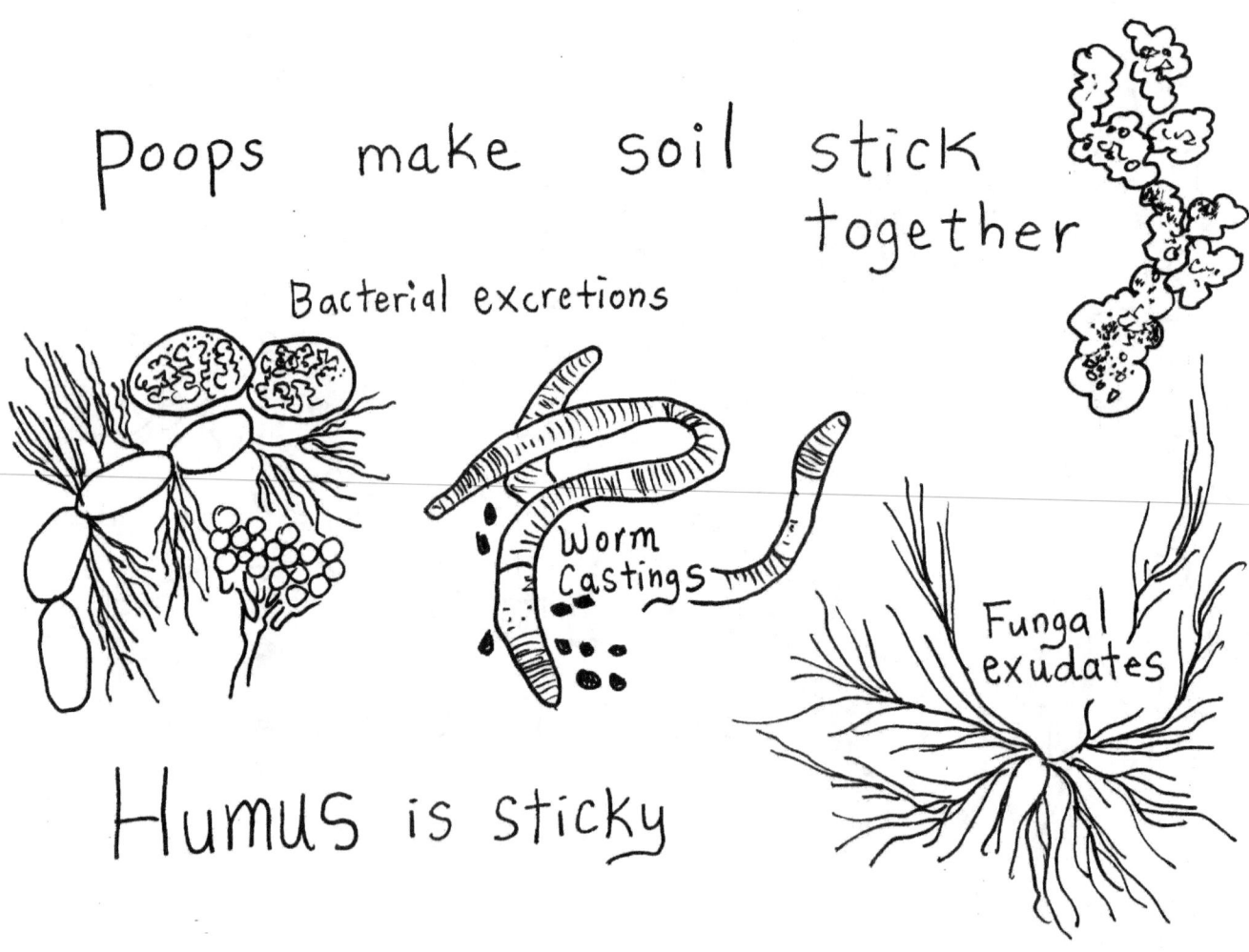

Let's give a big round of applause for the greatest movers and shakers of the earth... ANTS!!!

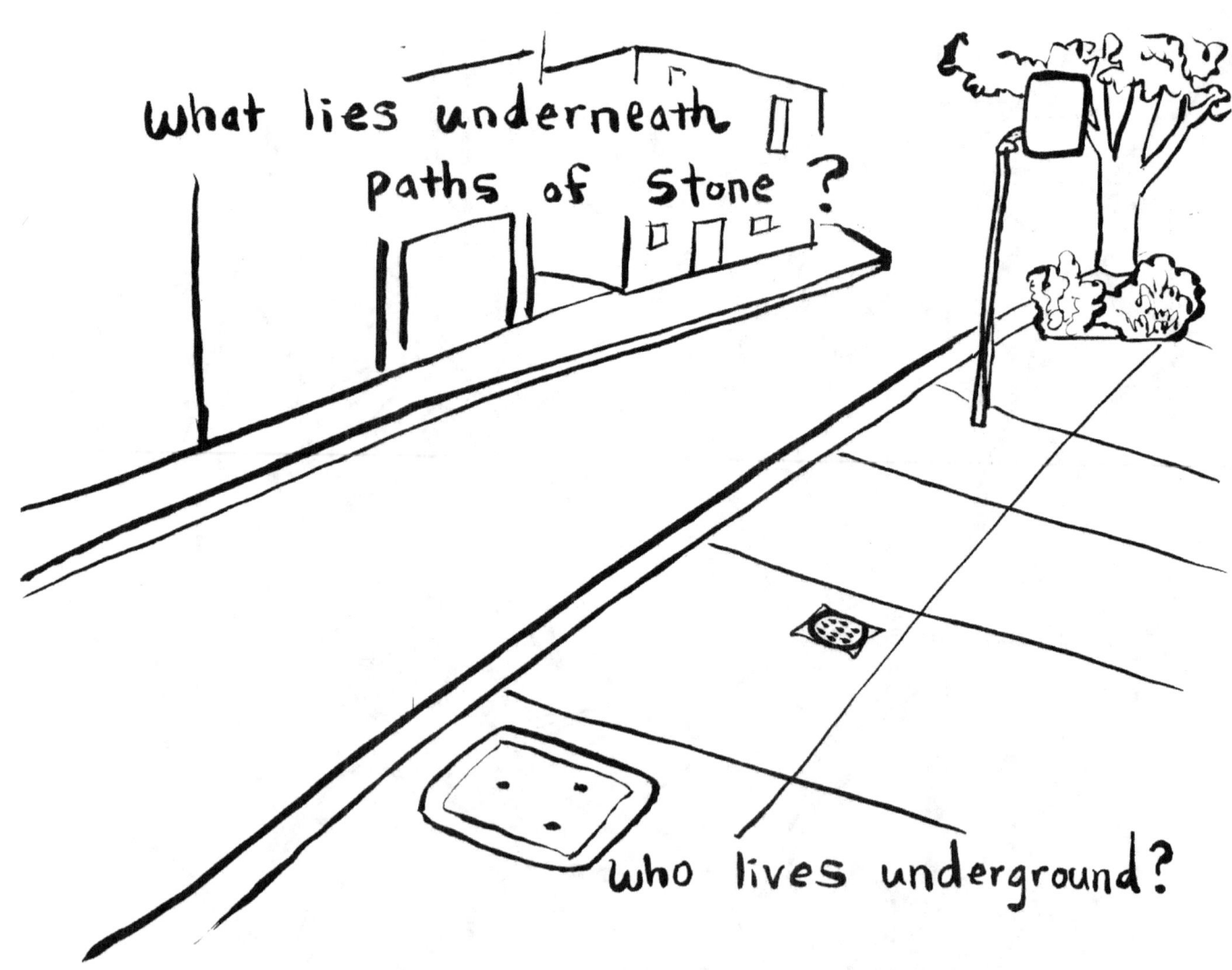

Squirrel road kill does not dream of acorns anymore

Ants! Take him back down into the earth...

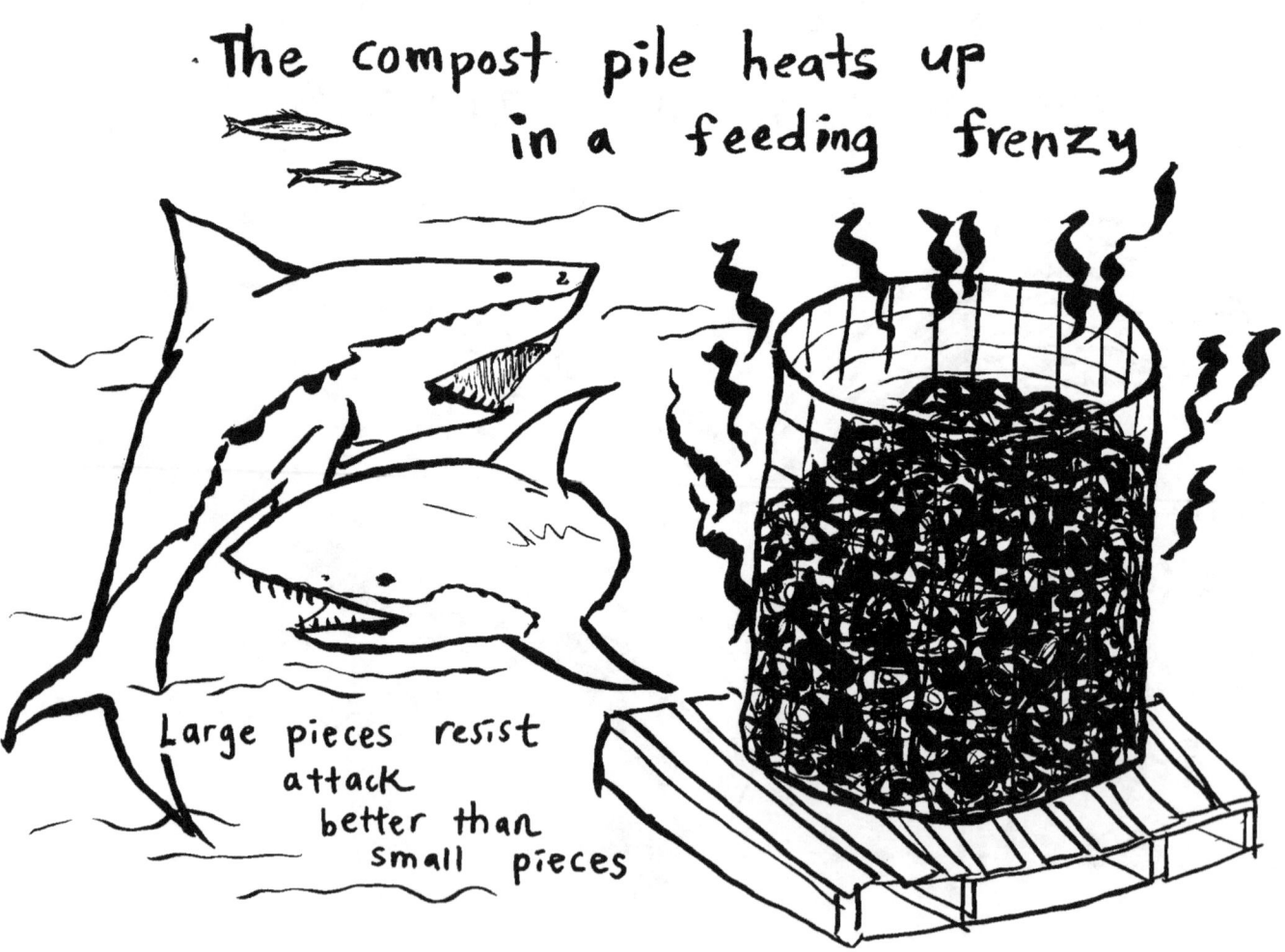

Fire and light

The sun is a fireball of exploding gases. There is a lot of light energy coming from very far away. The sun is the power source of the green and blue world we live in. It blows, big time. The power of the atom at its finest.

The earth has a fire of its own inside that spits up lava and warms hot springs. Once in a while, a volcano explodes its top and coughs up mountains of ash.

From time to time, lightning strikes, flames are lit, and fire scorches the land. Black ashes cover the earth. This process frees up all the nutrients in the bodies of trees, bushes, and grasses. It opens shaded woods, and wakes up seeds sleeping in the ground.

The sun warms the bark and kisses the leaves. Wake up! The world is full of light. Go outside and check it out.

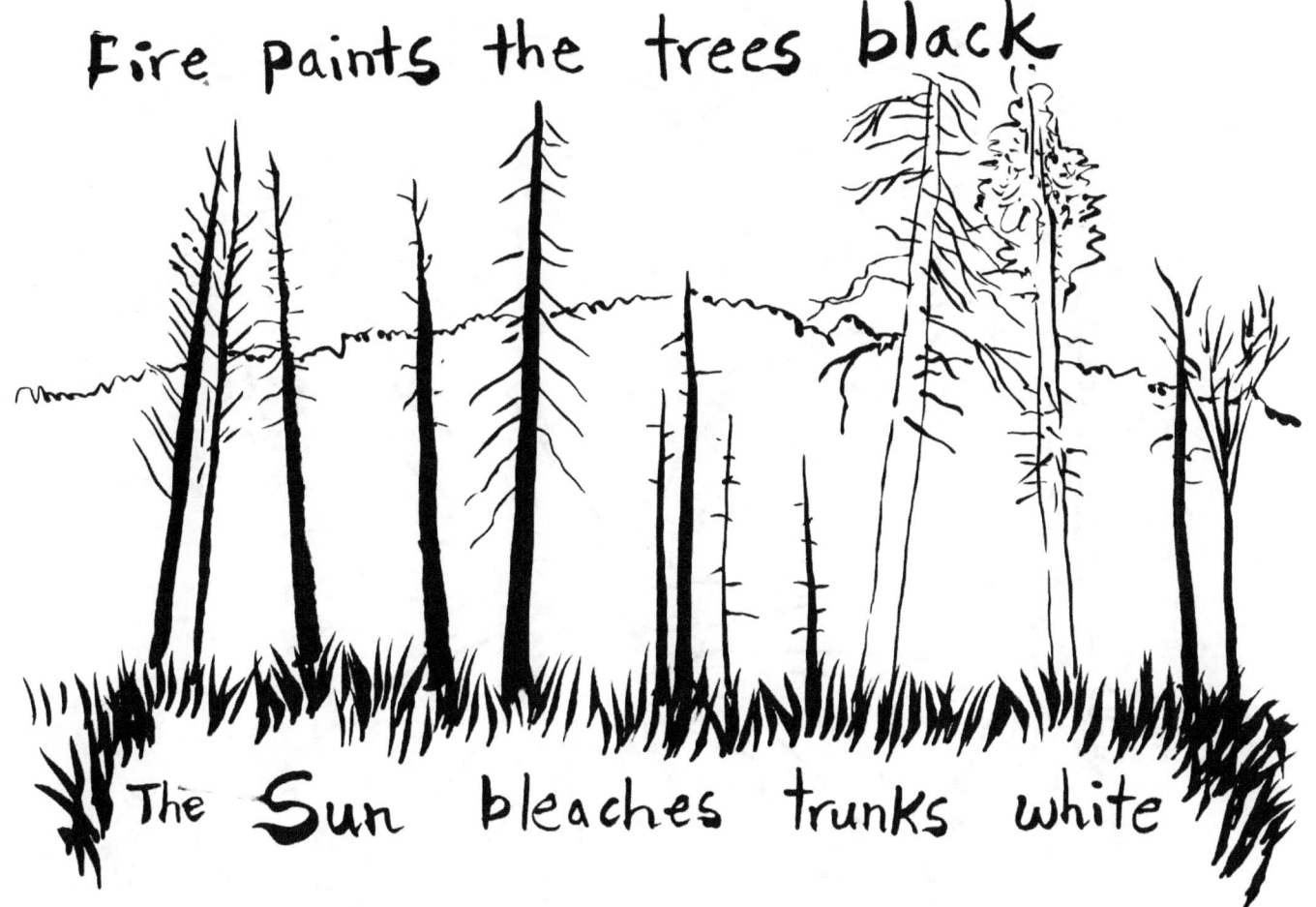

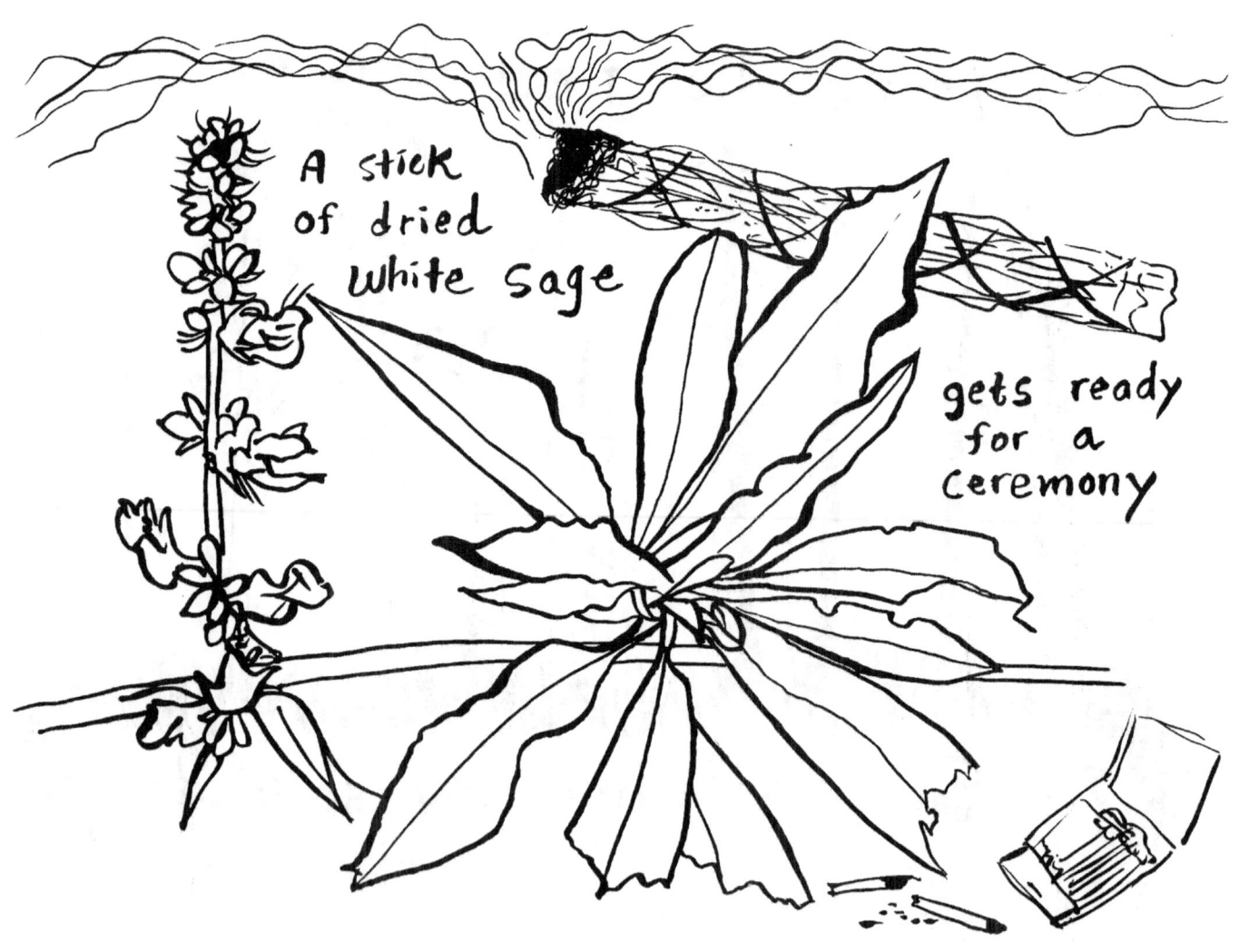

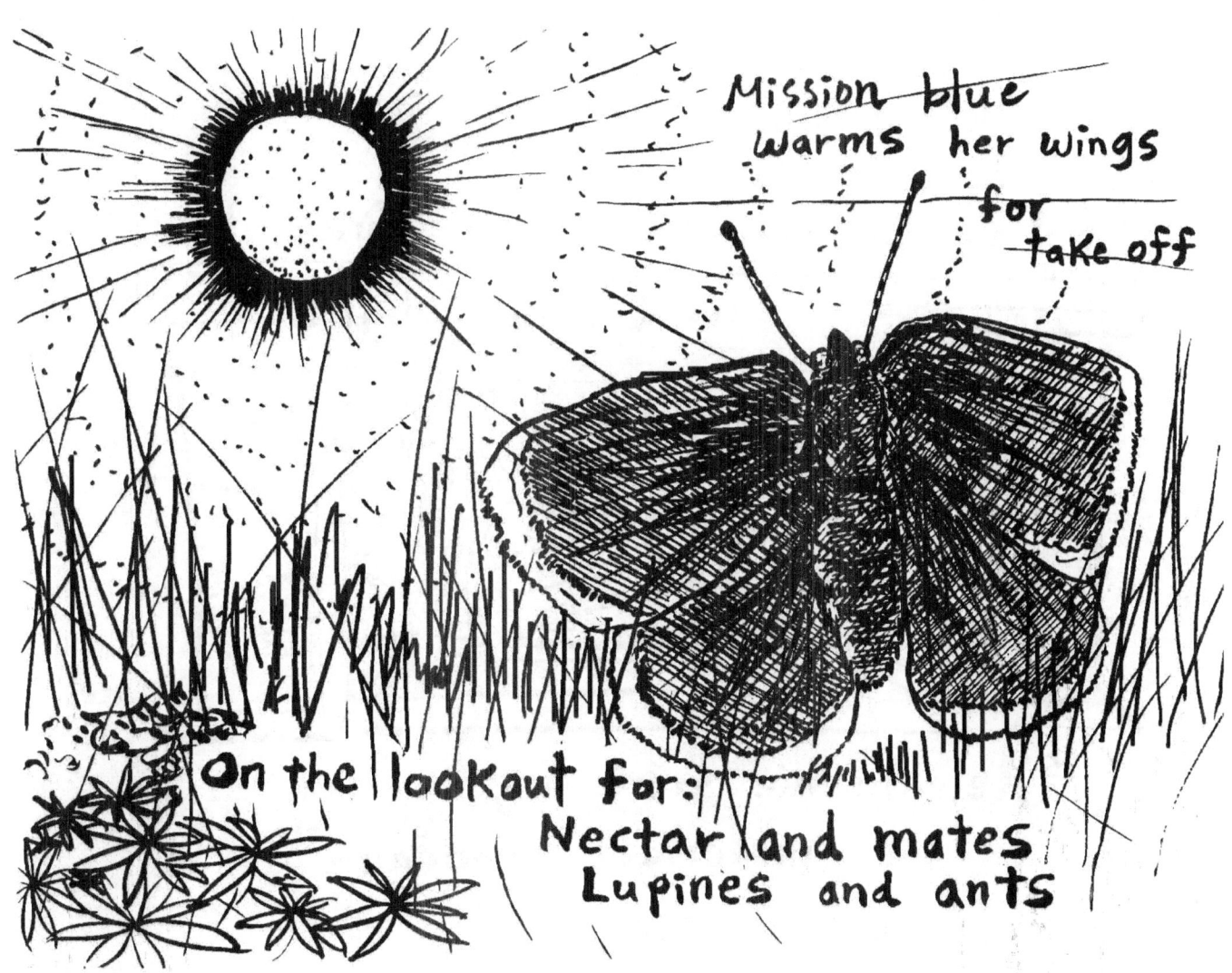

From roots to spores

There are just a few basic plant parts, with endless variations and adaptations. Out of a few simple ingredients, the plants create chains of life and webs of relatives. Patient observation and wanderings, near and far, will clarify the contents and details of this green world.

Roots

Roots go wide and deep in the soil to anchor plants, and keep them from falling down. Root caps and hairs poke this way and that way seeking water and minerals, and then suck them up into the plant. As a plant grows, roots become swollen with food made by the leaves.

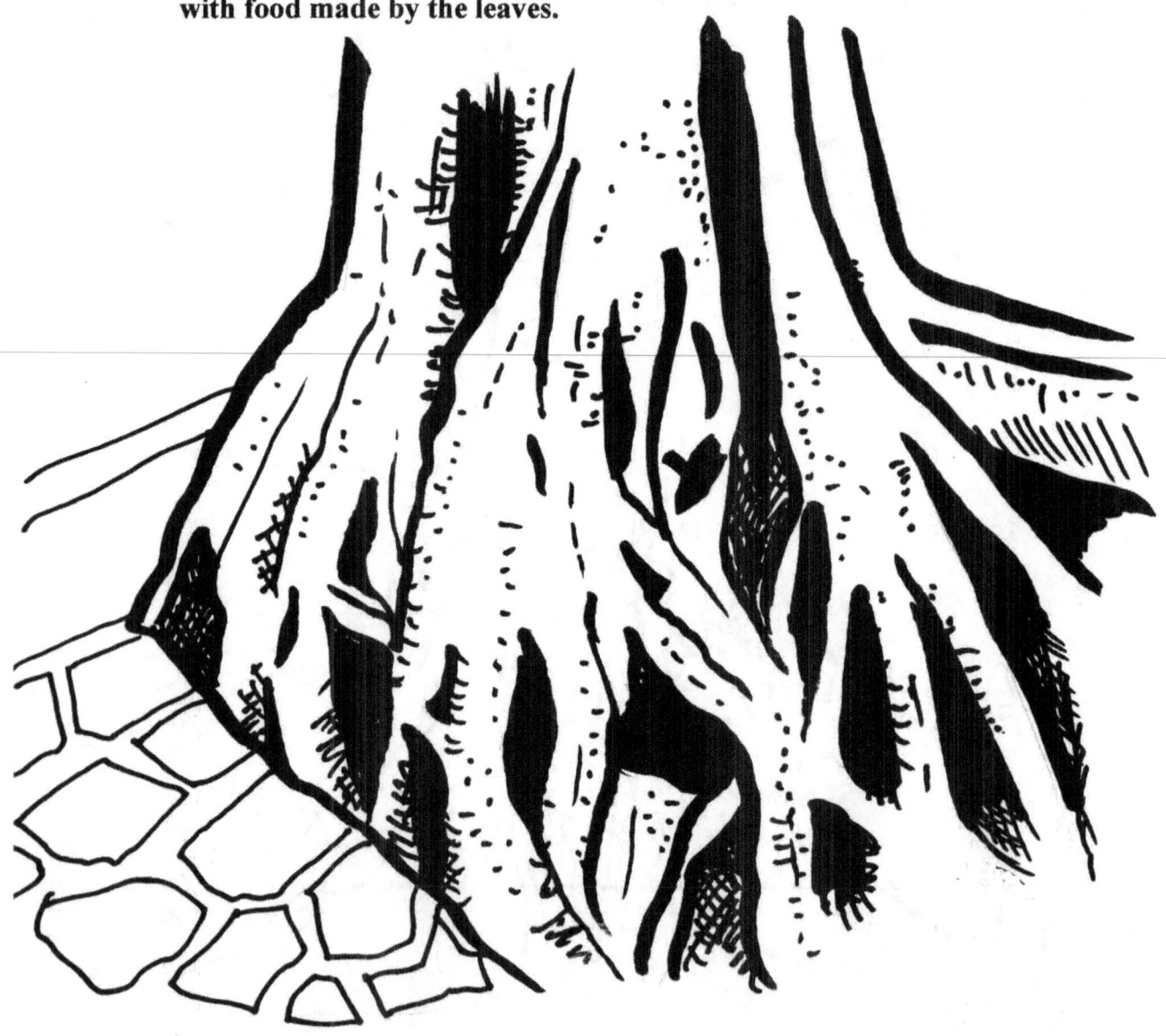

Laurel
Roots stretch across the earth and hold the soil.

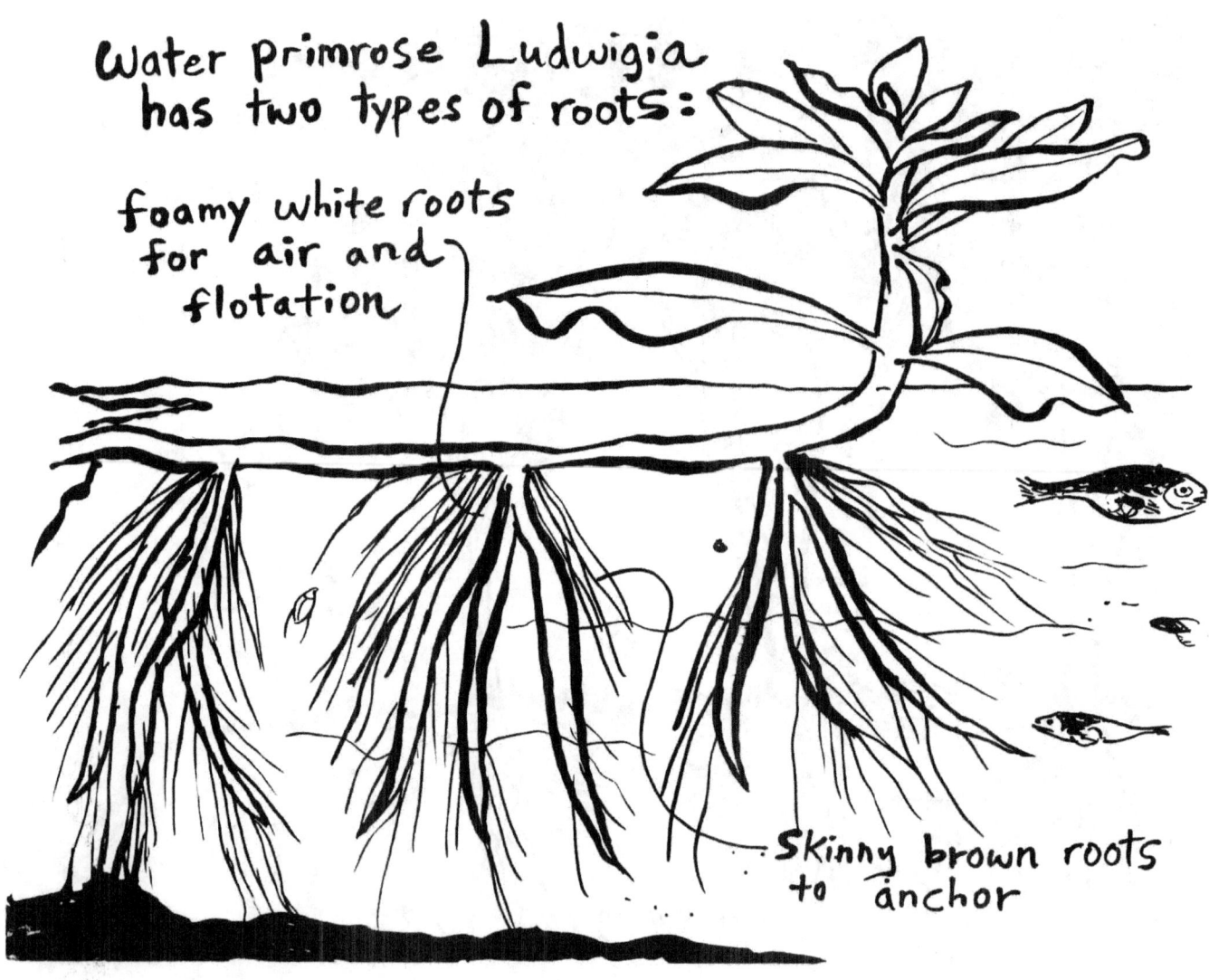

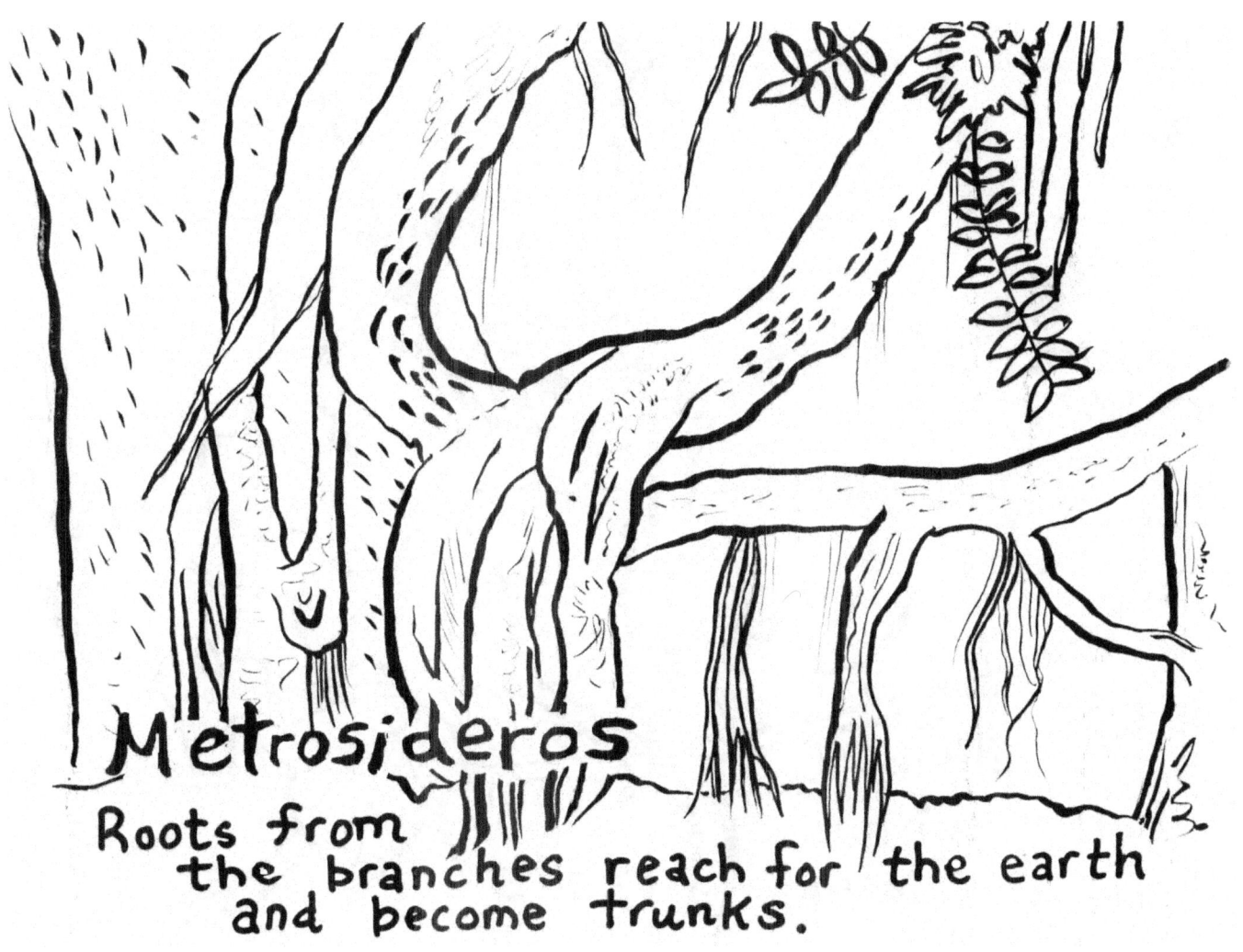

Metrosideros
Roots from the branches reach for the earth and become trunks.

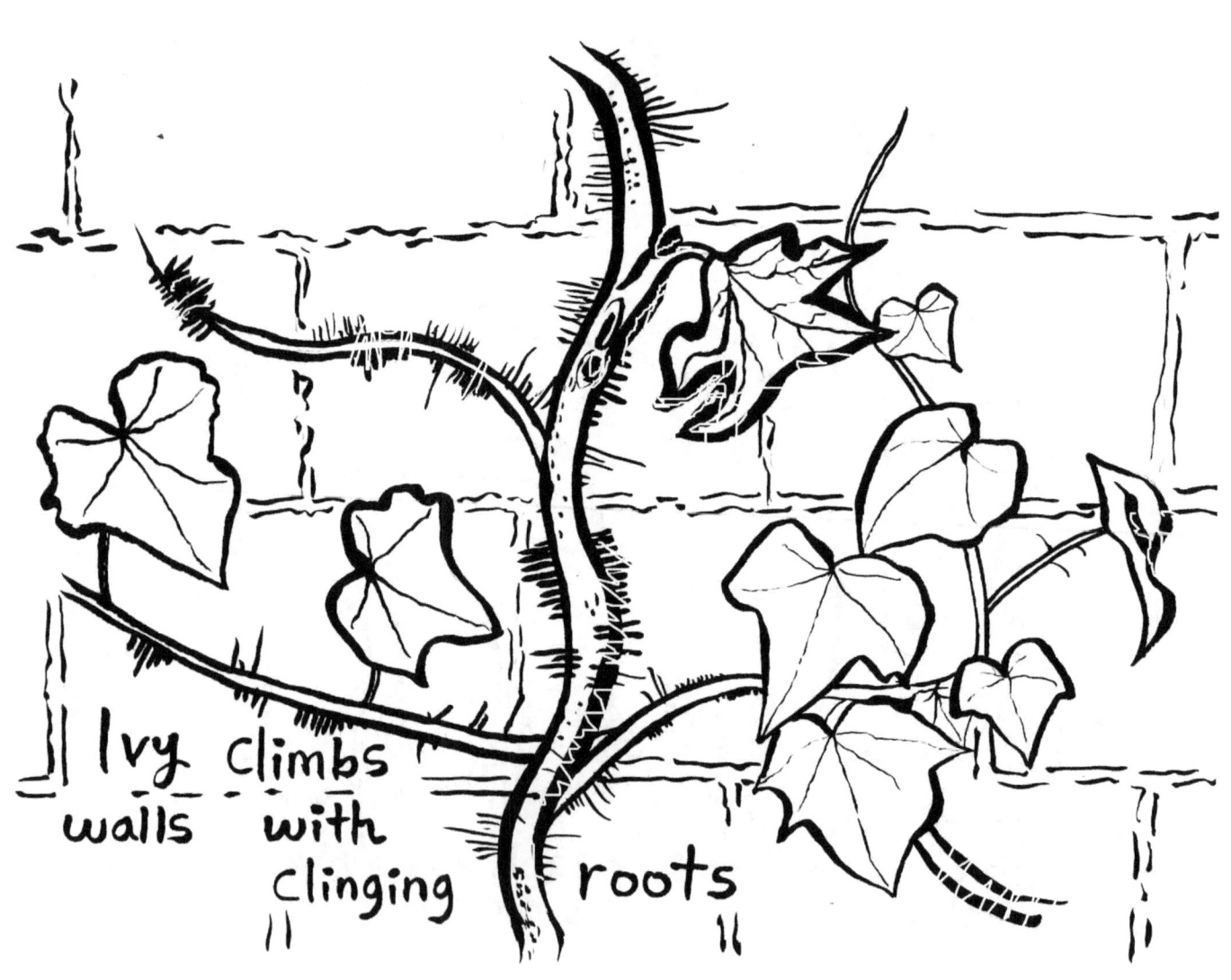

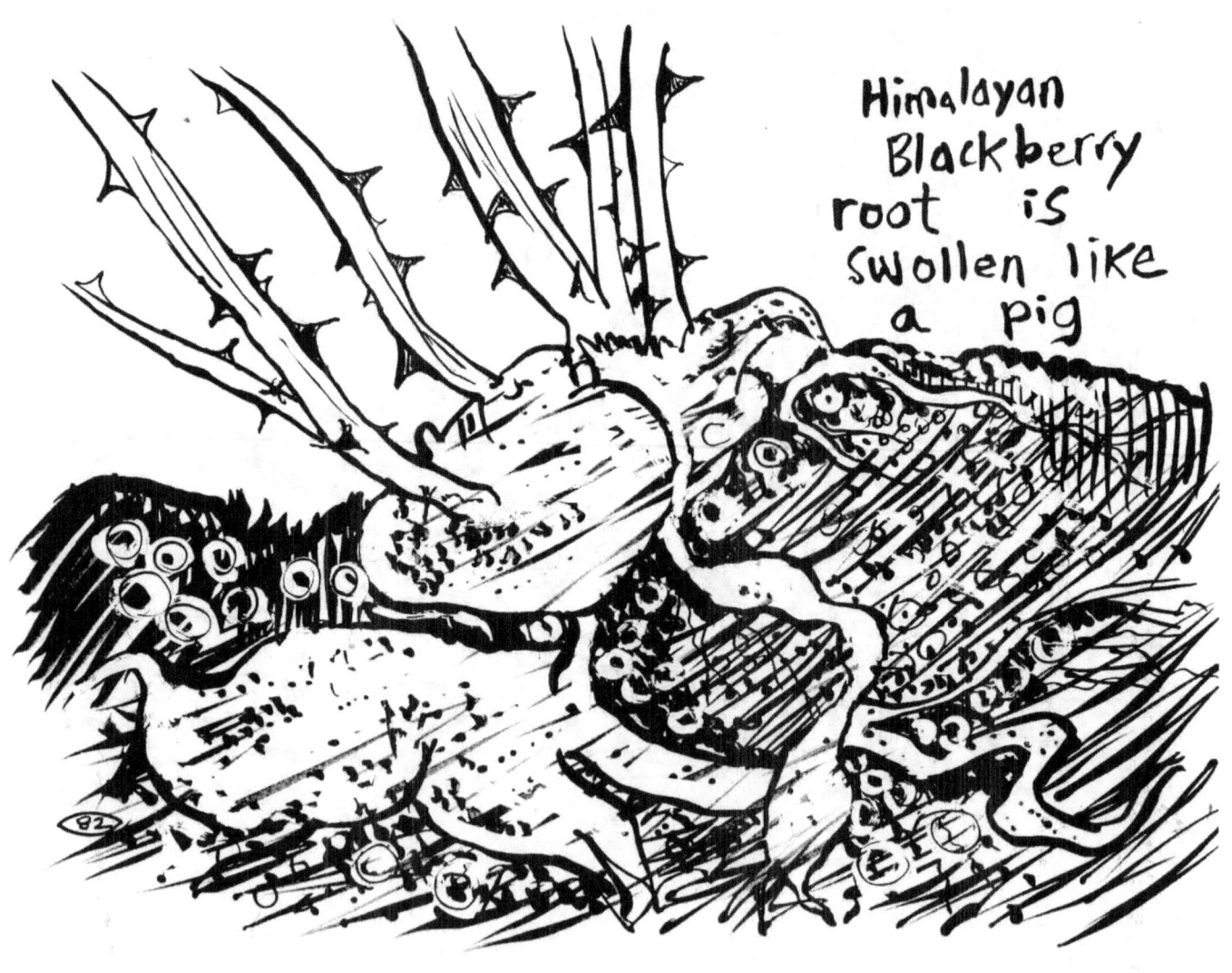

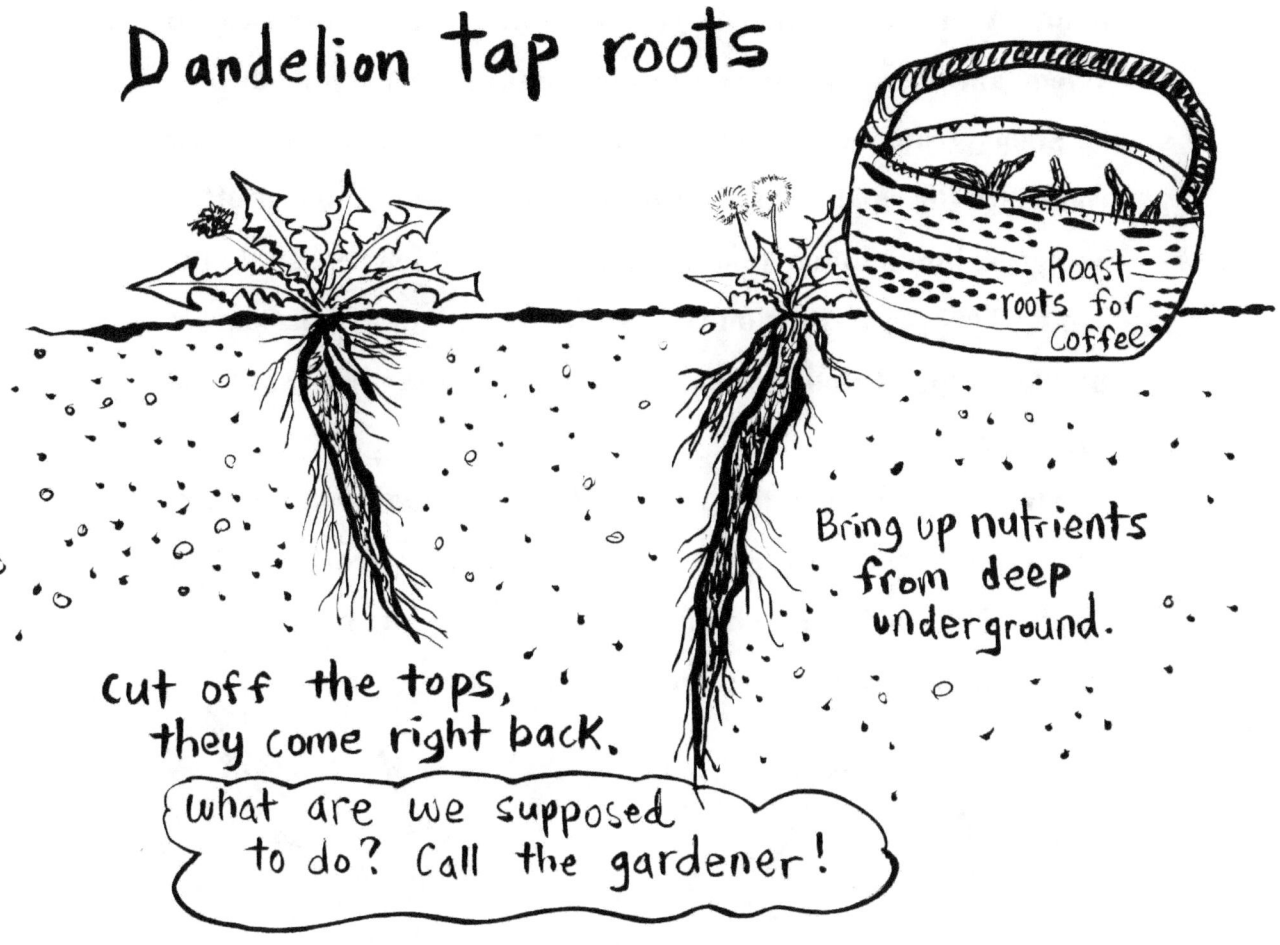

Stems

Stems are the great highways along which water, minerals, and sugars move. Swollen liquid pressure helps to hold up the plant. Water and minerals travel up the stem in tubes called xylem, and sugars go down the stem in tubes called phloem.

Stems grow leaves and flowers towards the sun, and grow roots into the earth. If a piece of stem is broken off or cut off, it can grow into another plant. Some roots and leaves can do the same. This piece is a clone of the original plant. If the parent plant had long tubular yellow flowers with waxy leaves, so will the clone.

Stems are another place to stash food made by the leaves. They enlarge into layers of hefty bulbs and fat corms. They stretch sideways into chunky rhizomes, and run above the ground to take over new territories as stolons or runners.

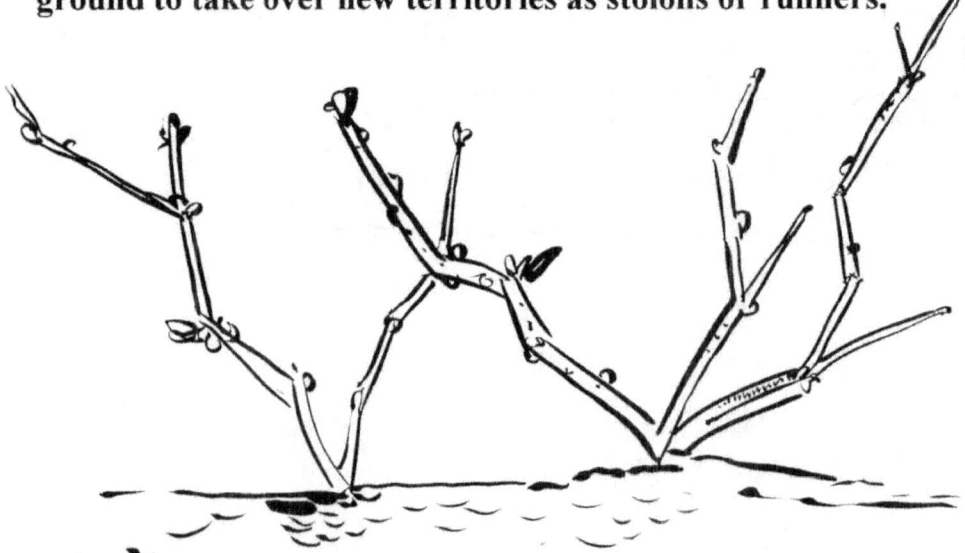

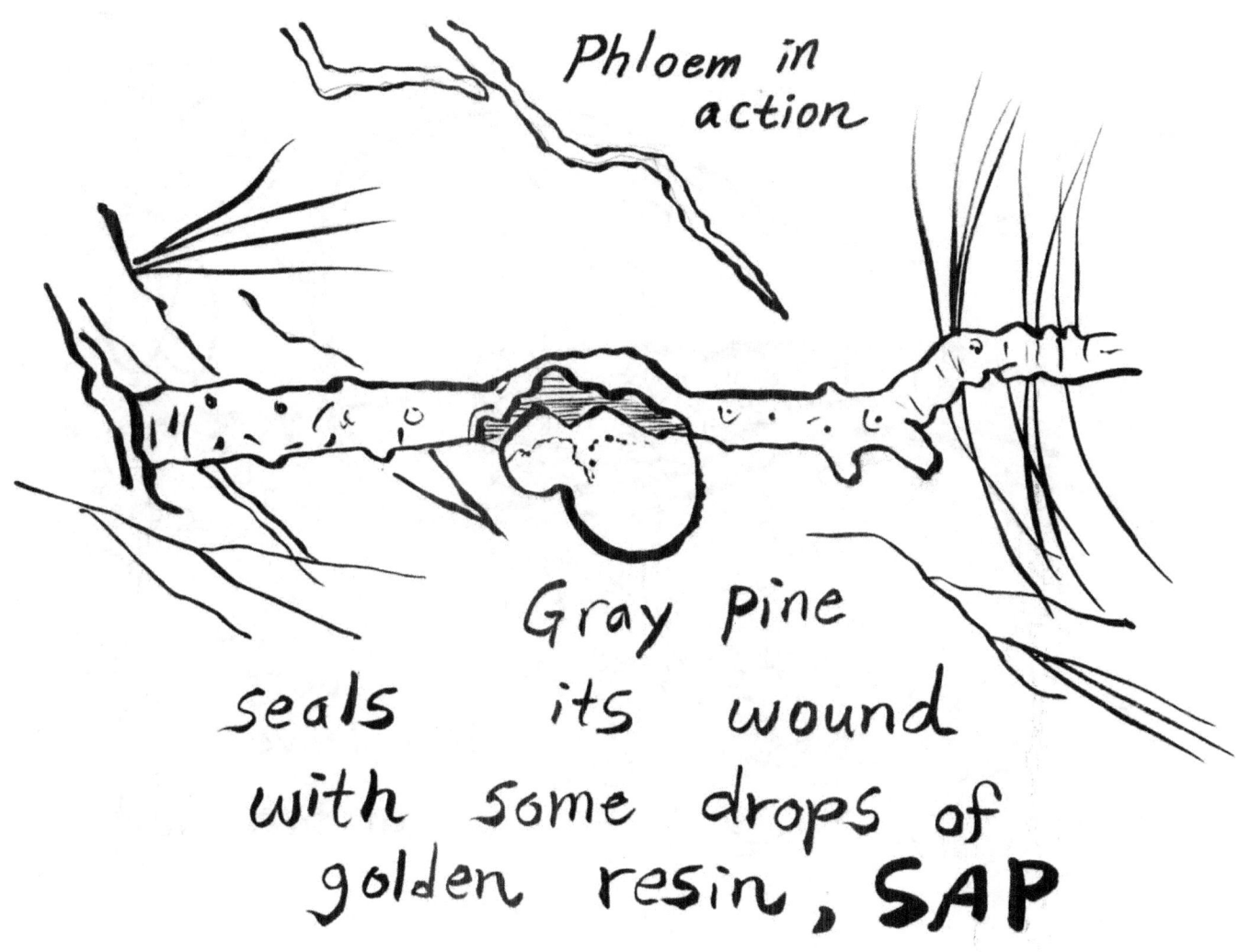

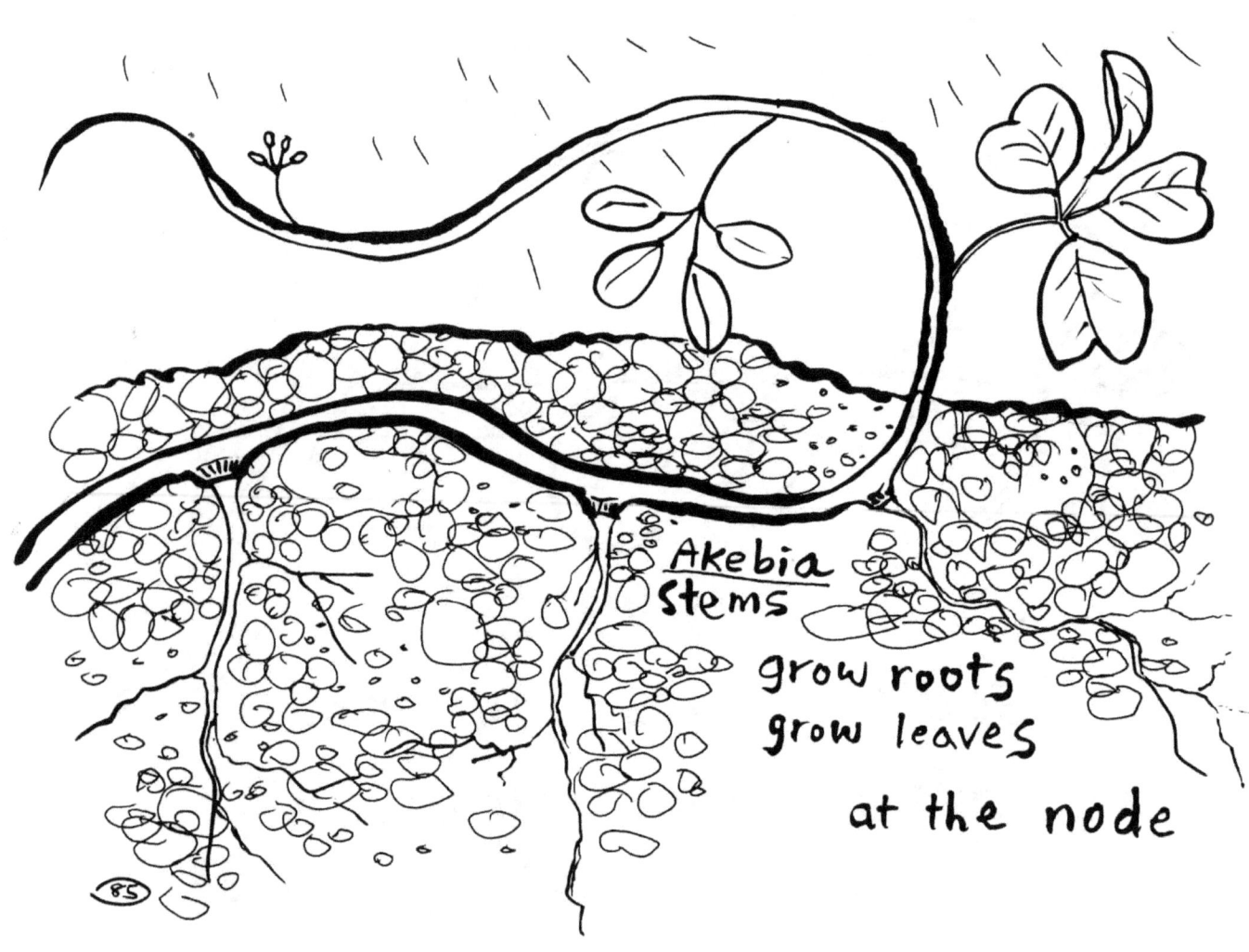

Air

Light

Water

Jasmin stem

two nodes

leaves

roots

A CUTTING

Still attached to its parent, _Kalanchoe_ clones already begin to grow roots

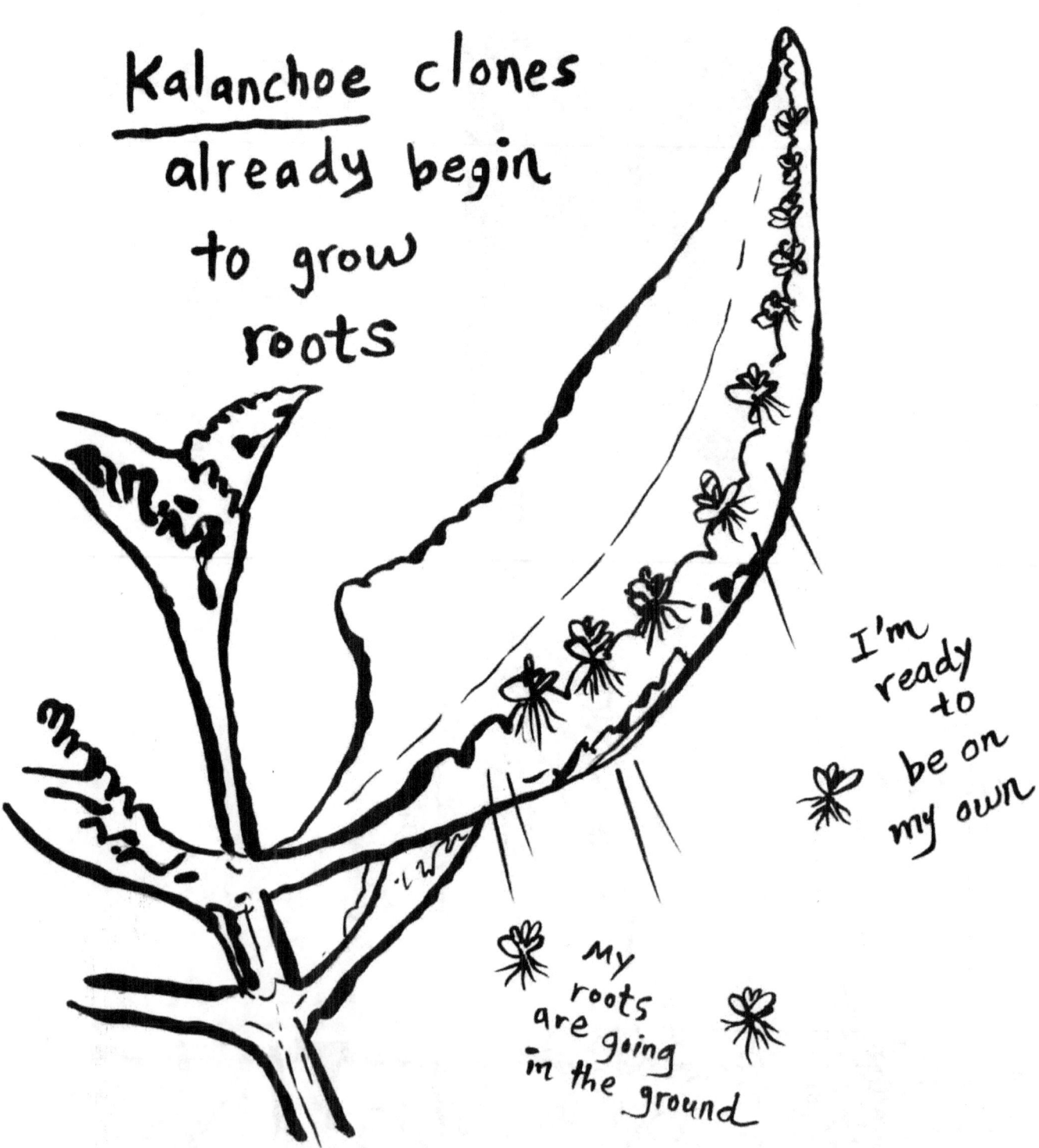

I'm ready to be on my own

My roots are going in the ground

Layers and layers of leaves and stems stored in a round ball

B _ _ B

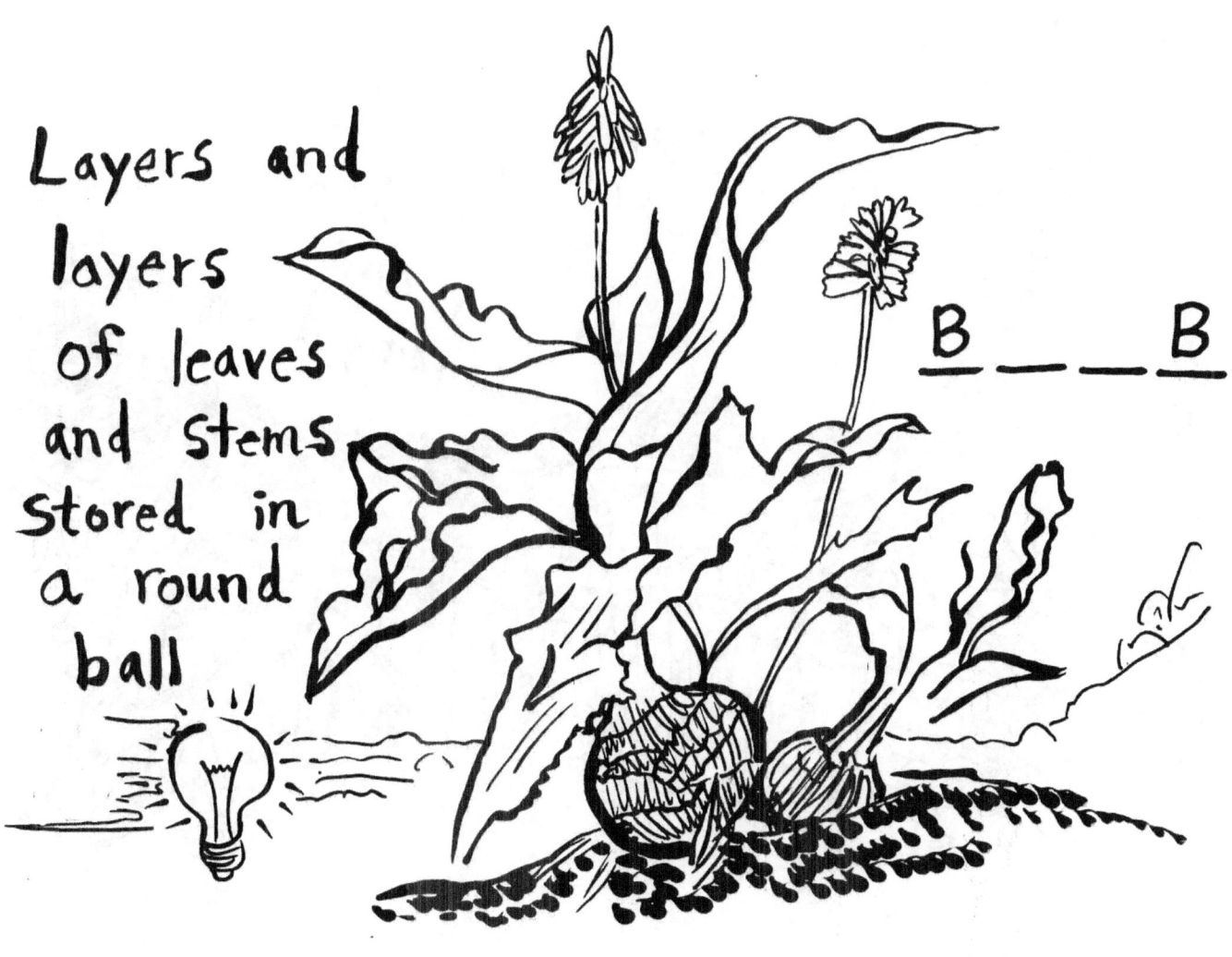

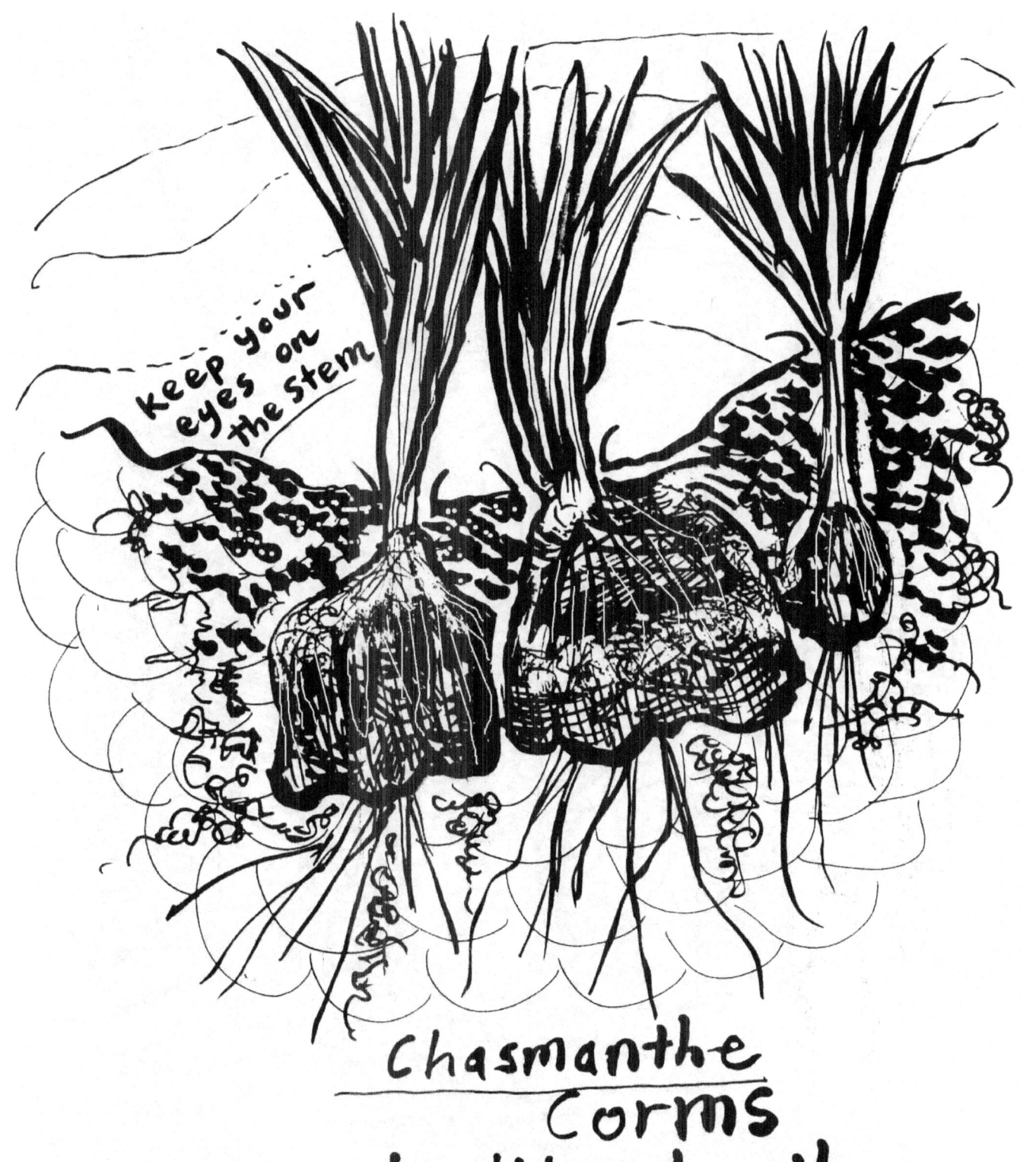

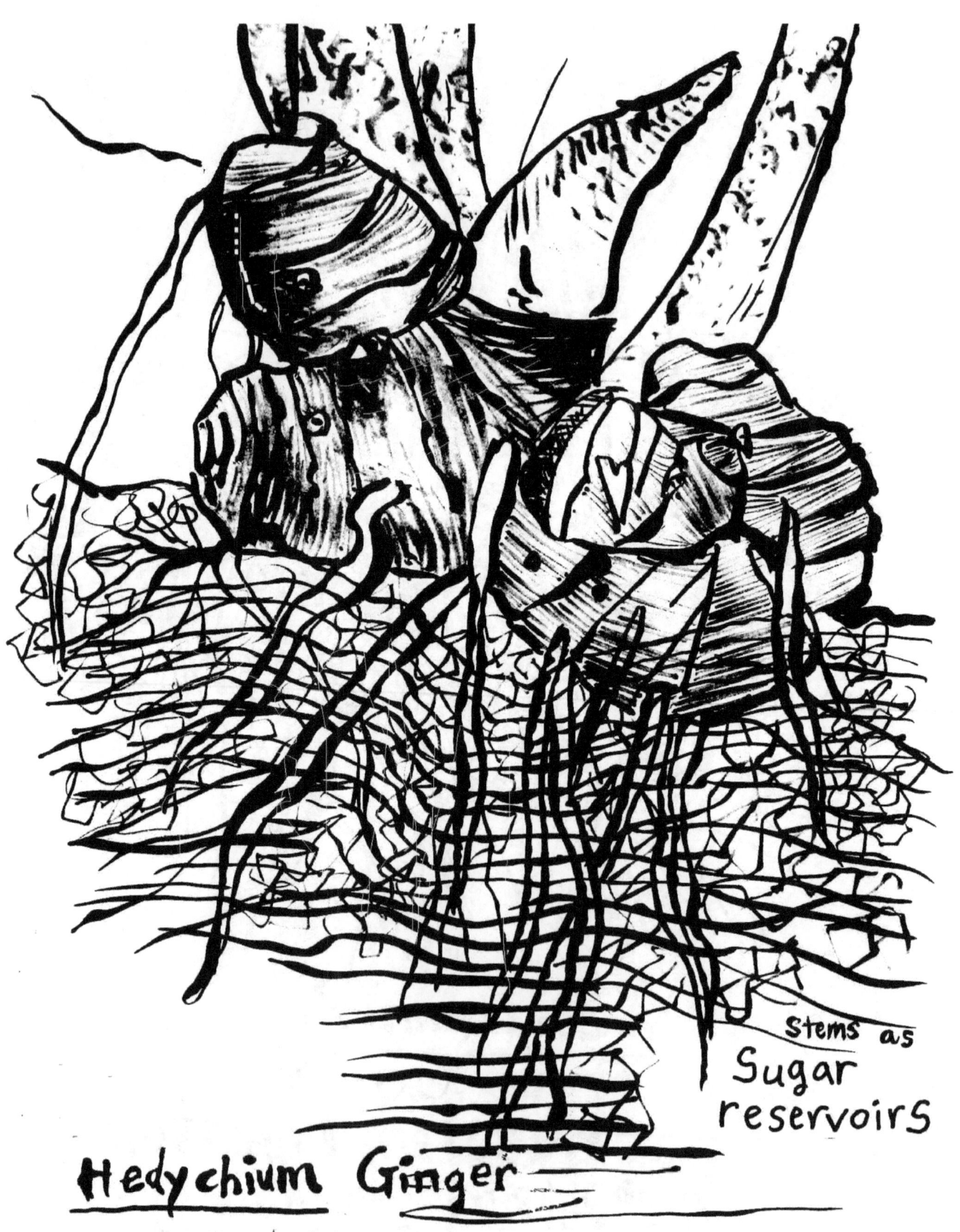

Hedychium Ginger — stems as sugar reservoirs

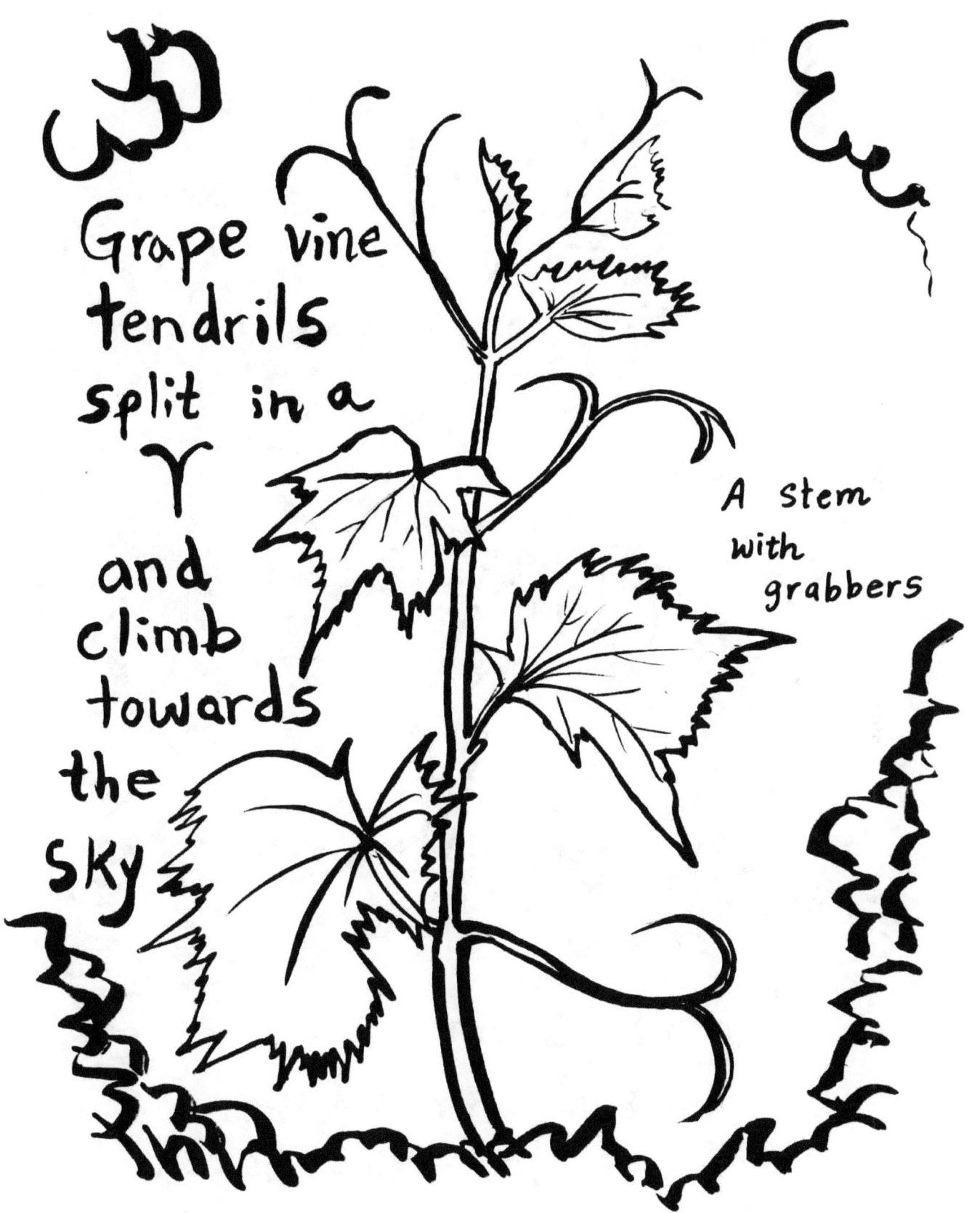

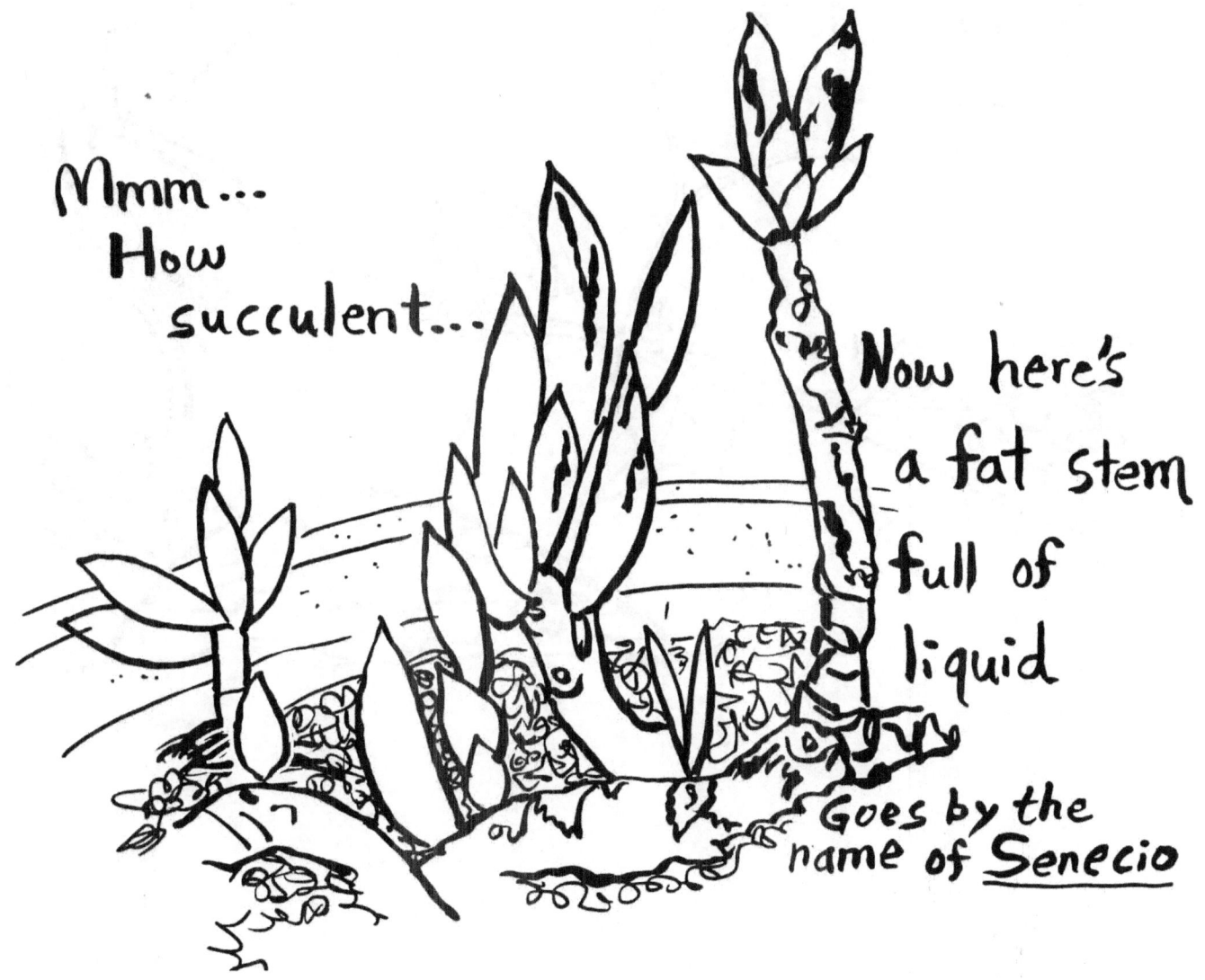

Wood

Sugars made by the leaves are transformed into wood - a hard and strong material that can help the plant stand tall and reach up higher for more light. Wood is made up of long threads of cellulose laid down around brown blocks of lignin; all are made from the sugars. Bark is protection for the sweet parts inside. Beetles, fungi, termites, goats – whoever can digest wood wants a piece of the sugar.

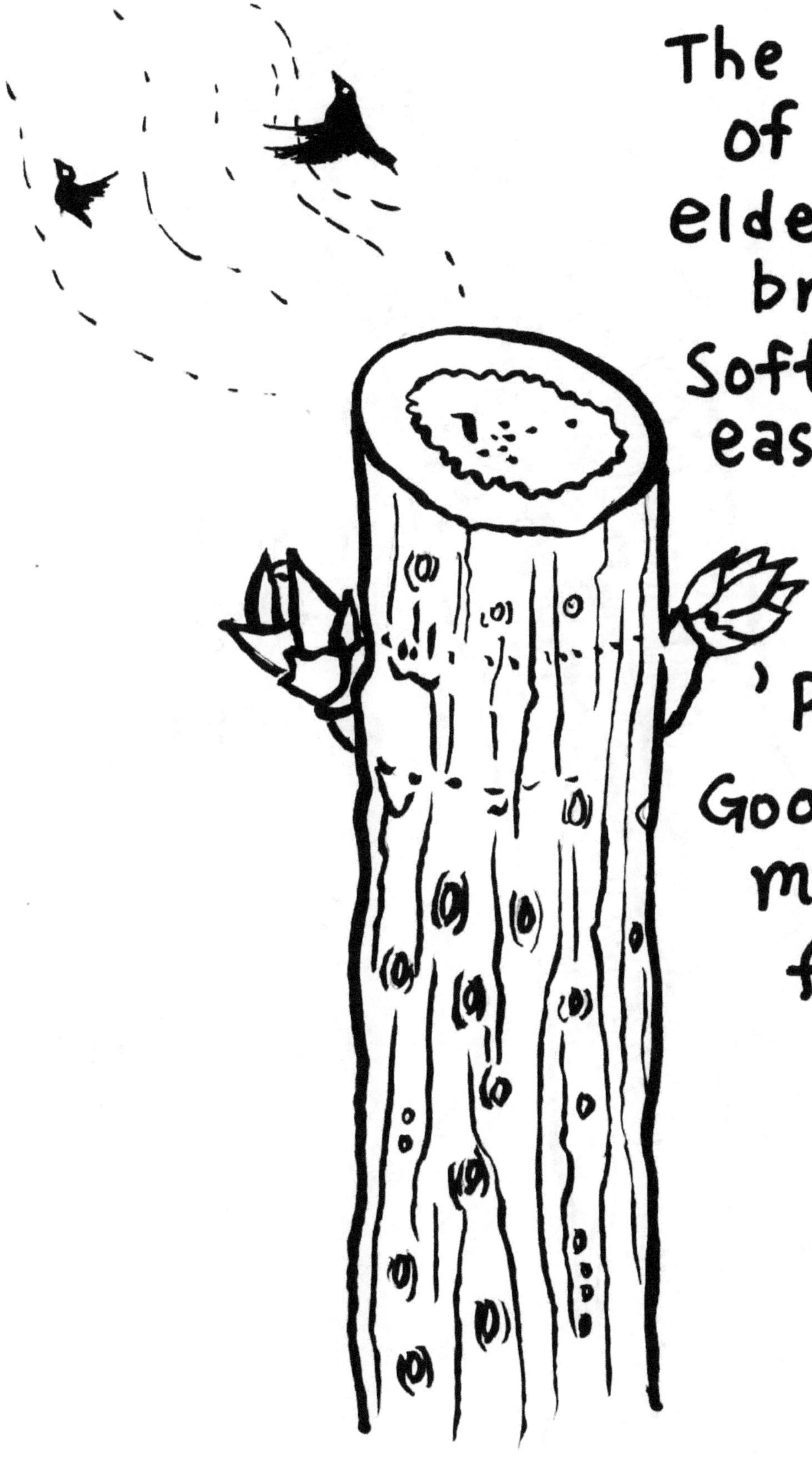

The center of an elderberry branch is soft and easy to hollow out. 'Pithy'. Good for making flutes.

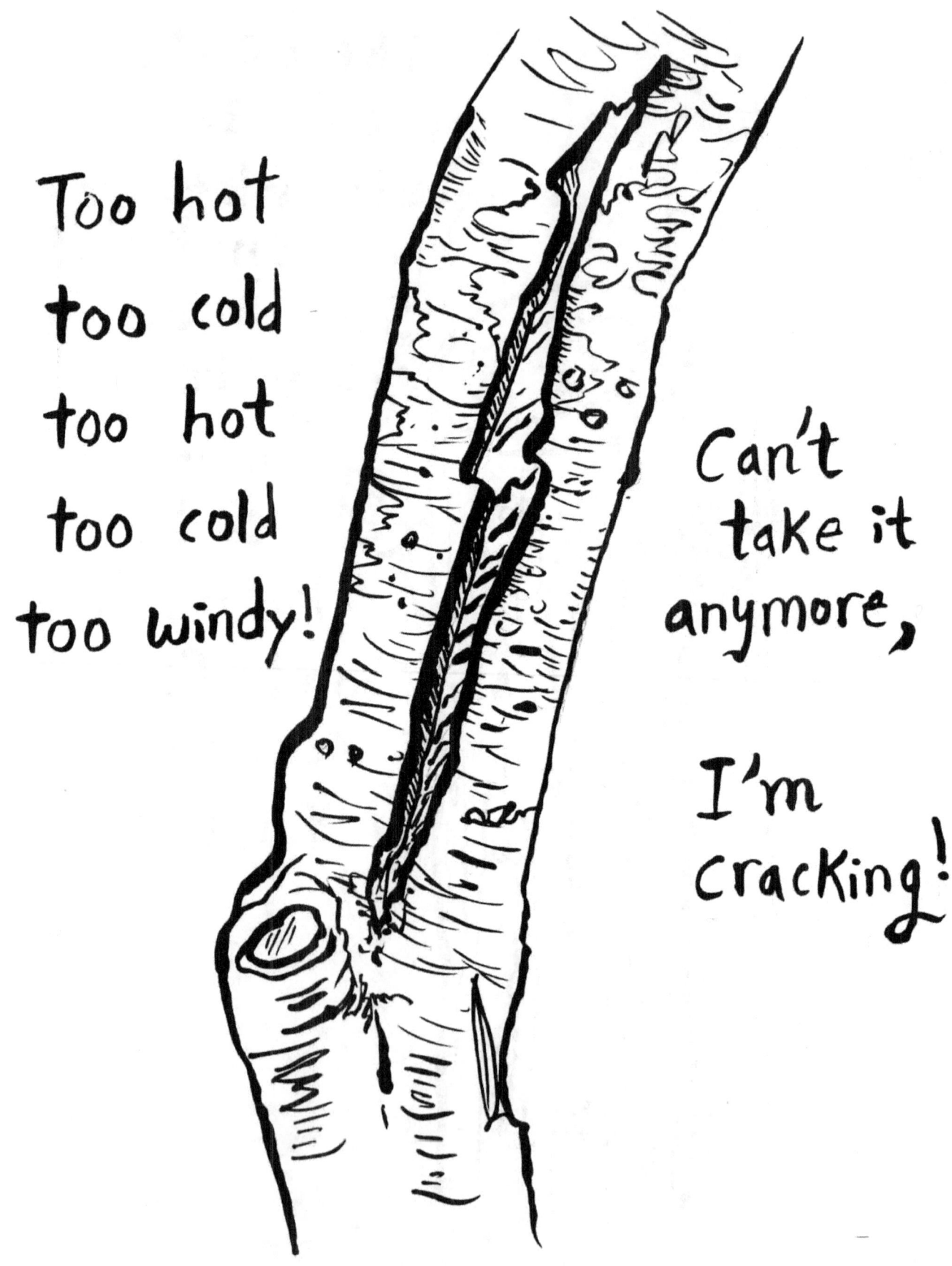

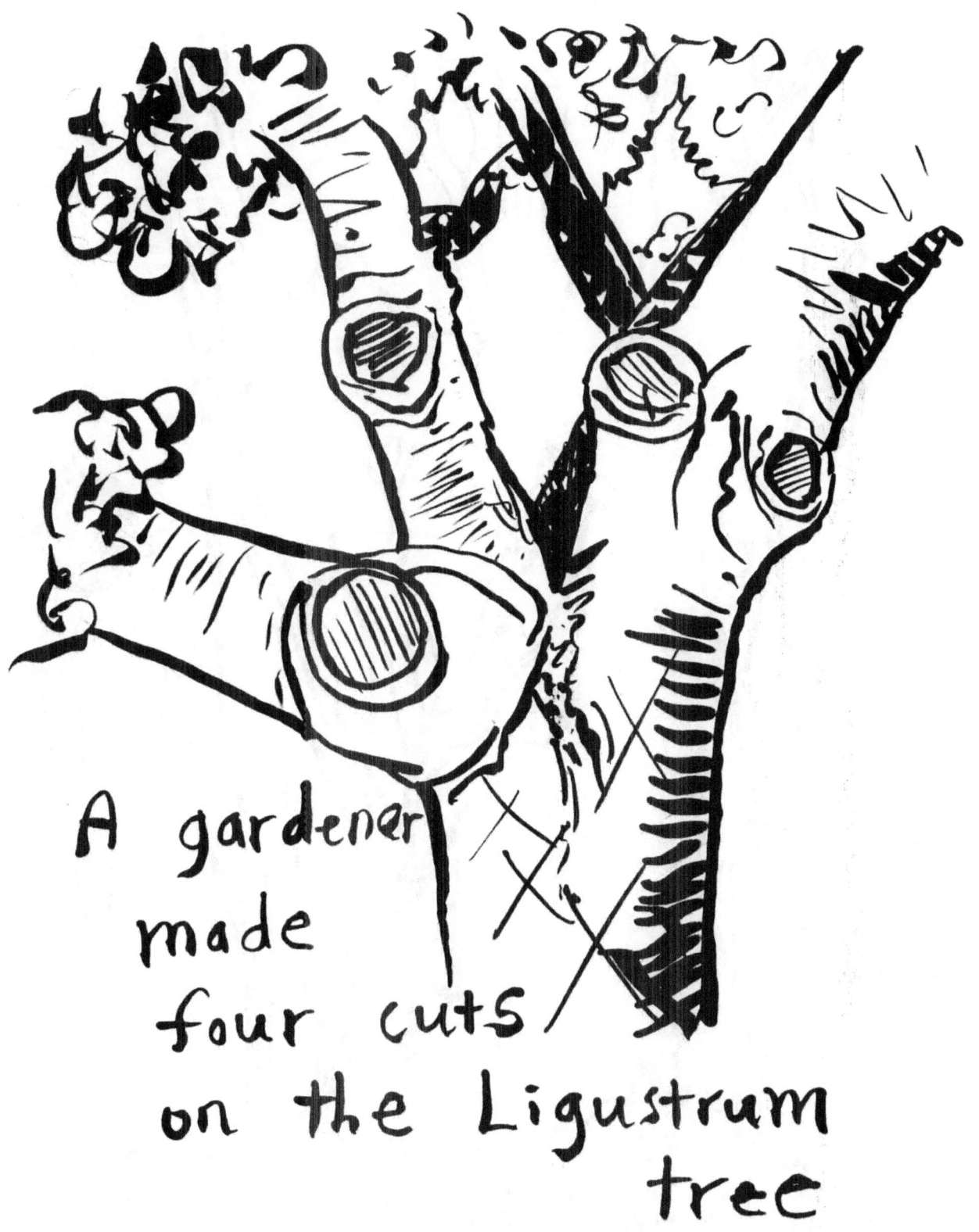

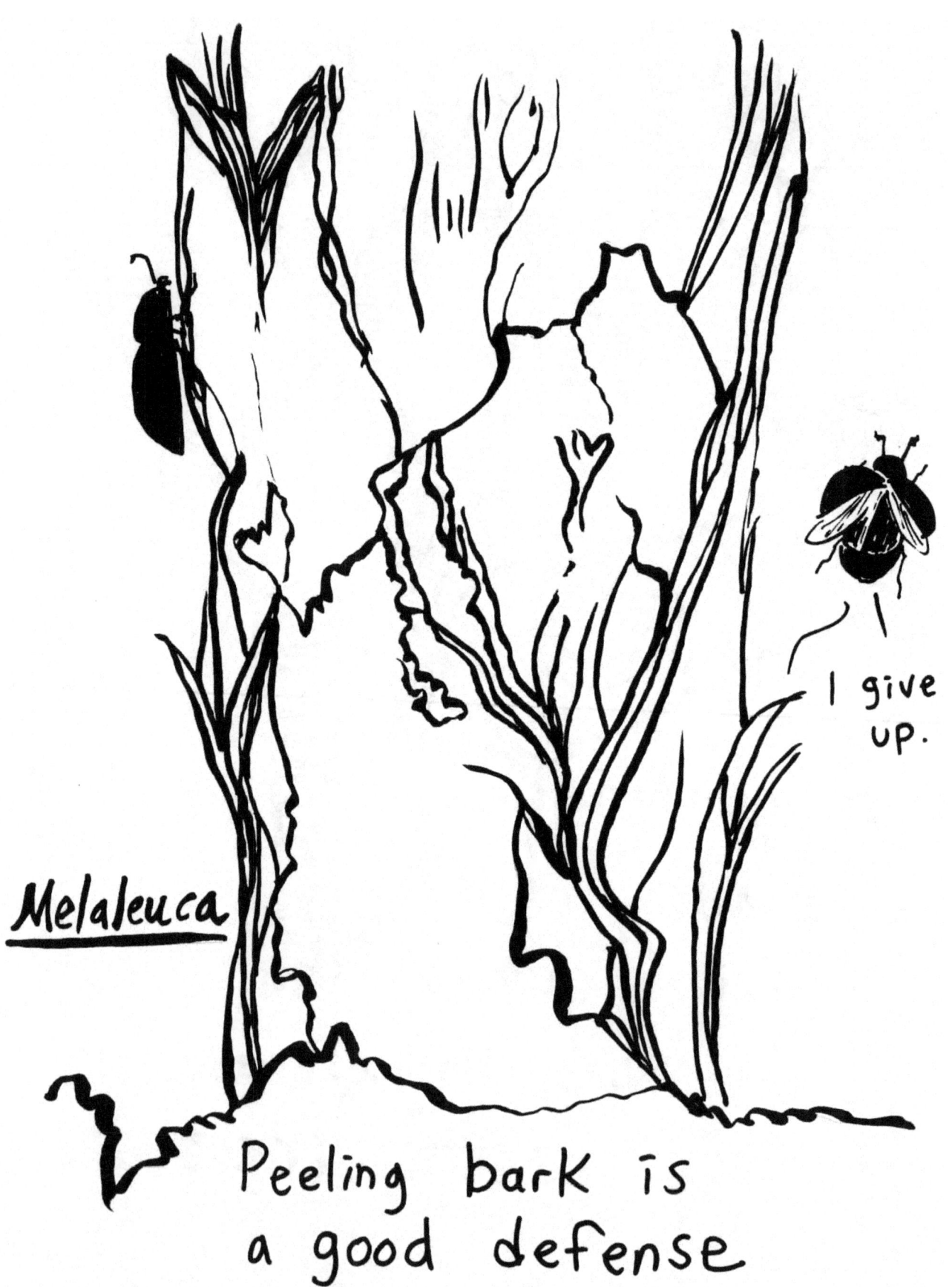

What's worse? Sapsucker holes or beetle larvae under walnut bark?

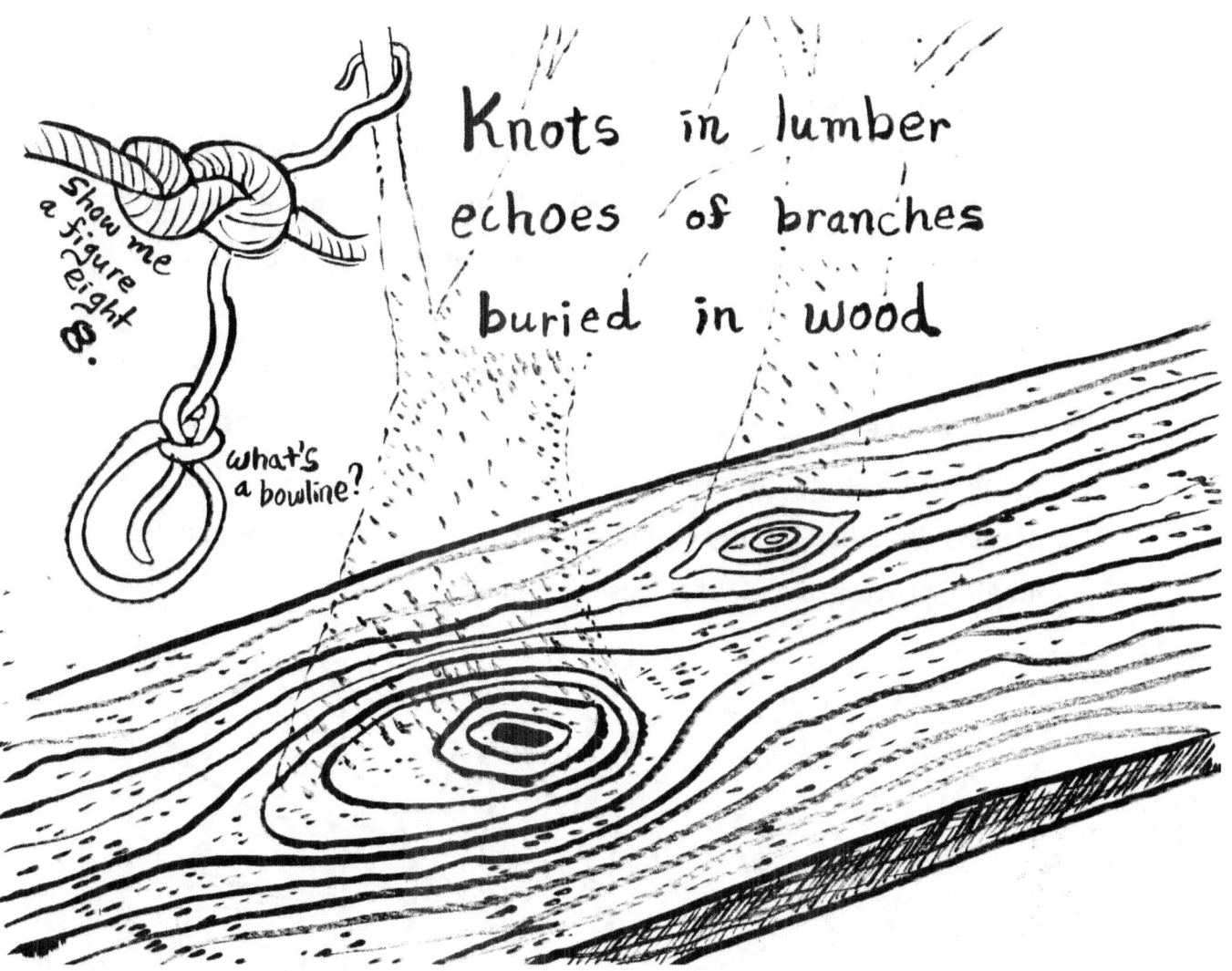

Leaves

Little green bits called chlorophyll in the leaves and stems gather the sunlight.

Water is sucked up the plant from the roots, runs through the stem, and into the leaf's veins. Tiny holes control how much water is lost into the air. Don't want to keep the holes open too long and dry out.

The holes breathe in and out carbon dioxide and oxygen. The leaf makes sugars by putting together three ingredients – warm sunlight, liquid water, and carbon dioxide gas. This process is called photosynthesis. At the end of the sugar making process, the plant releases oxygen.

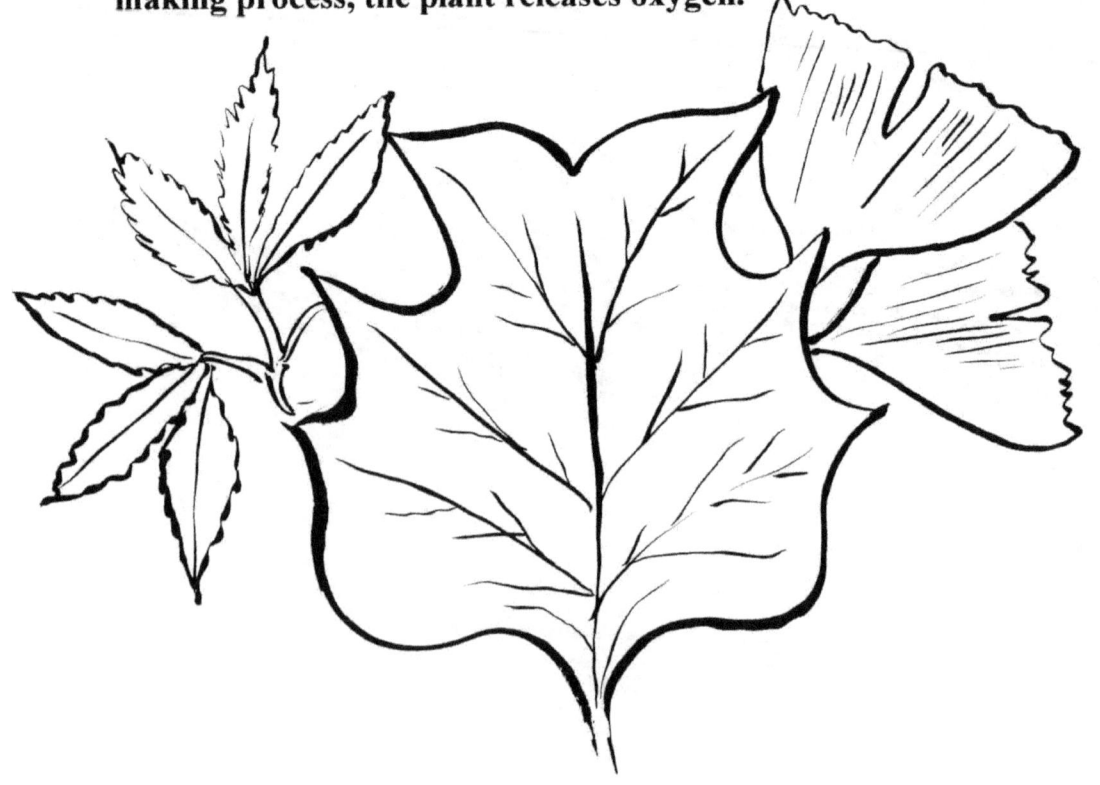

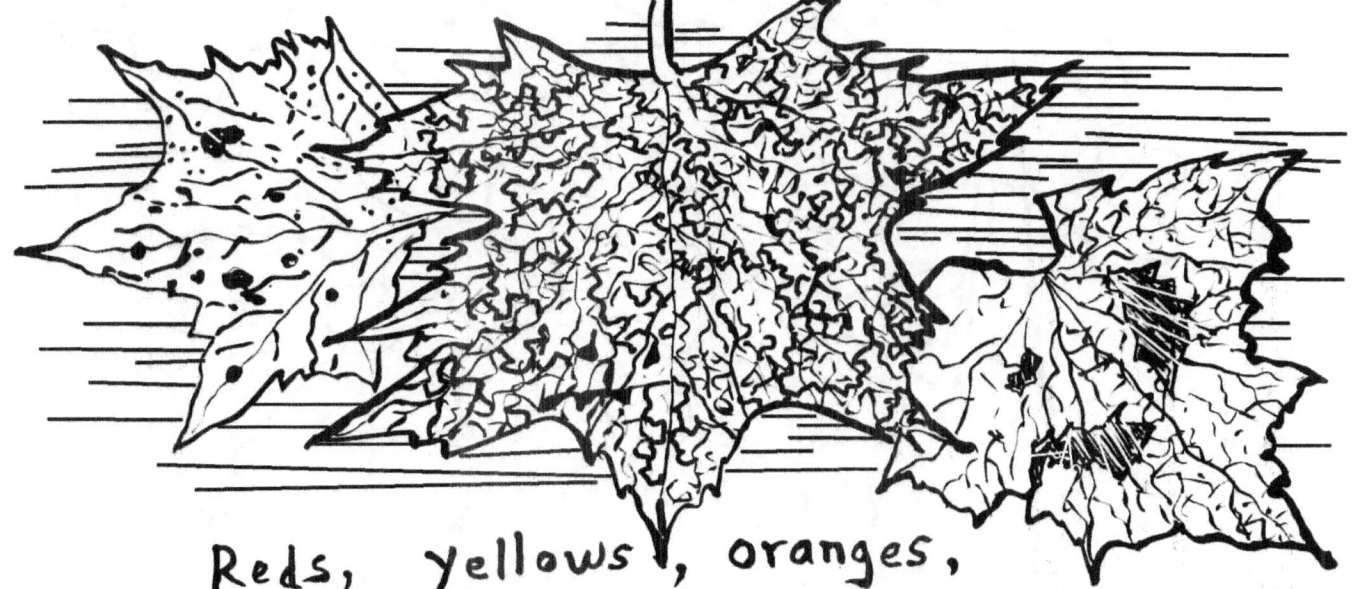

All the green chlorophyll has left the maple leaf

Reds, yellows, oranges, leaf skeletons and veins remain

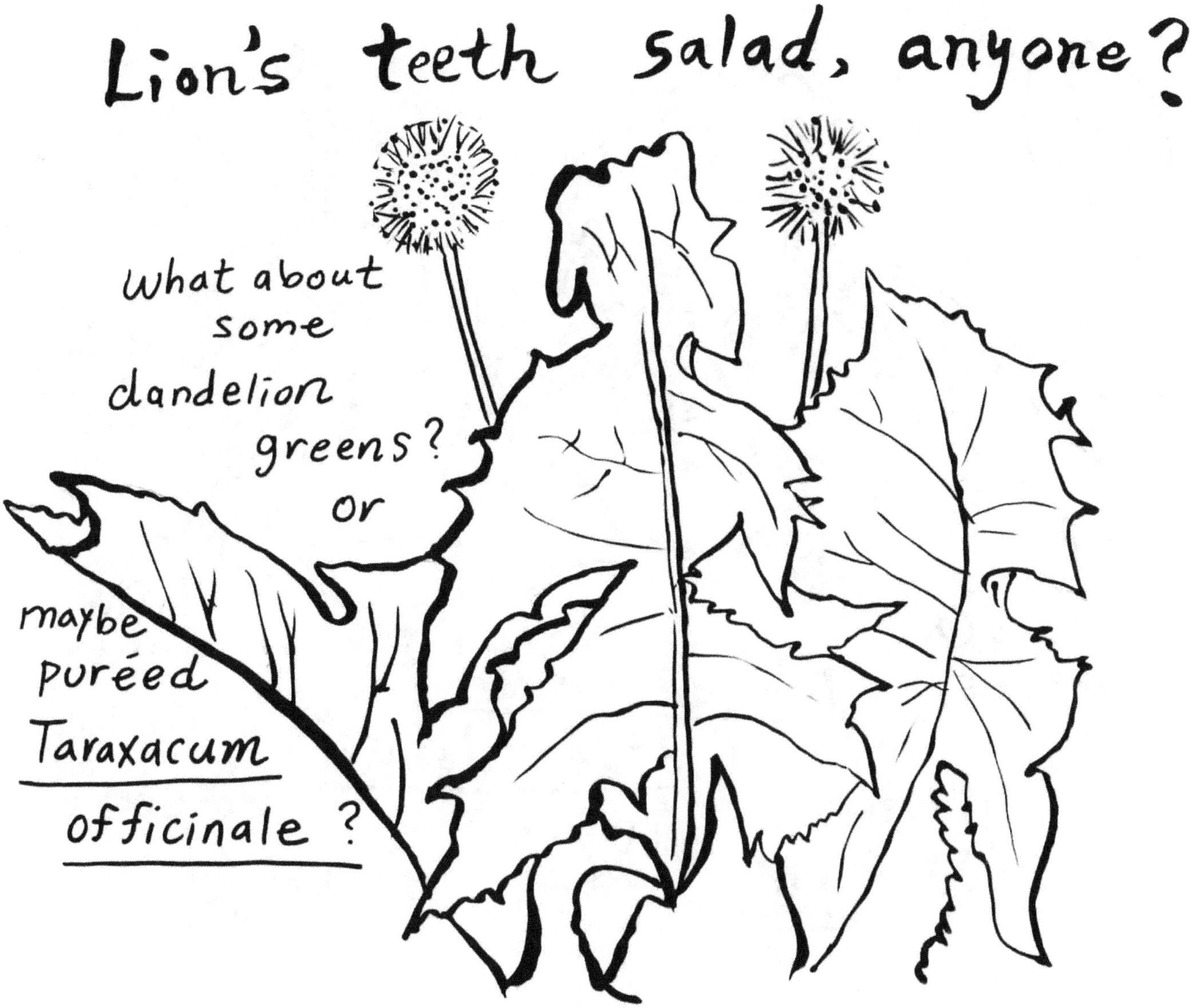

Lion's teeth salad, anyone?

What about some dandelion greens? or maybe puréed <u>Taraxacum officinale</u>?

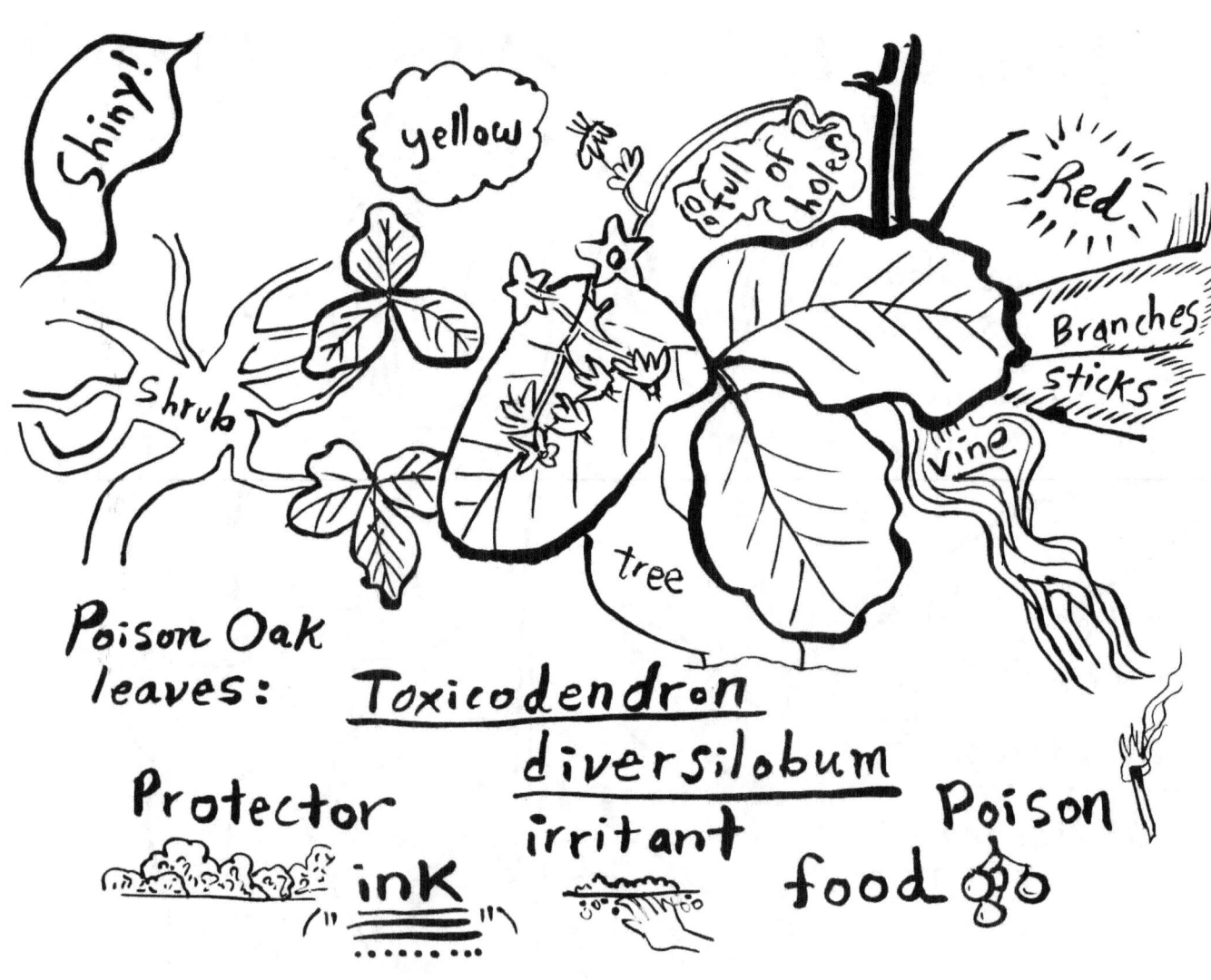

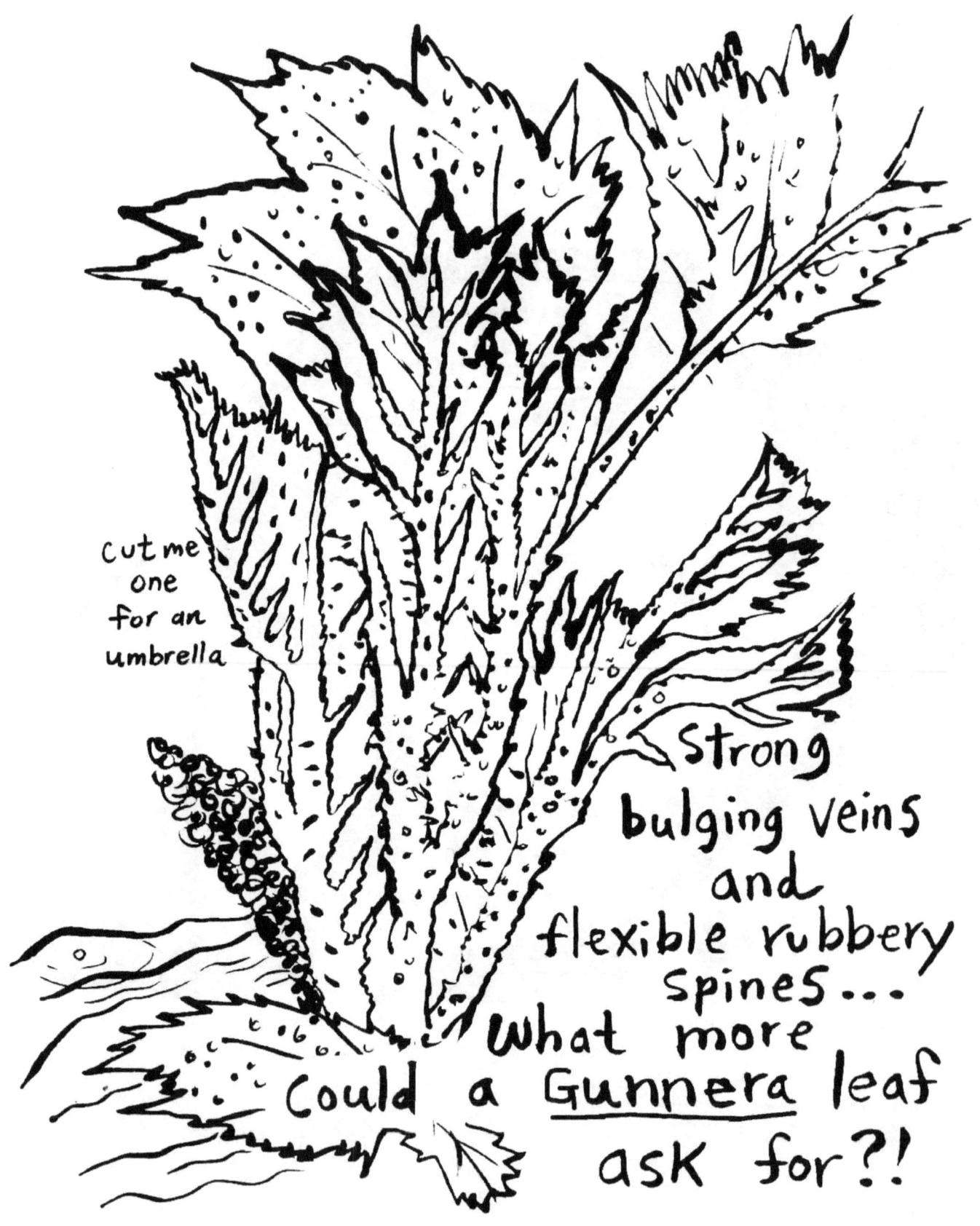

A blanket of
White hairs
on
Oregano
leaves

Cool in the summer
Warm in the winter

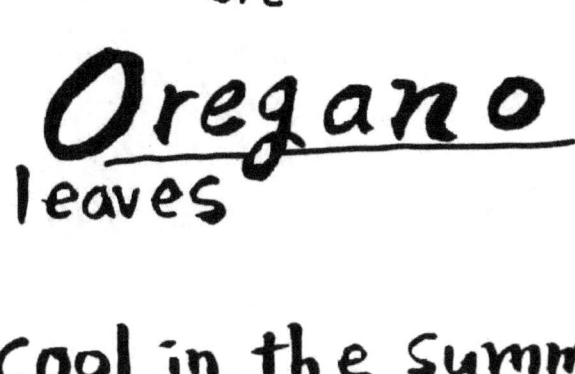

Gonna repeat
  this question
    one more time—
  who are you
    working with
       and
  How many
     are you?

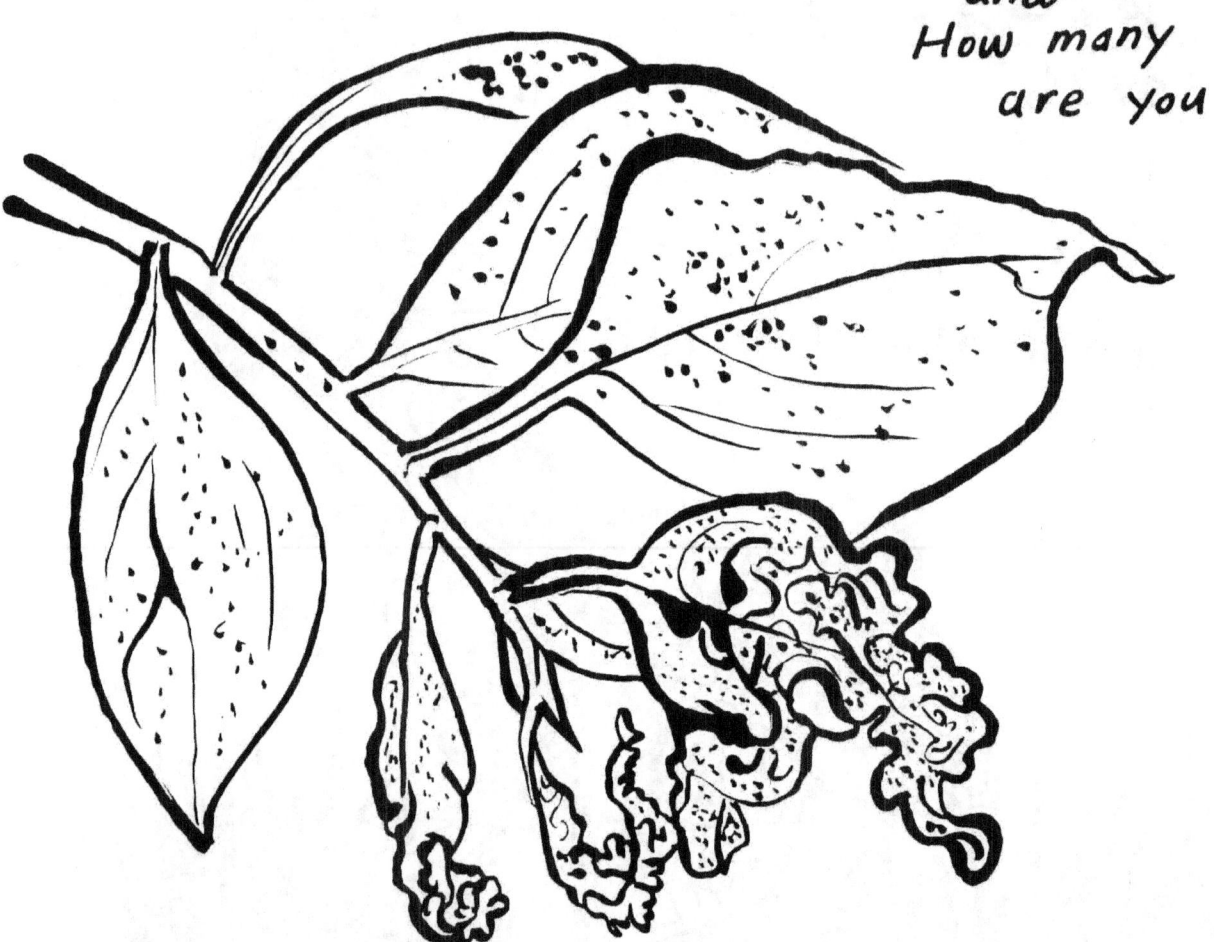

<u>Myoporum</u> leaves have twisted and gnarled tips who is the culprit?

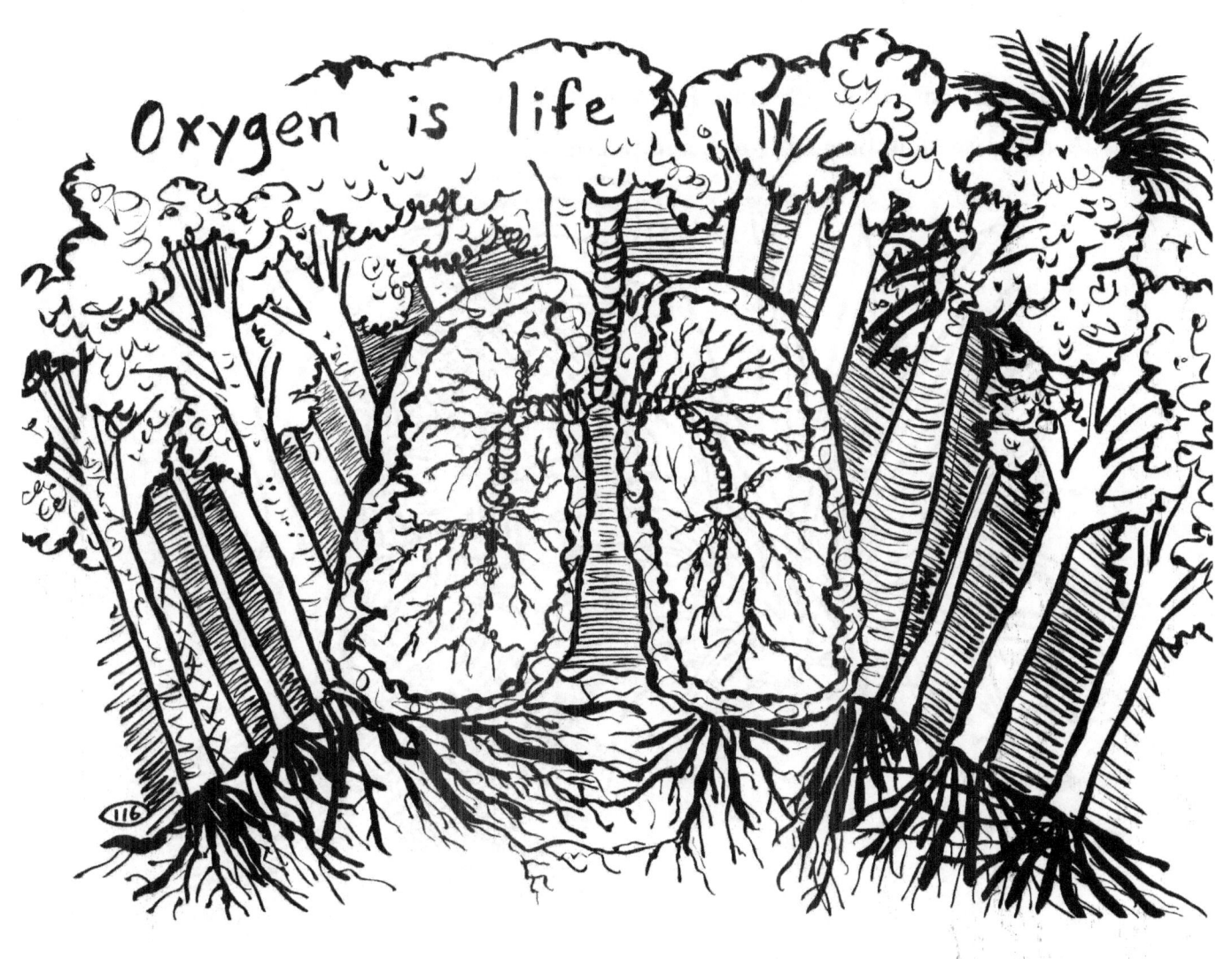

Growth and repair

Sugar made by the leaves is moved to different parts of the plant. Sugar's basic building blocks are taken apart and assembled, together with other components, into starches, proteins, oils, hormones, alkaloids, and fibers. These become part of the fruits and seeds, the stems, and the roots.

To grow bigger or seal off a wound, a plant uses some of the stored energy. In this process, plants breathe in oxygen and breathe out carbon dioxide. This is called respiration. Animals do it, we do it, bacteria do it, and plants do it.

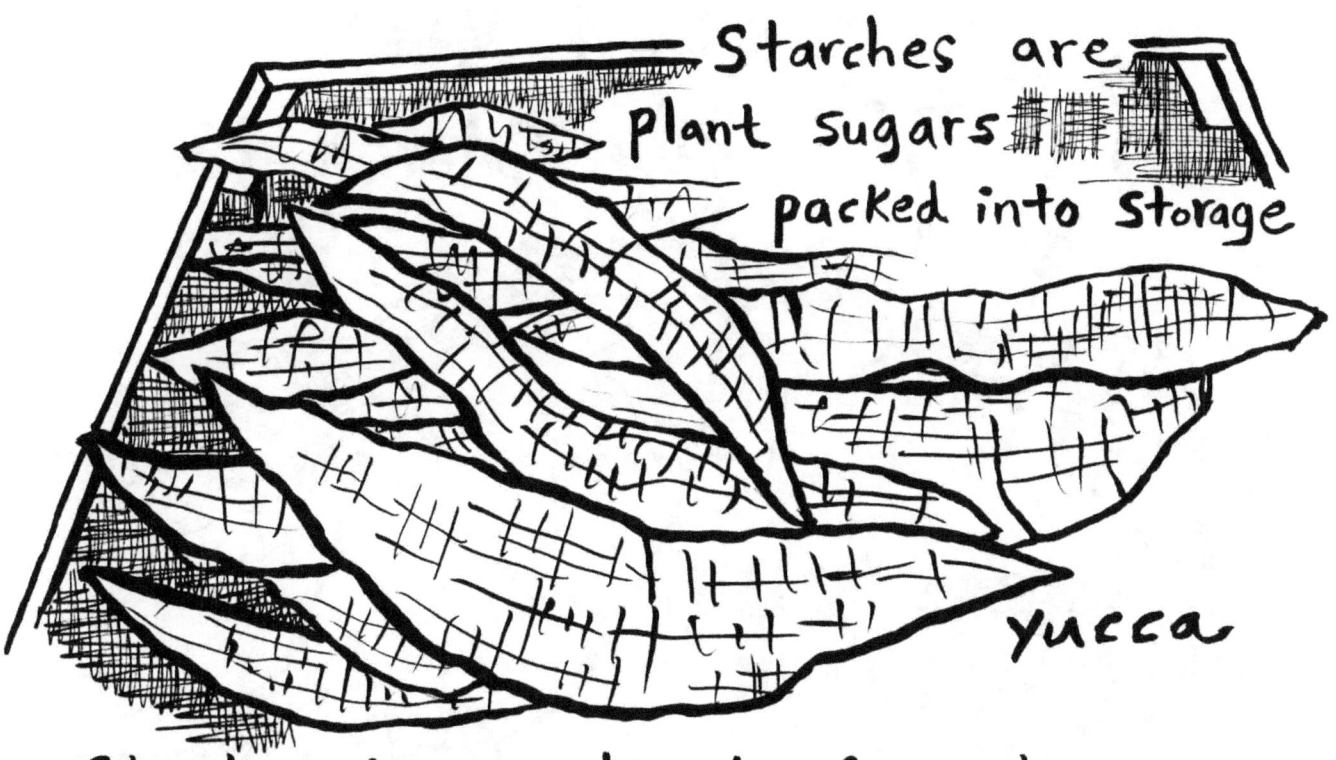

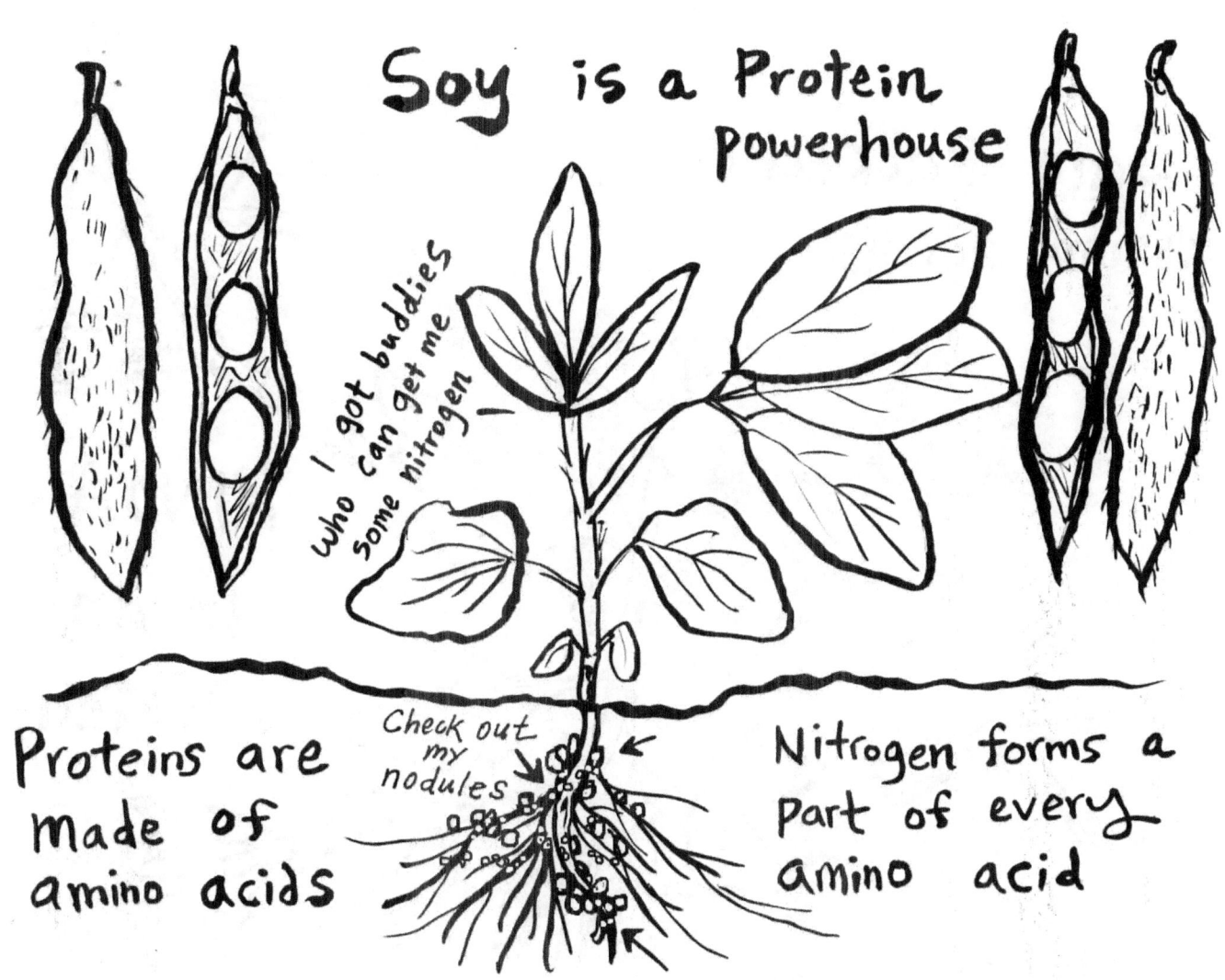

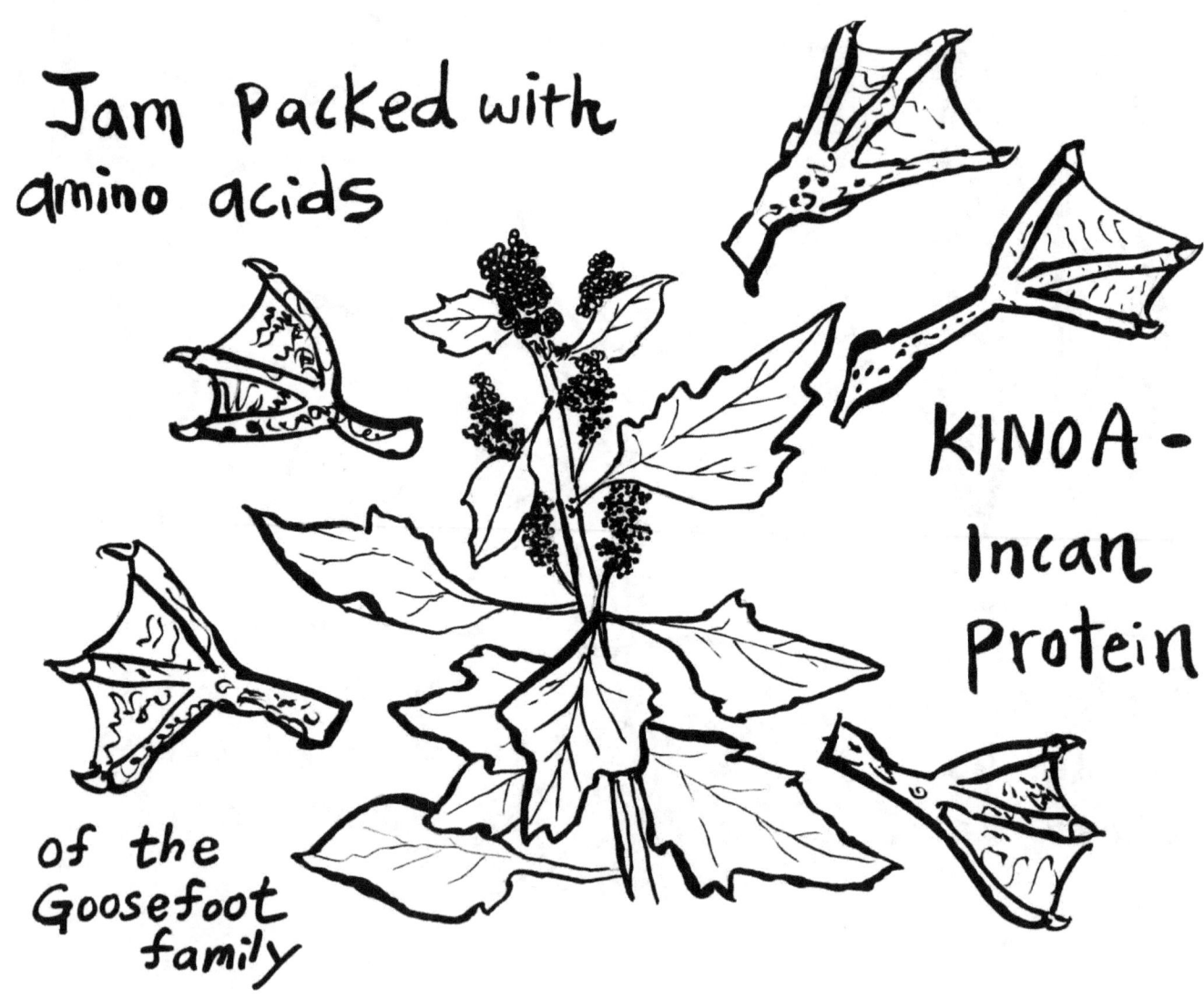

Oil is pressed and squeezed from bulbs, fruits, and seeds

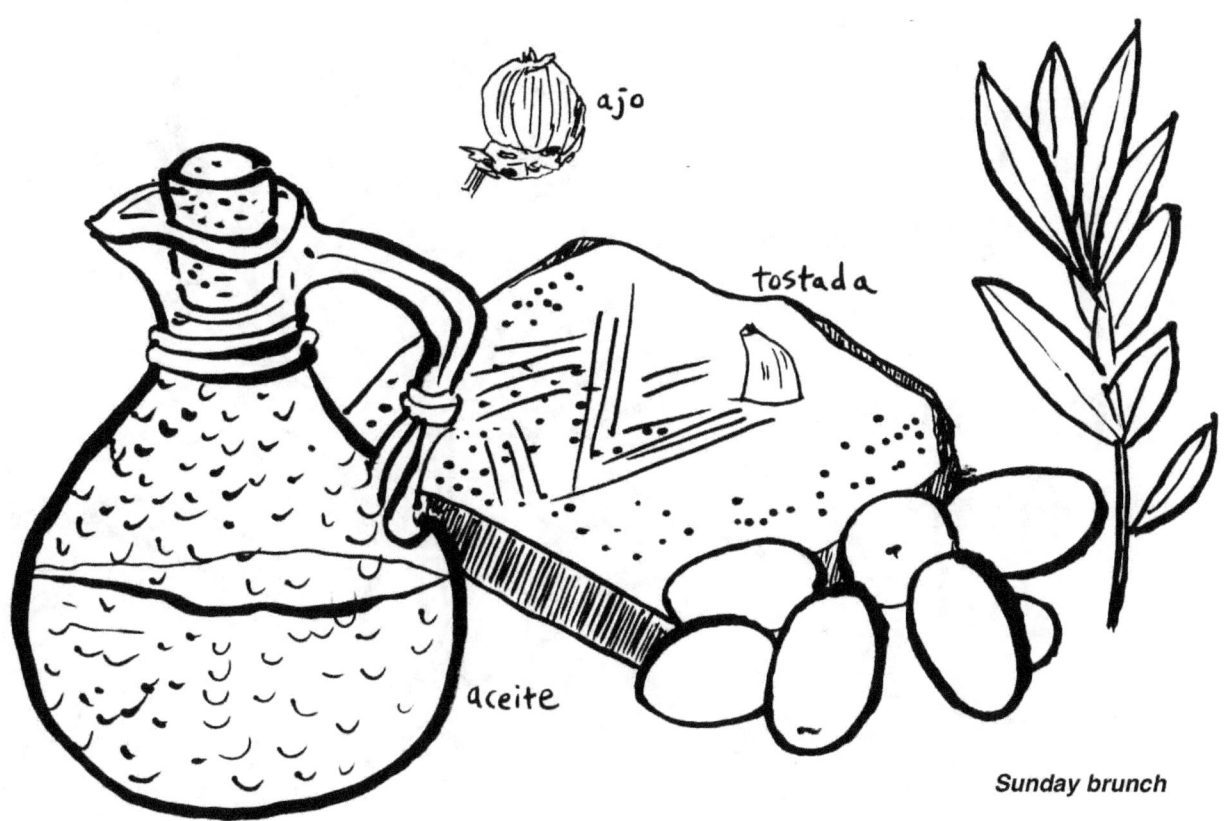

Sunday brunch

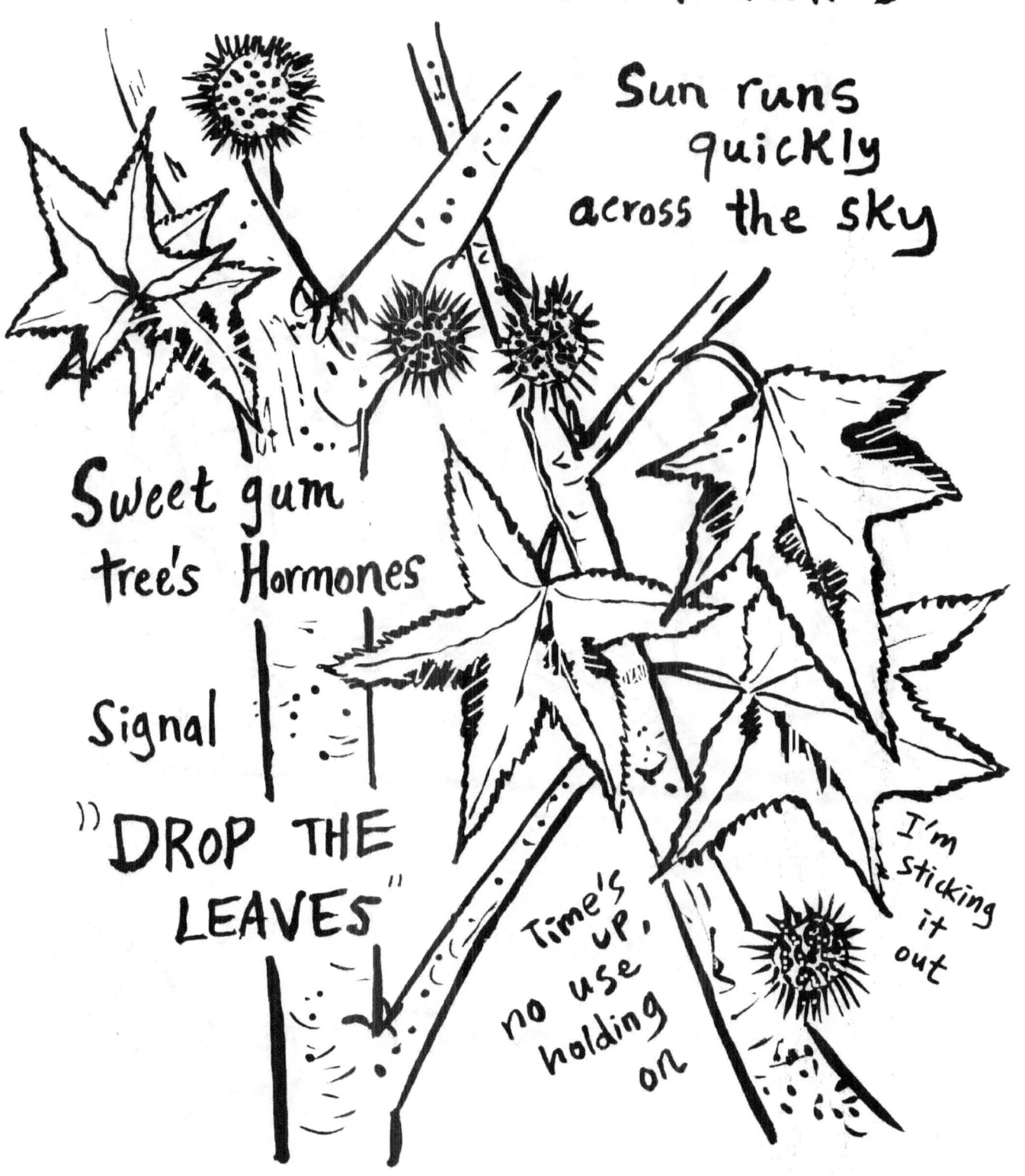

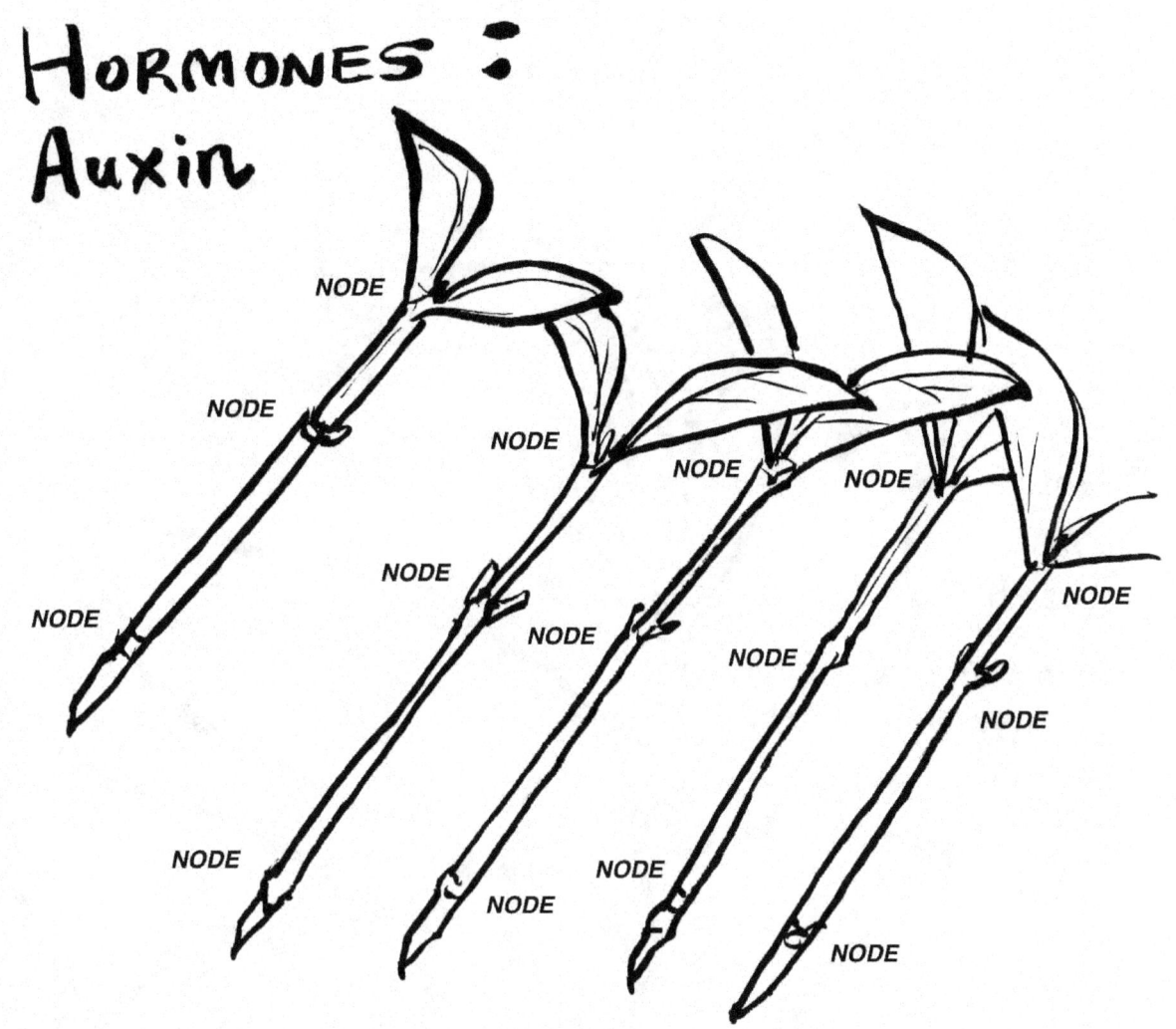

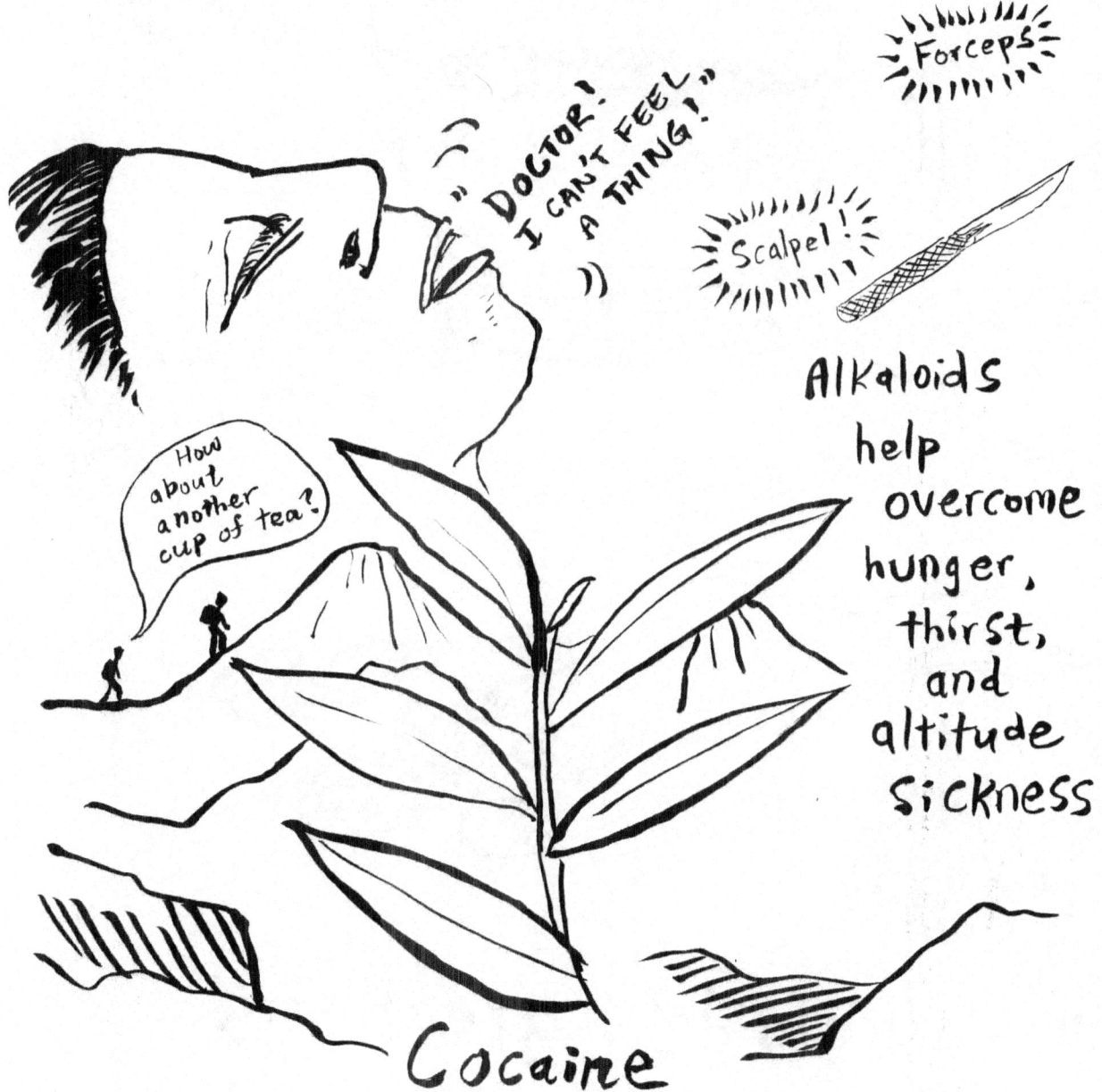

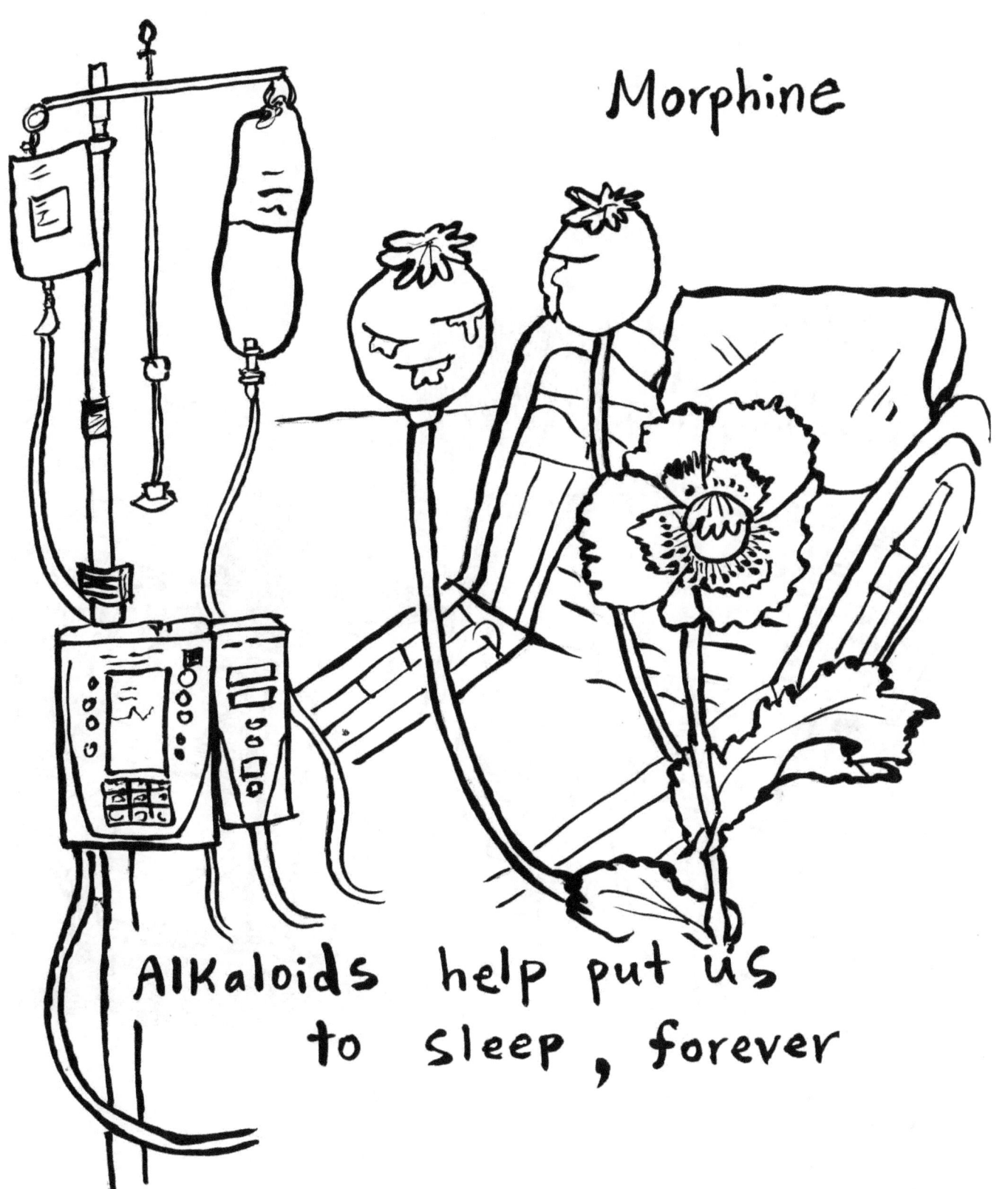

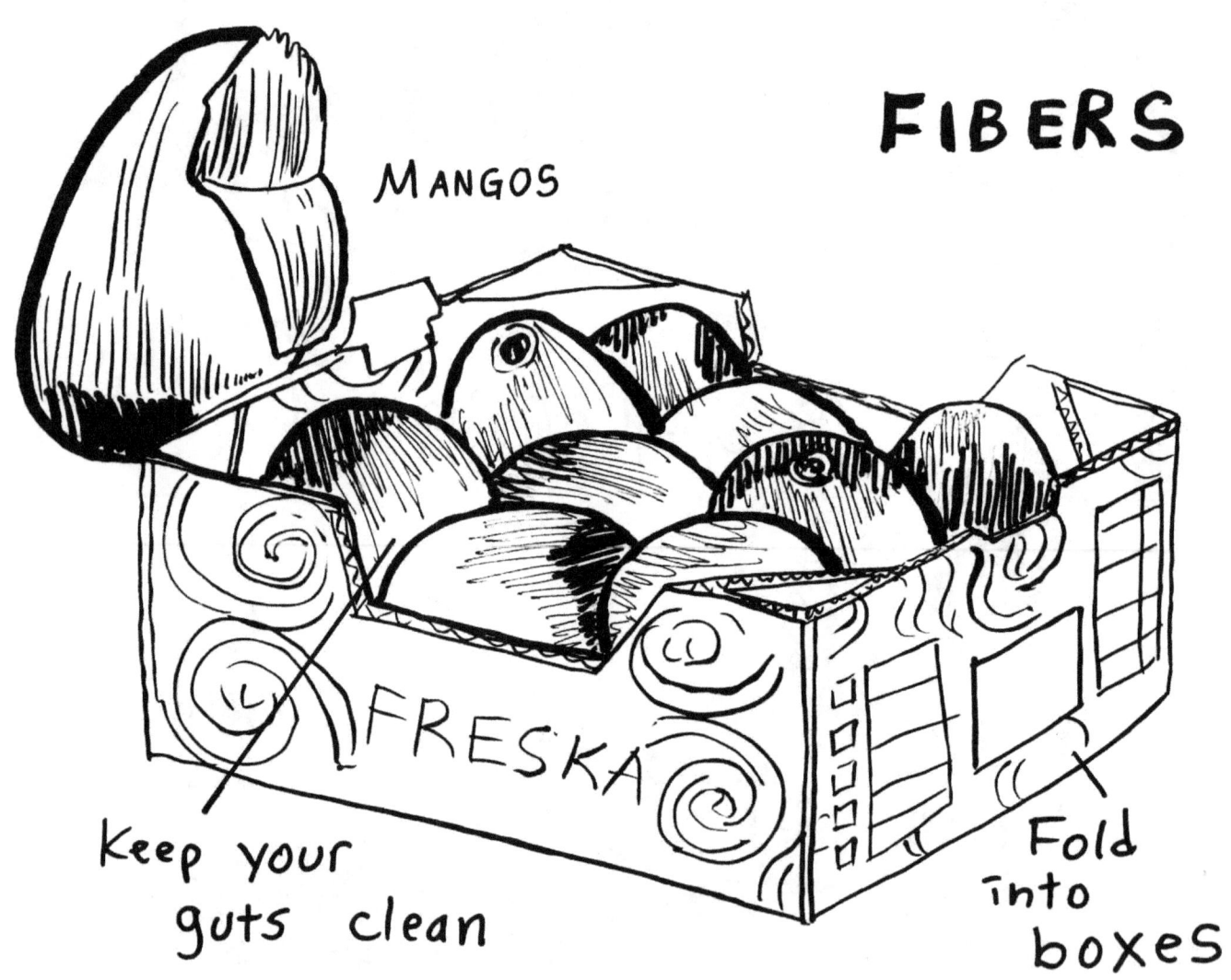

Cotton fibers protect cotton seeds

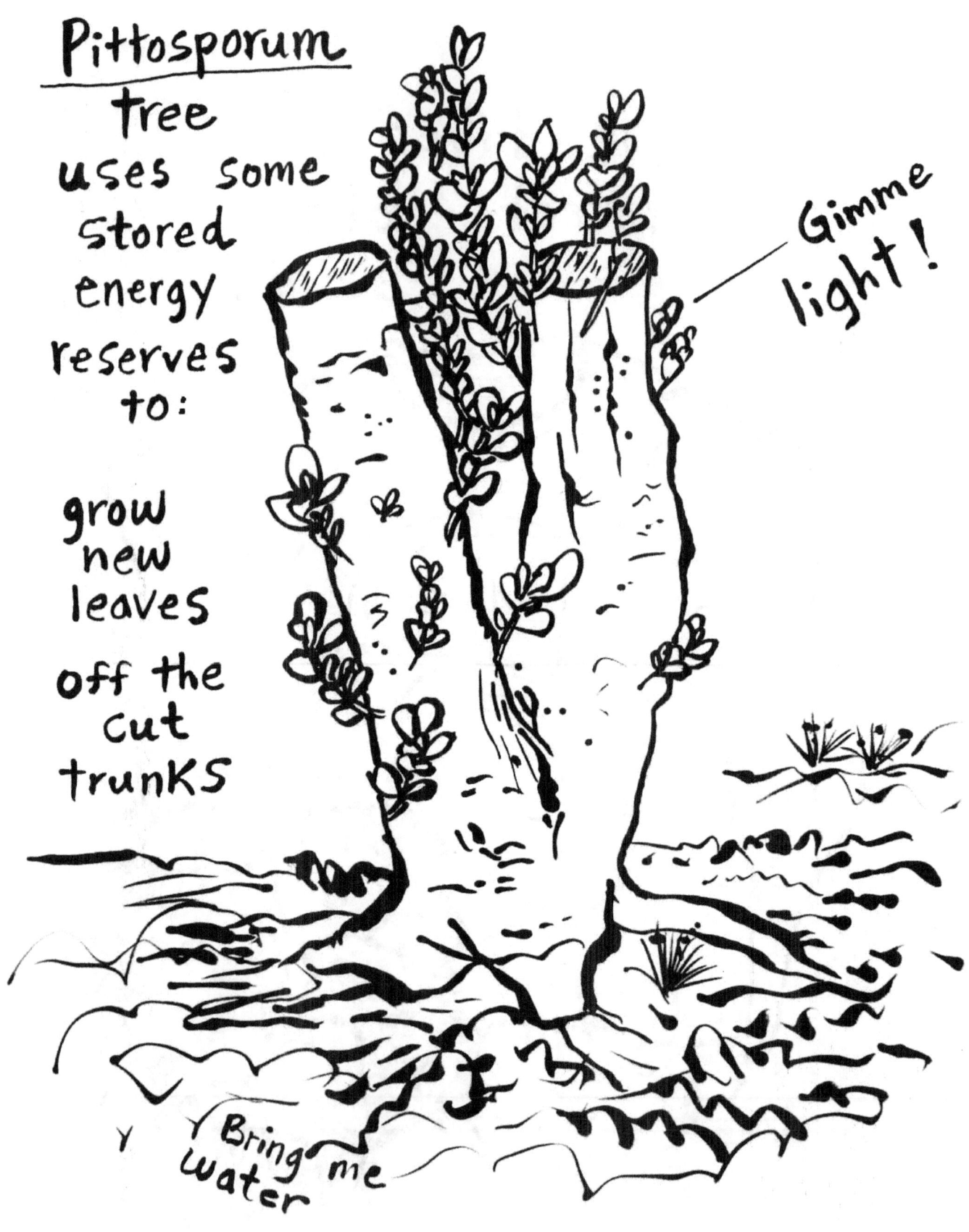

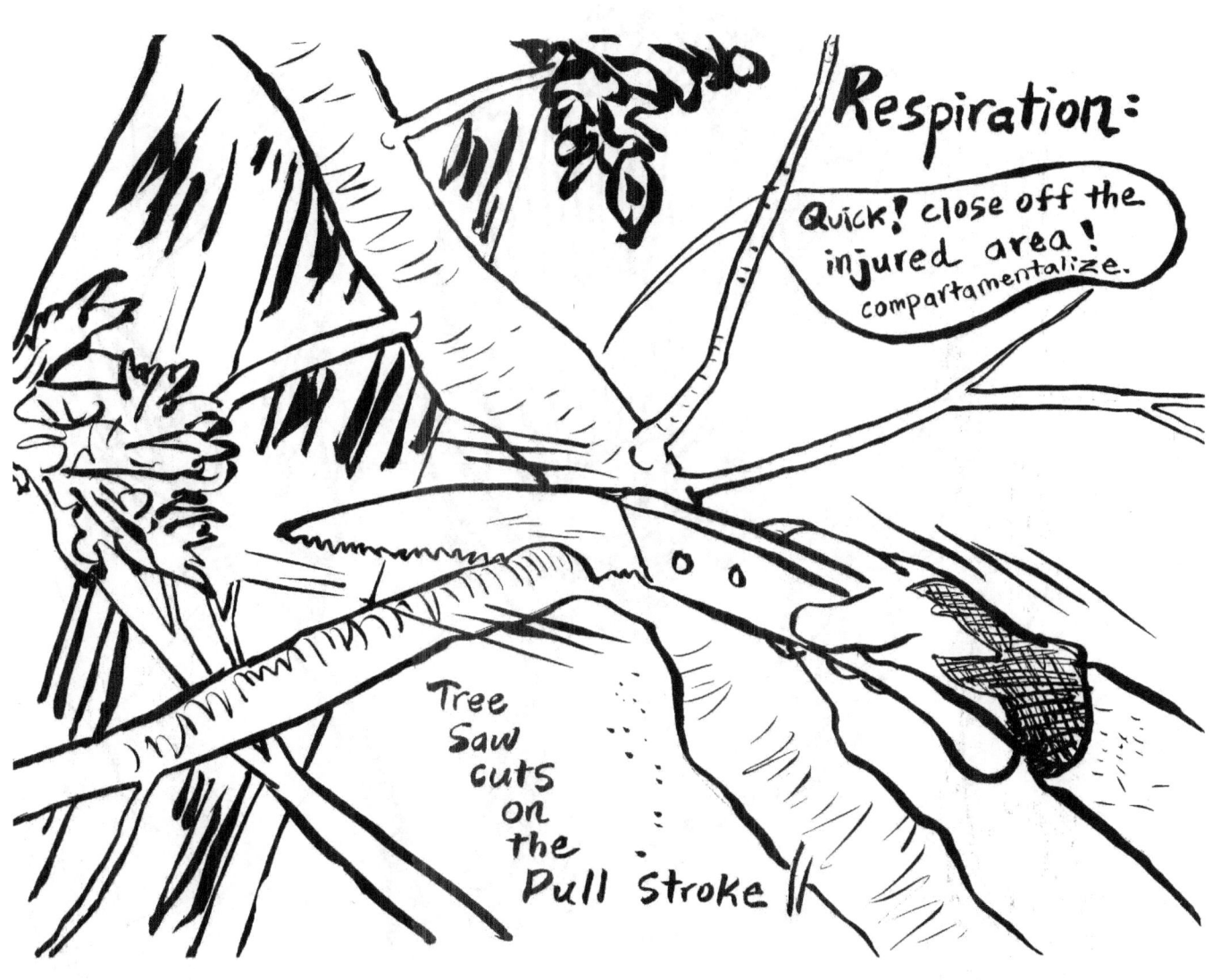

Respiration

Spring leaves unfurl
 Beech tree
 Energy in action

Flowers

Flowers exist so that a plant can make more plants. Before the young flower is mature, the sepals cover and protect it. As the weather warms and time passes, the petals emerge. The show's curtains open. Some flowers sit by themselves; others clump together into wide platforms and tall towers, or unfurl like scorpion's tails.

A flower can have both male and female parts together, only male parts, or only female parts. Stamens are the male parts in flowers. They release pollen - male sperm cells. The pistil is the female part of the flower. At the base of the pistil is the ovary. The ovary is the home of unformed baby seeds - ovules.

Sepals protect the young petals of the Angel's trumpet

White gum covers the young *Grindelia* flower.

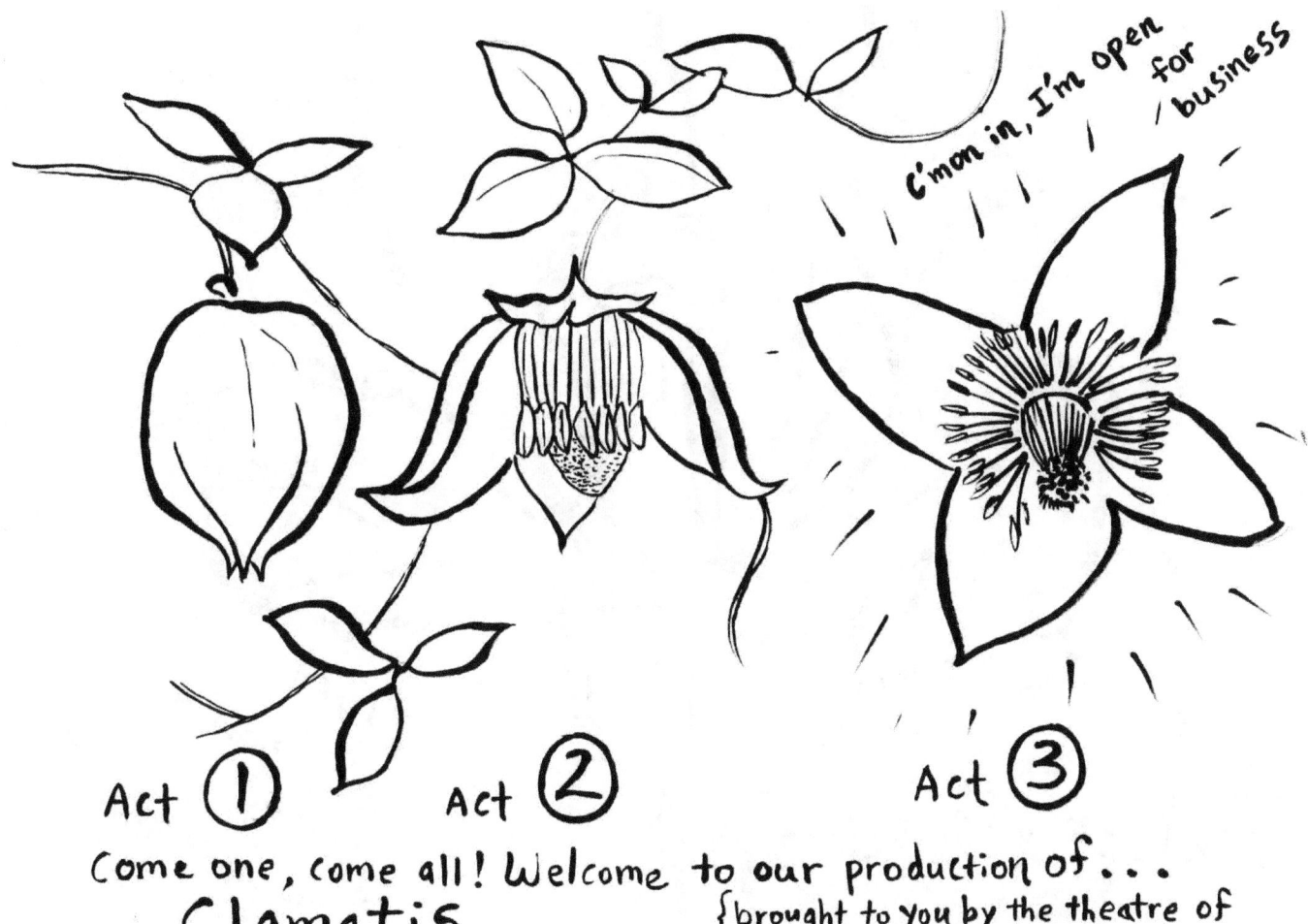

Tulip flower presents its parts to pollinators.

"Well, c'mon now, say something!"

Lewisia displays a cross shaped stigma.
{The stigma is the tip of the flower's female part.}

The ovary of the opium poppy is surrounded by lots of stamens

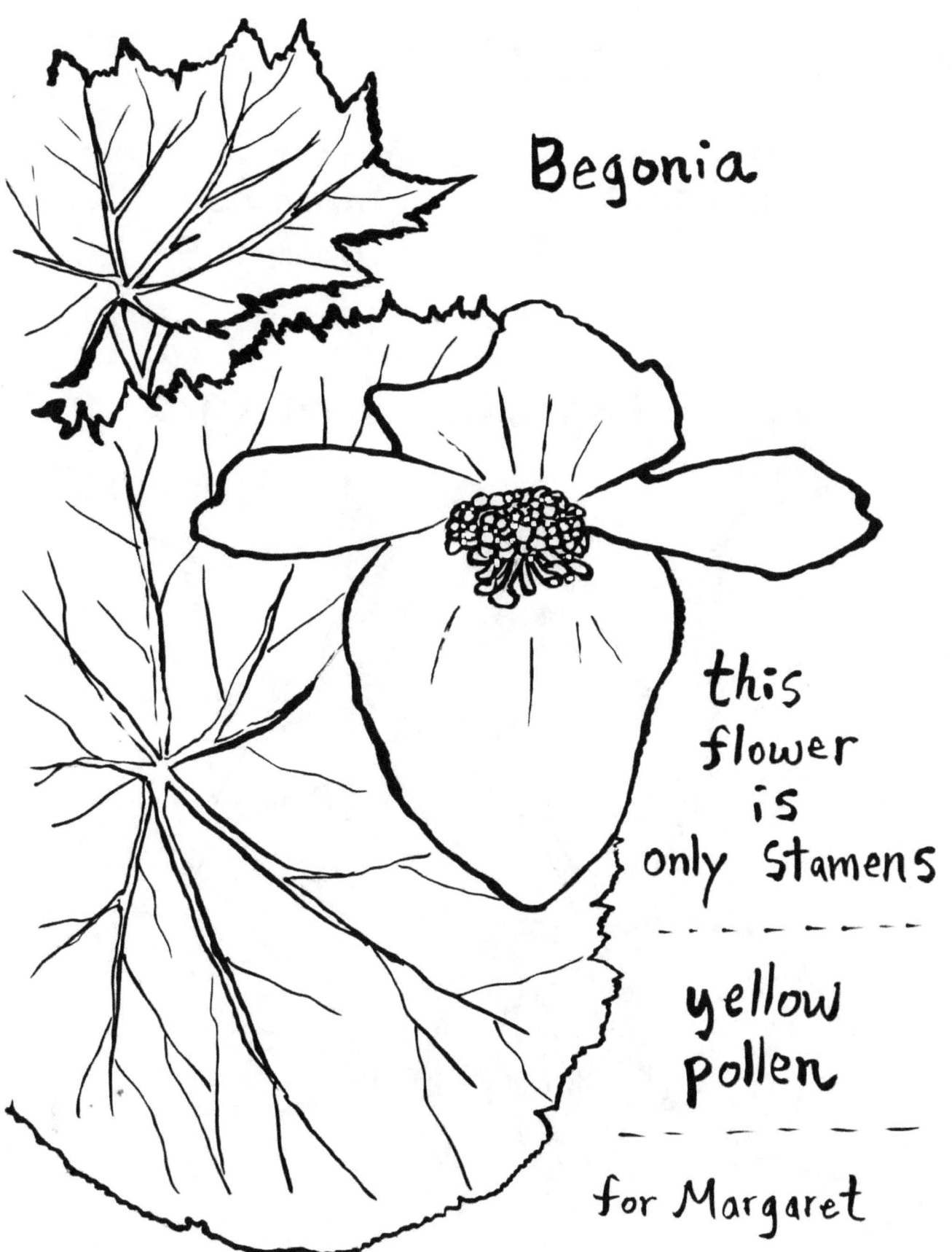

A bowl of greens:
- lettuce
- arugula
- carrots
- spinach
- almonds
- walnuts

top with borage flowers

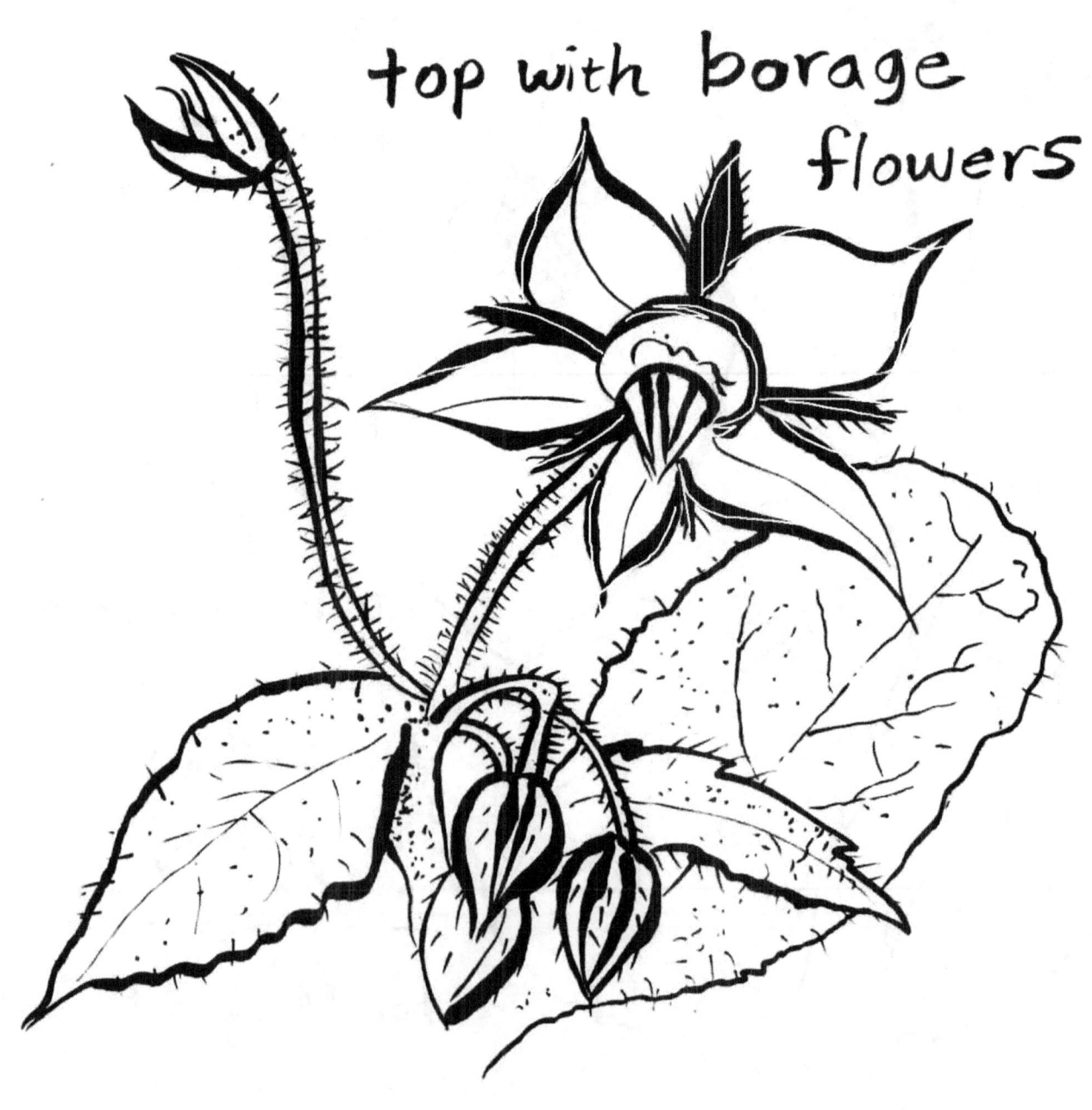

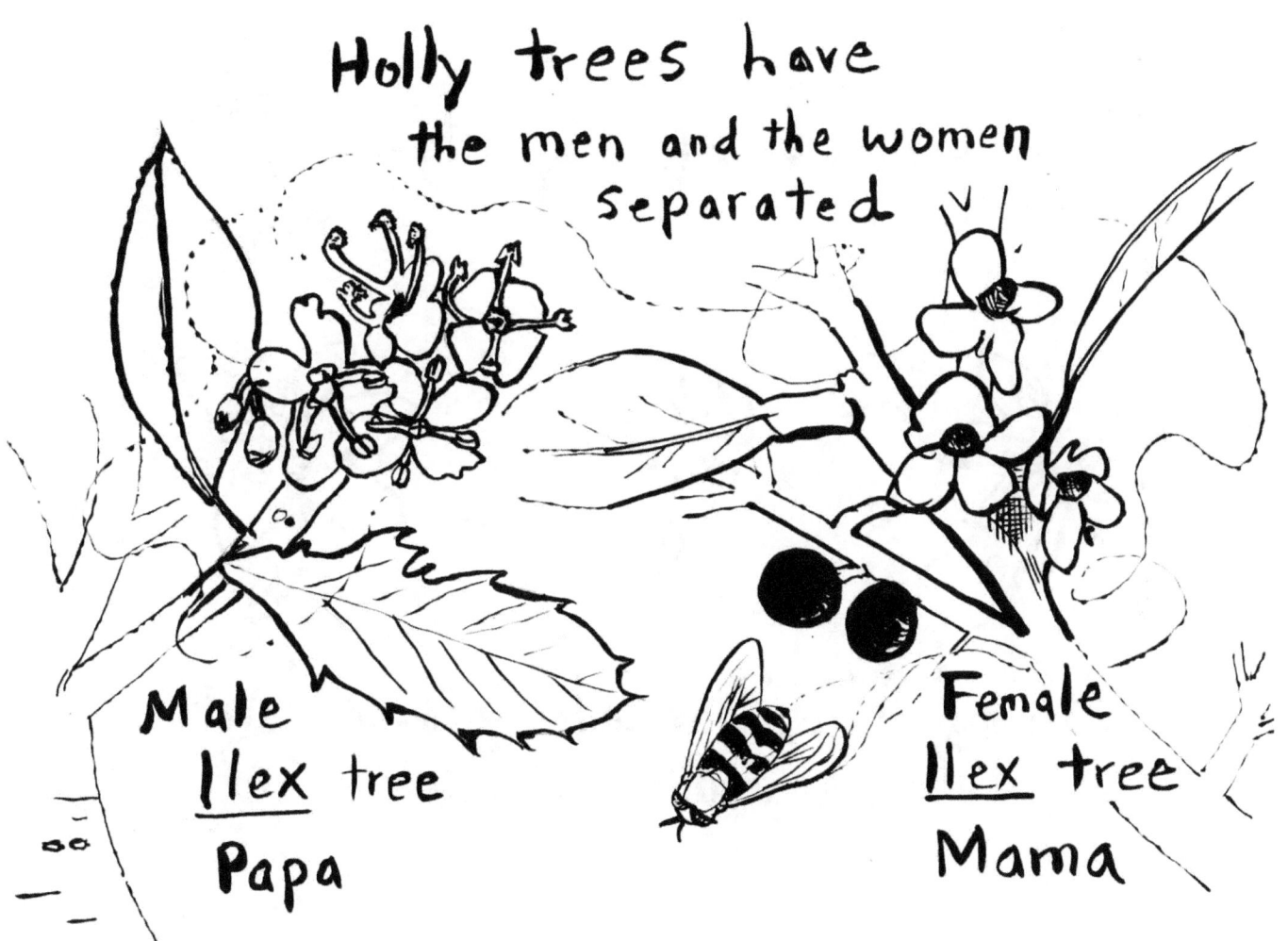

Timing keeps avocado flower from mating with itself

Pollination

For some plants, water and wind bring the male and female parts together. These kinds of flowers are usually small and not showy.

In other plants, go-betweens, or pollinators, bring the pollen to the pistil. The flower offers colors (petals and bracts), smells (perfume), food (pollen), and drink (nectar). While flying from here to there, the hummingbird smears some male parts from one flower onto the female parts of another flower.

To direct pollinators, petals may have dotted guidelines like the lights on the airplane's runway. Some flowers smell sweet, while others stink of rotten flesh. These flowers are attractive to flies and their little babies – maggots.

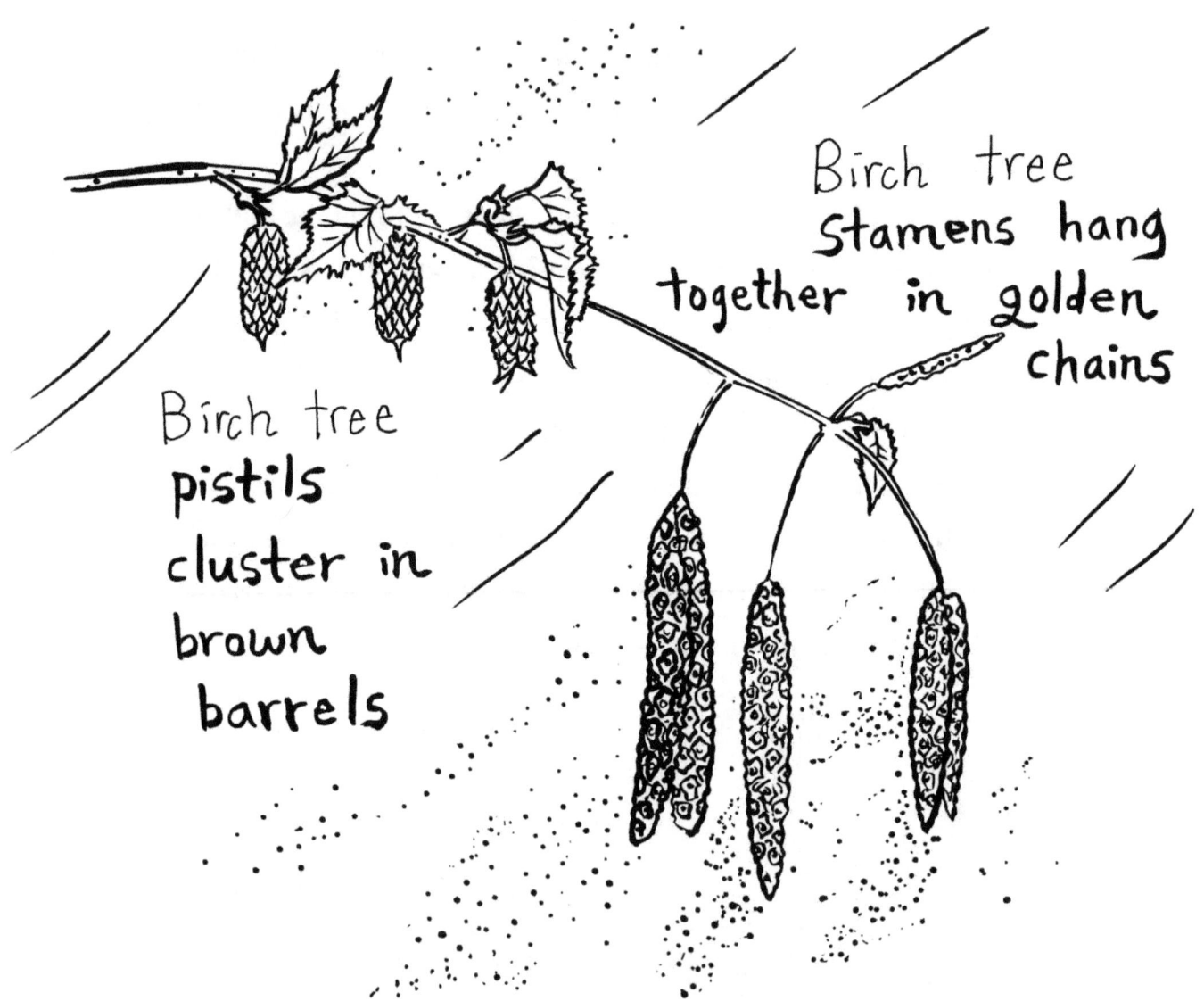

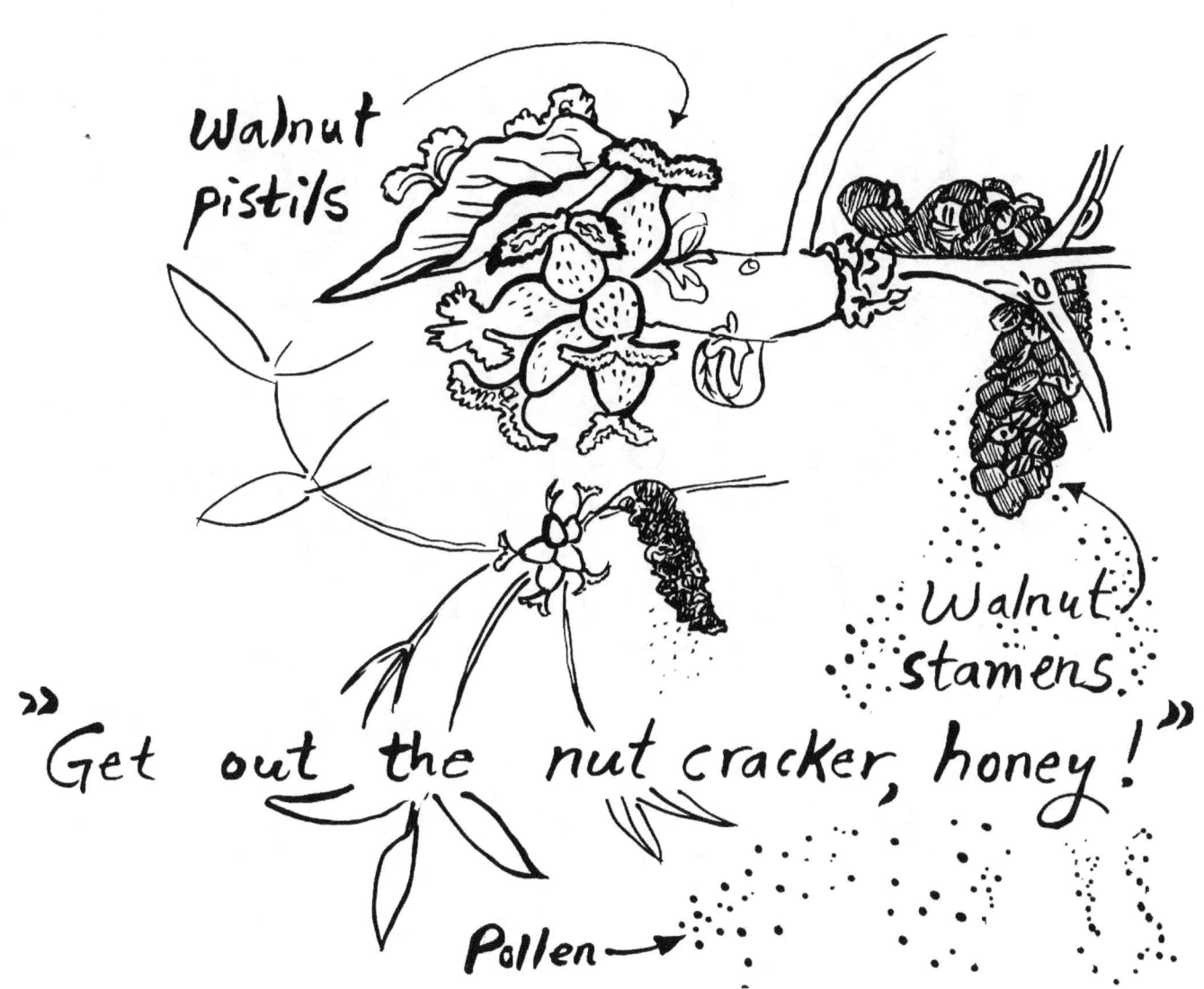

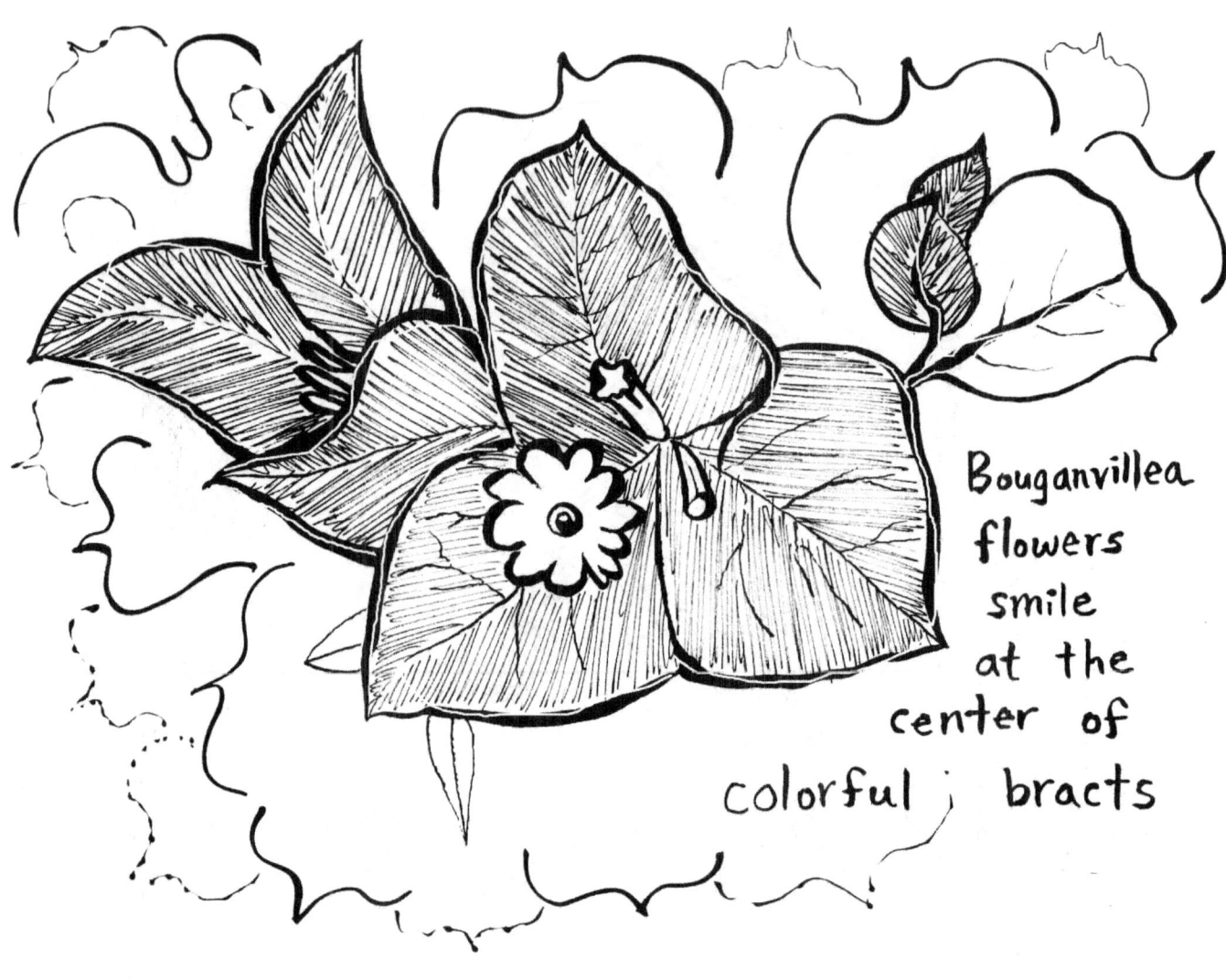

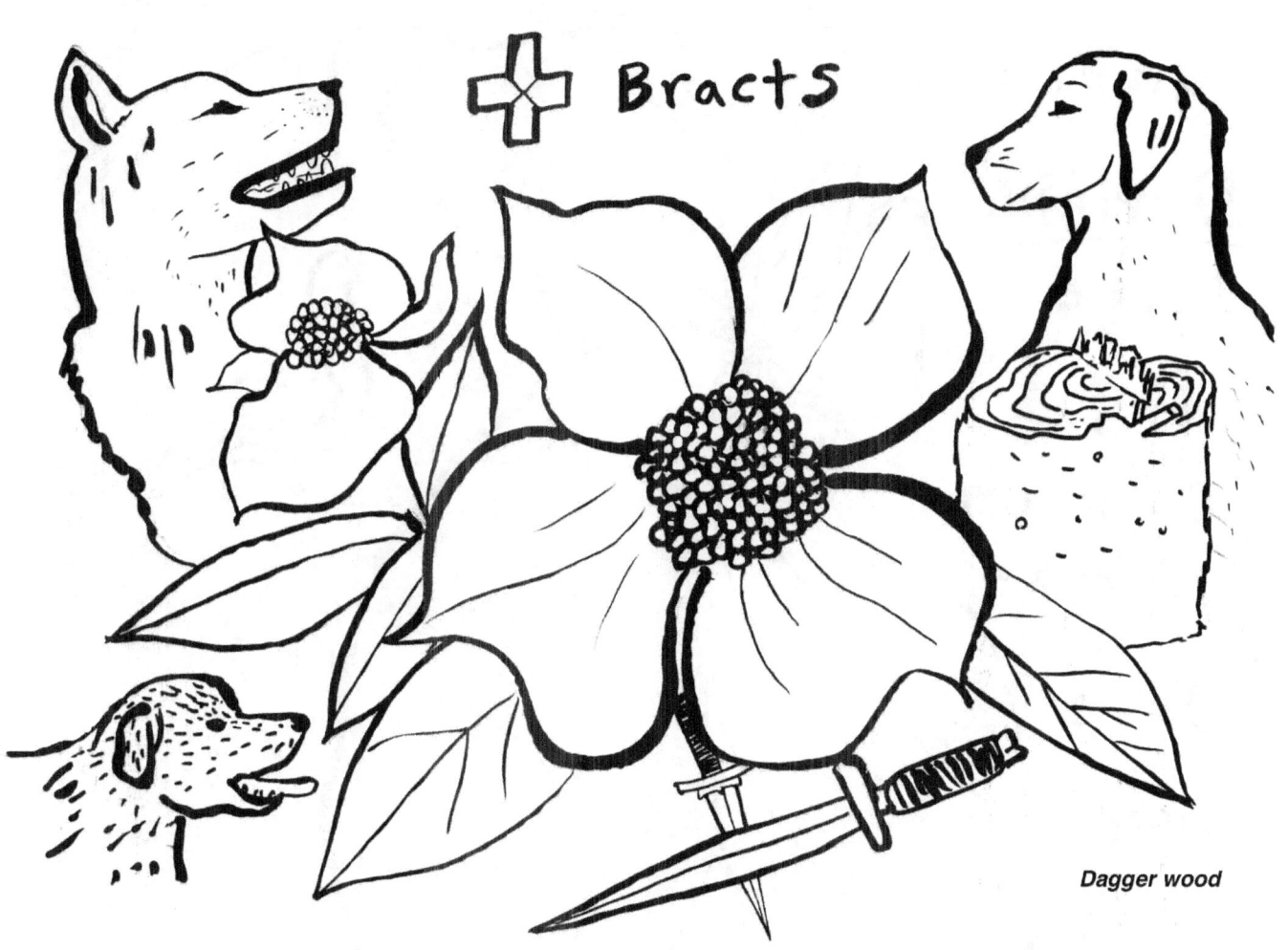

Dagger wood

White bracts give the <u>Davidia</u> tree its common name: Dove tree

Chrysanthemum flowers shout,
"Land here! Land here!
We got sweets!"

Alstroemeria flower
 is marked with lines and dots for pollinators to follow

Hey bug! c'mon in!!

Chiranthodendron tree
pentadactylon

Oh
what
deep
nectar
cups
my
sweets

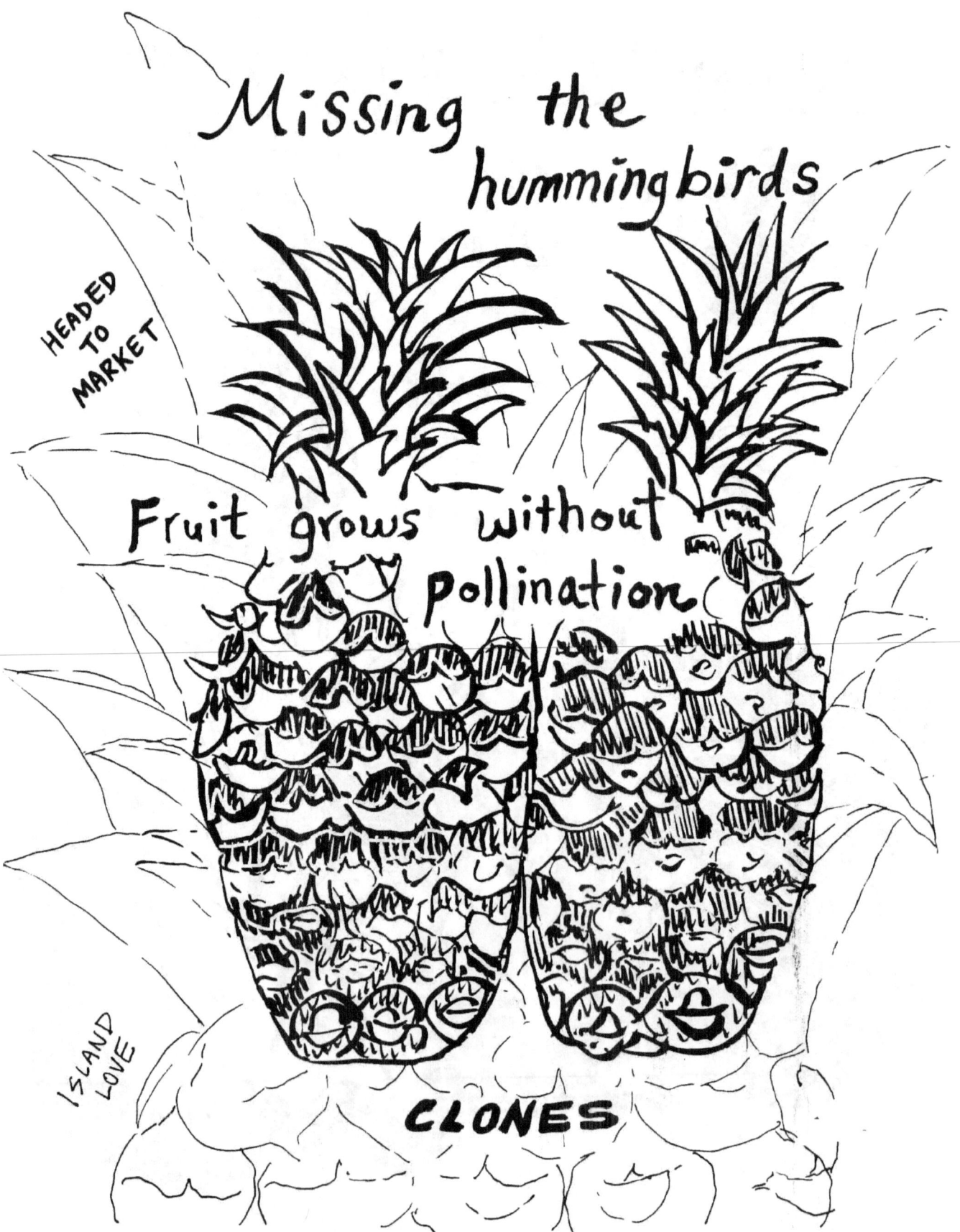

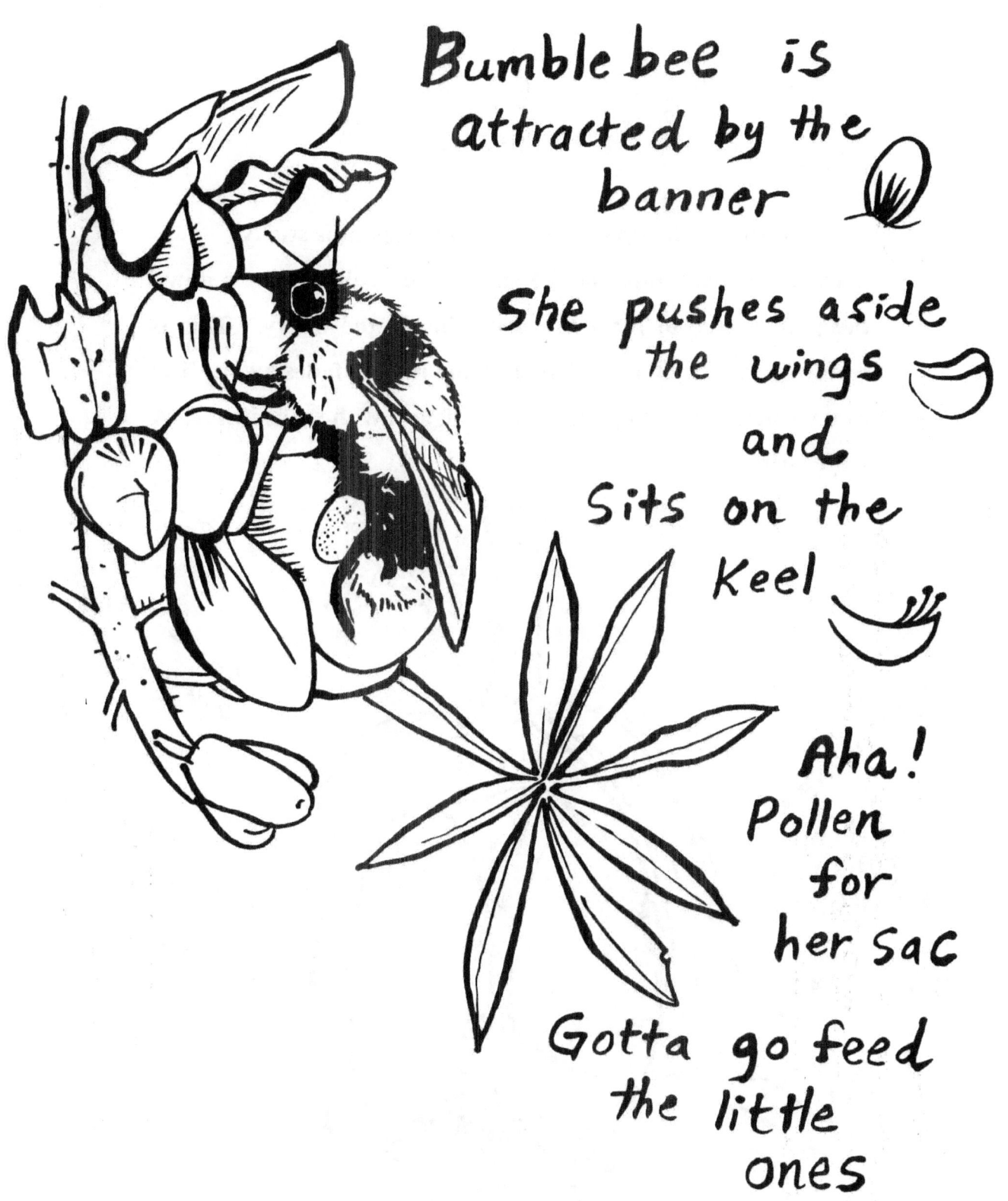

At the lupine blossum

Fertilization

At maturity, the tip of the pistil (the stigma) is sticky. Once the pollen lands on the stigma, the pollen travels down the pollen tube to meet the ovule inside the ovary. This is fertilization! The flower, having done its job, fades away. The ovary starts to swell up bigger and bigger, with seeds inside. A fruit forms.

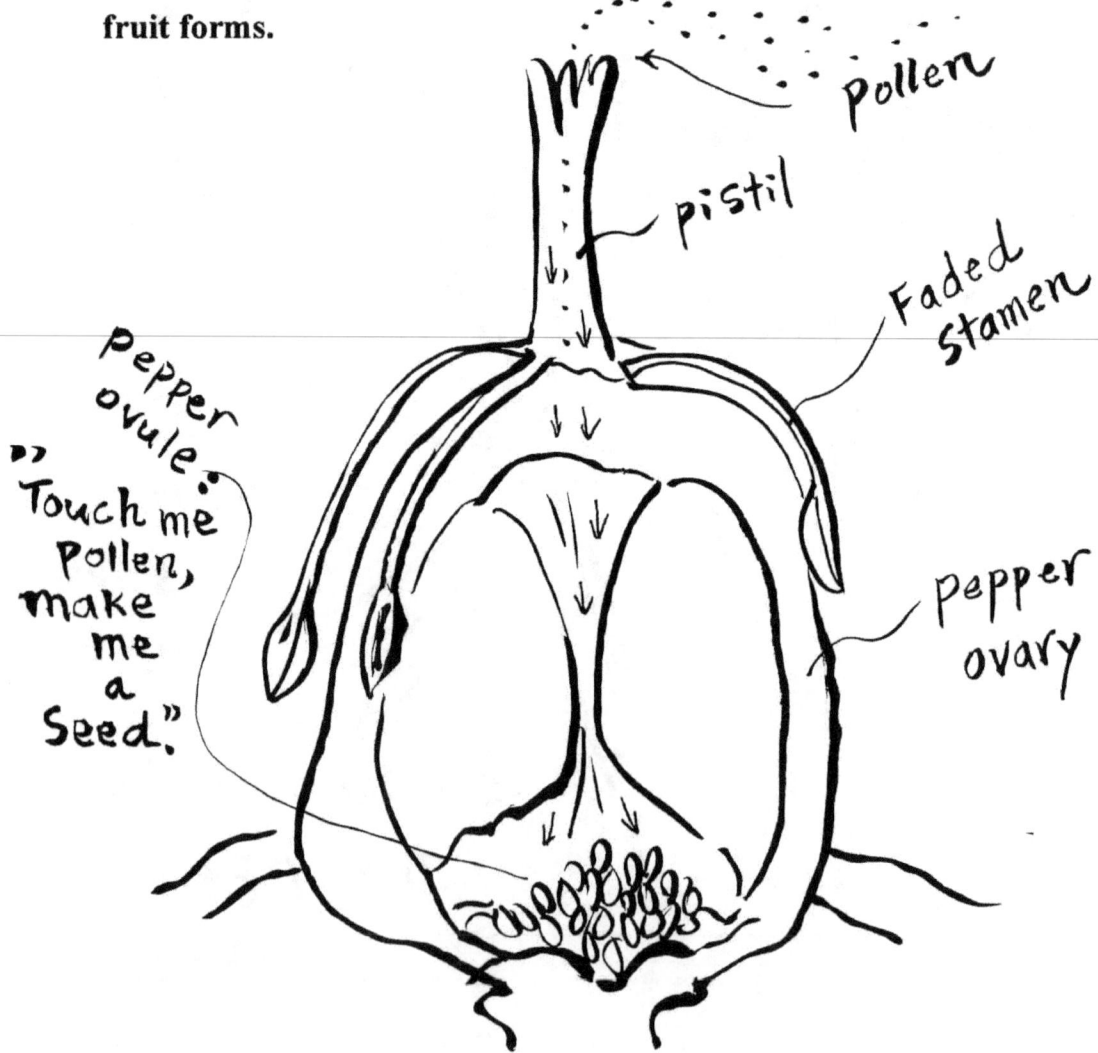

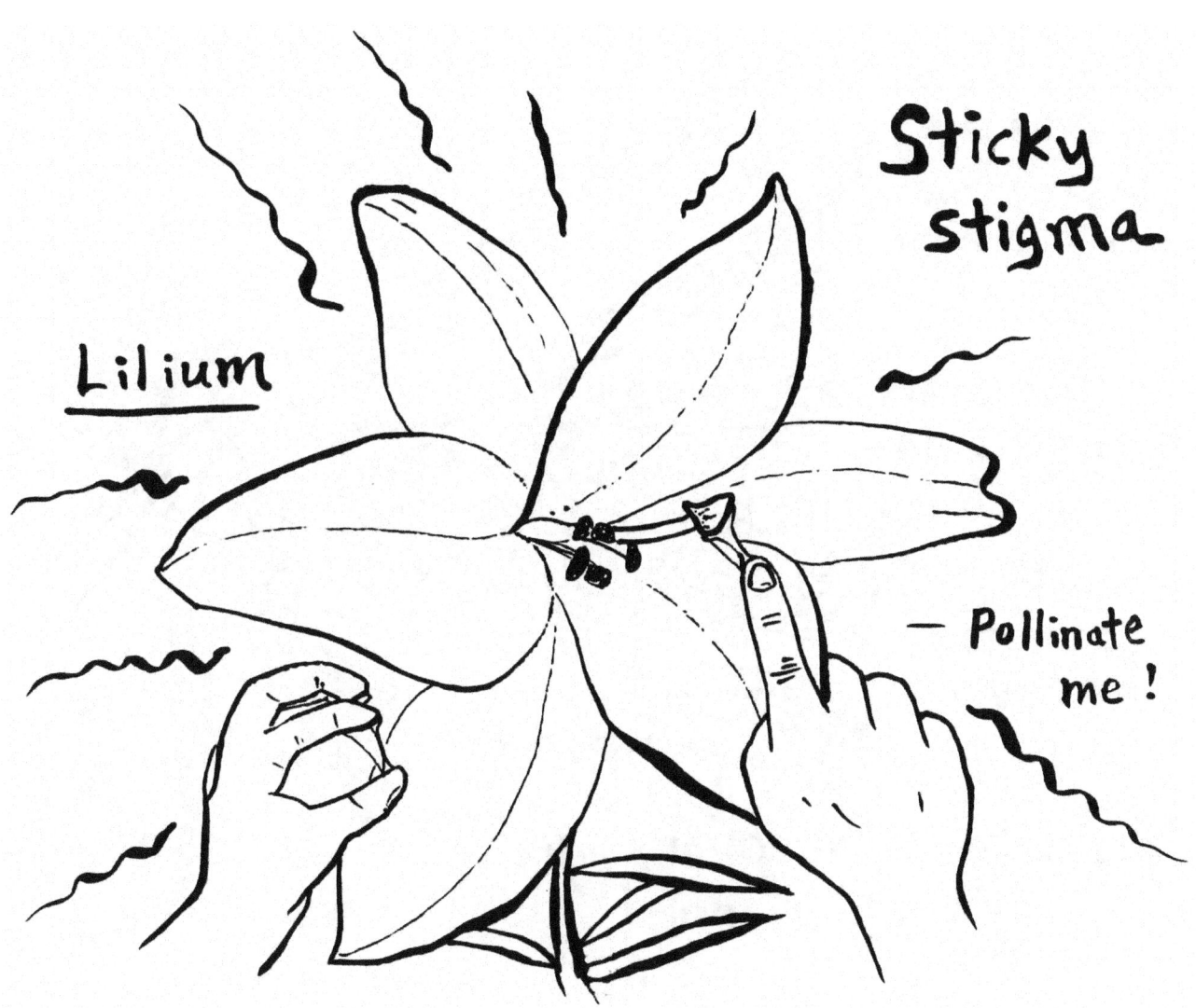

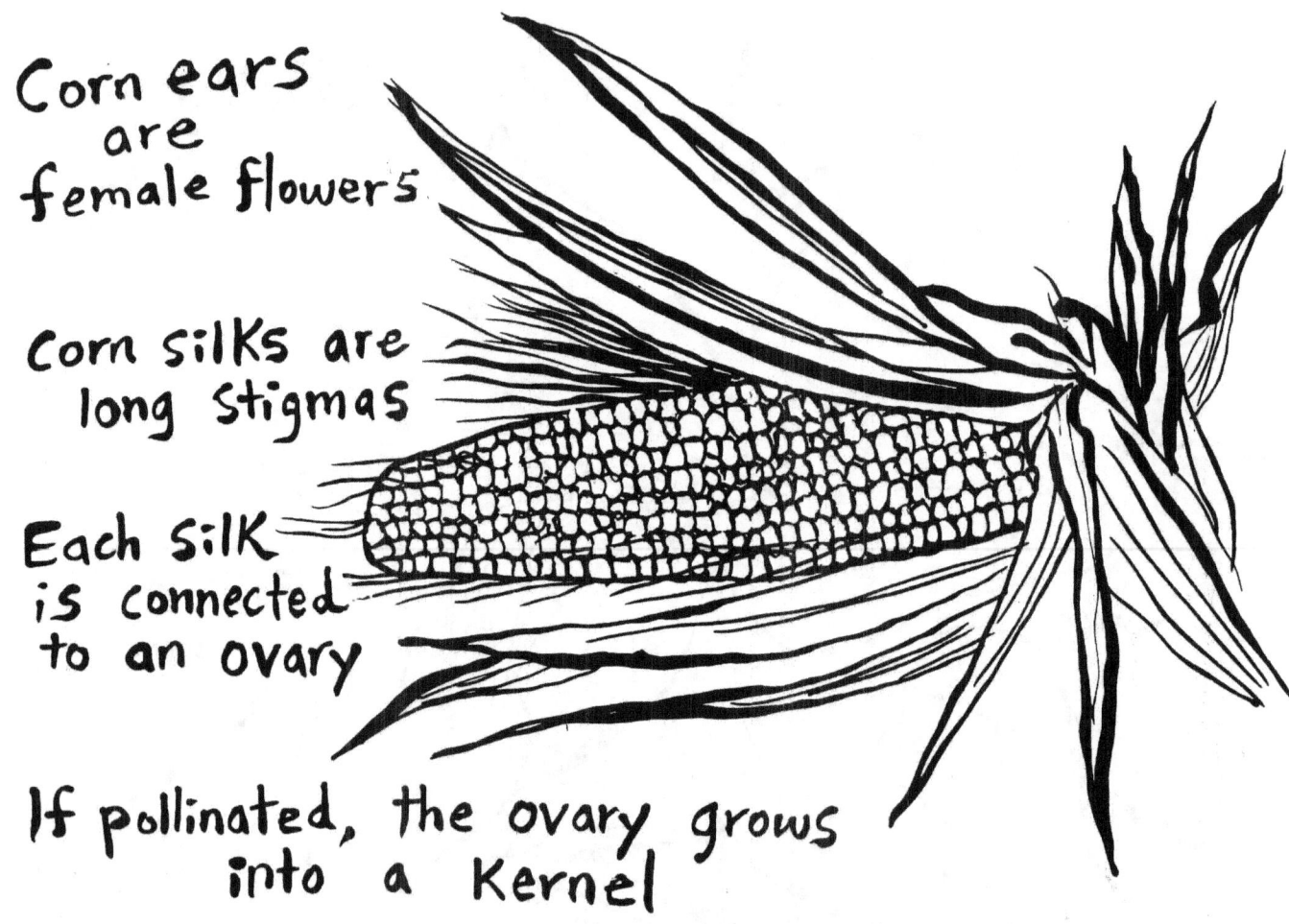

Tulip has dropped its petals.

The fruit is starting to swell up.

Baby seeds are growing inside.

The Power of creation

Baby maple tree fruits start off with wings

Fruit

A fruit is a container for seeds. A cone serves a similar function, with seeds sitting at the base of a cone scale. Parent plants want their seedlings to grow up a little away from them. This way, the plant babies have their own space, and are not shaded by adults. There are many ways seeds travel and find their place in the world. Fruits are the taxi, parachute, and boat for many seeds. Away they go!

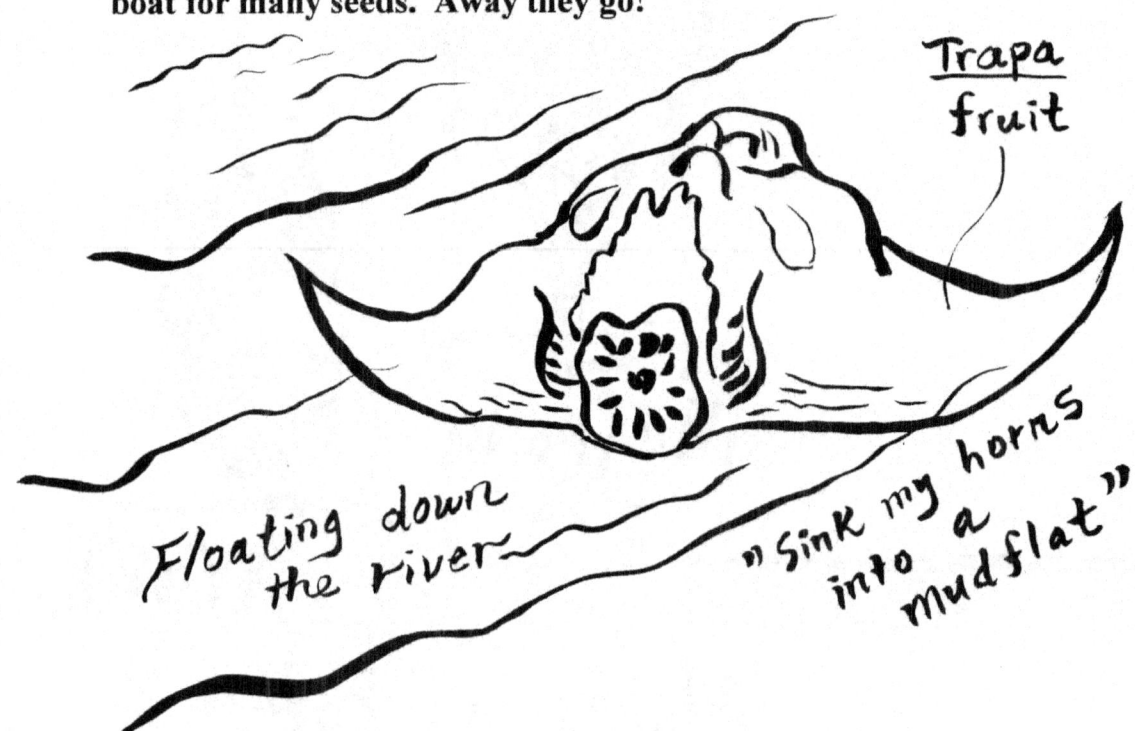

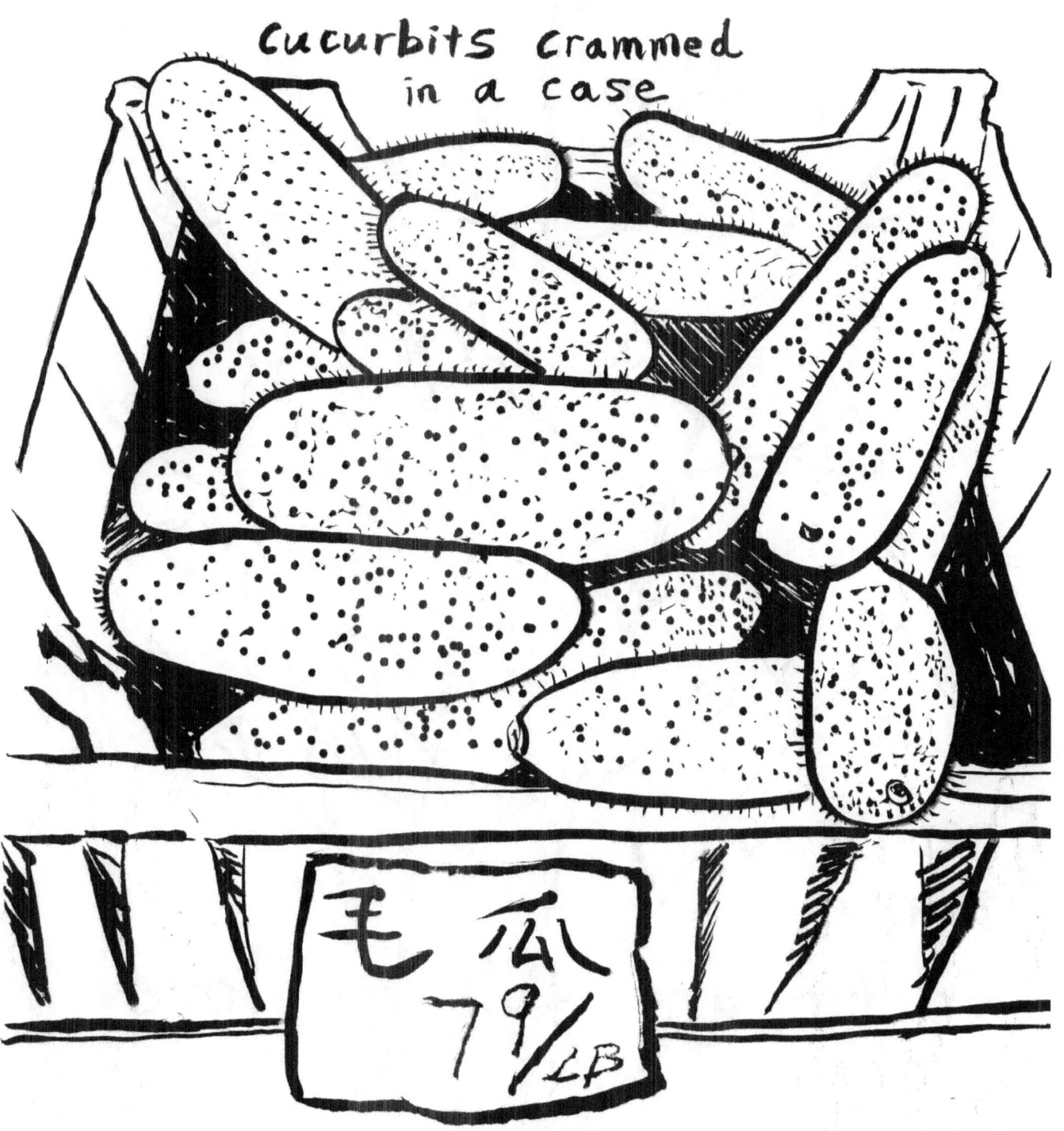

Furry fruits
Cucurbits crammed in a case

毛瓜
79/LB

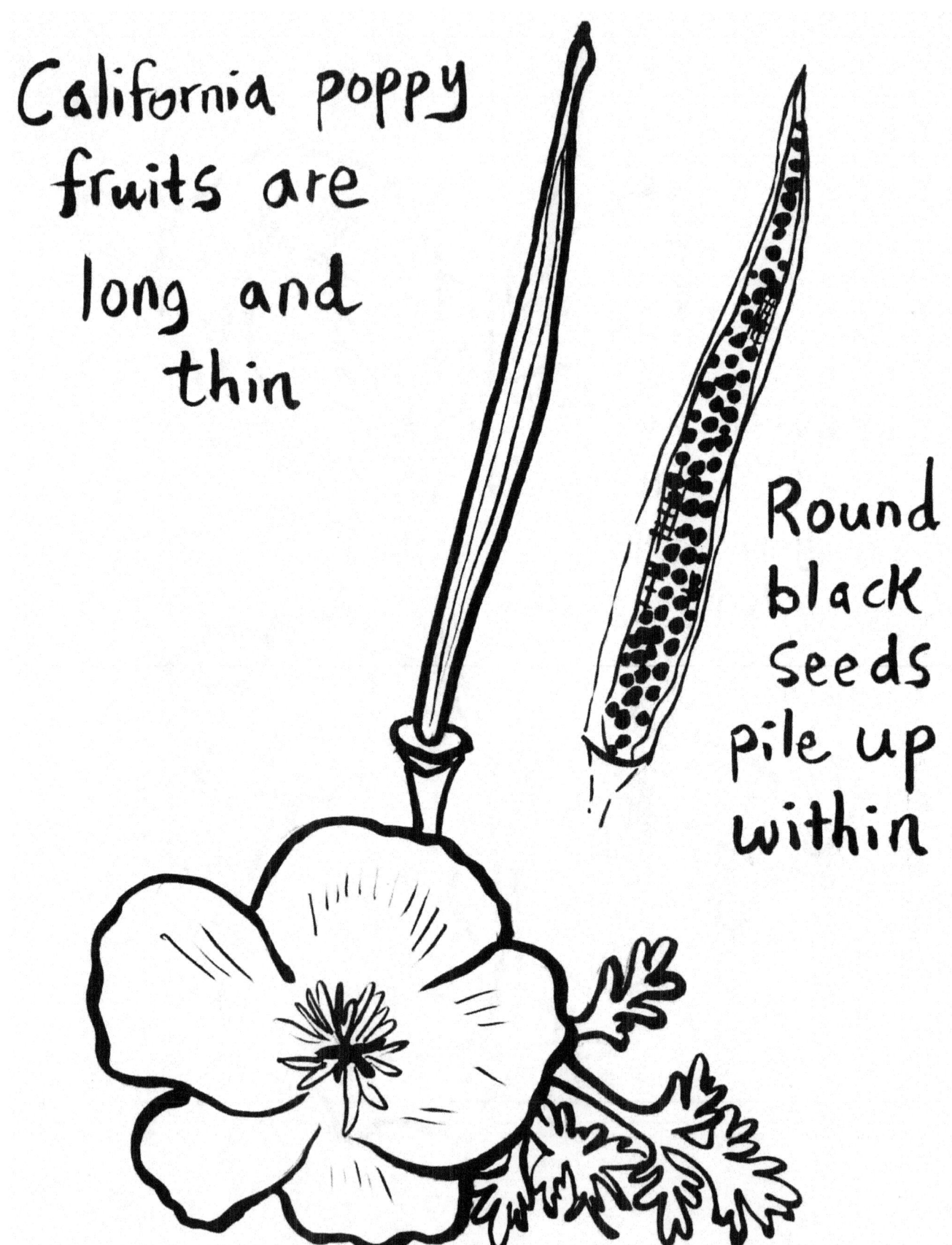

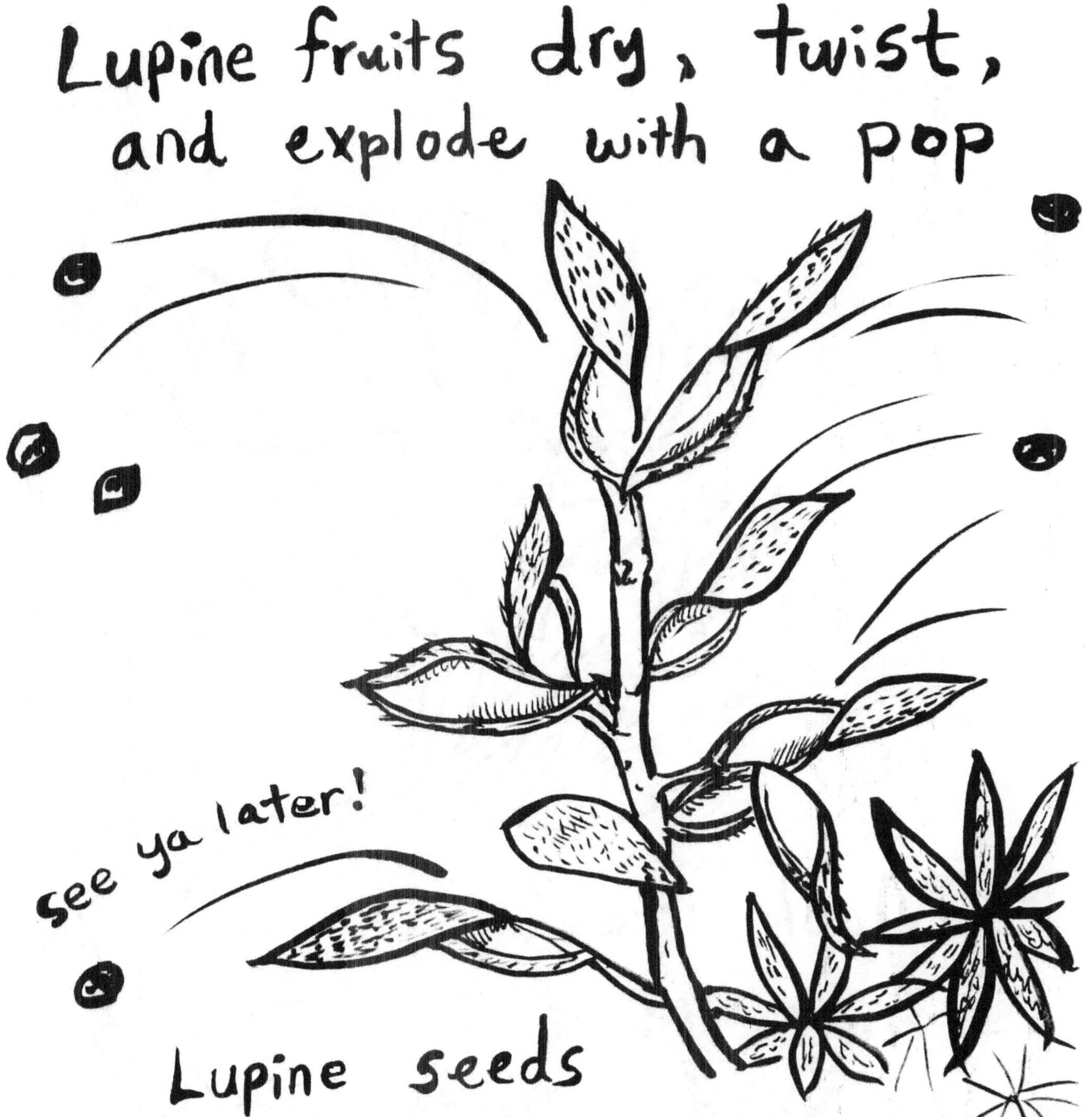

Lupine fruits dry, twist, and explode with a pop

see ya later!

Lupine seeds go-a-flying outa there!

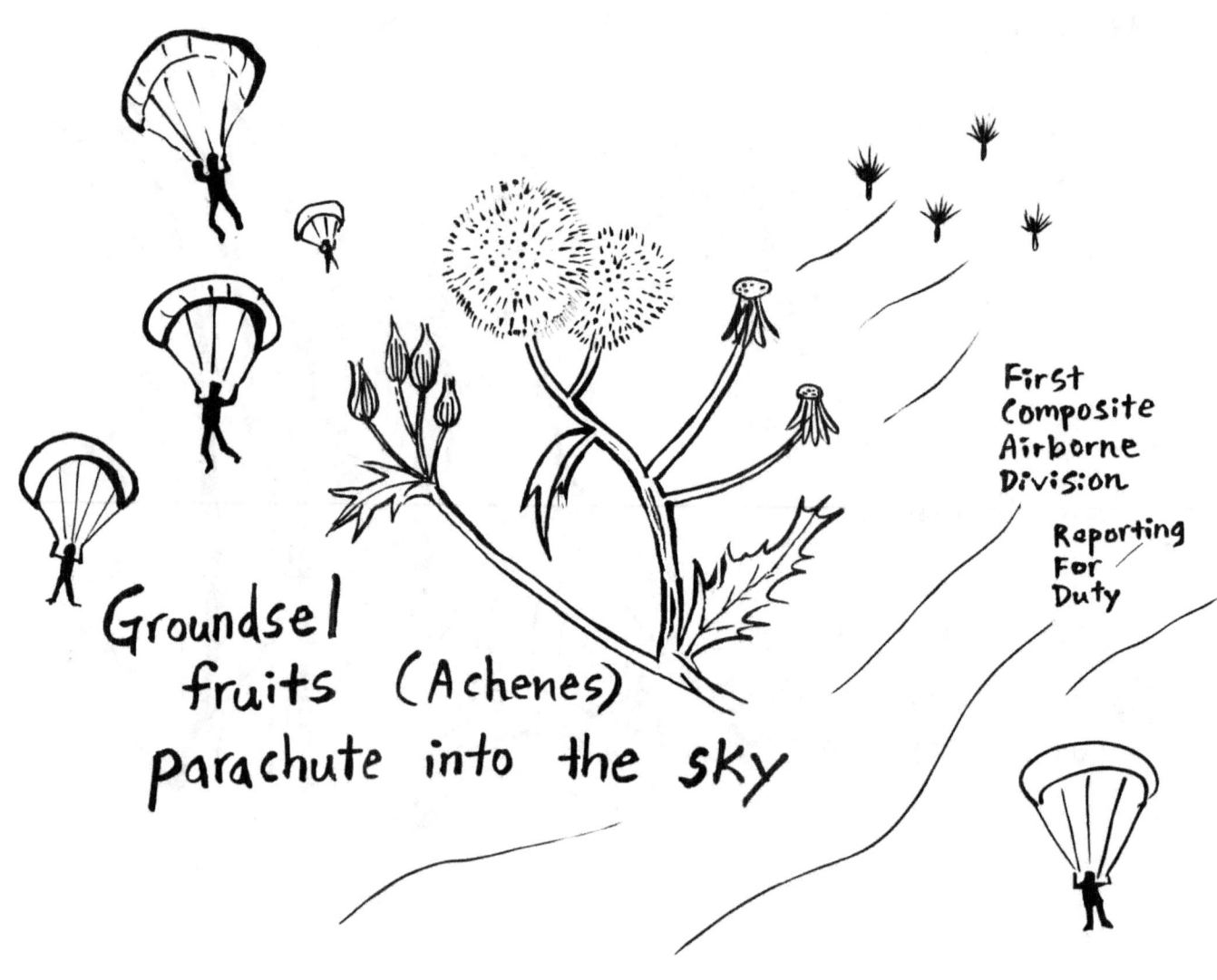

This gourd is a bumpy fruit.

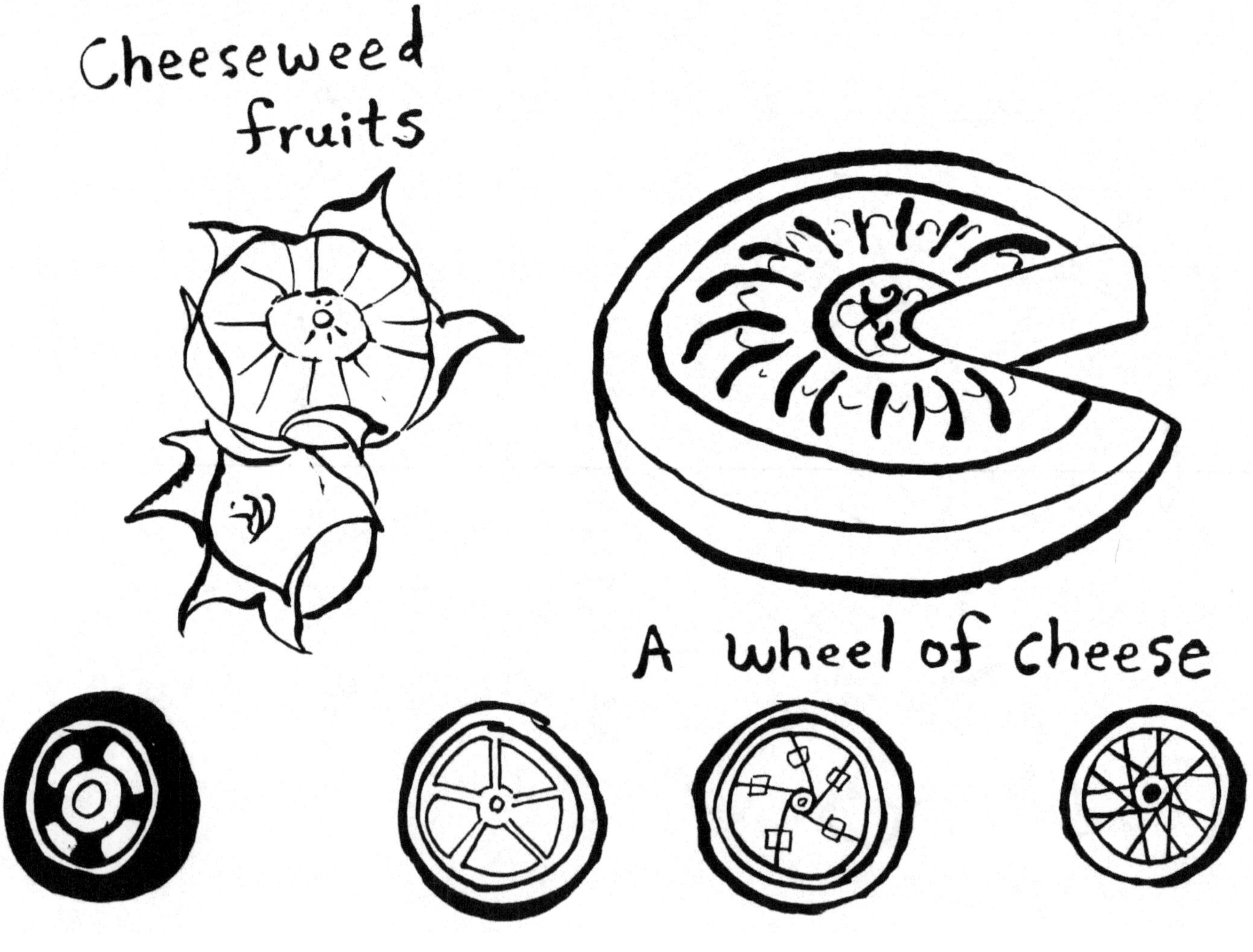

Cheeseweed fruits

A wheel of cheese

A capsule is a dry fruit.
To let the seeds out,
it splits open.

Or, it opens little round holes.

Some capsules don't open at all.

who will let the seeds out?

Who's the nut?
(A nut is one seeded dry fruit with a hard shell) (a,d)

One flower, many ovaries:

Hmm... blackberry pie!!

Many flowers, many ovaries in a cluster

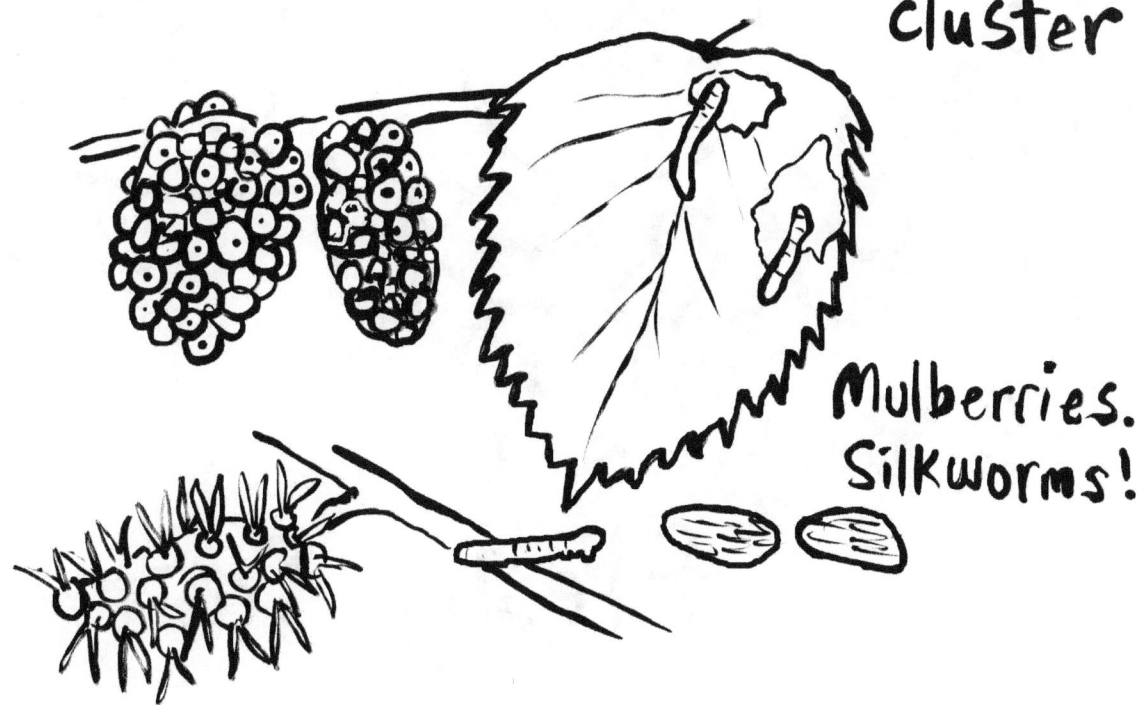

Mulberries. Silkworms!

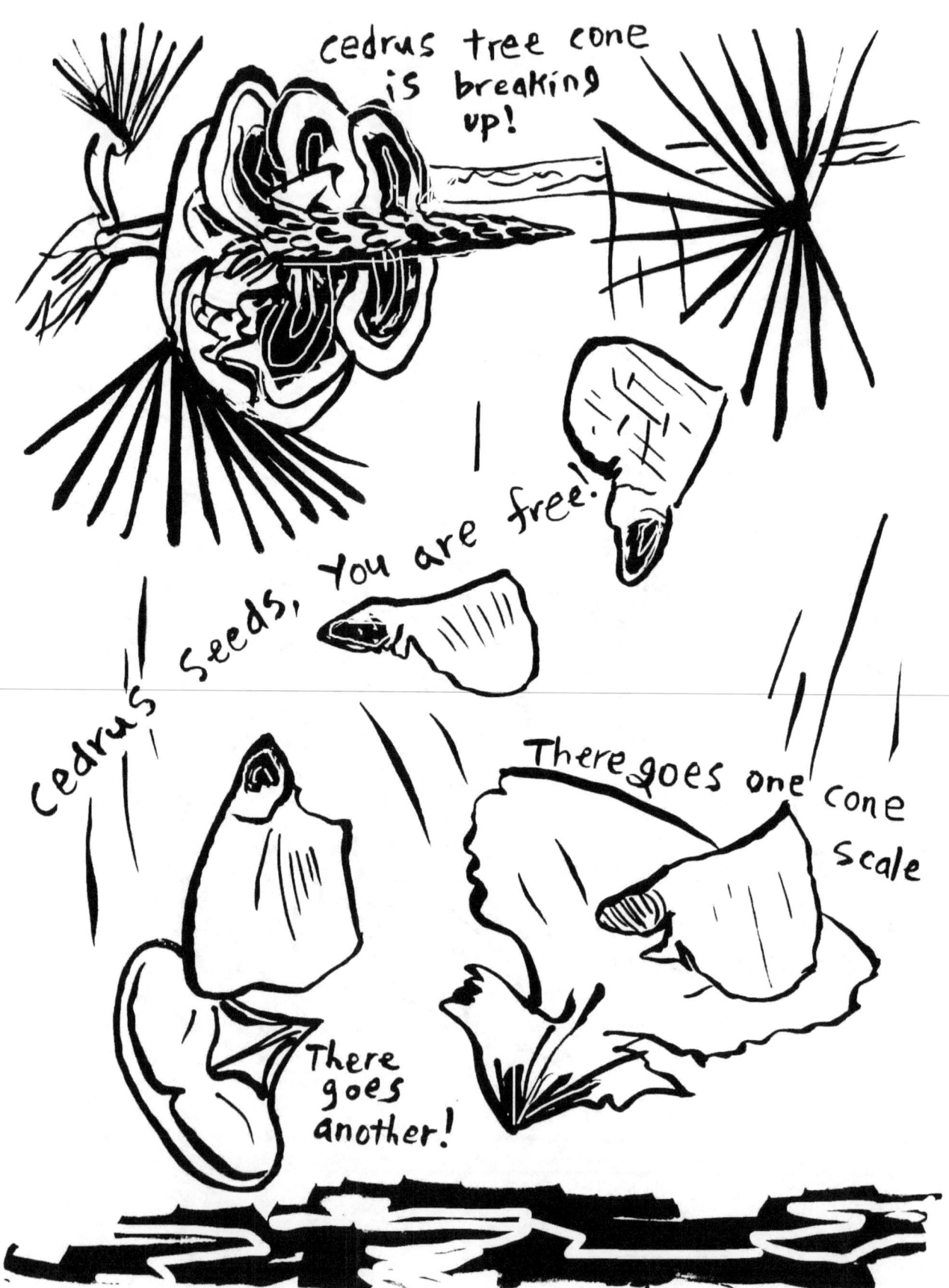

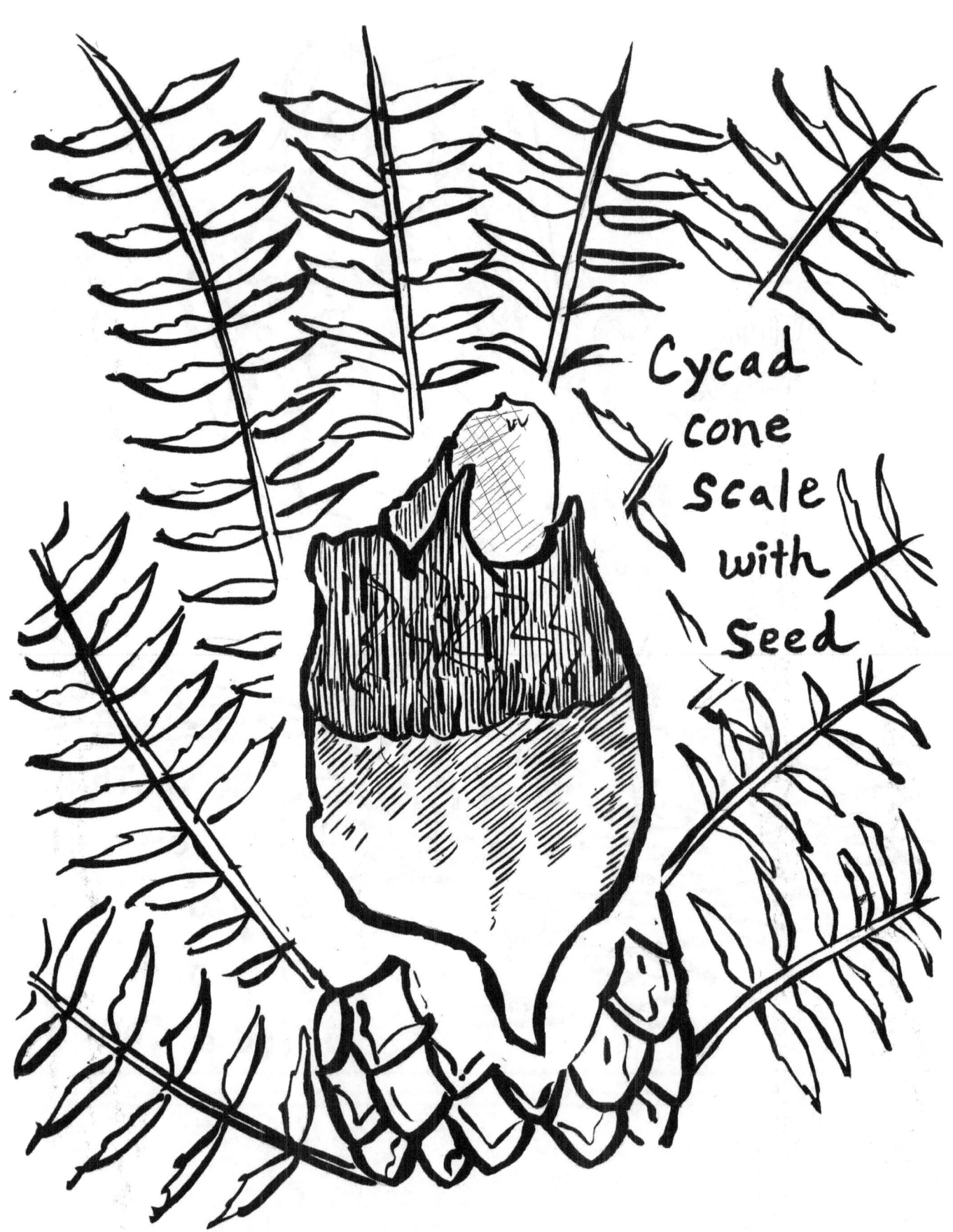

Seed

Seeds are the union between male and female contributions. Each seed is unique. Seeds are tough on the outside, with a supply of food for the growing plant baby (the embryo) on the inside. Seeds can survive the acid bath of a coyote's stomach, a watery ride down the river, or a fire on the grasslands.

Plants drop, splatter, and bury their seeds into the soil. When the conditions are just right, like on a warm day a bit after the rain, little seed leaves open and the roots head down into the ground. This is germination.

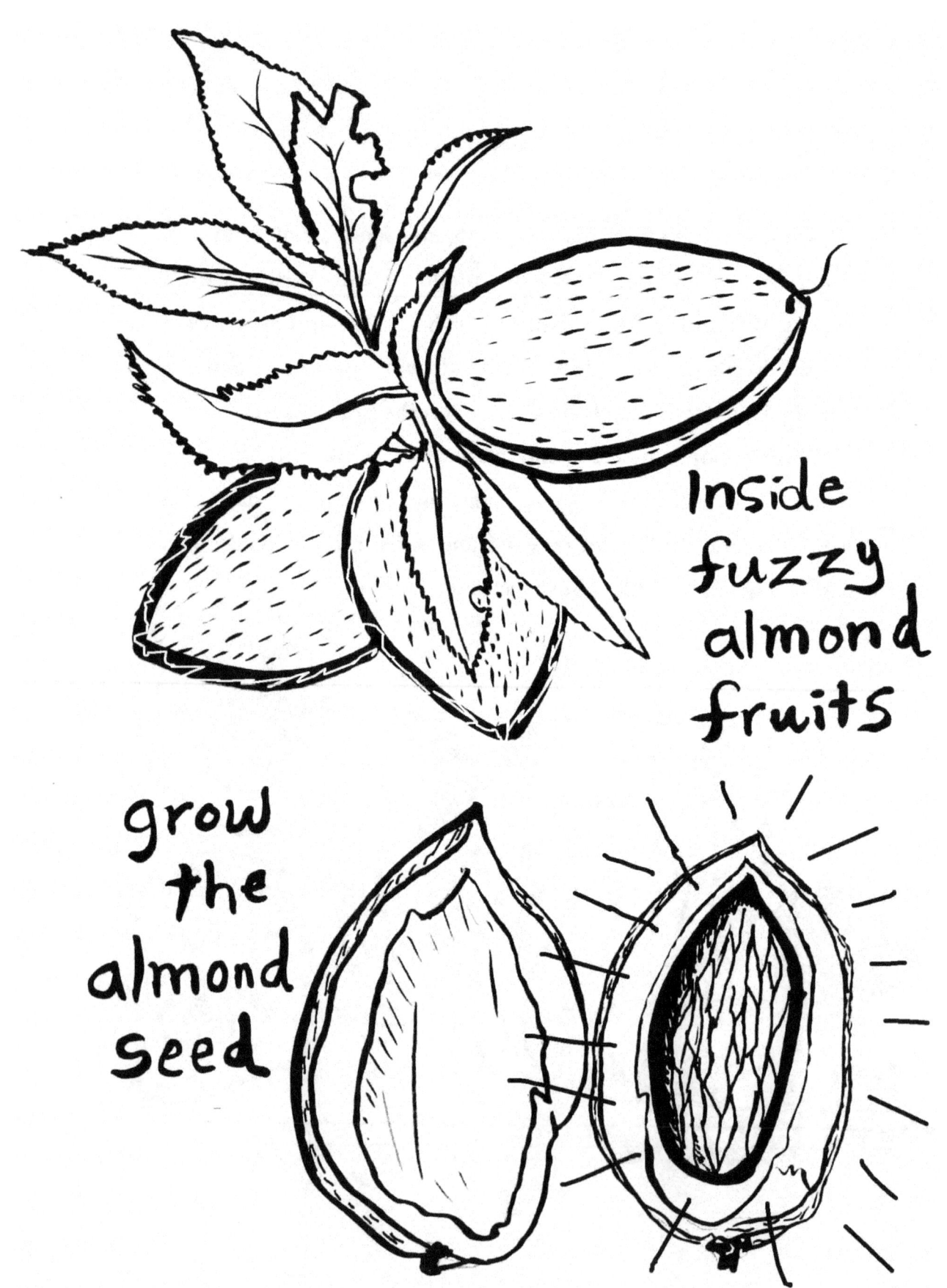

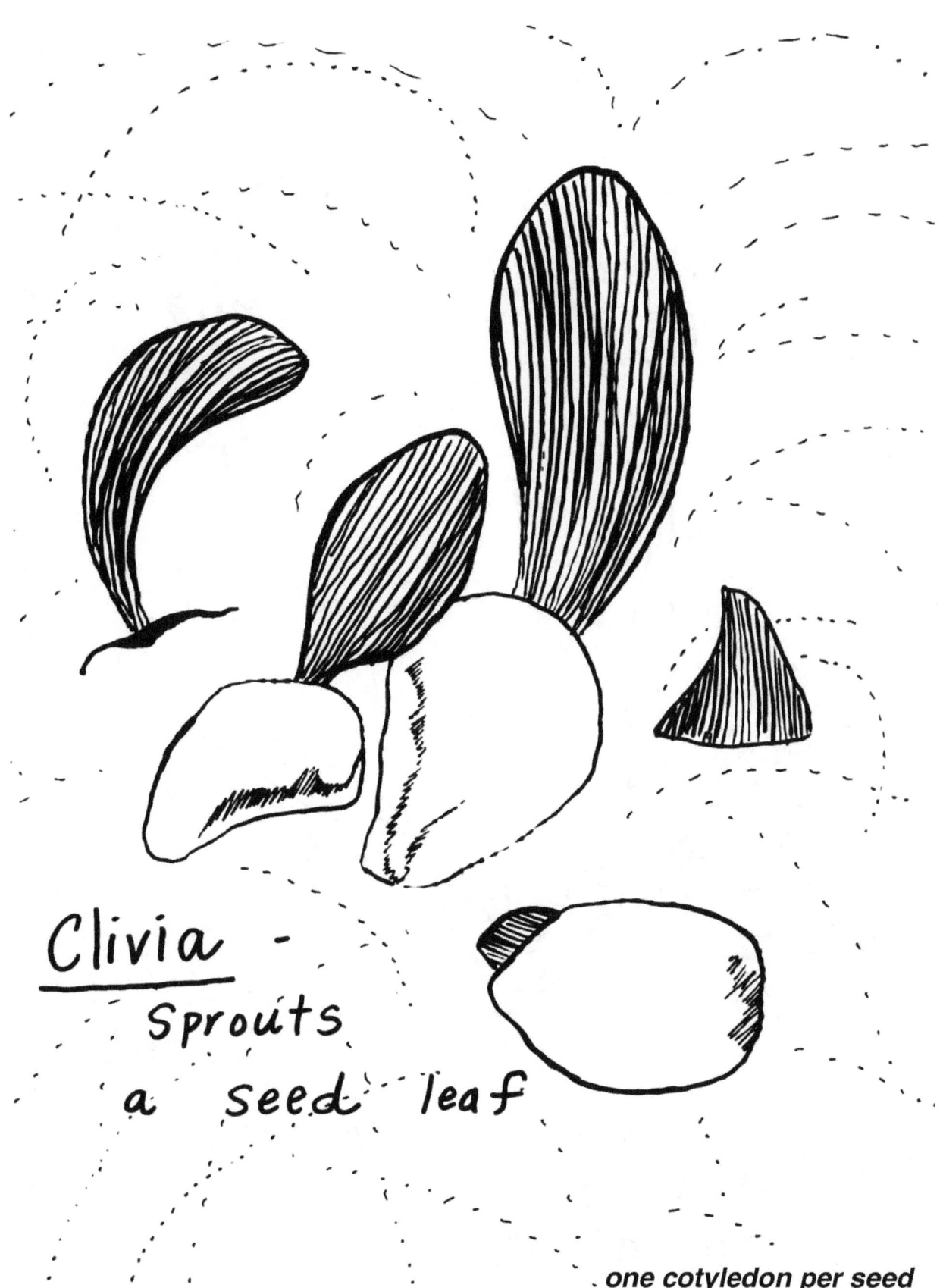

Clivia – sprouts a seed leaf

one cotyledon per seed

Garden snail plants strawberry seeds along its slime trail

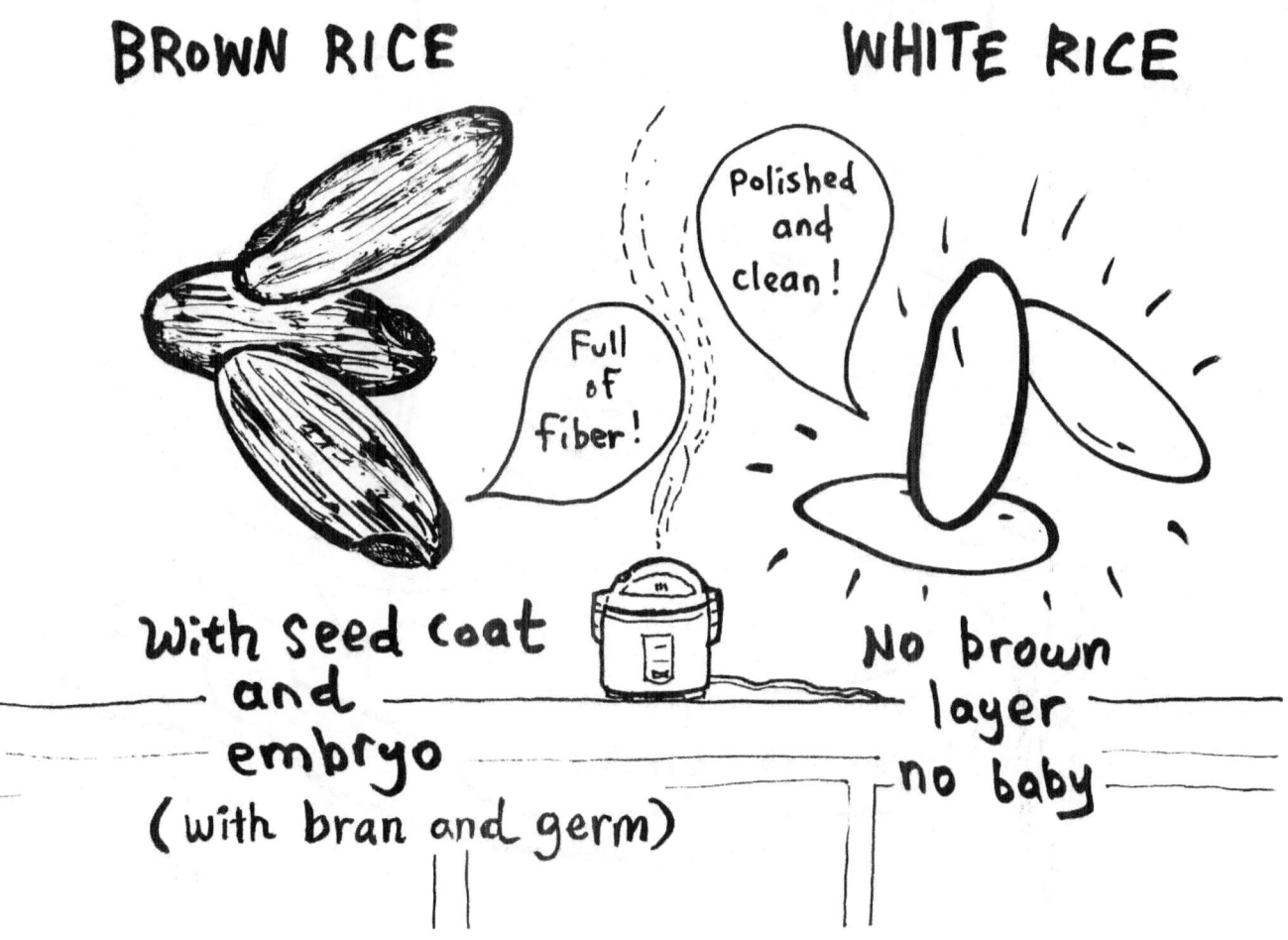

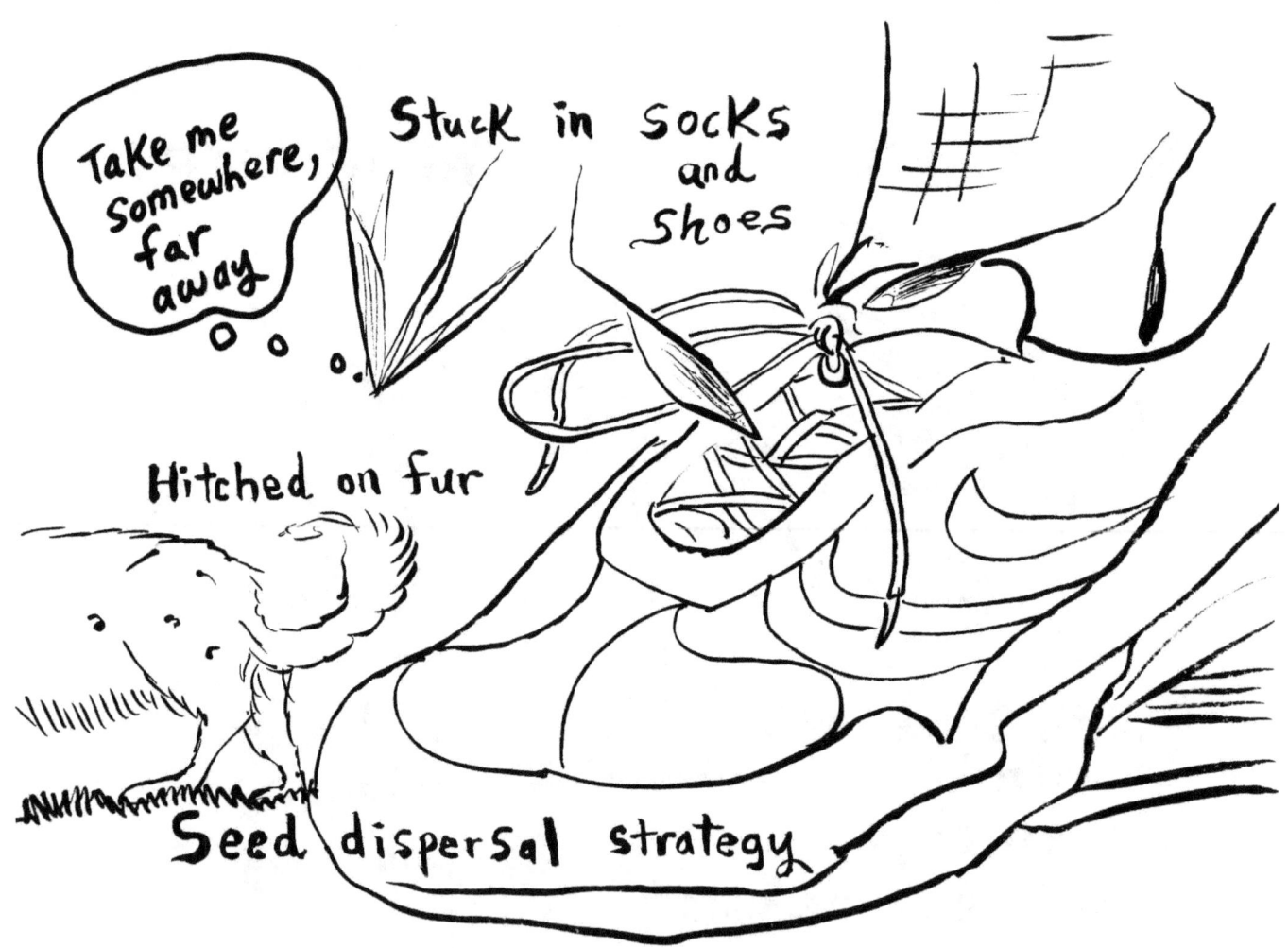

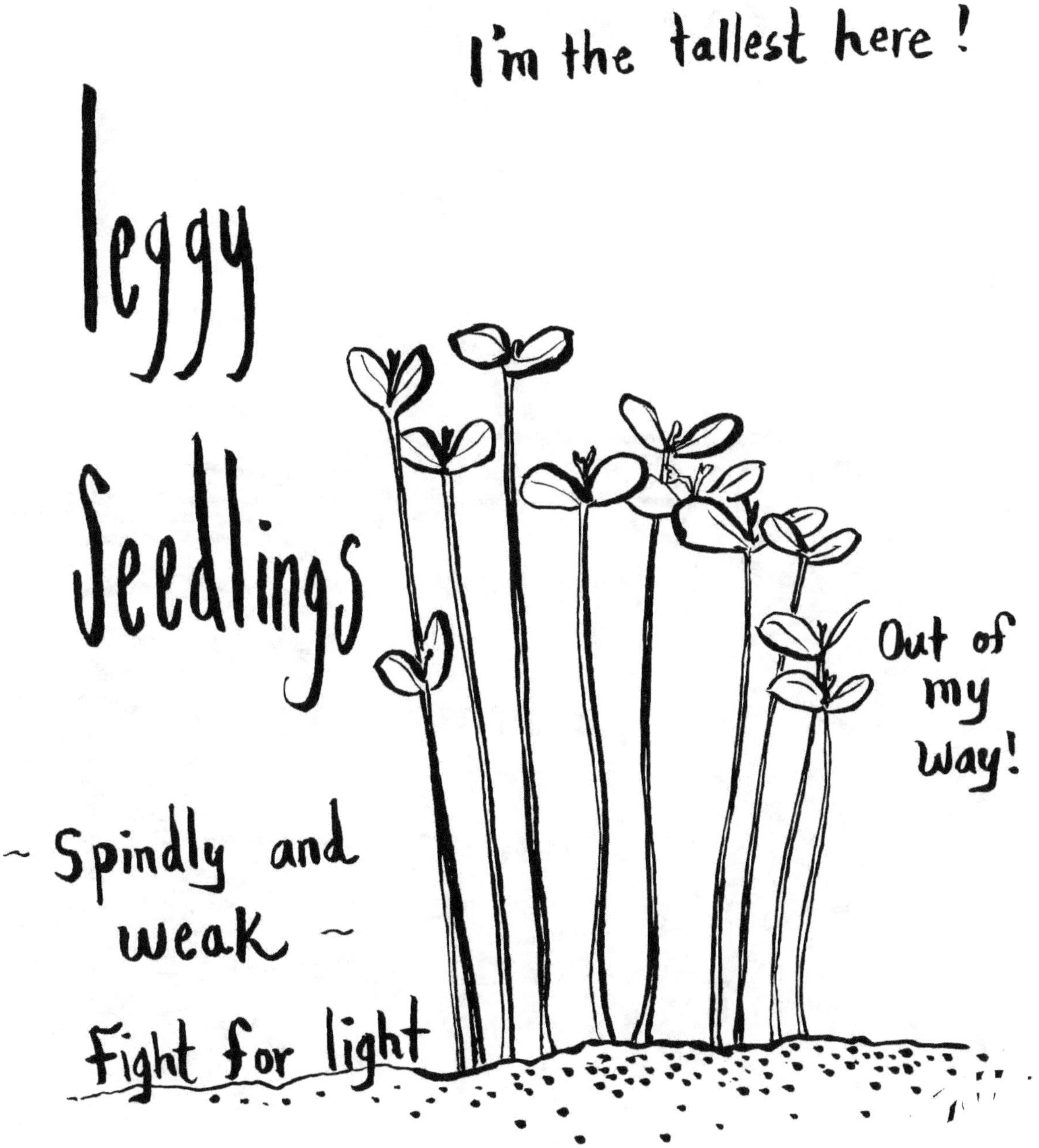

leggy seedlings

I'm the tallest here!

Out of my way!

- Spindly and weak -

Fight for light

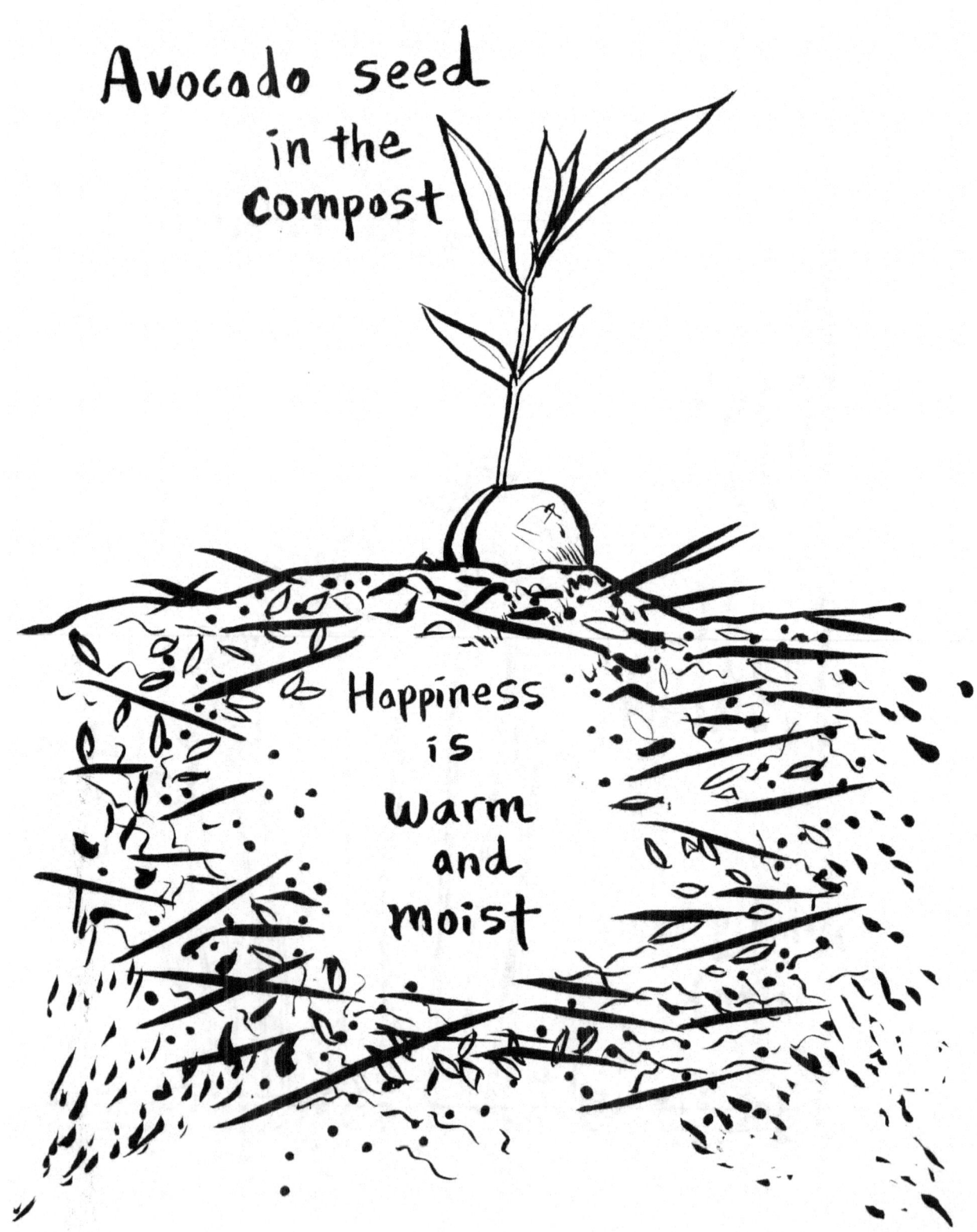

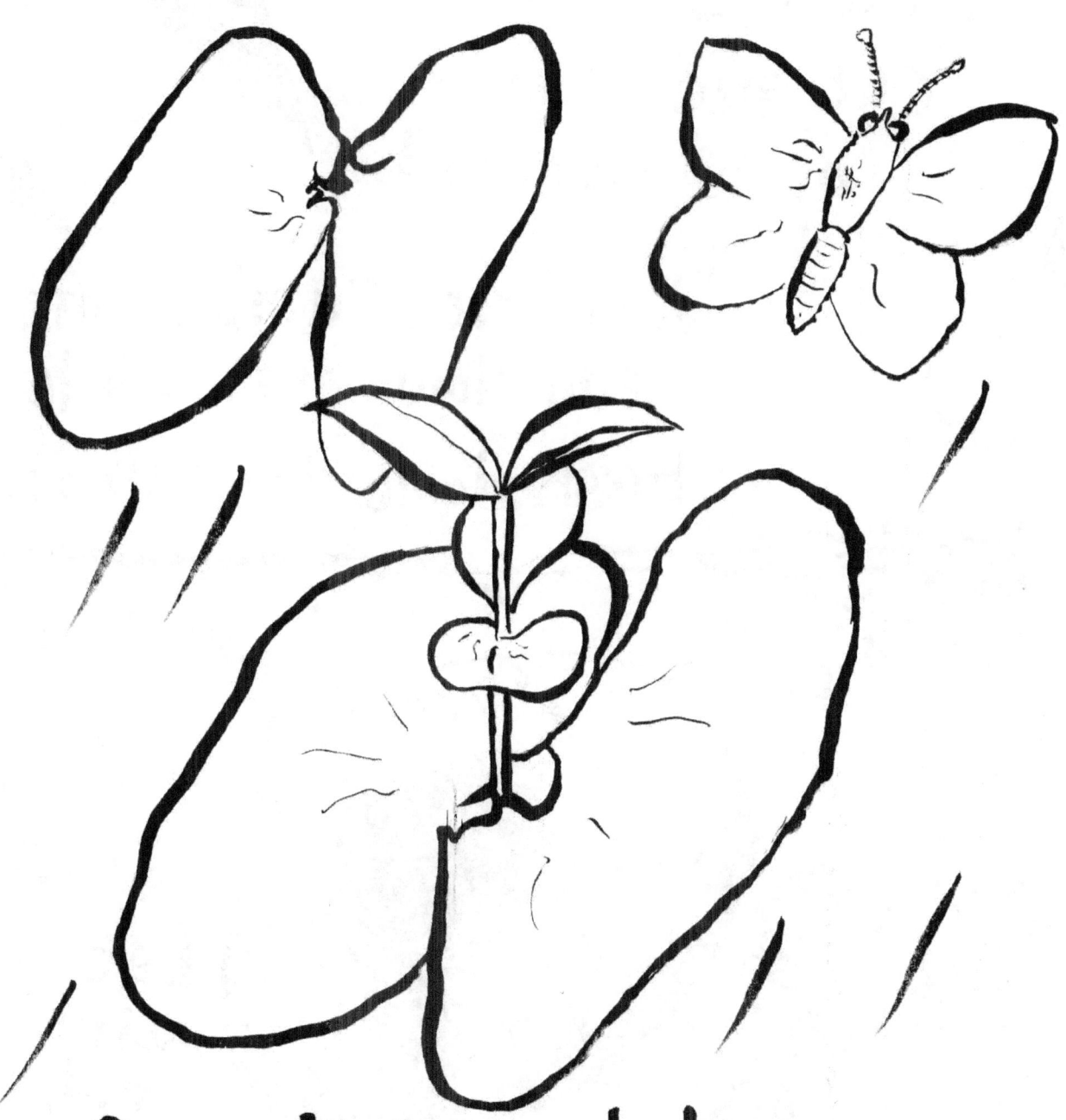

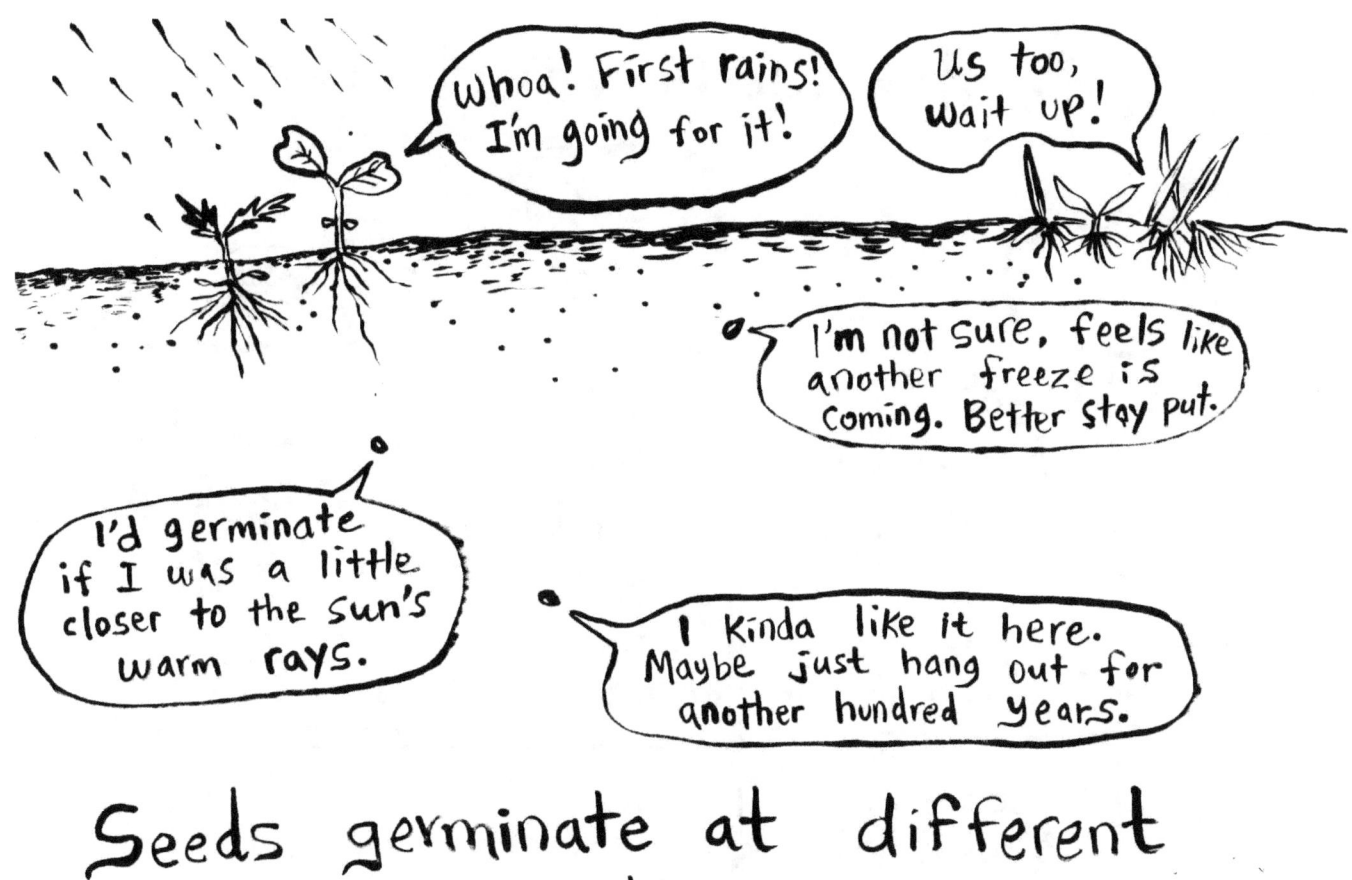

Seeds germinate at different times

Go into the world with a little help.

Bean: "I got a couple of seed leaves to pull me through."

Corn: "Yep, pure starch energy for me."

Chicken: "Got a yolk!"

"I'll have the huevos rancheros!"

Spore

Not all plants have seeds. Ferns, mosses and horsetails grow from a spore. Spores come from a time before the evolution of flowers, fruits, and seeds. Spores belong to ancient plants that made the jump from the sea to the land. They established their territories in wet places.

For the most part, spores do not have the extra food reserves like seeds do. They survive dry times in a dormant state - hang out and wait for good growing conditions.

Where it is moist and warm, spores awaken and grow. The plant cells divide and enlarge. In the green wetness, the male cell (a little sperm) swims over to the female egg chamber and KAPOW fertilization! Here begins the life of a spore bearing being.

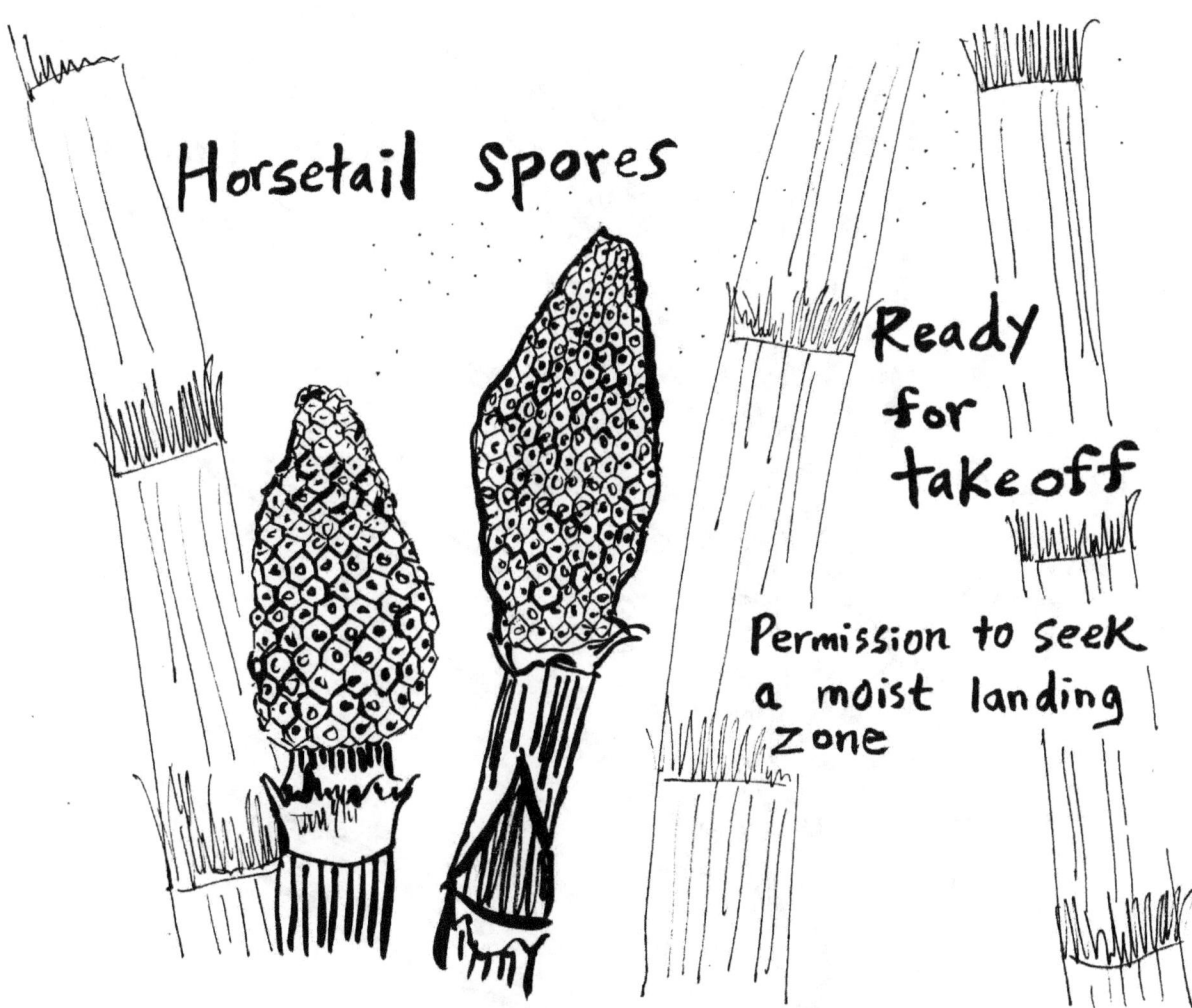

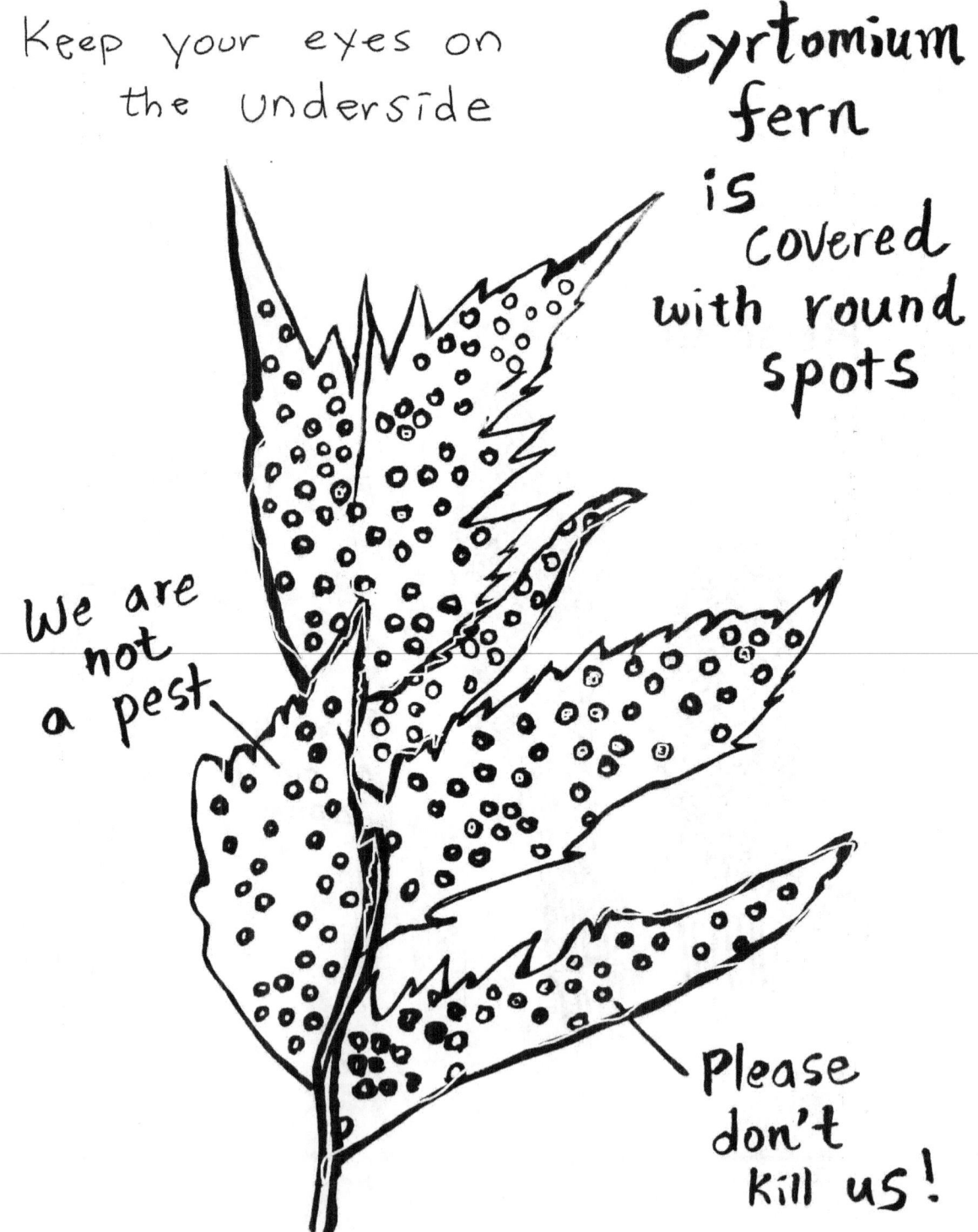

Amongst friends and decomposers

Plants are our closest energetic link to the sun. The sun's power is transferred from the sun to plants to you, via food.

The bonds between plants and other life forms are tight and ancient, woven of the strongest fibers. Plants are food and shelter. In exchange, creatures assist plants with their survival and dispersal. Once you fall in love with plants, the rest of creation tags along.

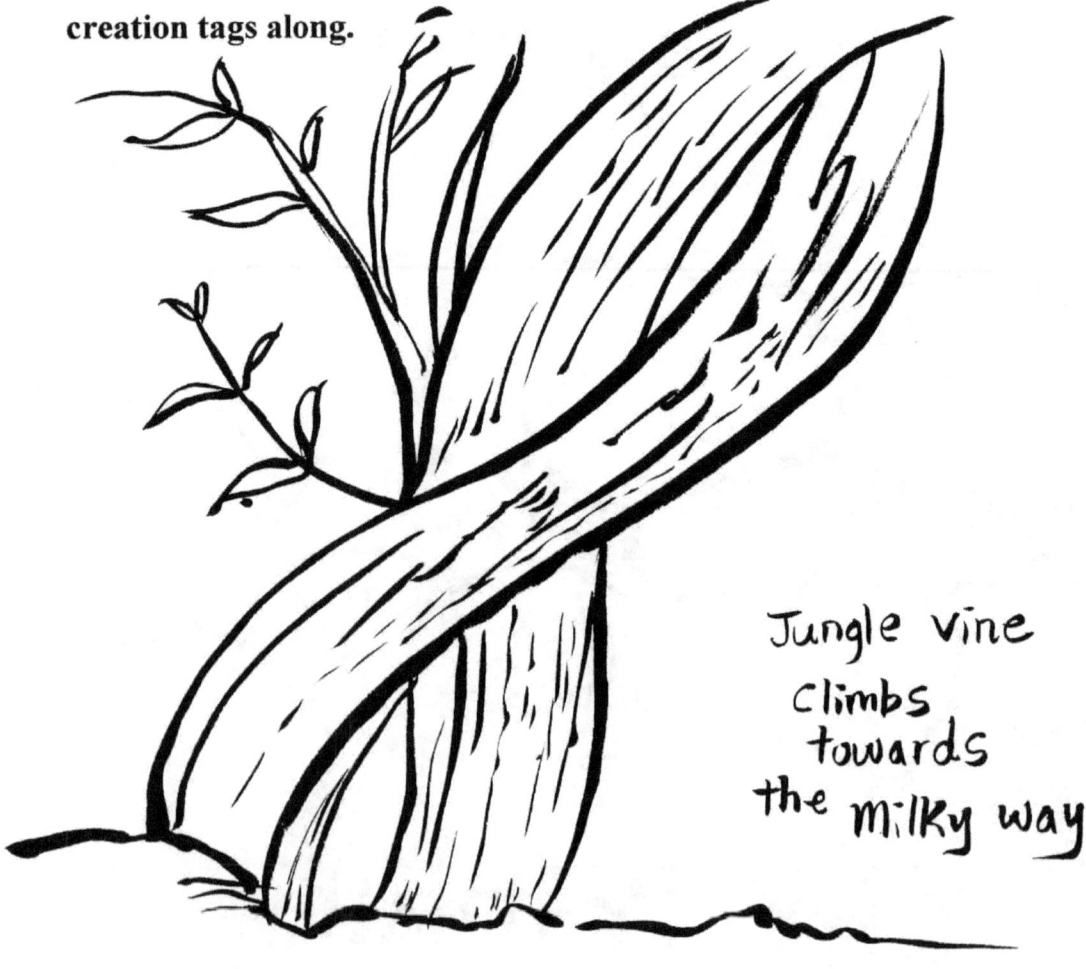

Jungle vine climbs towards the milky way

Plant parasites

There are a number of plants that do not photosynthesize well or not at all. They cannot make their own food from the sun. These plants don't have much chlorophyll, and rely on the sugary storehouses of others.

Parasites latch onto the roots and stems, tap in, and suck up what they need to survive. Many are fantastic colors of reds, oranges, and yellows.

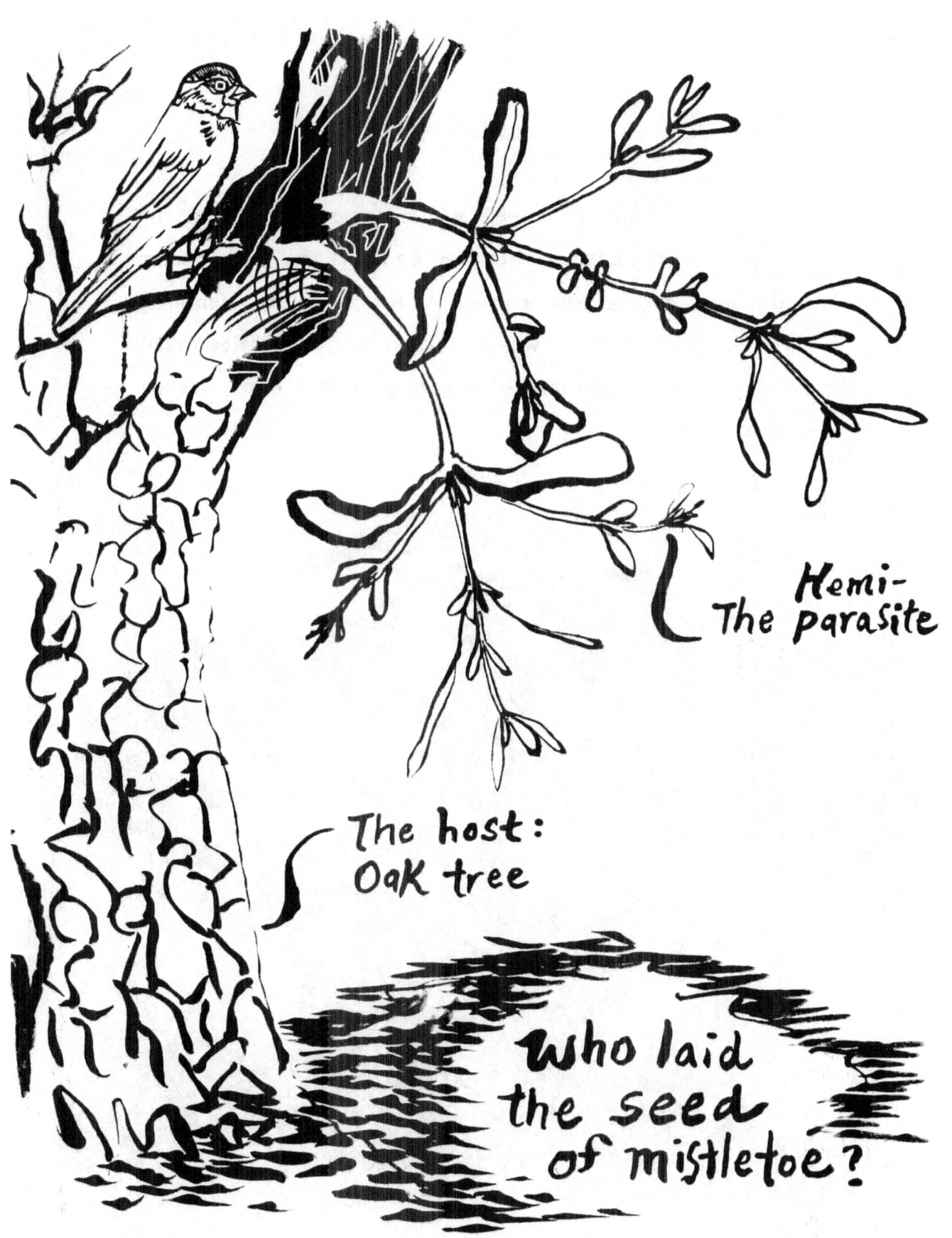

Birds

Birds are feathered angels whose songs greet us in the morning. In the garden, they feed on seeds and fruit, nectar and beetles, earwigs and worms. As they raise their families, birds eat garden pests as well as our garden plants. Red tailed hawk screams. Hummingbird goes blip blip blip. Raven cackles hahaha.

Mammals

Sometimes I would rather not see mammals in the garden. They are always causing mischief as they go - under and over, into and around, up then down - our beloved plants. This is not to mention their constant chewing, chipping, chomping, scratching, stomping, smearing, burrowing and badgering, rubbing and ripping habits.

Nevertheless, mammals are our close kin, a cousin of a cousin of a cousin. They are usually cute as babies, warm and furry, and breathe air into their lungs through a nose. The garden would not be the same without our fun and fantastic friends.

Luckily, mammals also help out the plants. Their tunnels bring air to roots; they plant trees as they bury seeds; they hunt and destroy colonies of caterpillars and termites; their feces and dead bodies return nutrients to the earth.

On the farm, mammals turn plants into muscles and fat, bone and blood, skin and fur. But that is a story for another day ... Let's go back to the garden.

Squirrels chew & scratch the bark and skin of the Magnolia tree.

Some mouse parts are not eaten.

Reptiles and amphibians

The garden is a wonderful home for reptiles and amphibians. A little water to drink, a fly to eat, and a chunk of wood to hide under are the essence of happiness. A frog or a salamander in the garden is a super sign of health. Listen to a ranalian love chant on a summer night go whoppa whoppa whoppa ong ong ong. Turtle bakes on hot rocks. A slithering snake takes us back to Eden and the paradise that is this earth.

Reptiles and amphibians have a mind that is best described as that of the Buddha. Look into the eyes of a newt and you will understand. Om……

Red legged frog gases out next to the primrose.

Meander yonder
Slender Salamander

under a log
in the fog

Take a nap

Next to an inky cap

Friendly pillbugs
and
centipede hugs

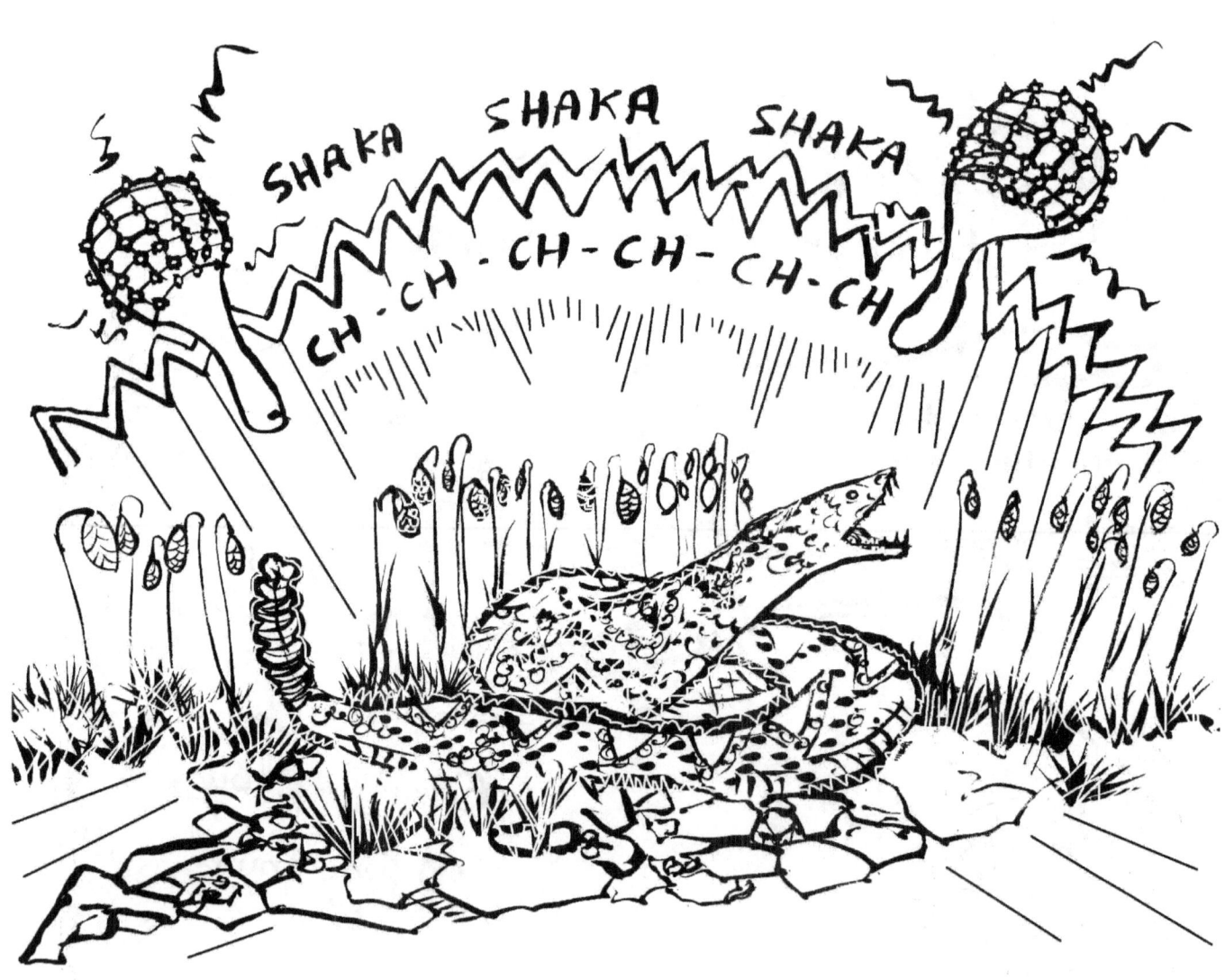

Arthropods of all kinds

Insects, spider, pill bugs, and their countless relatives are the mini rulers of the earth. A few common features are hard shell skeletons, plenty of legs, and segmented bodies. Their brains are tiny! In spite of this, they have tremendous organization, and the ability to adapt quickly over time. We stand in awe of hundreds of million years of evolution. They have much to teach us about chemistry and survival.

Eyes of a fly
Body like a bee

Hover in the sky
Pollinate a tree

Flower to flower
Nectar Power!

Family Syrphidae

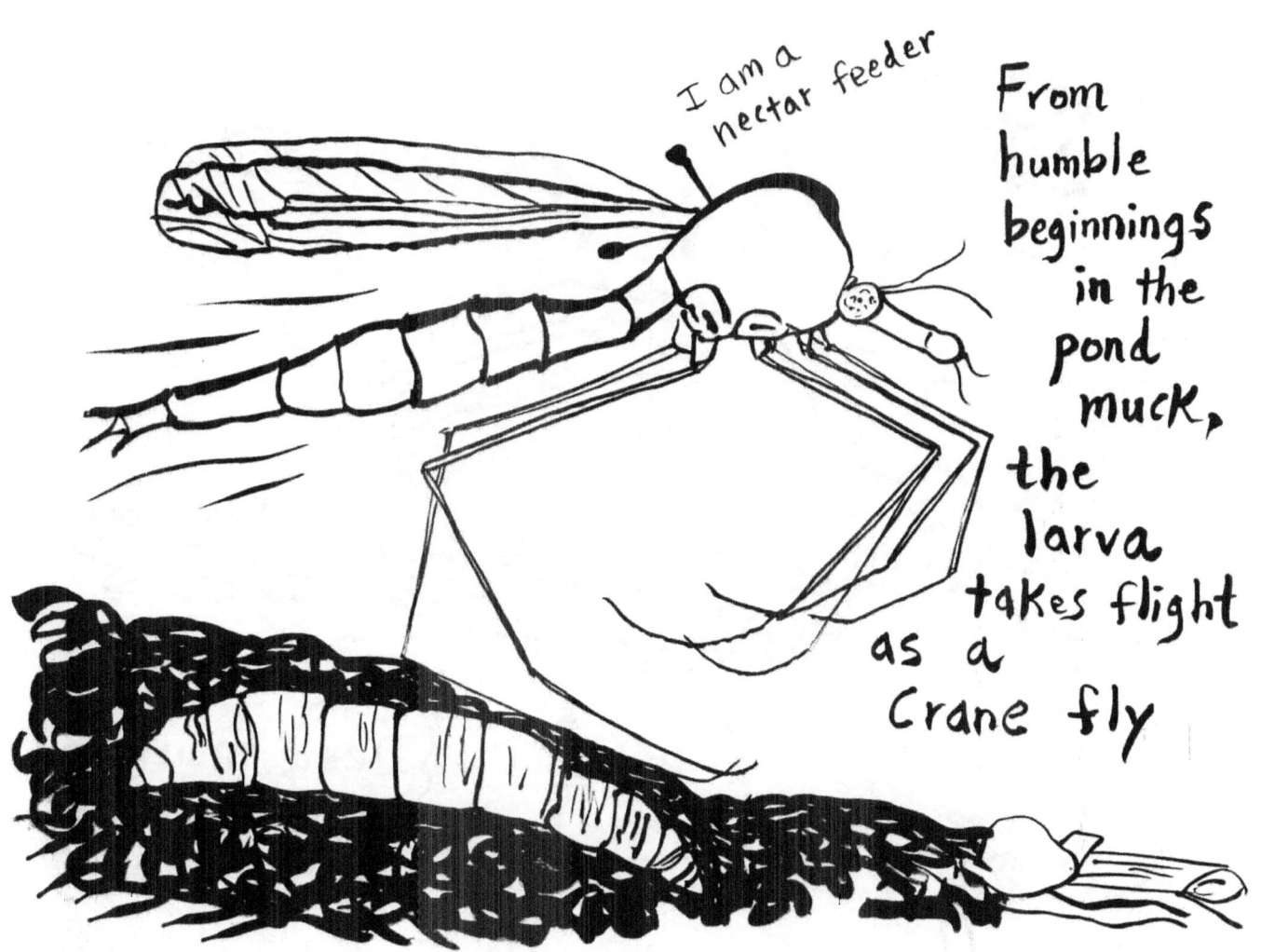

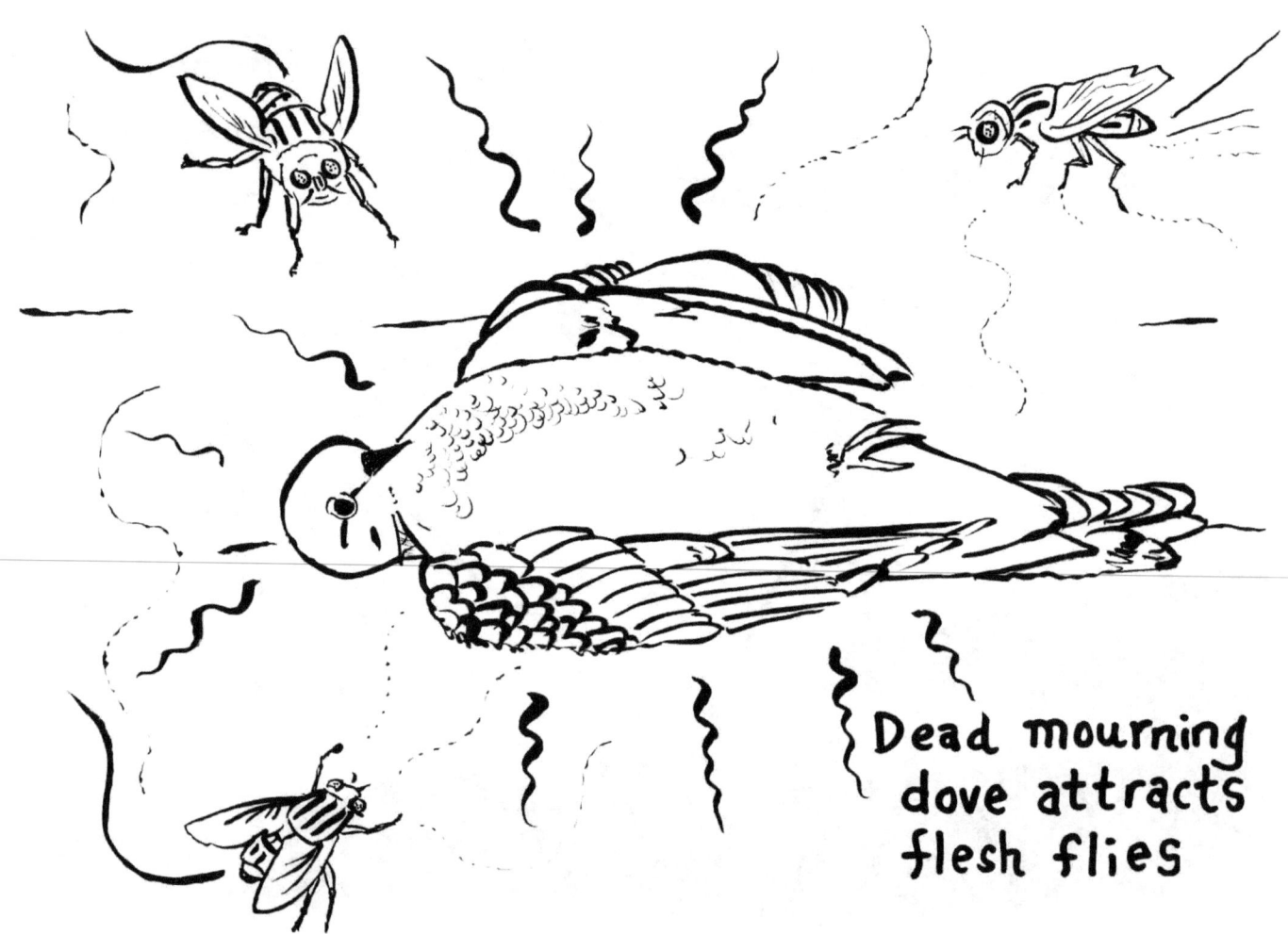

Hunger - love - food - mate - aphids - babies - chewing mouth parts - eggs - sugar - happiness

Ladybug ecstacy on a lupine

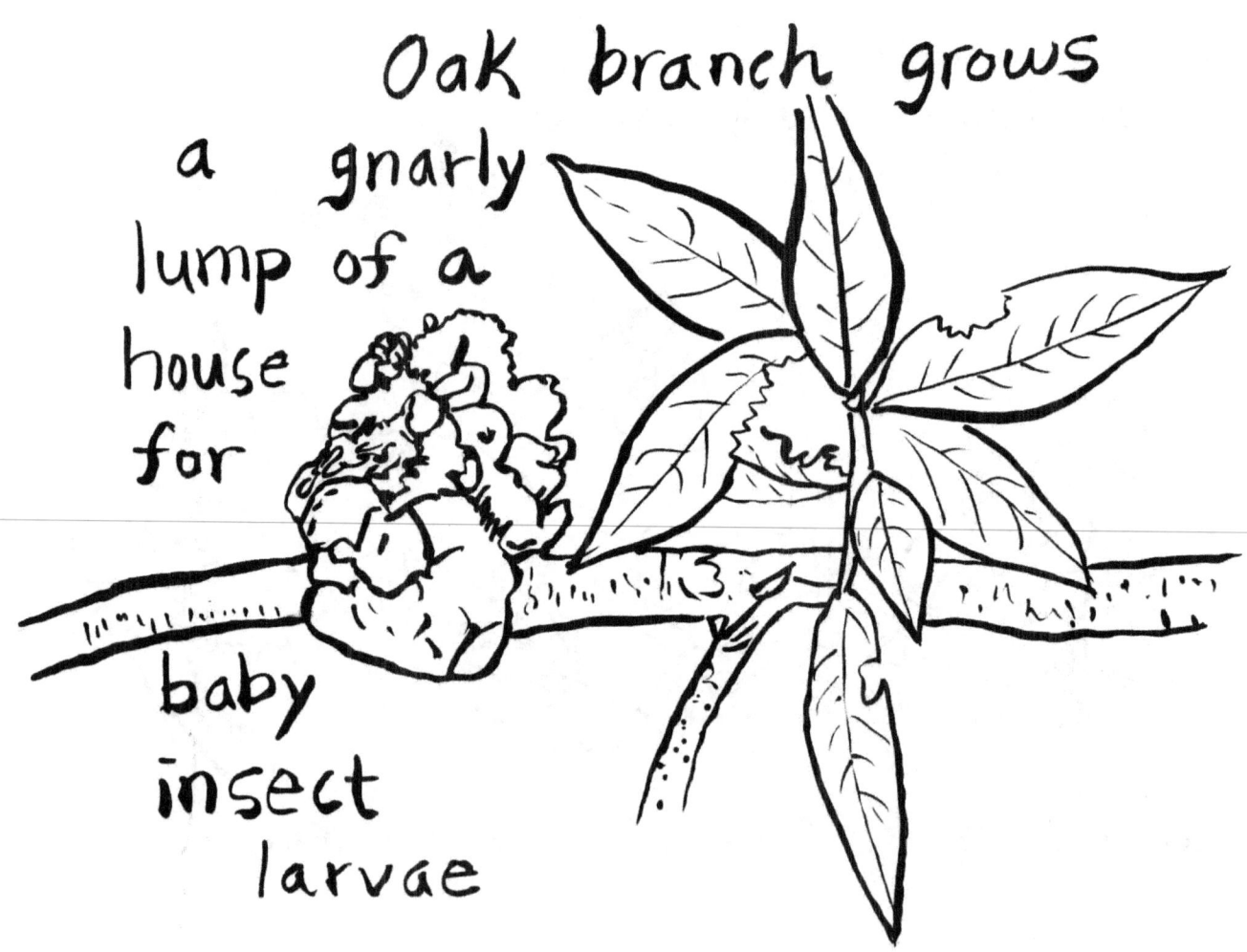

Oak branch grows a gnarly lump of a house for baby insect larvae

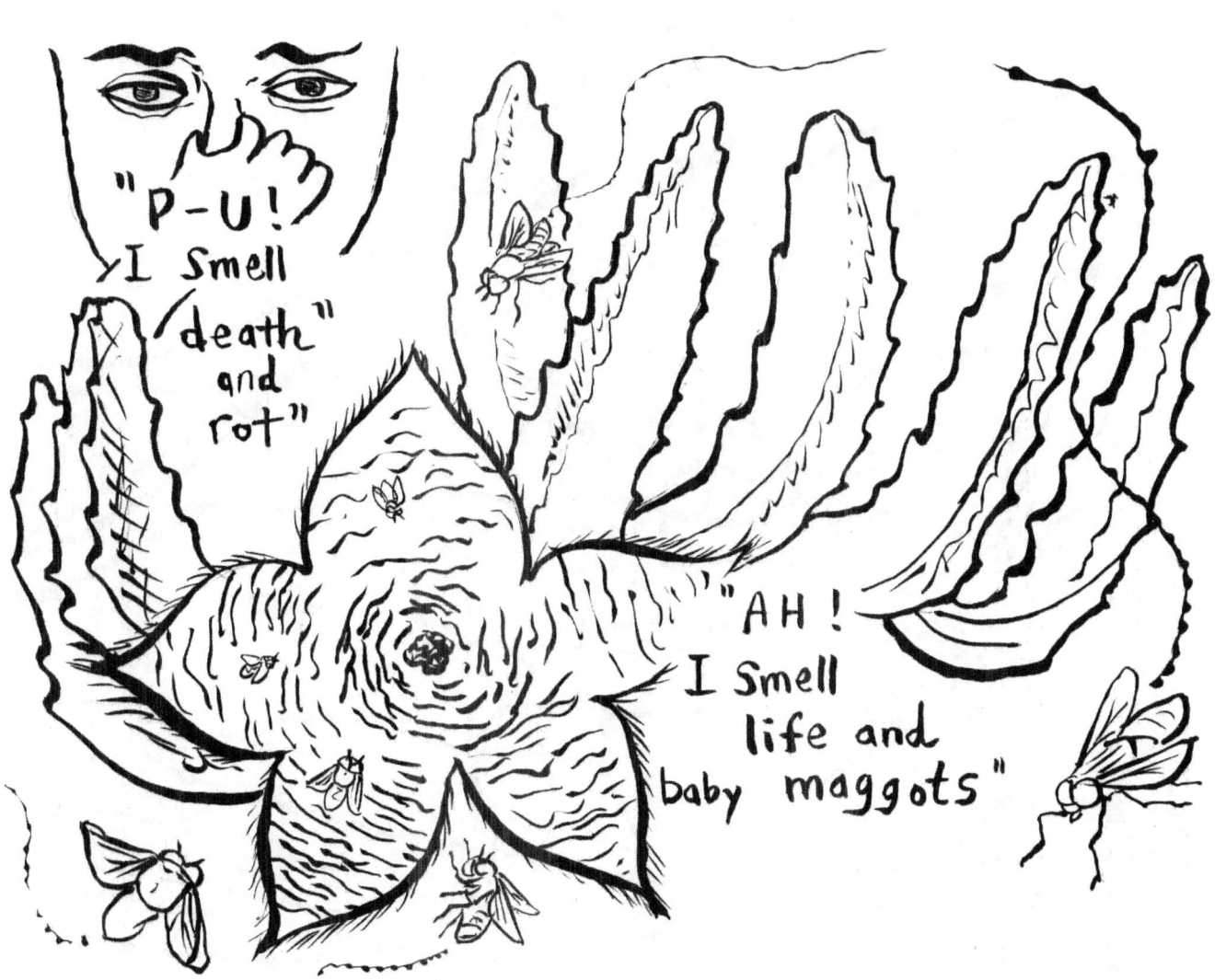

Aphids suck the sweet flow of the Alstroemeria flower.

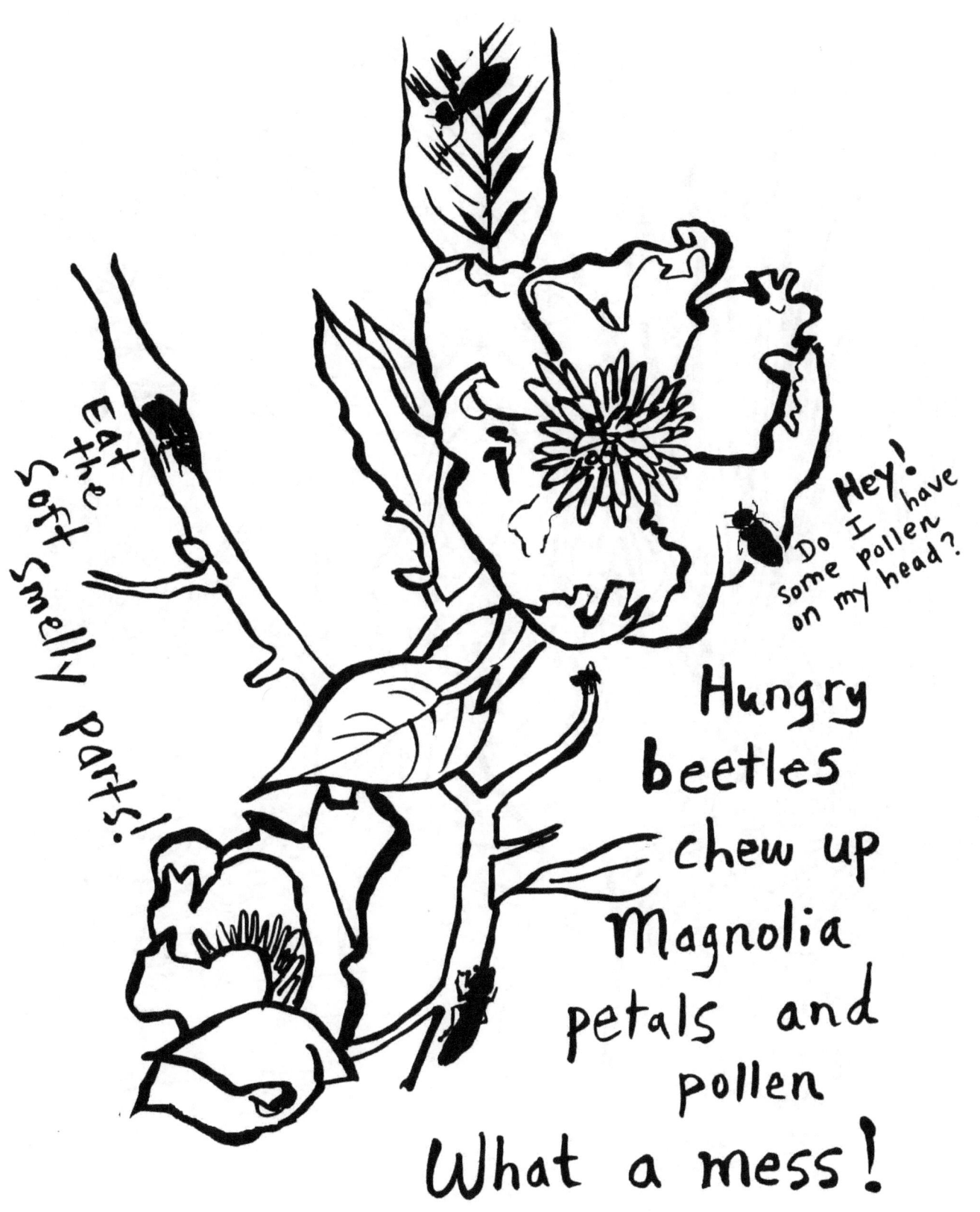

Fungi

Fungi are delightful creatures to meet and know. They are the master bosses of this planet. When our bodies return to the earth, fungi are there to greet us. Their web and chain networks cover the earth in dominant and spreading patterns. Their spores float into open bottles of spaghetti, and wait patiently on ripening grapes.

Many fungi feed on dead stuff. They are responsible for rot and decay. In the process, they break down and recycle the world. They release nutrients into the soil that plants can use. Fungi keep this world from being filled with thousand-year old logs and leaves, fruits and feces.

There are also a great number of fungi that are friends to plants. They live in, or on, the roots of plants, and barter with plants. There are also fungi that feed on live plants - eating leaves, sucking juices, and clogging plant pipes. These are plant killers and parasites – fungi that bring down the tallest pine trees, and hollow out the fattest trunks.

Turkey tail fungus
eats the
fallen douglas fir log

Just putting
things back
where they
belong

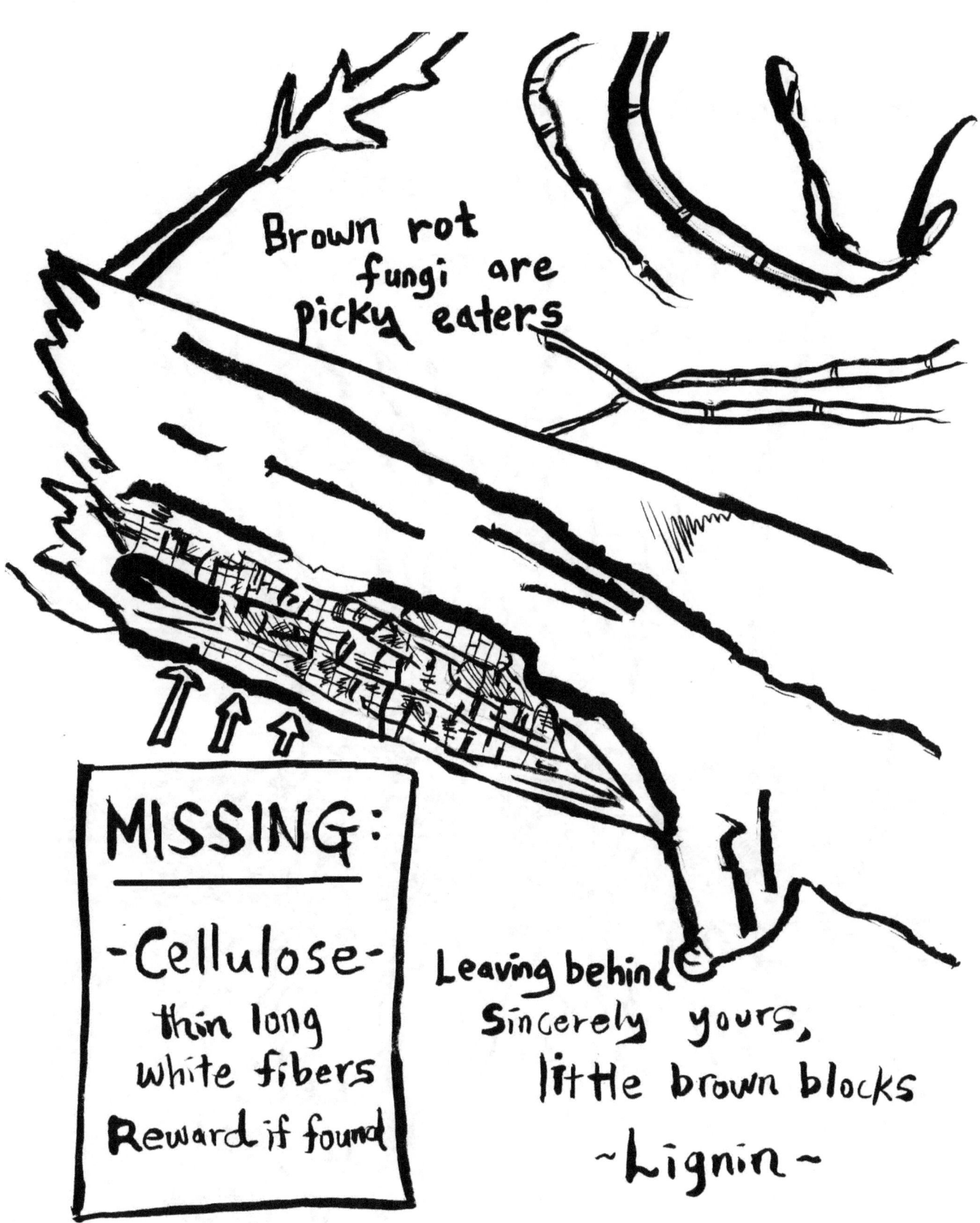

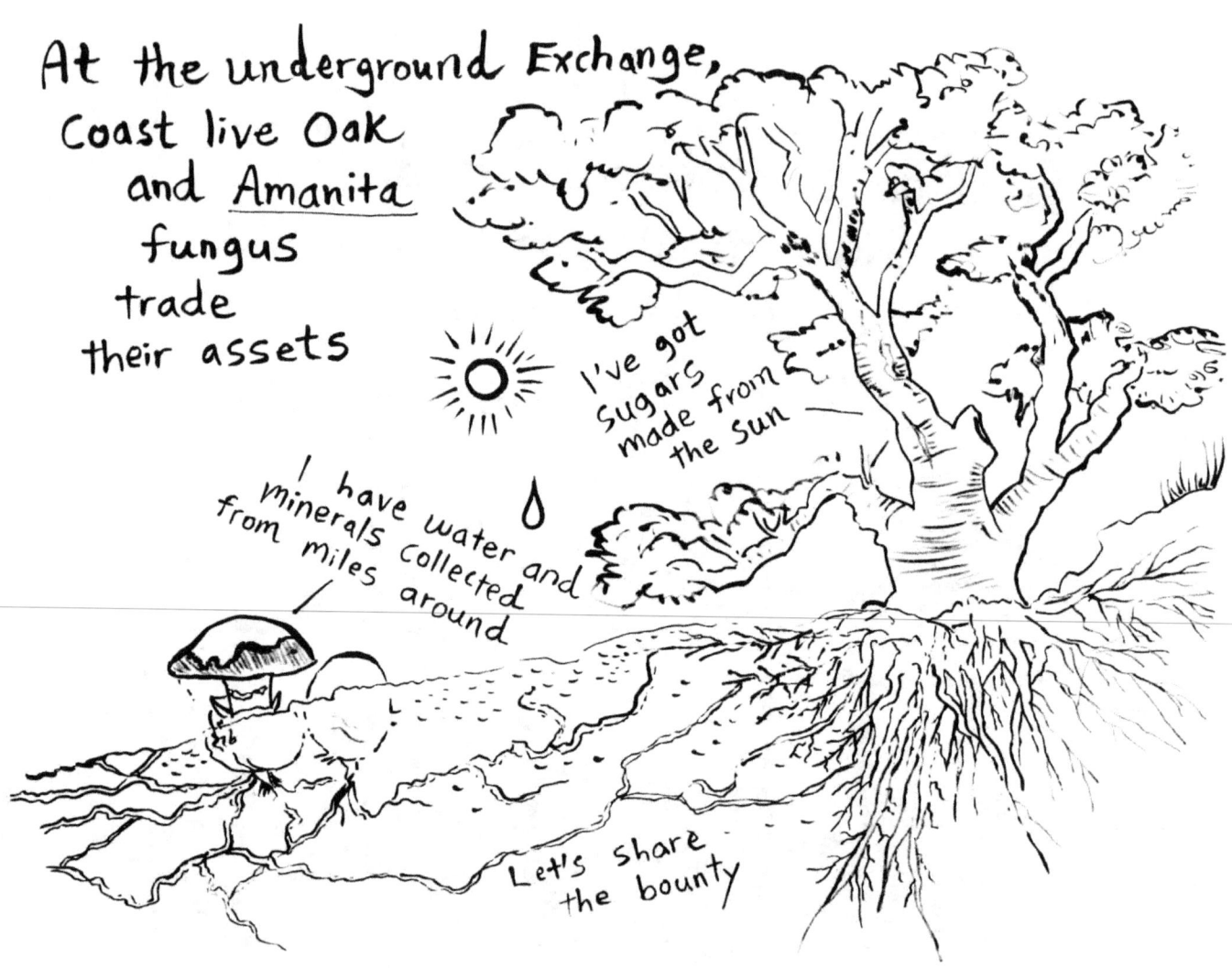

Psilocybe mushrooms wave their caps with joy as they eat the Eucalyptus wood chips.

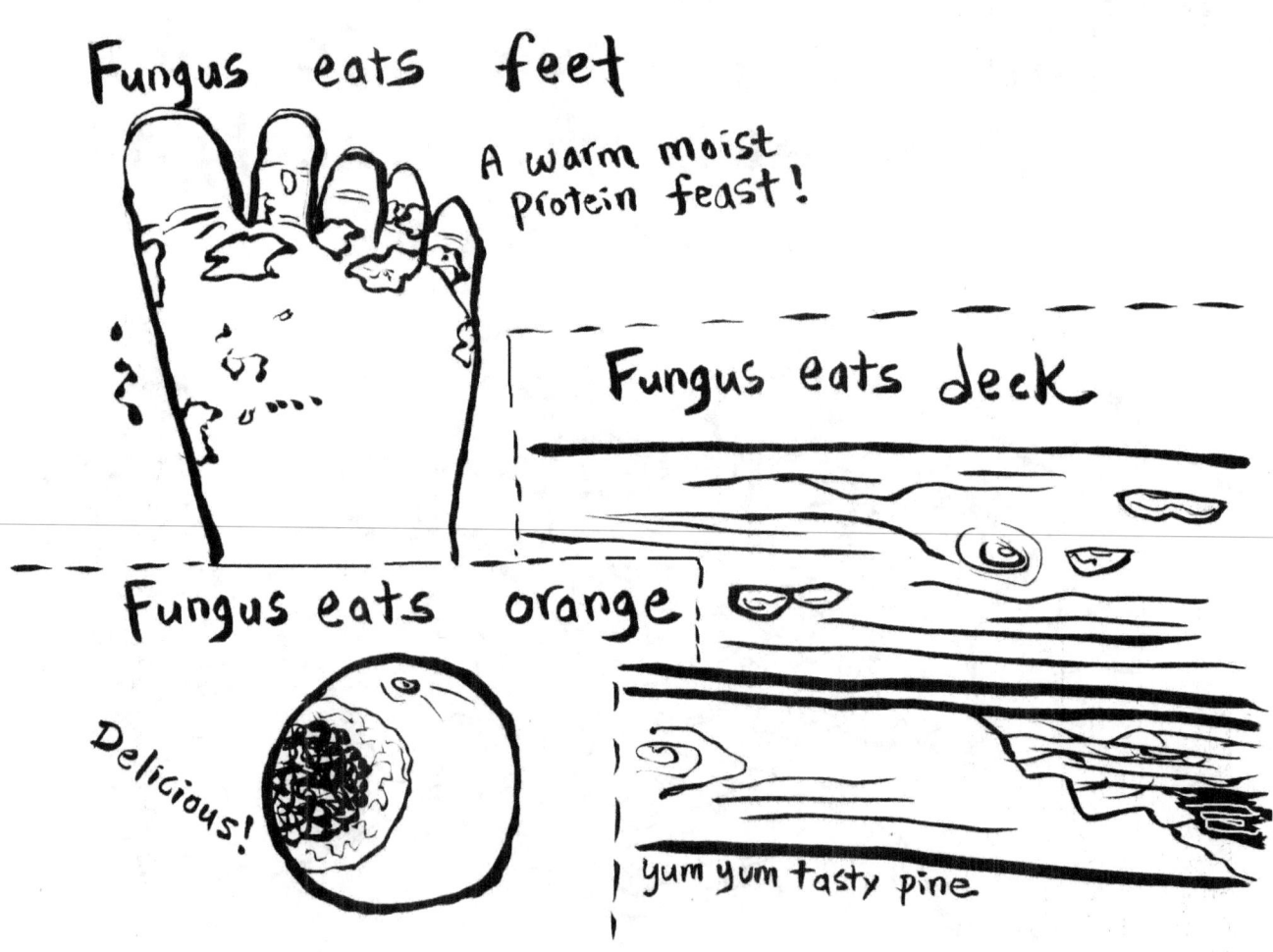

Worms

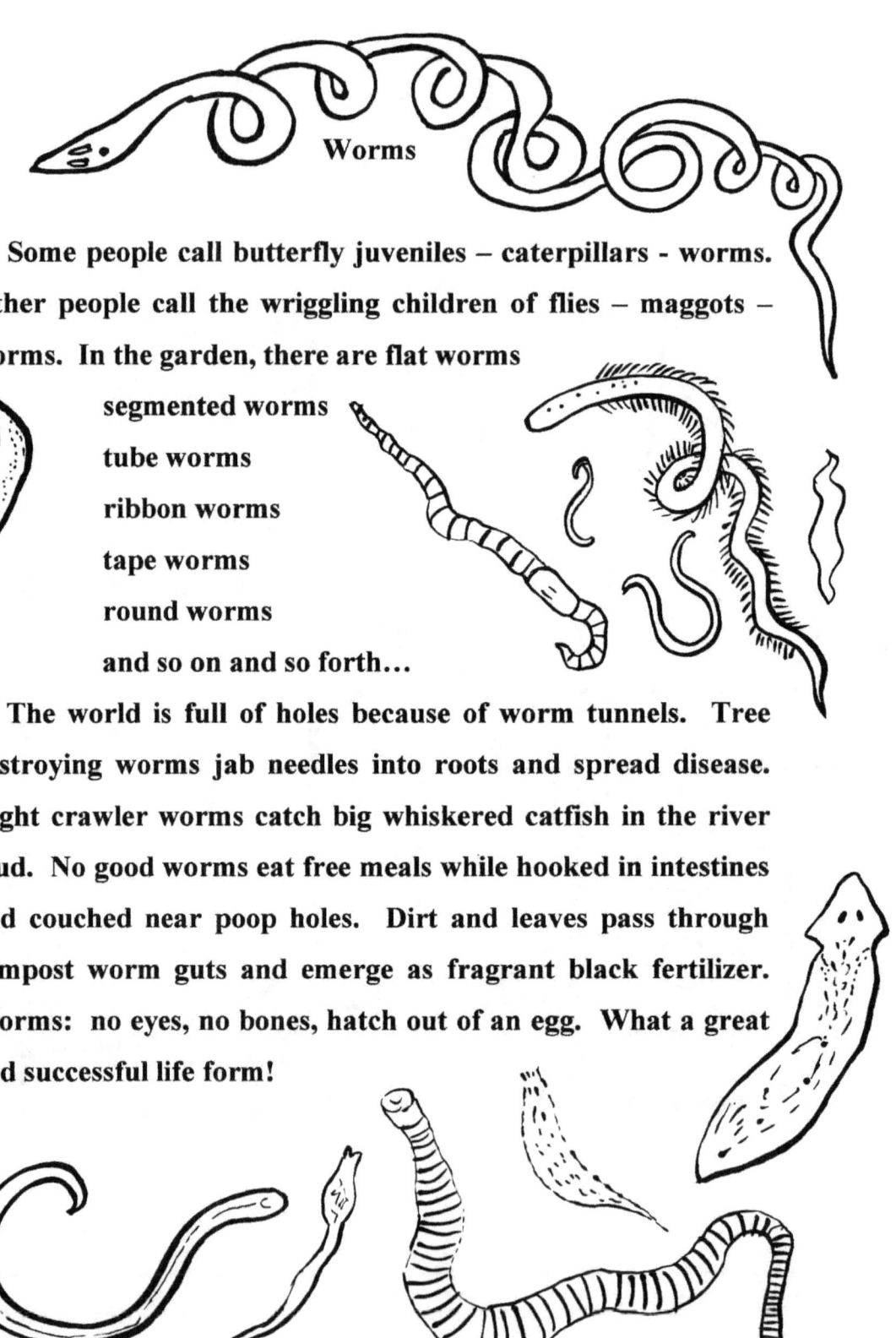

Some people call butterfly juveniles – caterpillars - worms. Other people call the wriggling children of flies – maggots – worms. In the garden, there are flat worms

segmented worms

tube worms

ribbon worms

tape worms

round worms

and so on and so forth…

The world is full of holes because of worm tunnels. Tree destroying worms jab needles into roots and spread disease. Night crawler worms catch big whiskered catfish in the river mud. No good worms eat free meals while hooked in intestines and couched near poop holes. Dirt and leaves pass through compost worm guts and emerge as fragrant black fertilizer. Worms: no eyes, no bones, hatch out of an egg. What a great and successful life form!

Snails and slugs

The row of lettuce you just planted, gone! The flowers and fruits of lupines, chewed to the nub! Who is responsible? You find shiny silver trails, munched leaves, and green and white coils of poop... In the garden, pill bugs are milling about, scavenging for the leftovers.

Snails and slugs are distant cousins of clams and squid. They have a buff muscular foot for movement, a body that is male and female, eyes on a stalk, and an armor of slime. A blanket of skin covers snails and slugs. It can grow a shell above, and cover the lungs and heart below.

Perhaps we can ask the snails and slugs to leave quietly from the garden. If they resist, I will have to use my secret arsenal of weapons: copper and beer, beetles and ducks, flashlights and the bottom of my sole.

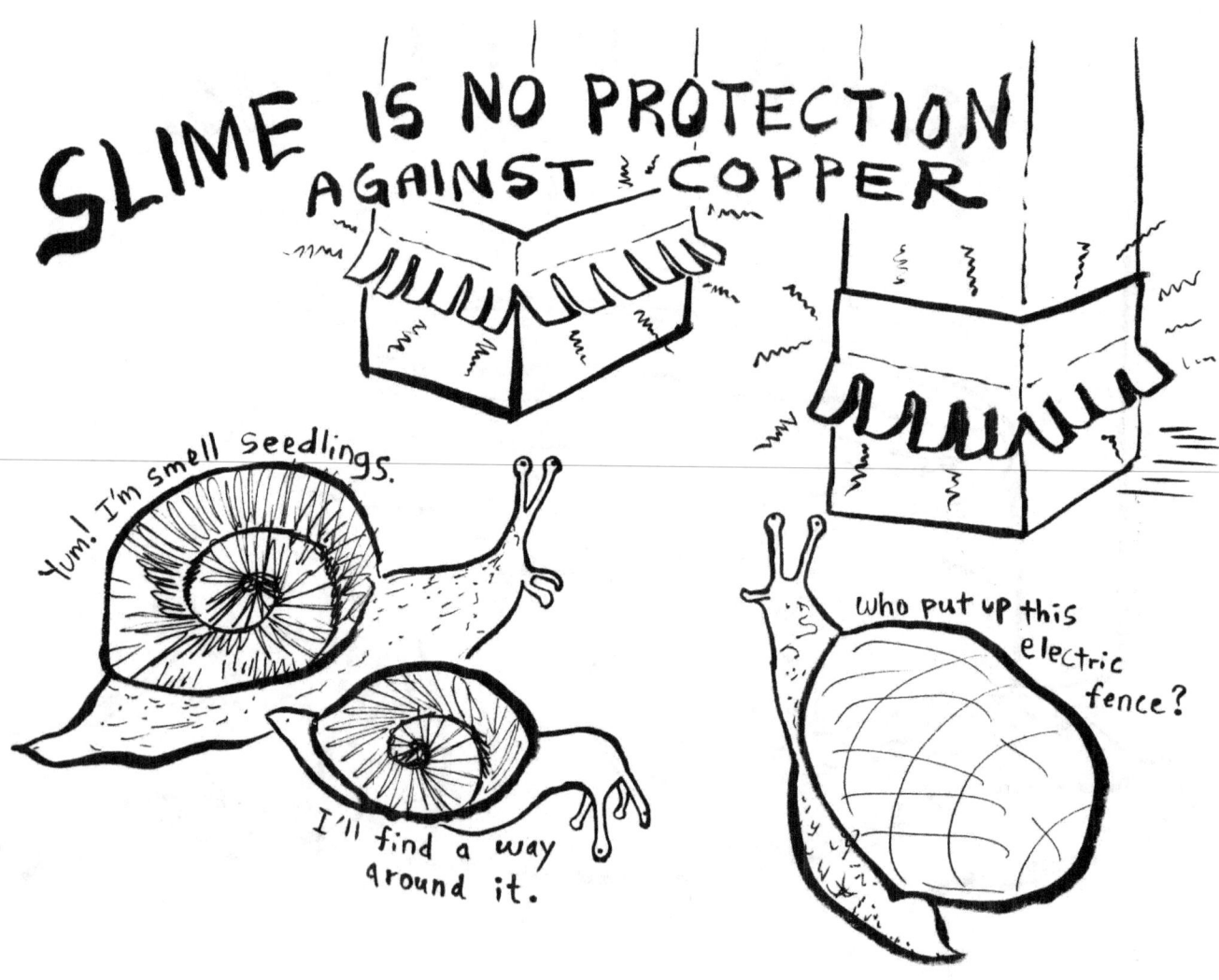

Bacteria and their even smaller relatives

Little eeny weeny creatures we can hardly see with our naked eye are tucked into the folds of the world. They cover every surface: bathtub tile and leather sofa, scruffy cedar tree and chunky elephant, icy mountain and steel warship. Bacteria are picky eaters that enjoy all kinds of food - plastic and rubber, warm and cold bodies, oils and sugars, metal and stone. Their happy homes are guts, armpits, boiling mud, and no oxygen caves. They survive in the hottest springs of the earth and the deepest seas. If chased by a hungry predator like a nematode worm, bacteria swim and nudge away.

Bacteria grow in clumps and chains, mats and layers. Large numbers of them form thin films that stretch and seal. In the blink of an eye, two bacteria have become twenty bacteria. Another pause, and twenty bacteria have become one thousand bacteria.

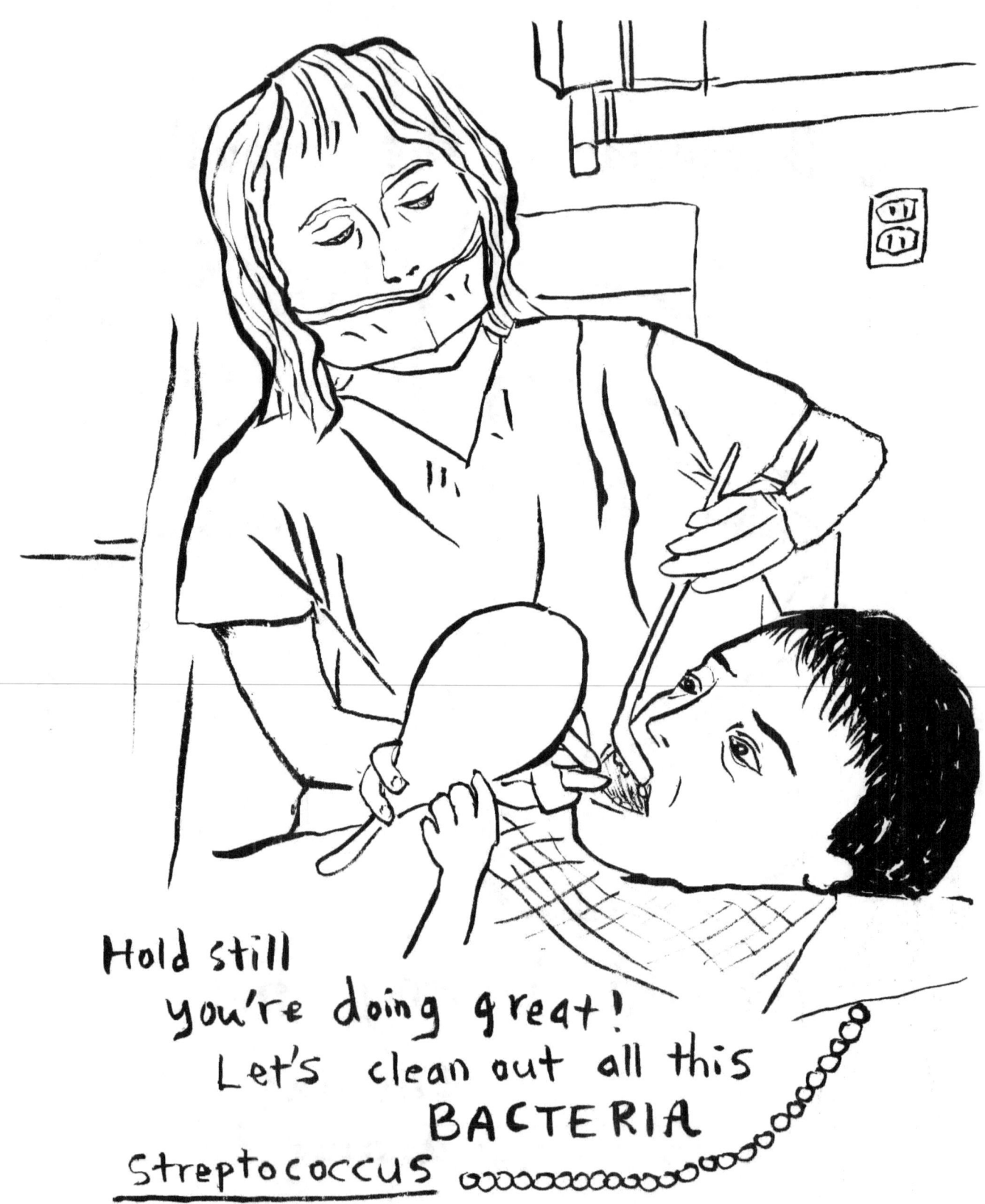

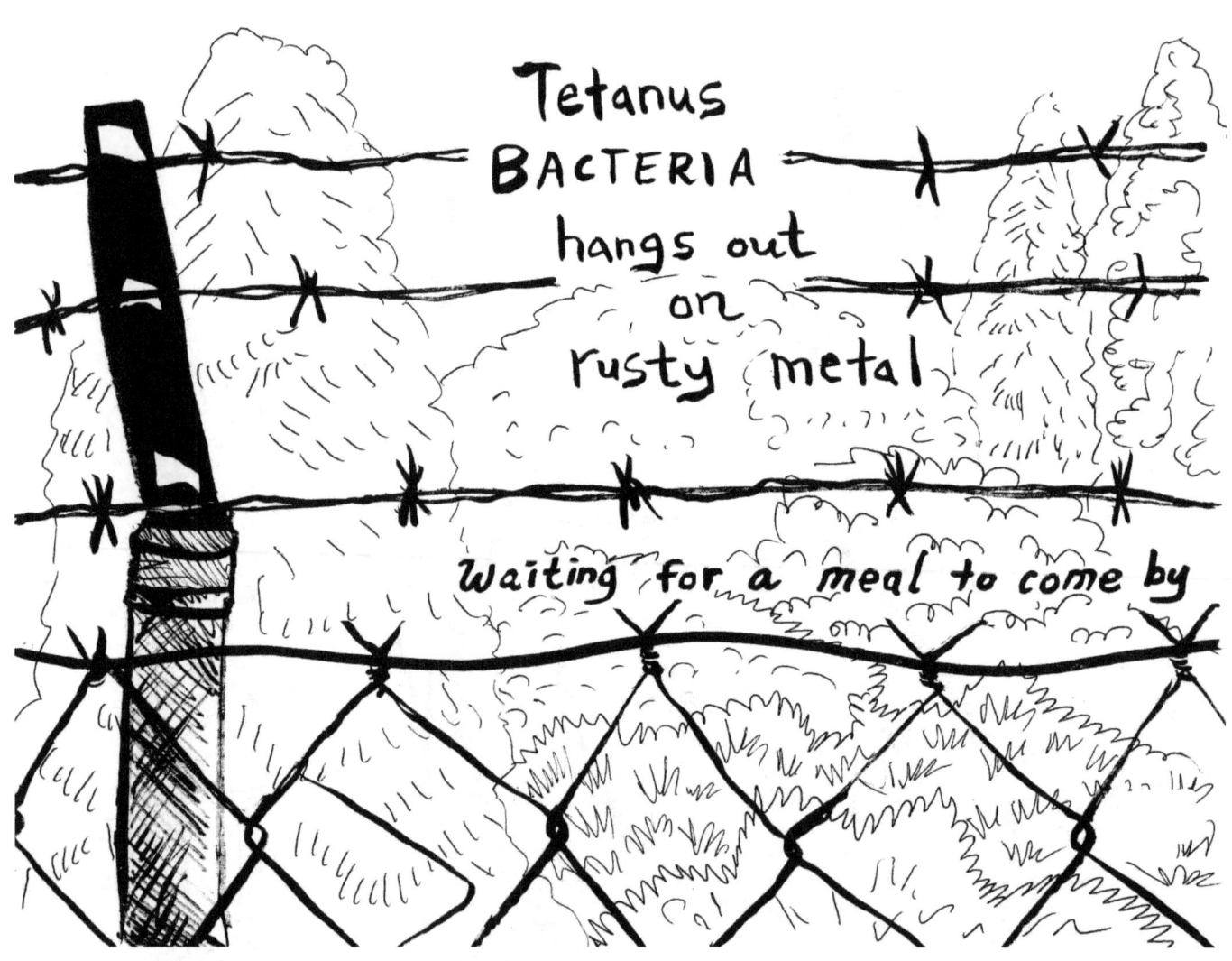

Bacteria are death's allies and undertakers. House cleaners call them germs and reach for a disinfectant like bleach. In the hospital's operating room, bacteria are contaminants. Alcohol kills 'em, iodine kills 'em, hydrogen peroxide kills 'em. Bacteria coat every crevice and pit, wait their turn to invade within, and then grow and spread like mad.

Bacteria are our most beneficial partners in this world. They turn milk into yogurt, and sewage into fertilizer. In your stomach, bacteria feast on corn and beans, fish and rice. Their acidic work breaks food down into tiny pieces the intestines can absorb. Bacteria putrefy protein bodies and ferment the sugary carbohydrates. Bacteria is passed from mother to baby, and shared in the family. Bacteria make life happen.

In the garden, bacteria gets around by hitching rides on insects and tools, wind and water. Bacteria keep the soil tidy, and move nitrogen into and out of the ground. Bacteria kill shrubs, fight with fungi, and paralyze caterpillars.

Gardeners respect bacteria for their work and power, and try to live with them in harmony. Wear gloves, wash your hands, and clean your cuts. Eat food in good company. Keep your immune system strong - live with love and forgiveness.

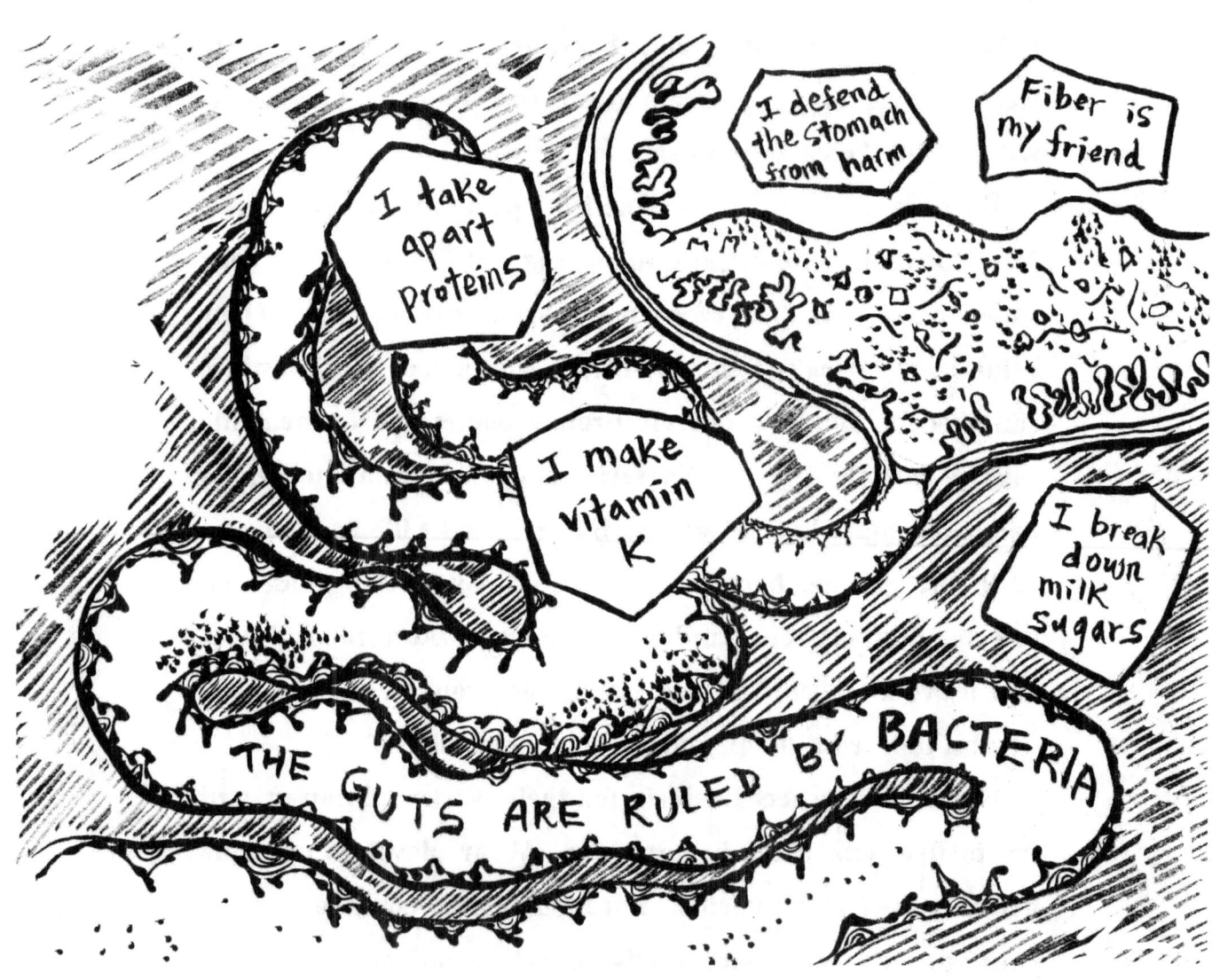

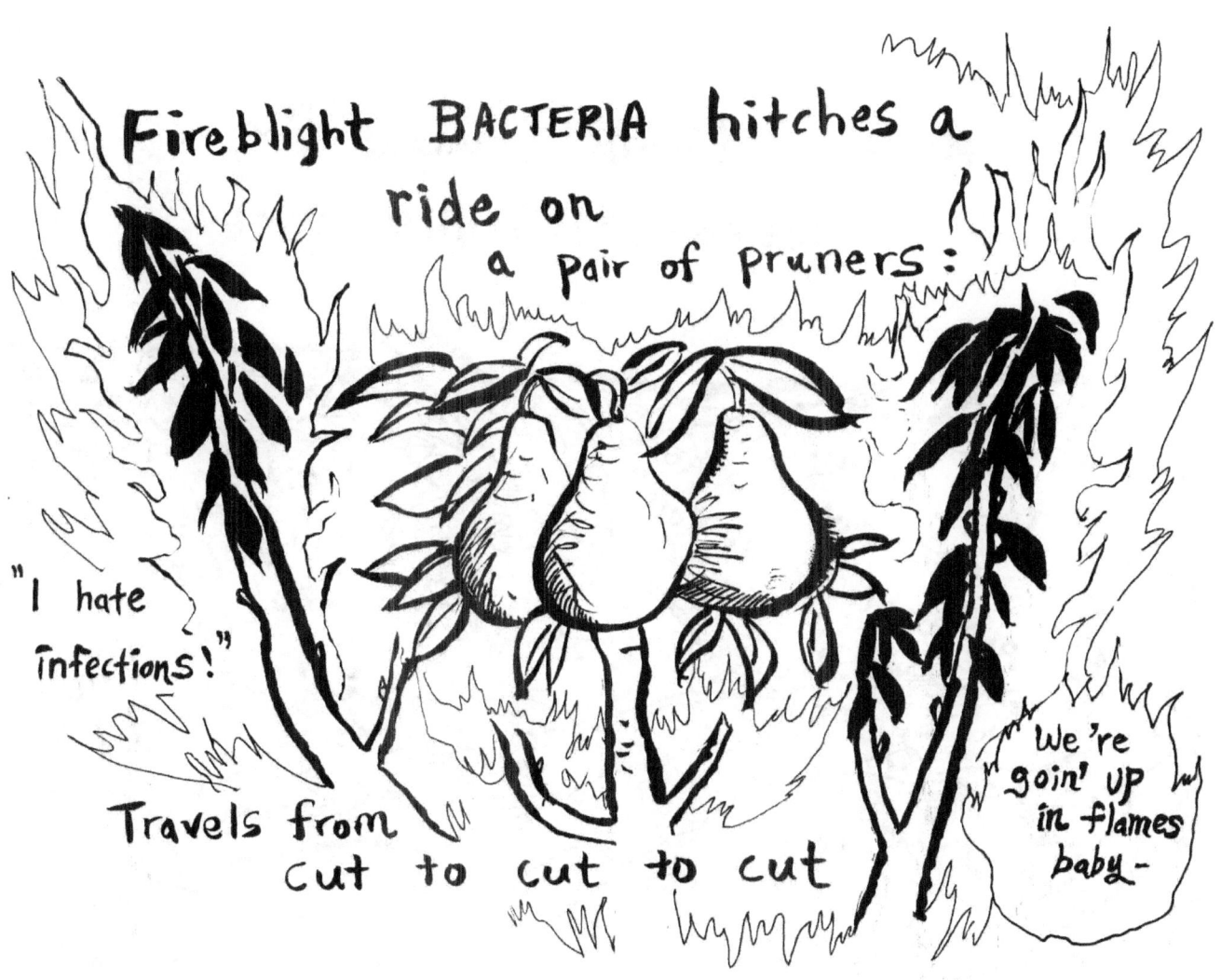

Bacteria fights fungus for leftovers in the soil

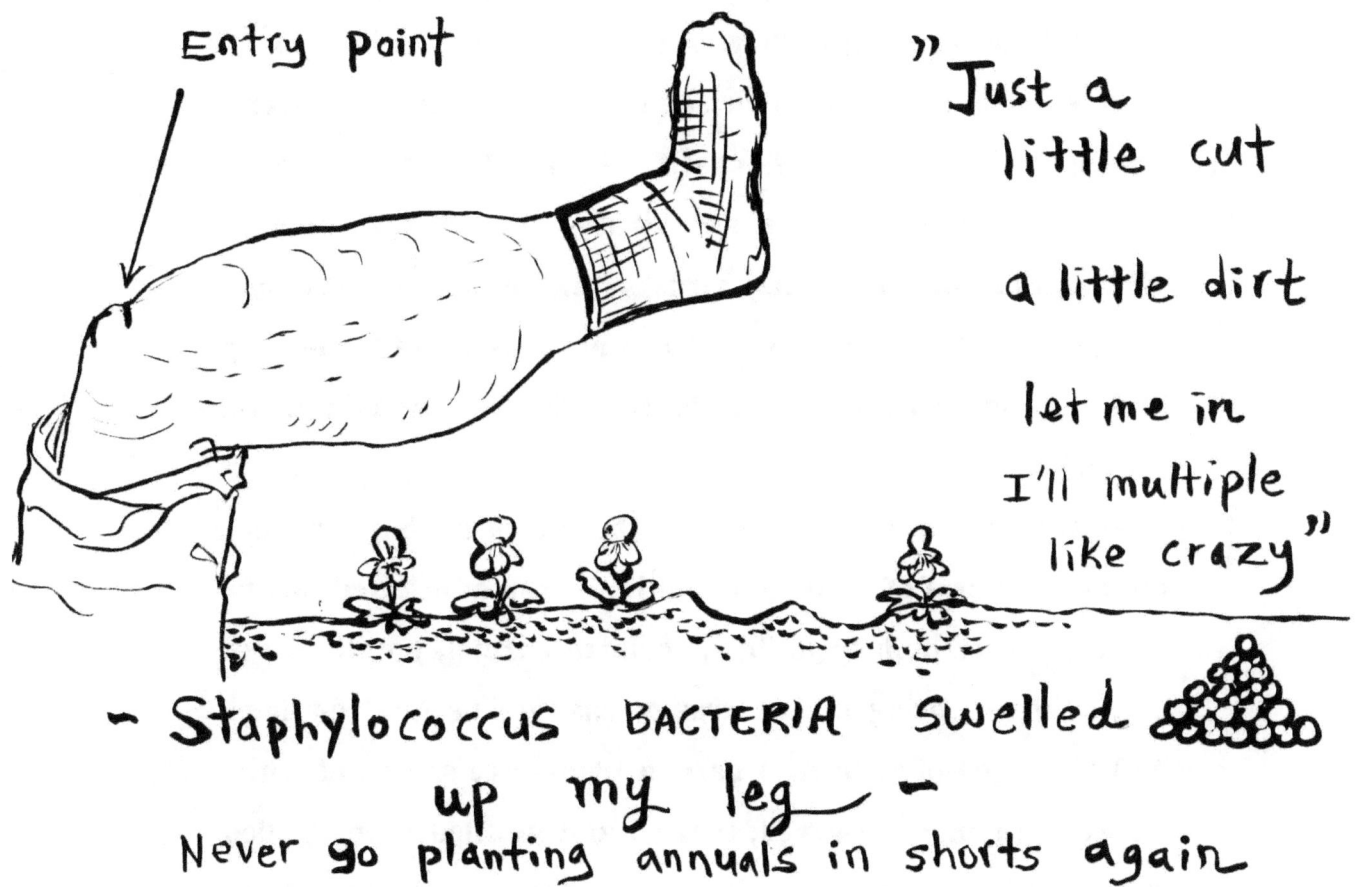

Viruses

There are creatures even smaller and more invisible than bacteria. Imagine a creature that cannot make more of itself without help. This is a creature that needs a host, somebody to invade, in order to reproduce. A virus.

A virus is a little protein shell and a strand of its secret message. Make more of myself. Destroy! Make more of myself. Destroy! There are viruses that attack animals, viruses that attack plants, viruses that attack worms, and viruses that attack bacteria. Viruses are masters of the mix-up and mutation, welding species together in chaos as they travel the globe.

In the garden, viruses travel in the spit of leafhopper bugs, on the dried leaf of cigarettes, and in the sap of infected plants. They go from bulb to bulblet, corm to cormel, potato eye to eye. Viruses bring about strange changes or fatal endings. Tell tale signs of viruses in garden plants are specks of white where it ought to be green, twisted and mottled stems, rolled and crinkled leaves. Prevention is priority number one, as there are no known cures... Keep it clean.

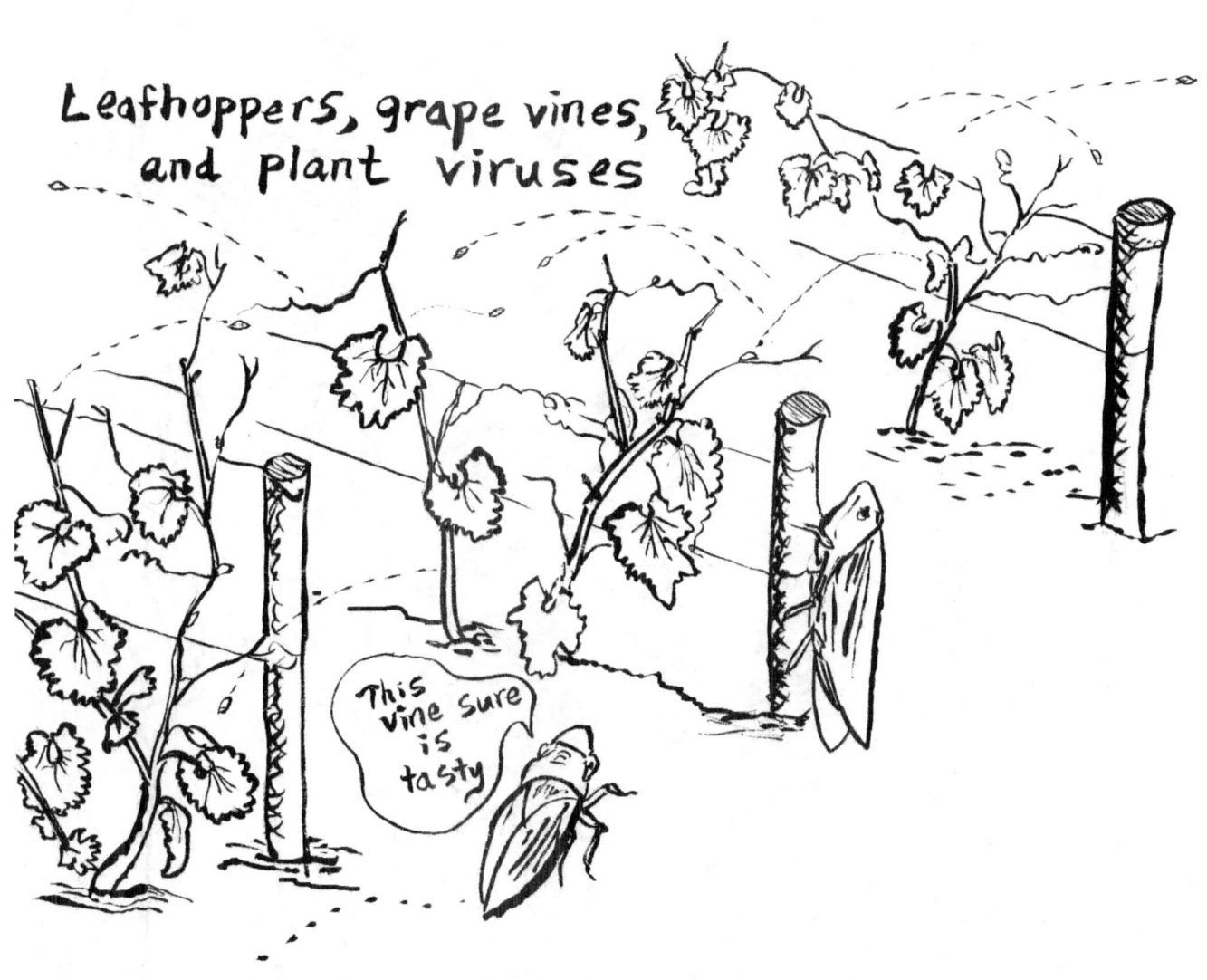

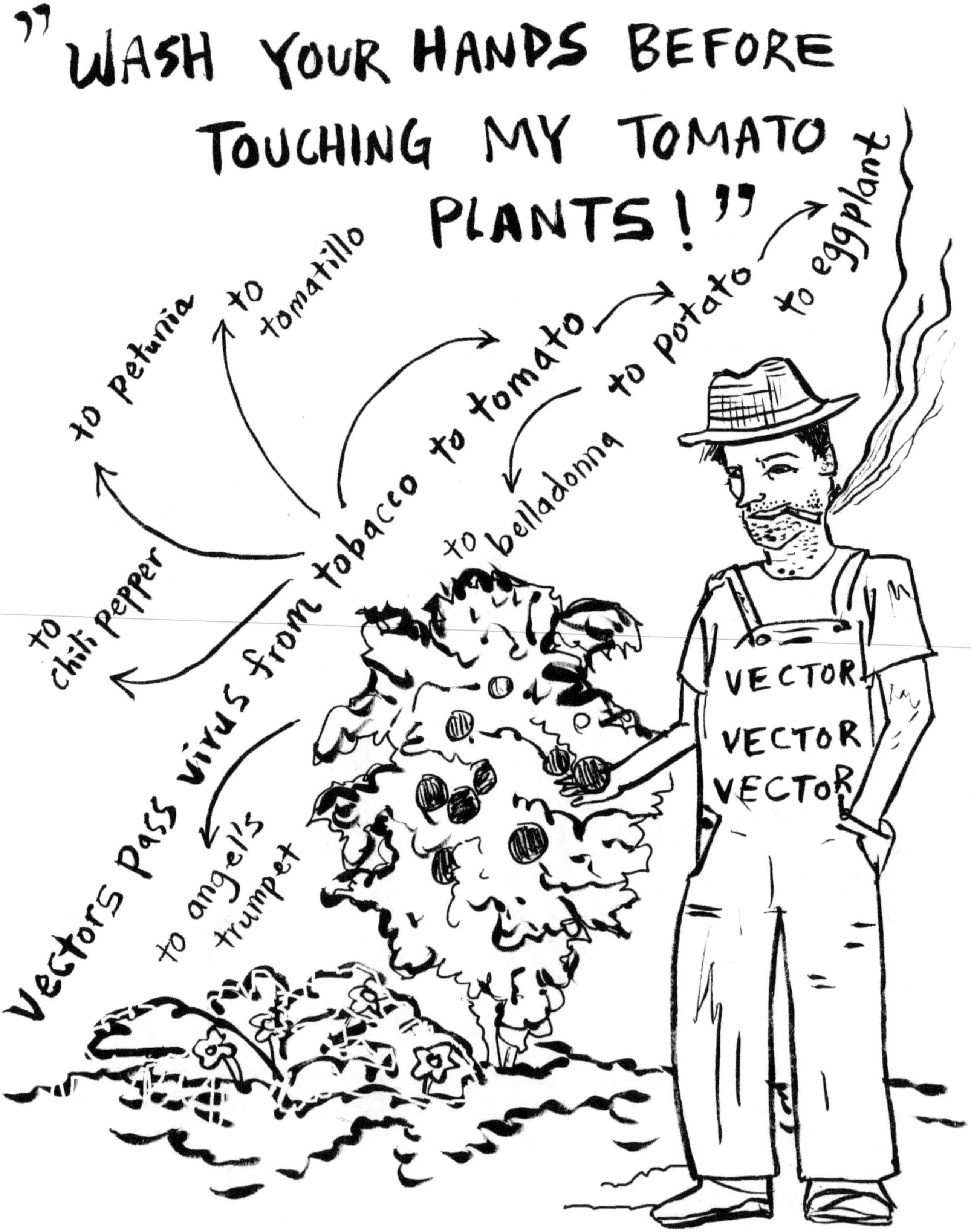

"WASH YOUR HANDS BEFORE TOUCHING MY TOMATO PLANTS!"

Vectors pass virus from tobacco to tomato
- to petunia
- to tomatillo
- to chili pepper
- to potato
- to eggplant
- to belladonna
- to angel's trumpet

VECTOR VECTOR VECTOR

Virus ↓↓↓ decreases photosynthesis

"Yep, this Acacia has got the 'yellow spots'."

"Do you mean 'variegation'?"

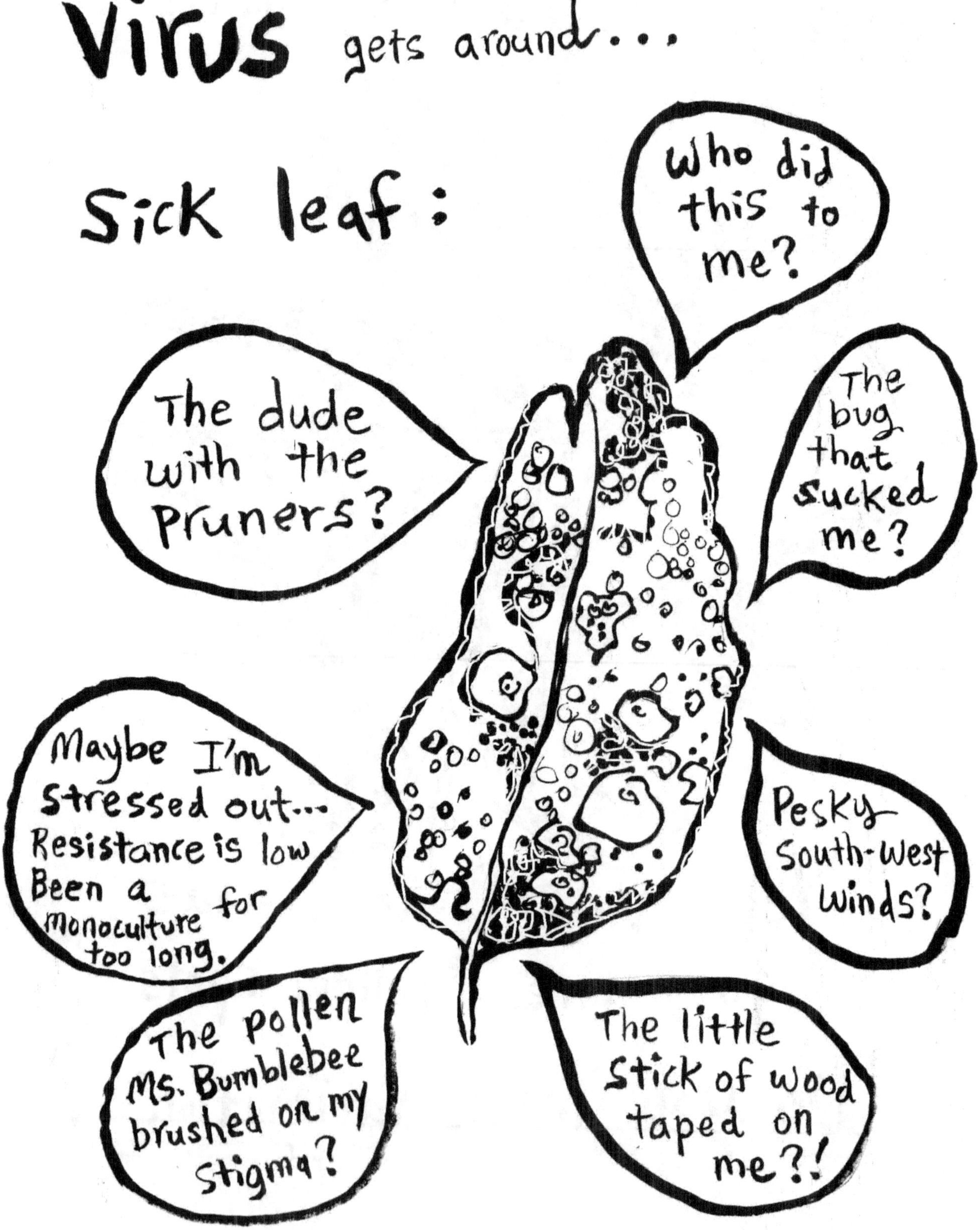

Virus gets around...

Sick leaf:

- Who did this to me?
- The dude with the pruners?
- The bug that sucked me?
- Maybe I'm stressed out... Resistance is low. Been a monoculture for too long.
- Pesky South-West winds?
- The pollen Ms. Bumblebee brushed on my stigma?
- The little stick of wood taped on me?!

Families and teachers

Plants are everywhere. How does one learn the names of plants and their habits? With time spent in the garden, you will gradually greet plants as teachers, recognize their families, and hear the laughter and chatter that is nature in daily rhythm and action. Begin to organize plants as groups of long lost relatives.

Cone or no cone

One way that botanists group plants is by how the seeds of the plant are held. Plants with pollen and seeds inside the woody scales of cones are Gymnosperms. These plants have no flowers. These are: pine cone, fir cone, redwood cone . . .

Plants with pollen, *flowers*, and seeds inside of a *fruit* are Angiosperms. The seed is surrounded by some kind of a fruity vessel; the vessel can be dry or juicy, pokey with hooks or smooth and long, fibrous or exploding.

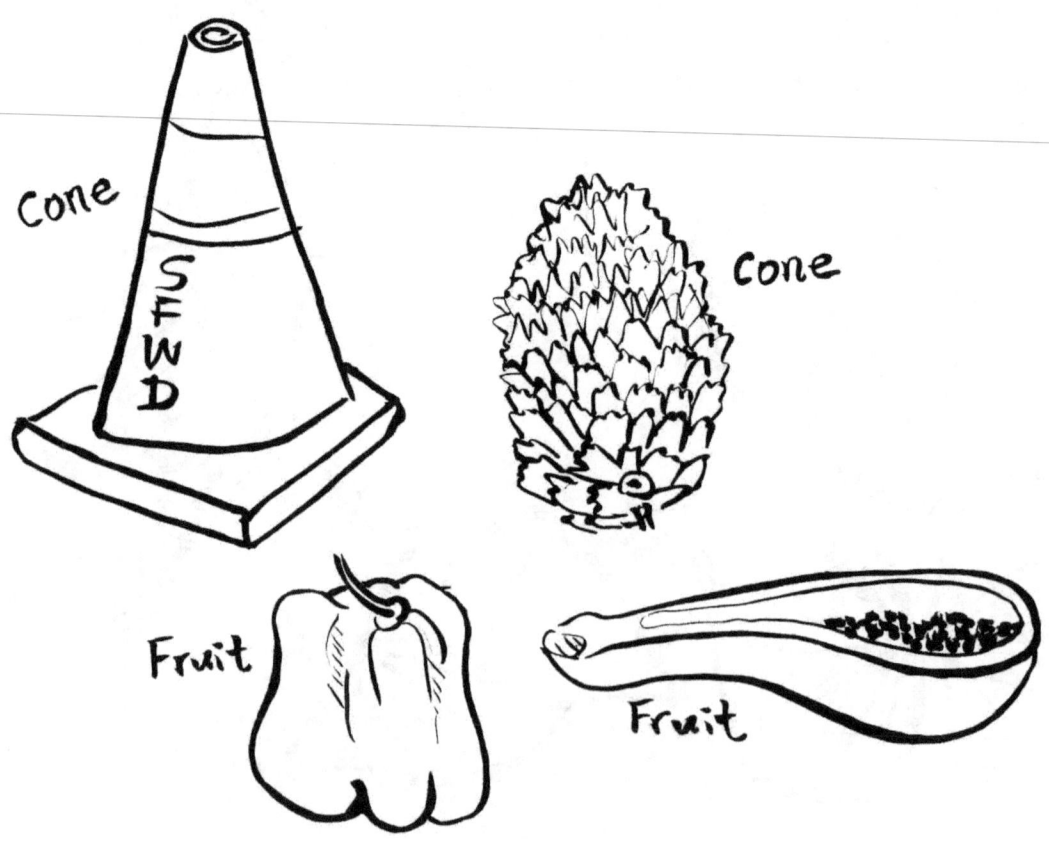

GYMNOSPERM CONES

Pollen drifts on the wind
Candles and yellow clouds

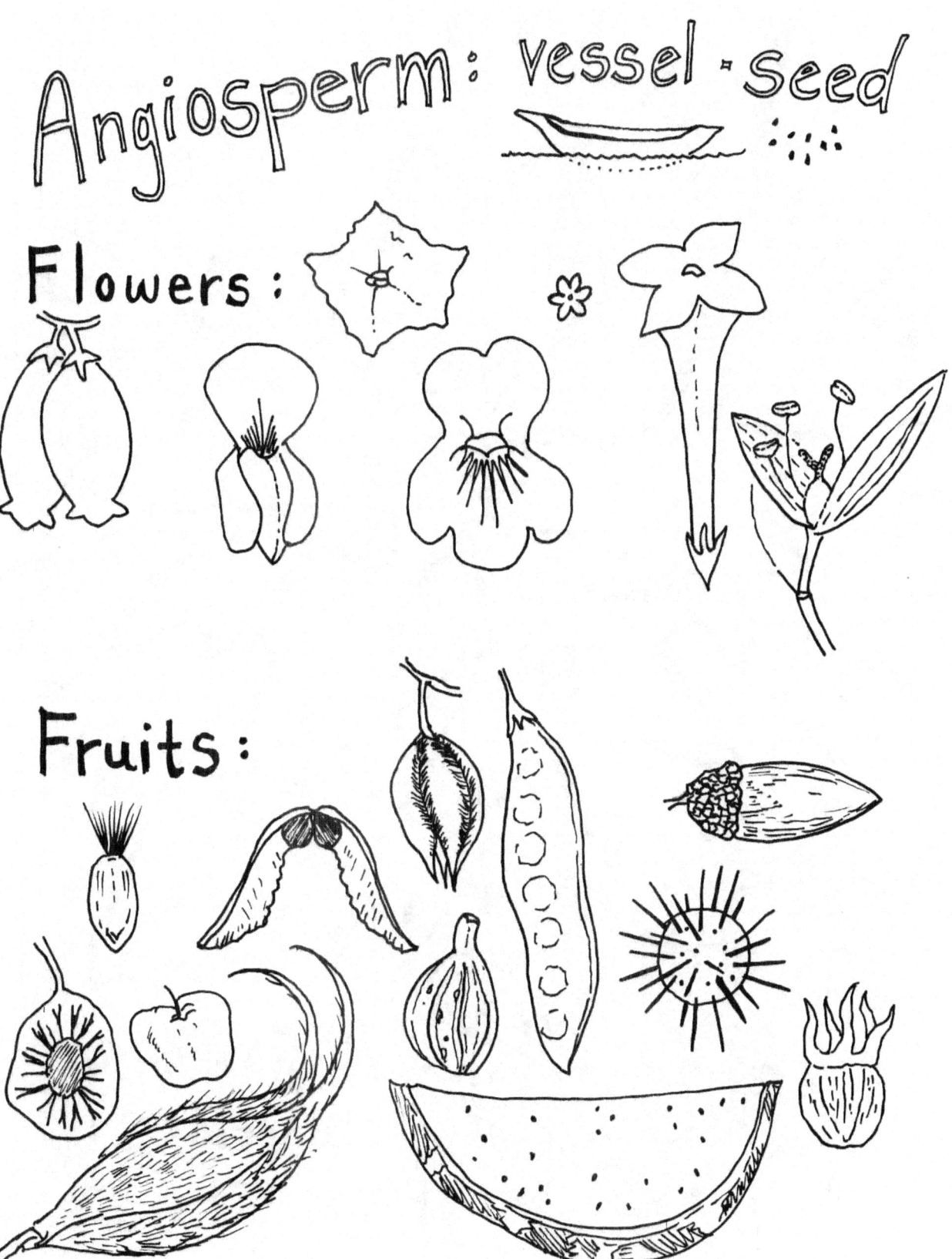

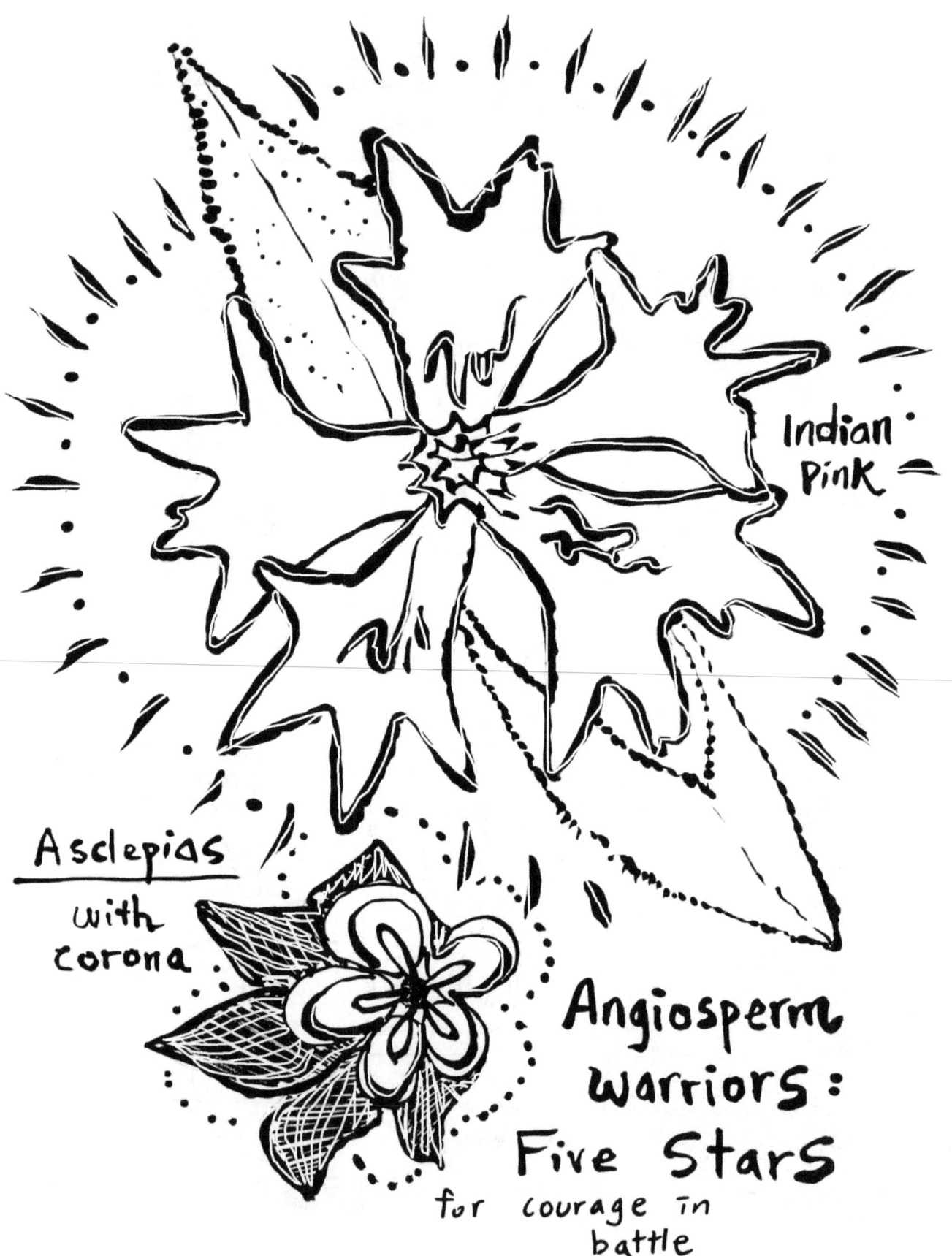

Yew tree is a gymnosperm with a fleshy berry like cone

Taxus
Yew tree

Banksia is an angiosperm with a cone like fruit — woody and hard

---

Not all boundaries are clear cut

Botany versus Horticulture

Botanists are plant scientists who travel the world counting the number of plant parts and looking at the shape and arrangement of flowers, fruits, and leaves. They lump similar plants into families, and trace their lineages back through time. They want to know who is related to whom, when they split off and so on. How can there be so many different kinds of plants!?

Horticulturists care for plants in the garden and fields. They may recognize plants based on its edibility or its shape. On when it flowers, or its colors in the winter. A fancy gardener is called a horticulturist.

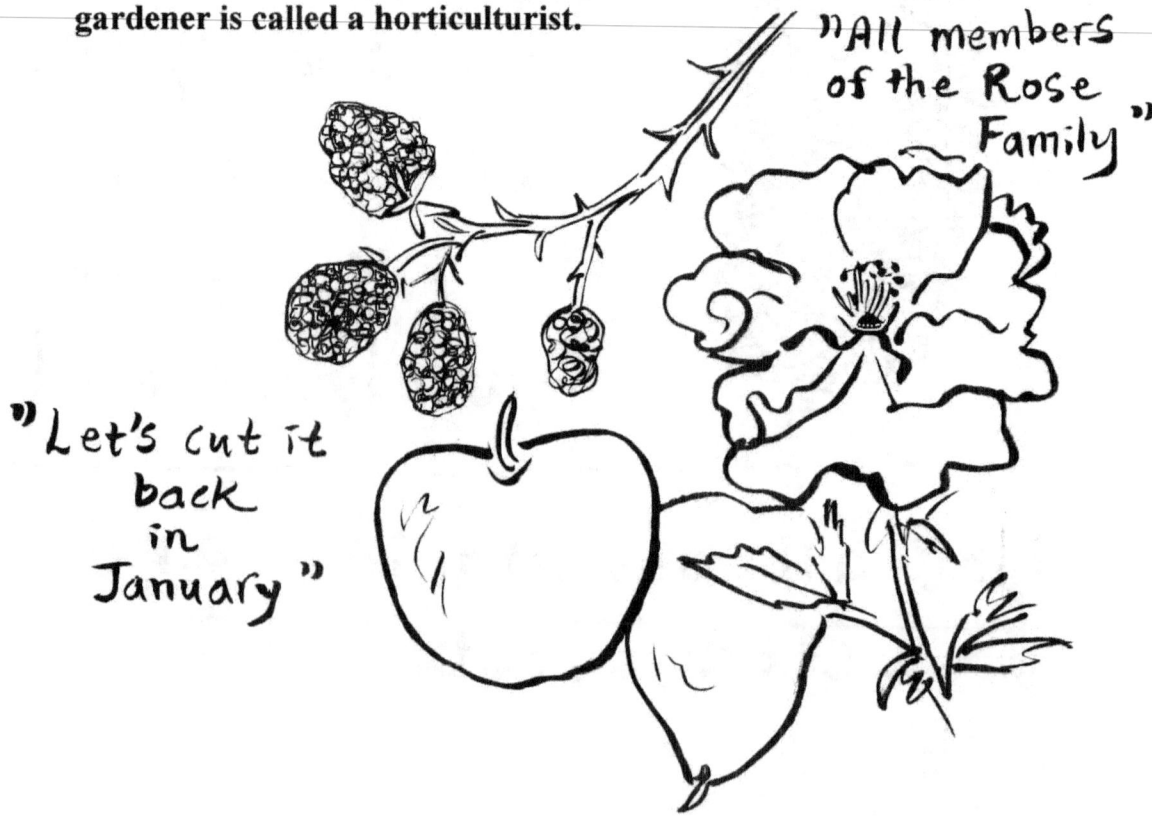
"Let's cut it back in January"
"All members of the Rose Family"

Heather family flowers dangle
Bells chime
Manzanita and Arbutus
<u>Agapetes!</u>

Mint family stems are sometimes square

Mint family flowers often have two big lips.

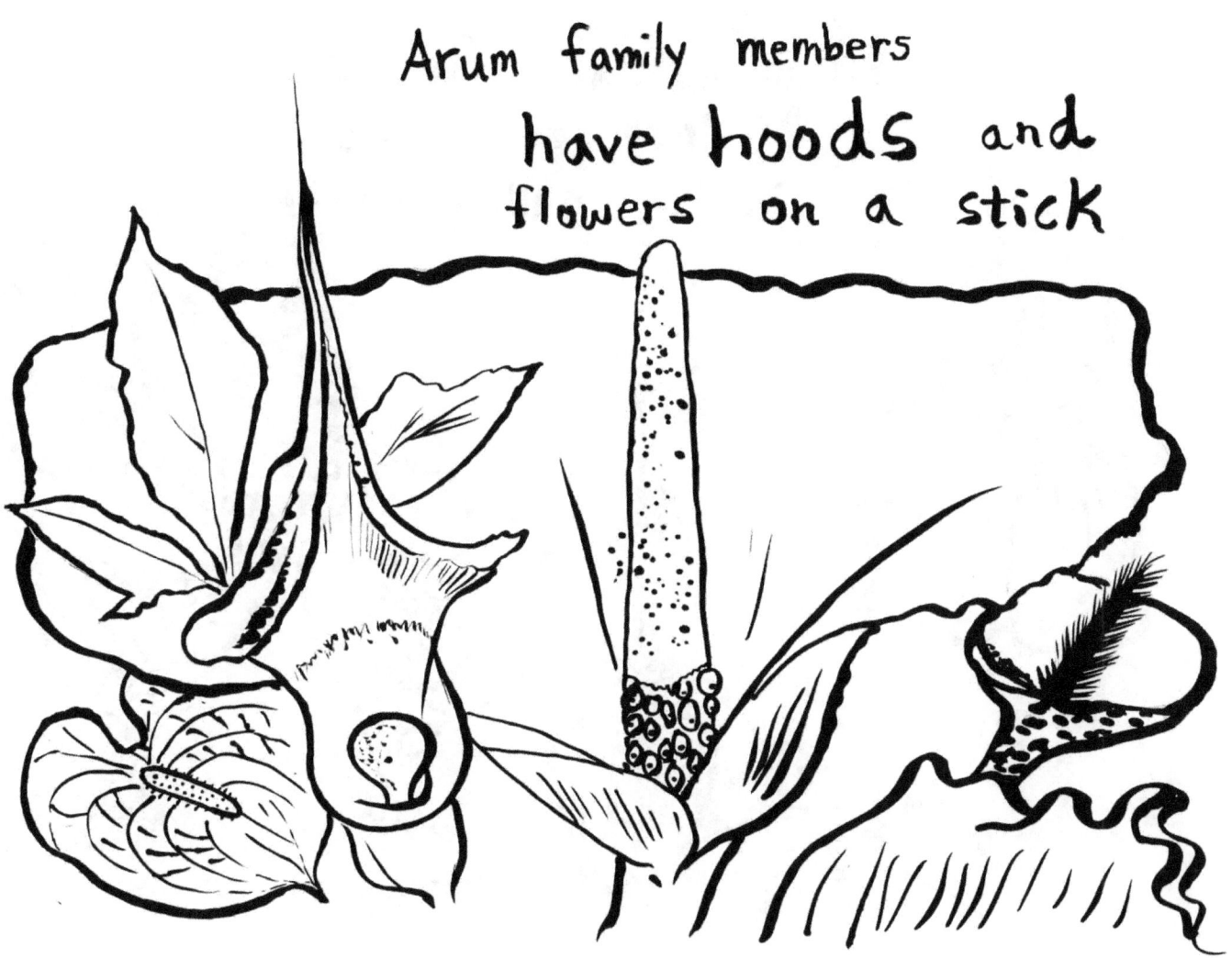

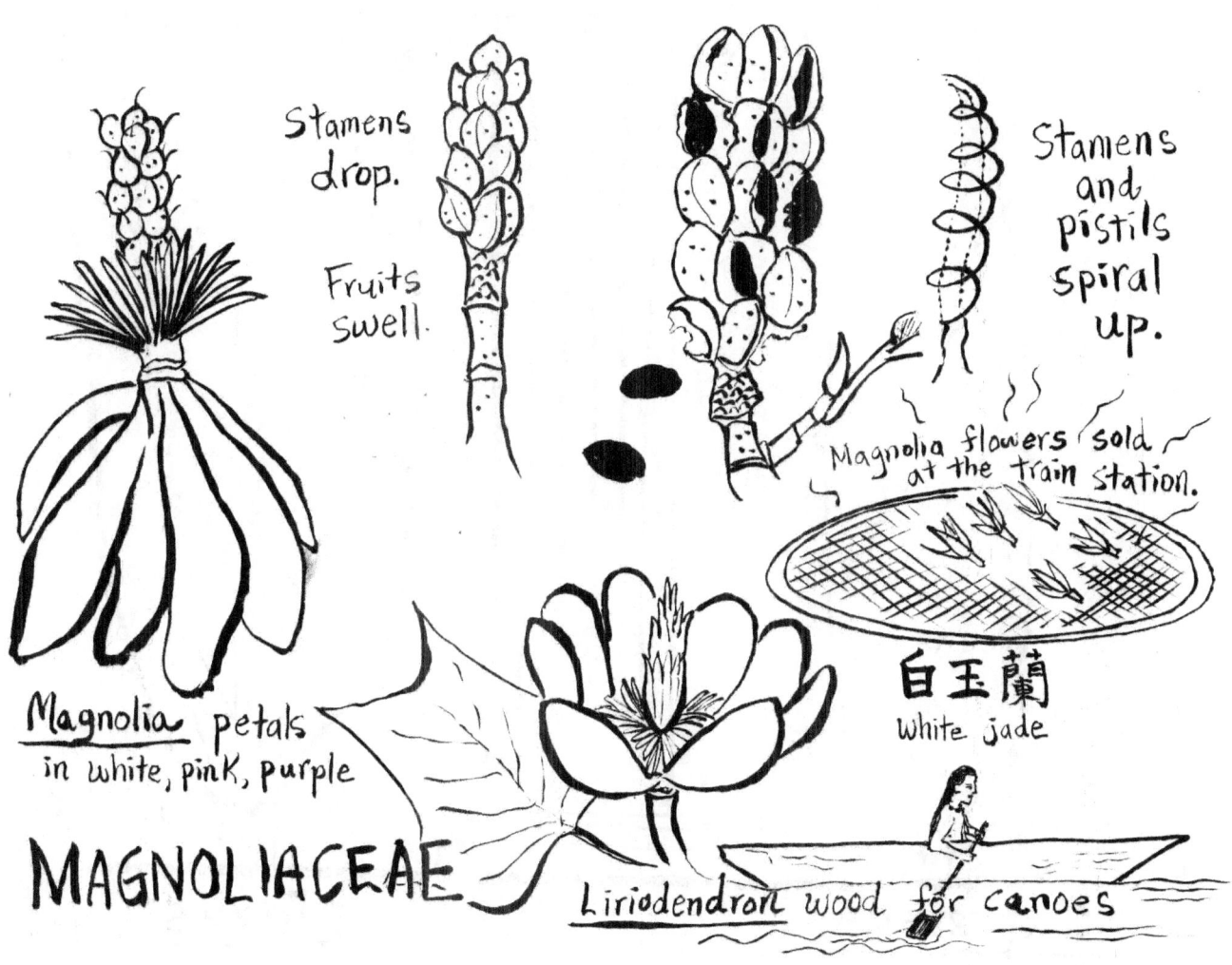

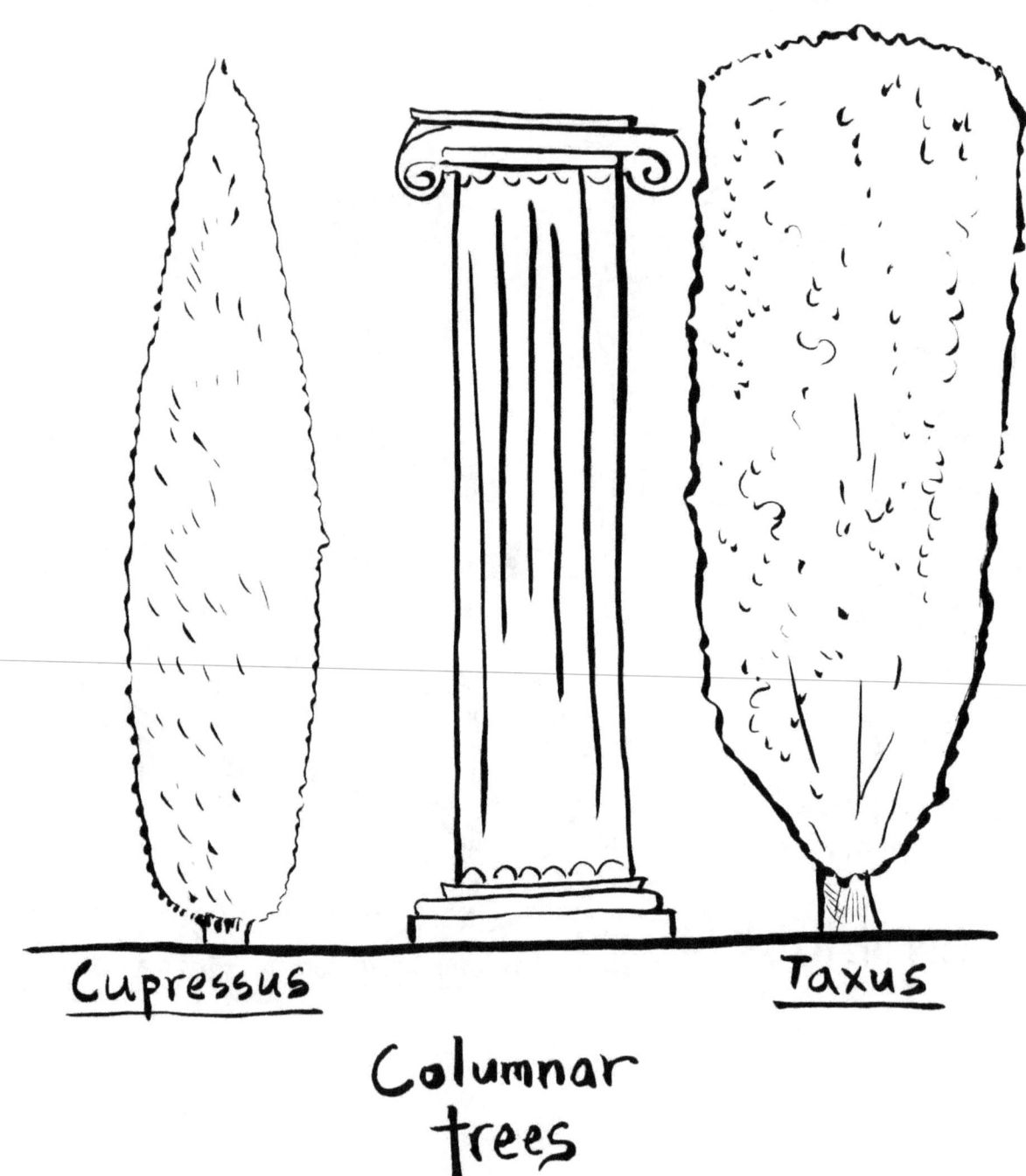

Columnar trees STAND STRAIGHT AND TALL

Woody plants:

Break and snap

Hard to gouge

Herbaceous plants:

Bend

Soft and squishy

Got water in my stem

Got water in my leaves

Succulence

Poky or not, it don't matter

Two groups of flowering plants

The flowering plants (Angiosperms) are further divided into Monocots and Dicots. Pay attention to the flowers you see. Start counting petals and feeling for veins. Nature is full of subtle variation and strange exceptions.

Monocot leaf veins
mostly parallel

Dicot leaf veins
mostly net-like

Monocot seedlings
one seed leaf

Dicot seedlings
Two seed leaves

Monocot flowers
Parts usually in 3's or 6's

Dicot flowers
Parts usually in 4's and 5's

Count 'em!
Dicot flowers in series of fours and fives

Milkmaids 1, 2, 3, 4

Buttercups 1, 2, 3, 4, 5

Vascular systems

In the Phoenix palm (a monocot), mineral drinks and sweet saps move up and down the plant in little straw like tubes across and throughout the entire stem. To grow fatter, the tubes enlarge and swell up. The palm does not grow more tubes.

In the dicot tree Magnolia, a ring of pathways in the outer layers of the trunk guide the movement of materials. As the tree grows, the tubes that once transported water retire. The tubes become heartwood; this wood helps to hold the tree up. The new water tubes grow, and so does the diameter of the trunk.

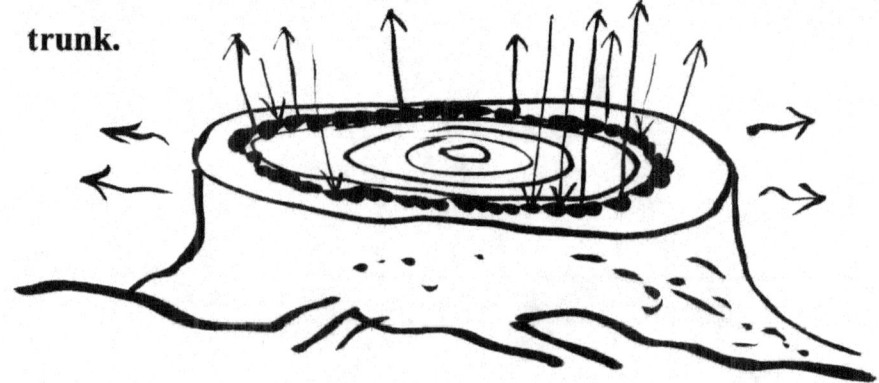

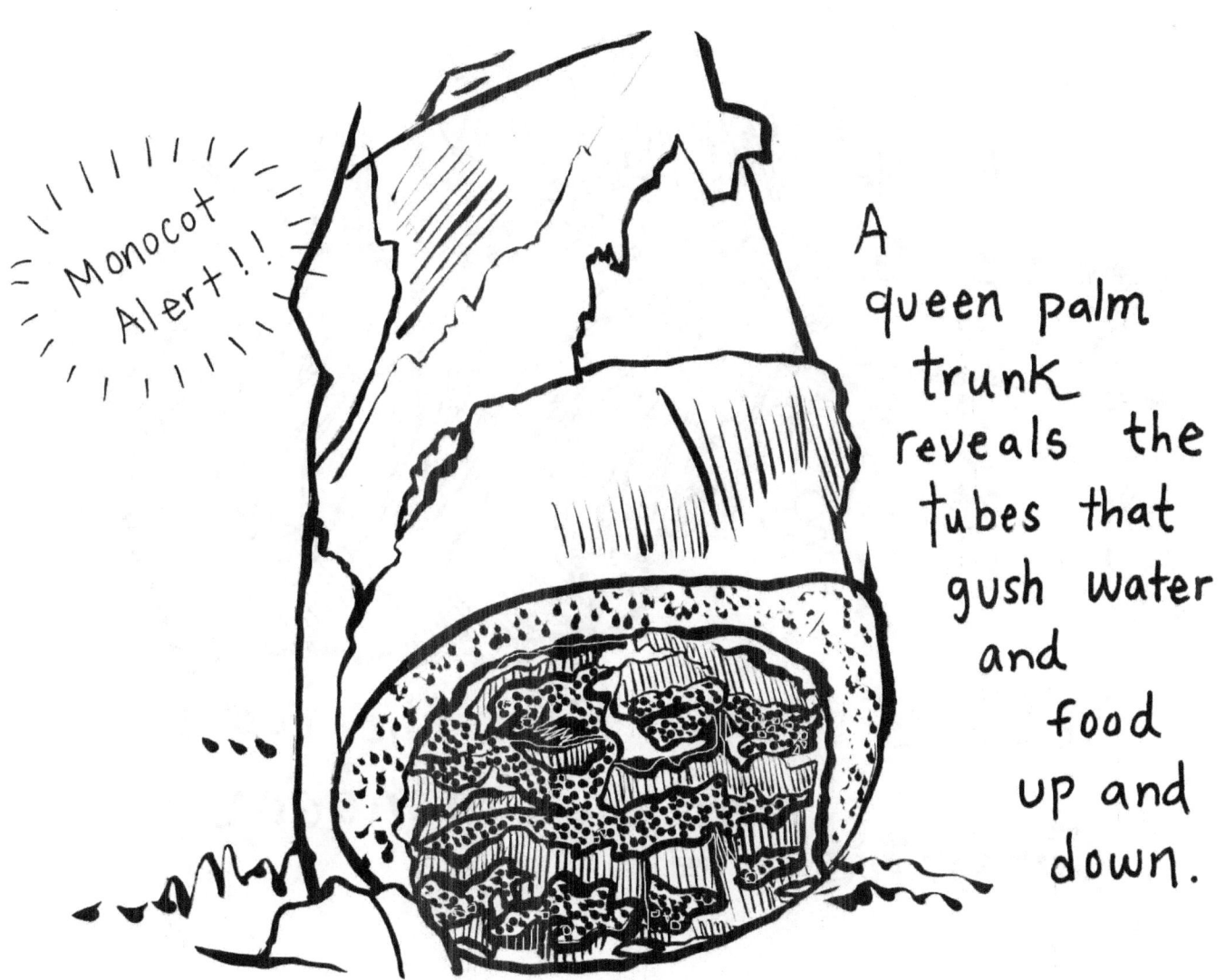

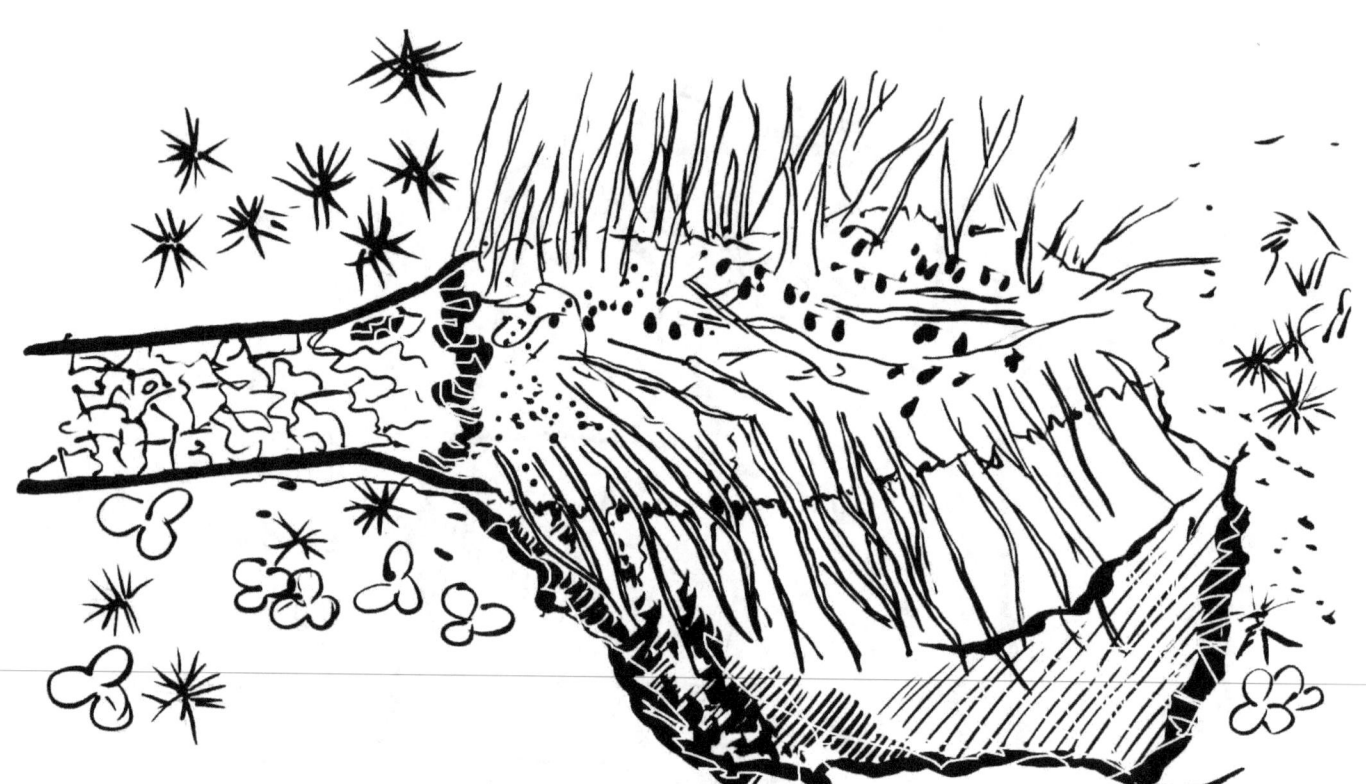

Yes! It looks like the roots of a monocot! *Cordyline* tree.

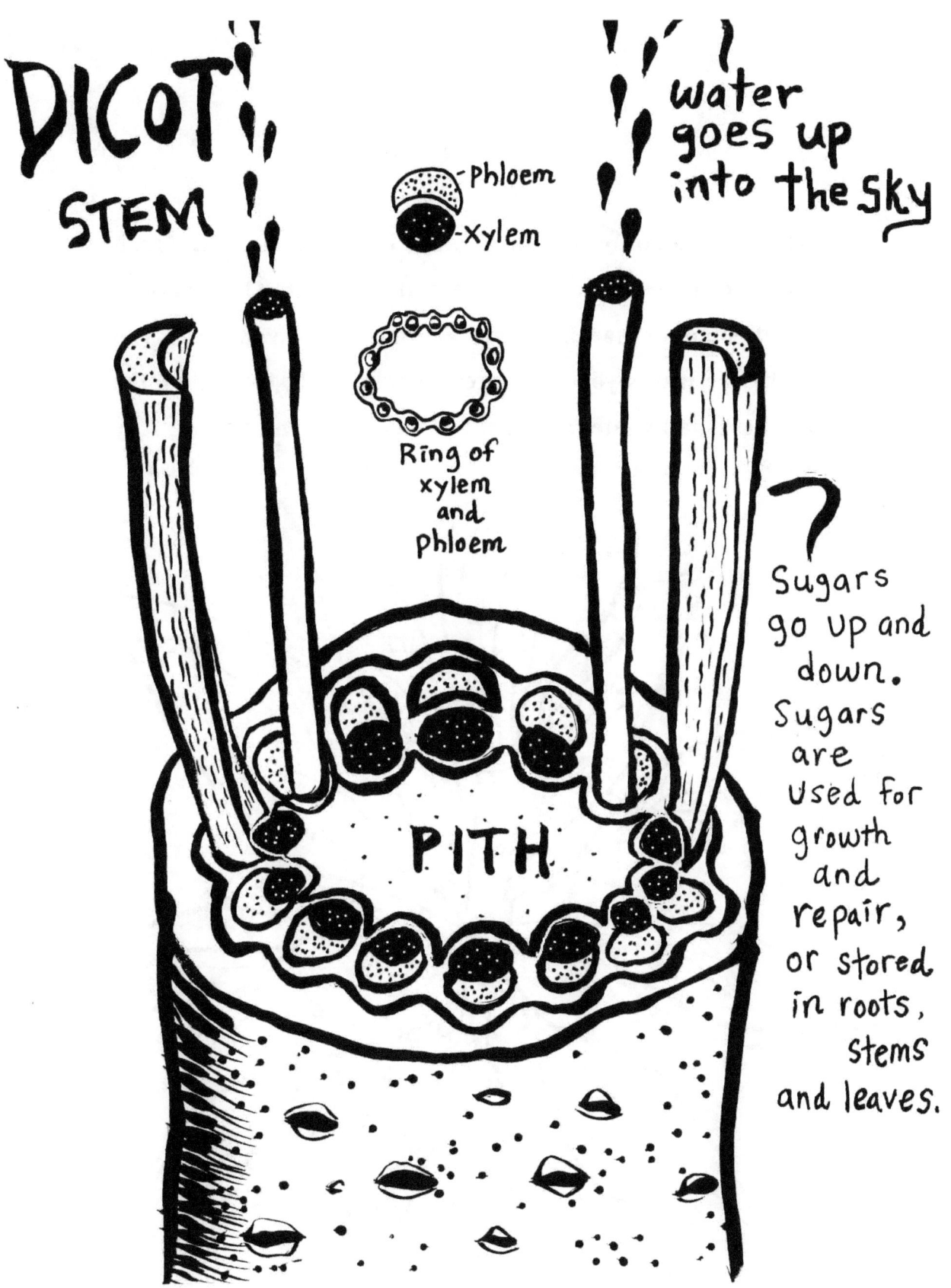

Leafy diversity

A leaf grows off of the stem or the branch at a node. Or, it grows out of the ground at the base of the plant. Observations of leaf shapes, margins, and arrangements will help you identify the plants you encounter. Look, smell, feel. Does the plant have milky latex? Are the leaves shiny and waxy? Any hairs?

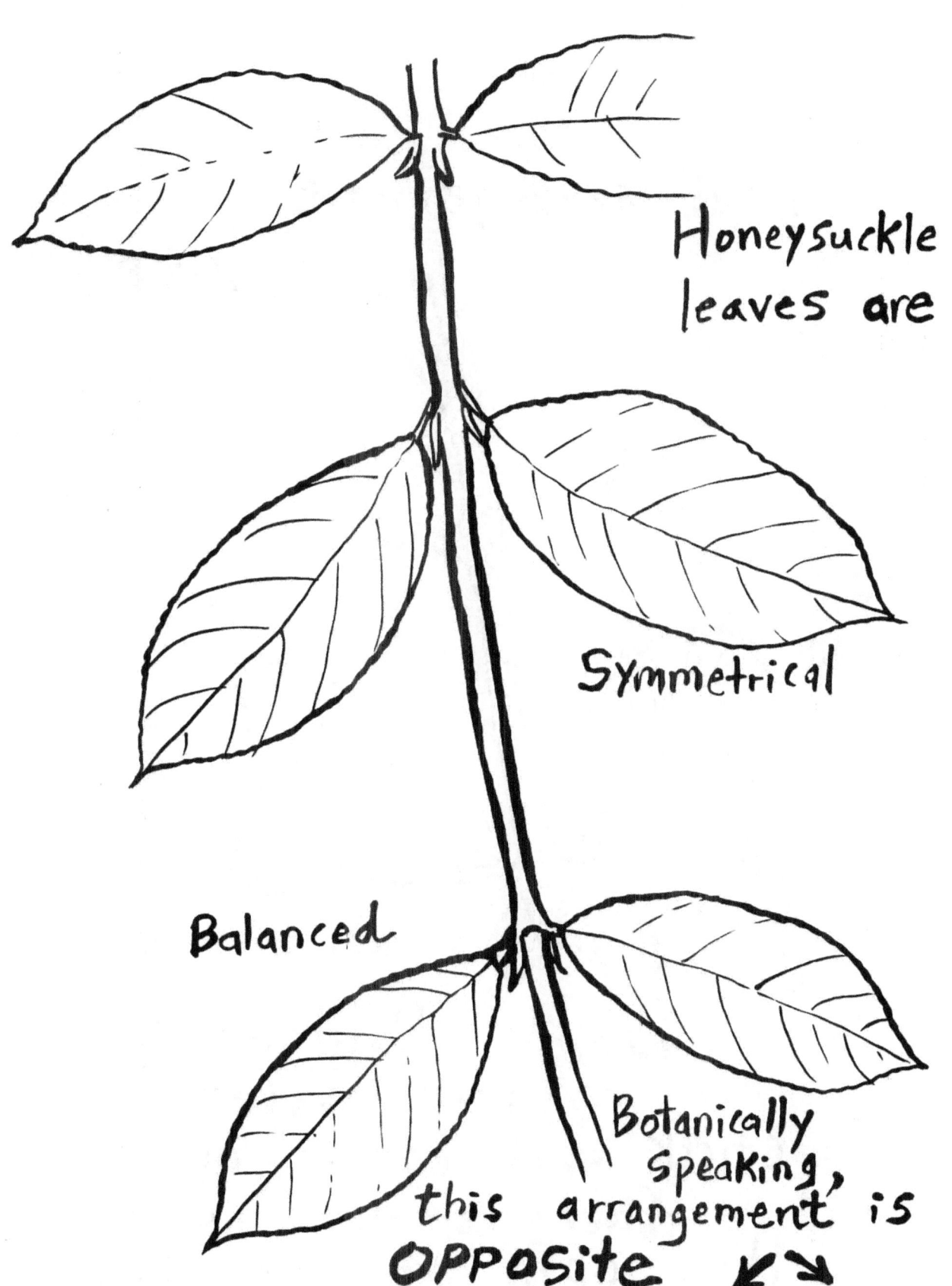

Leaf arrangement is opposite.

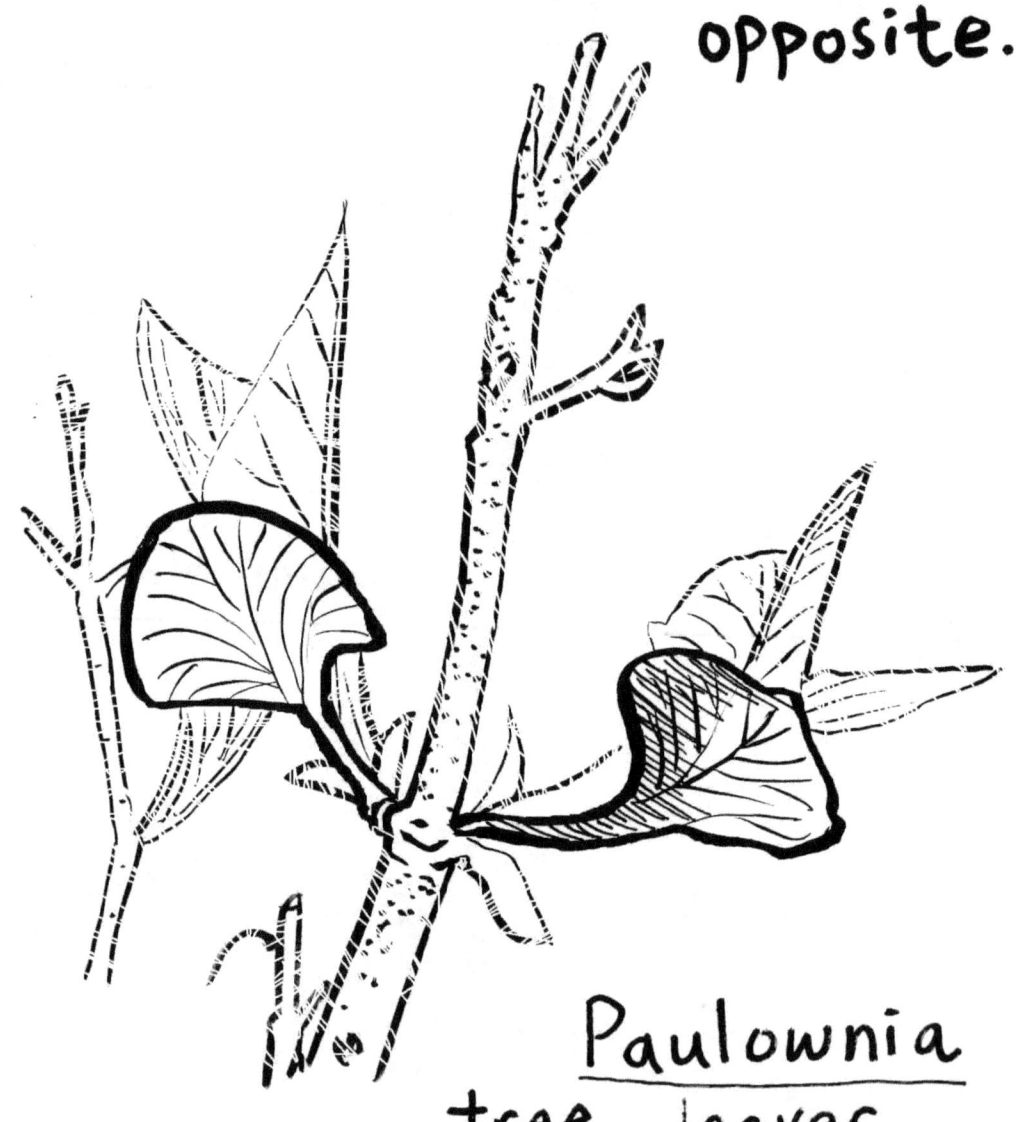

Paulownia tree leaves check each other out face-to-face as they open to the sun.

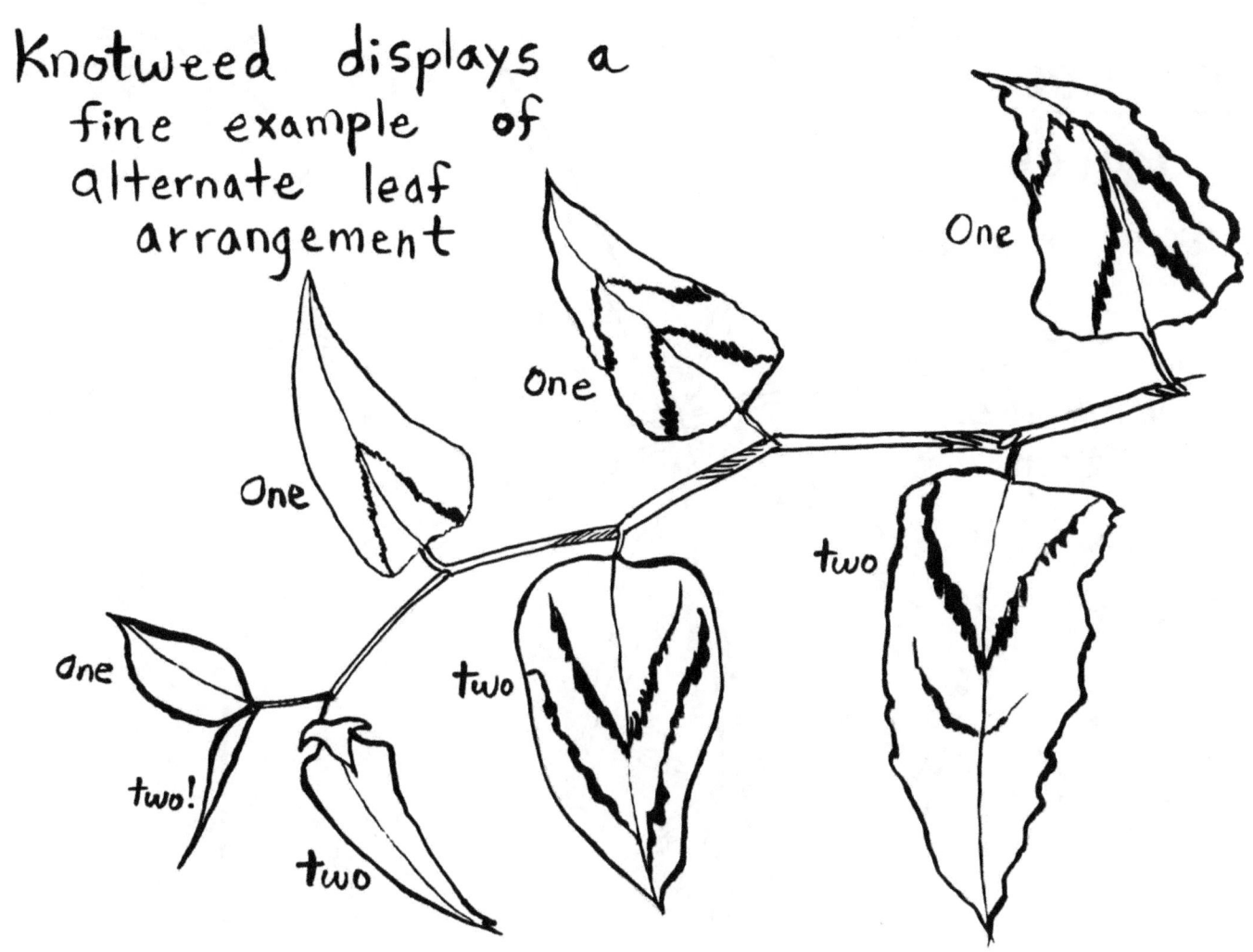

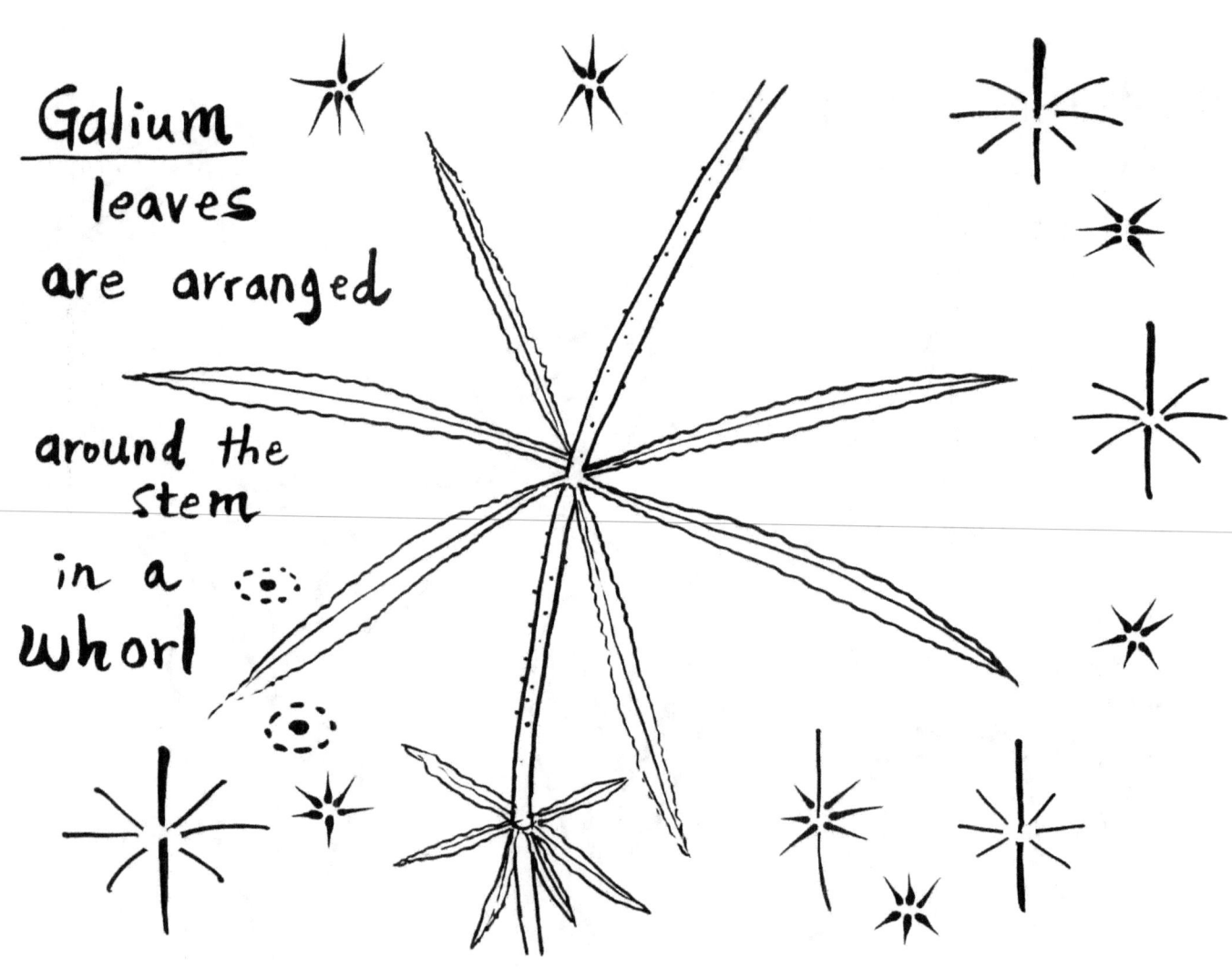

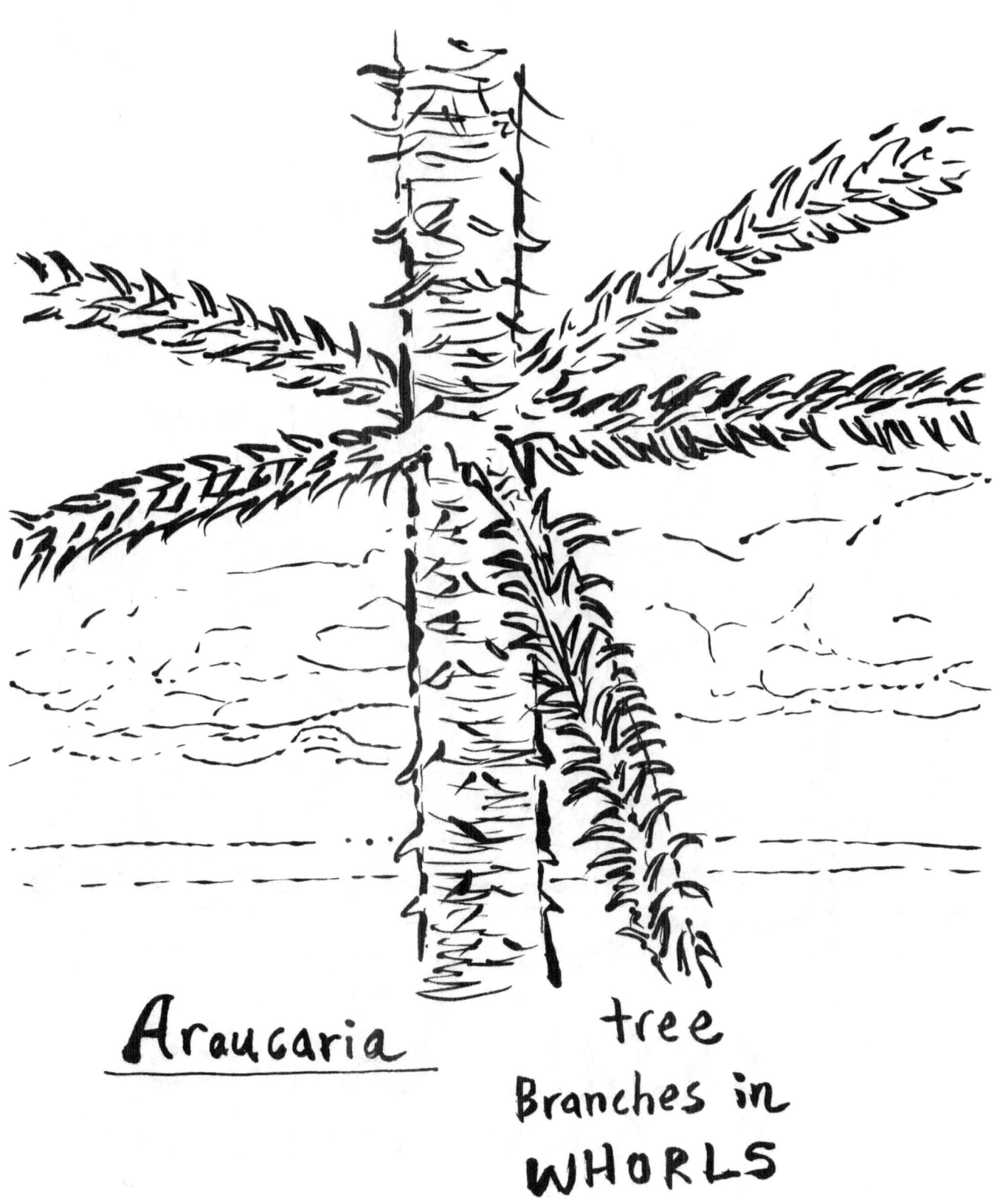

Araucaria tree Branches in WHORLS

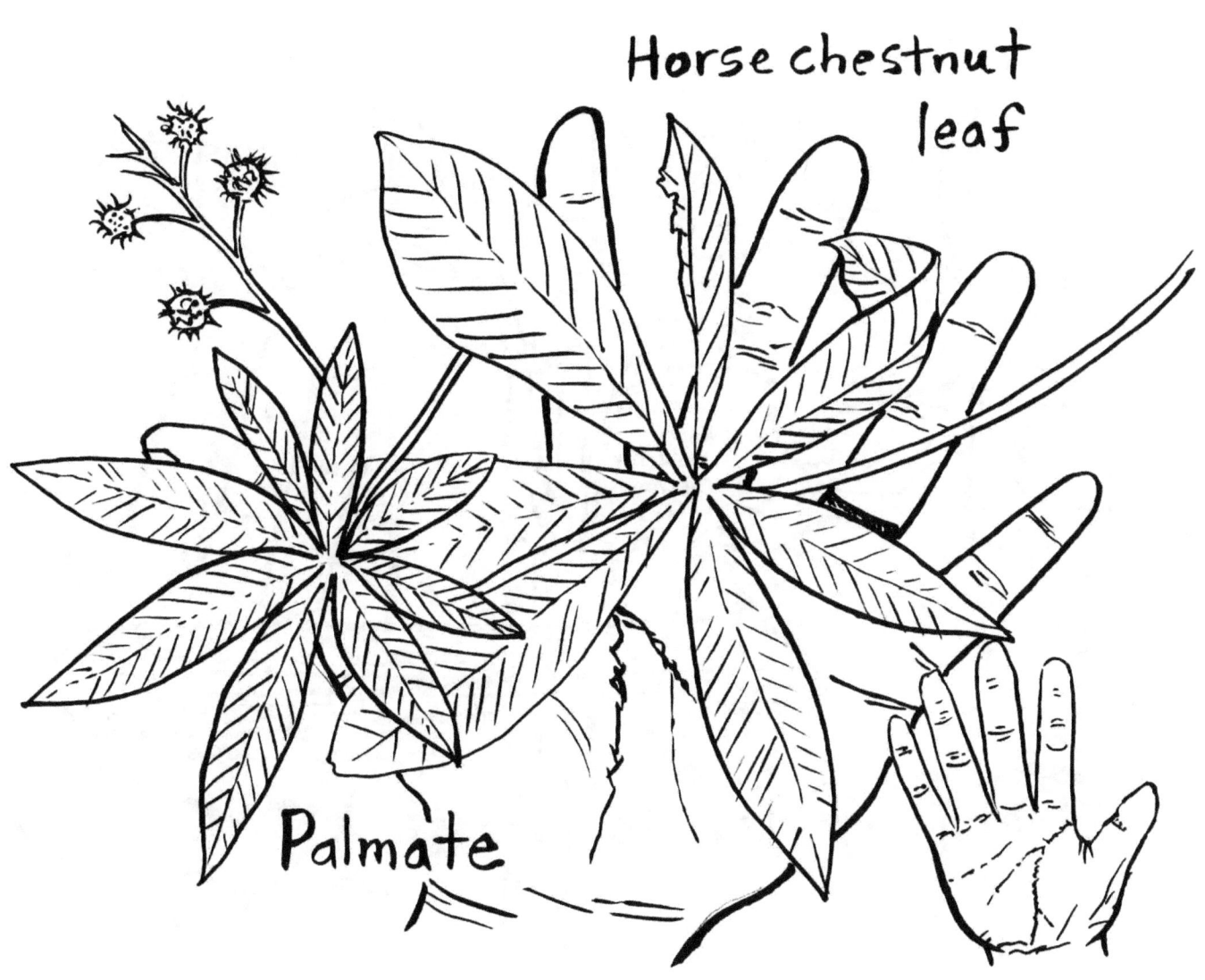

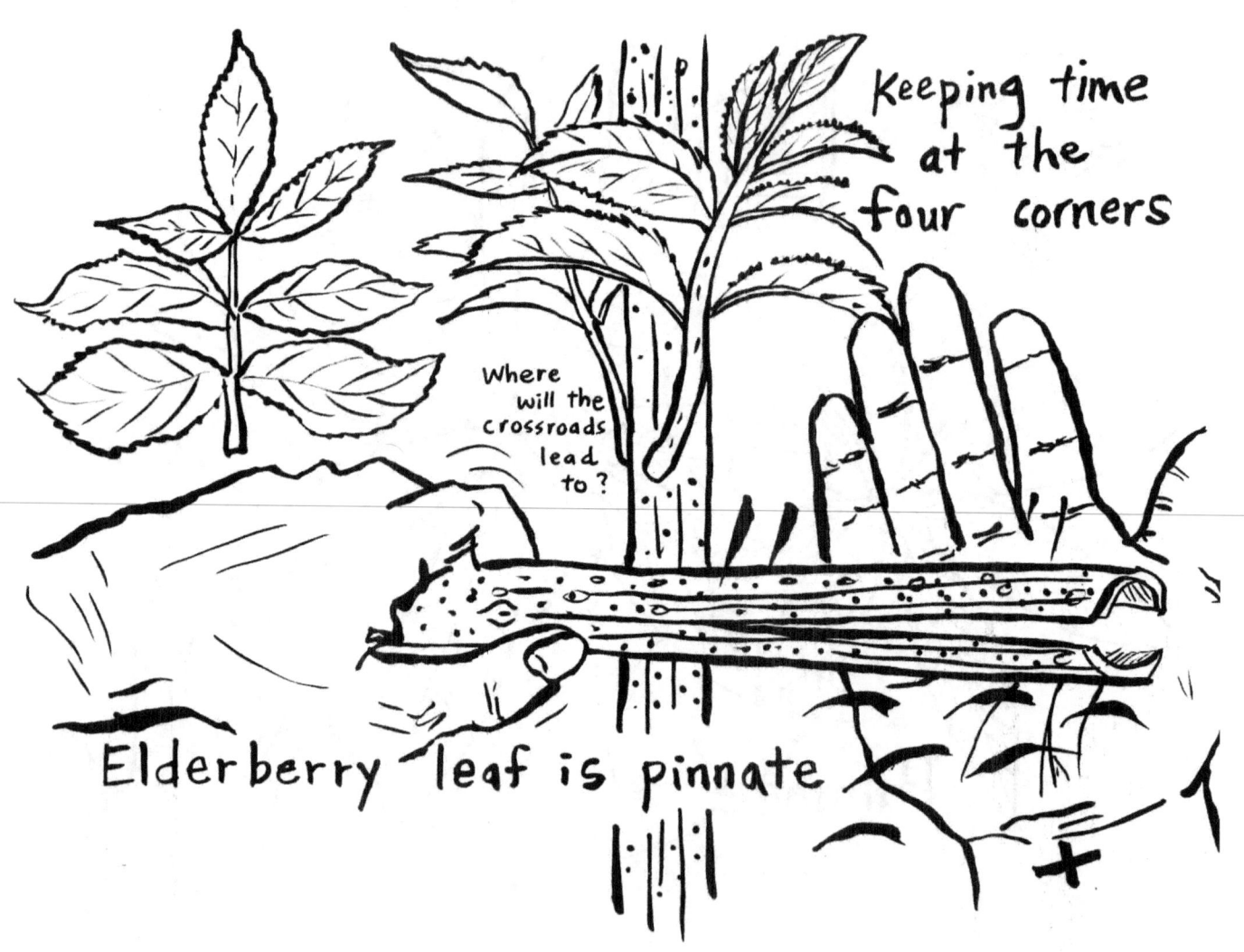

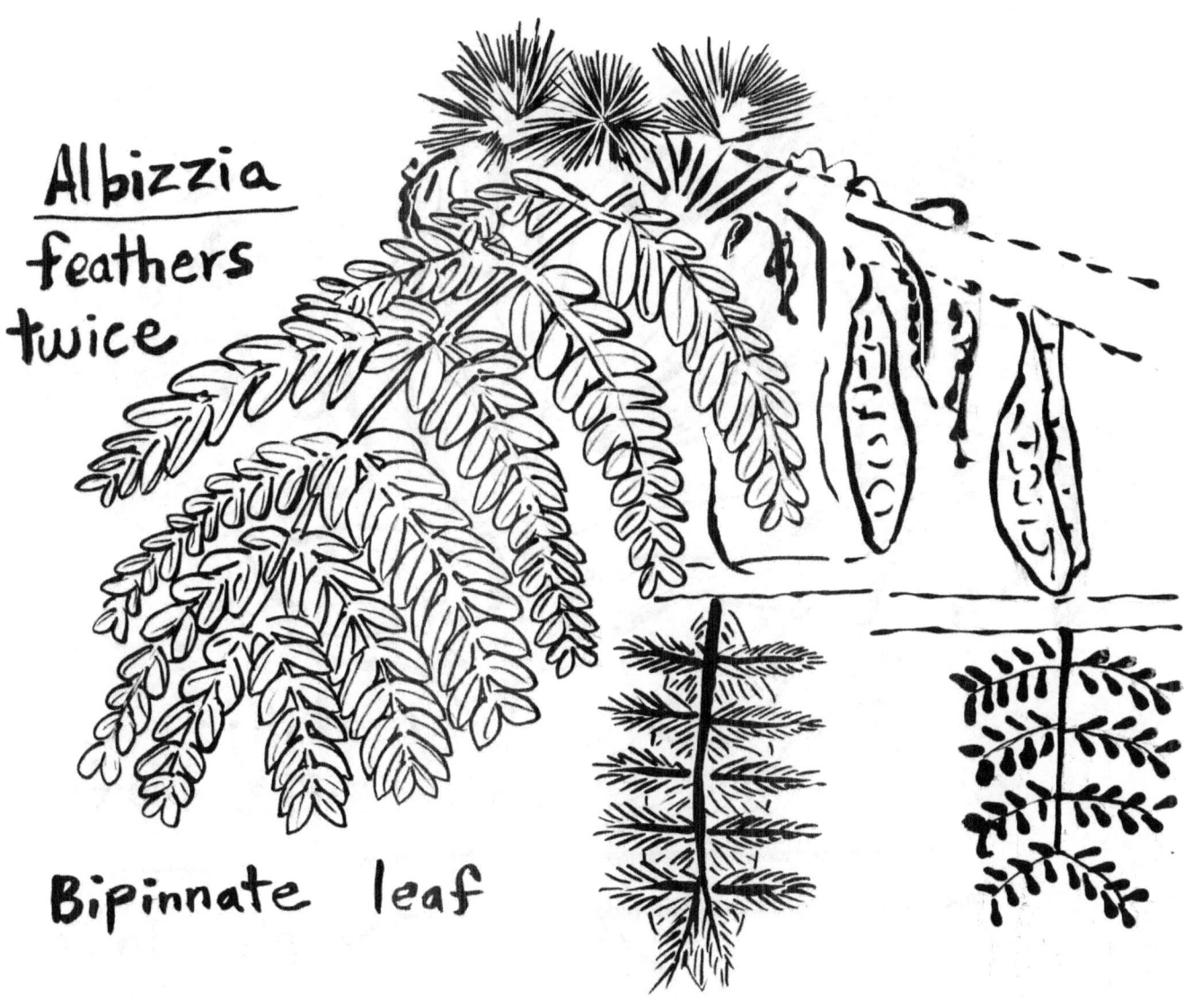

Matilija poppy leaf

Deeply lobed

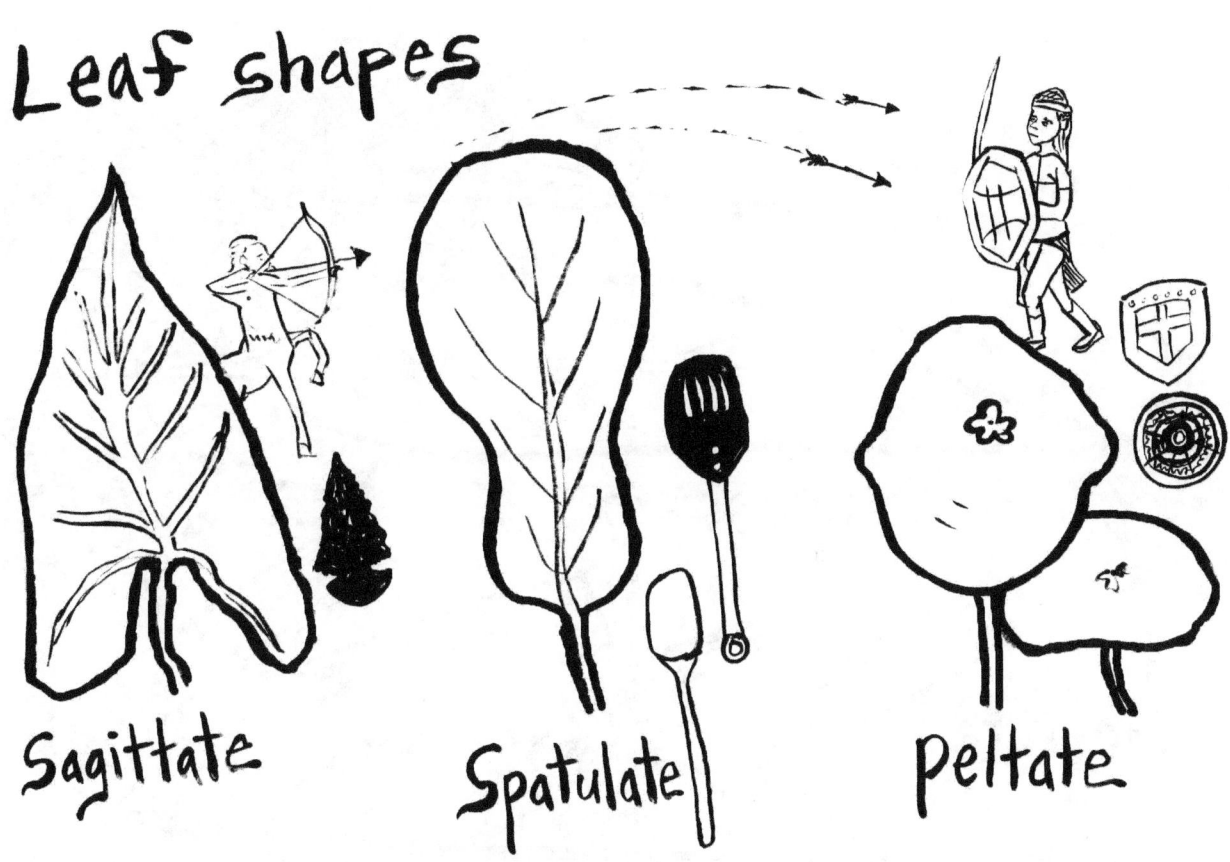

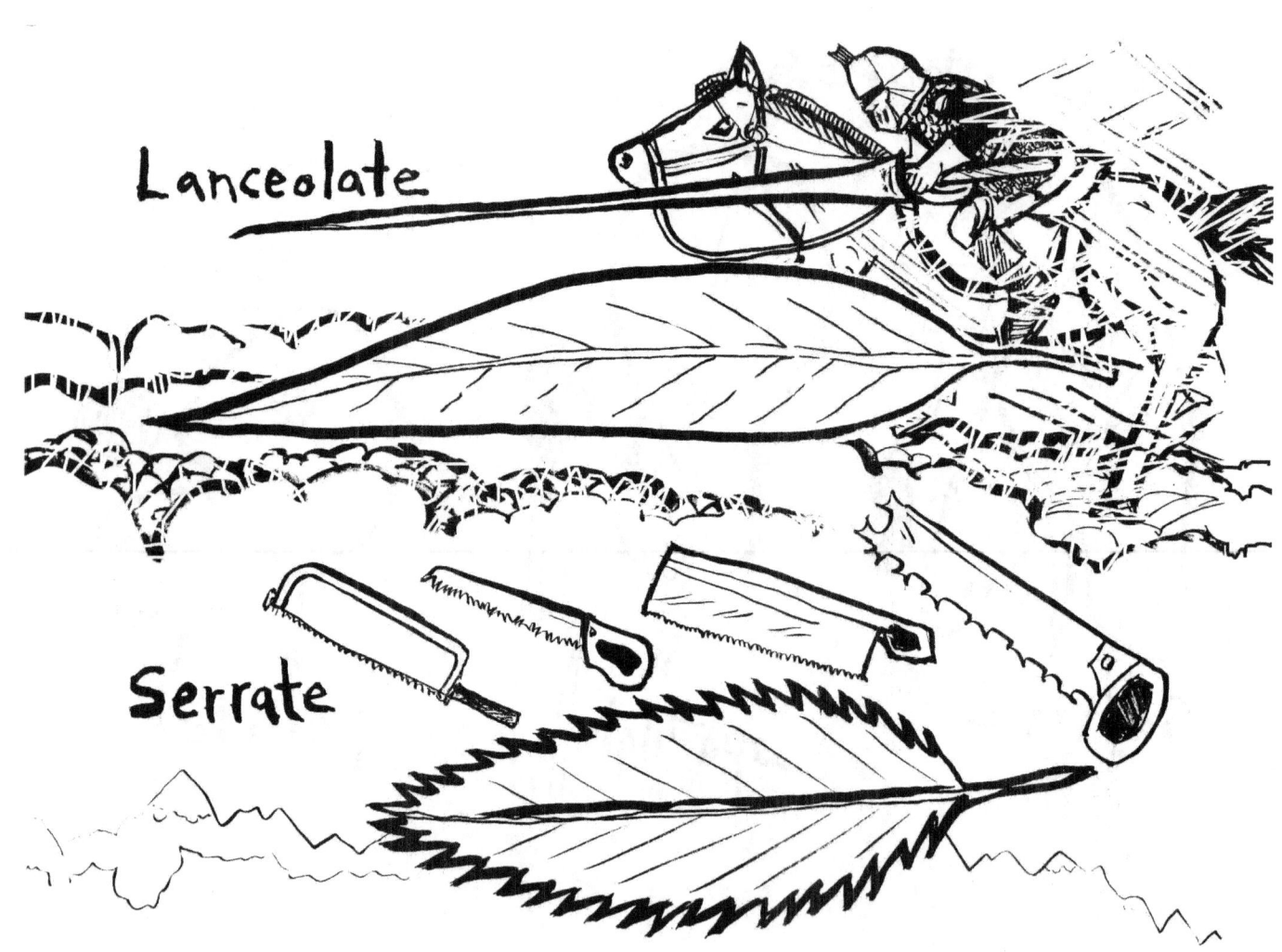

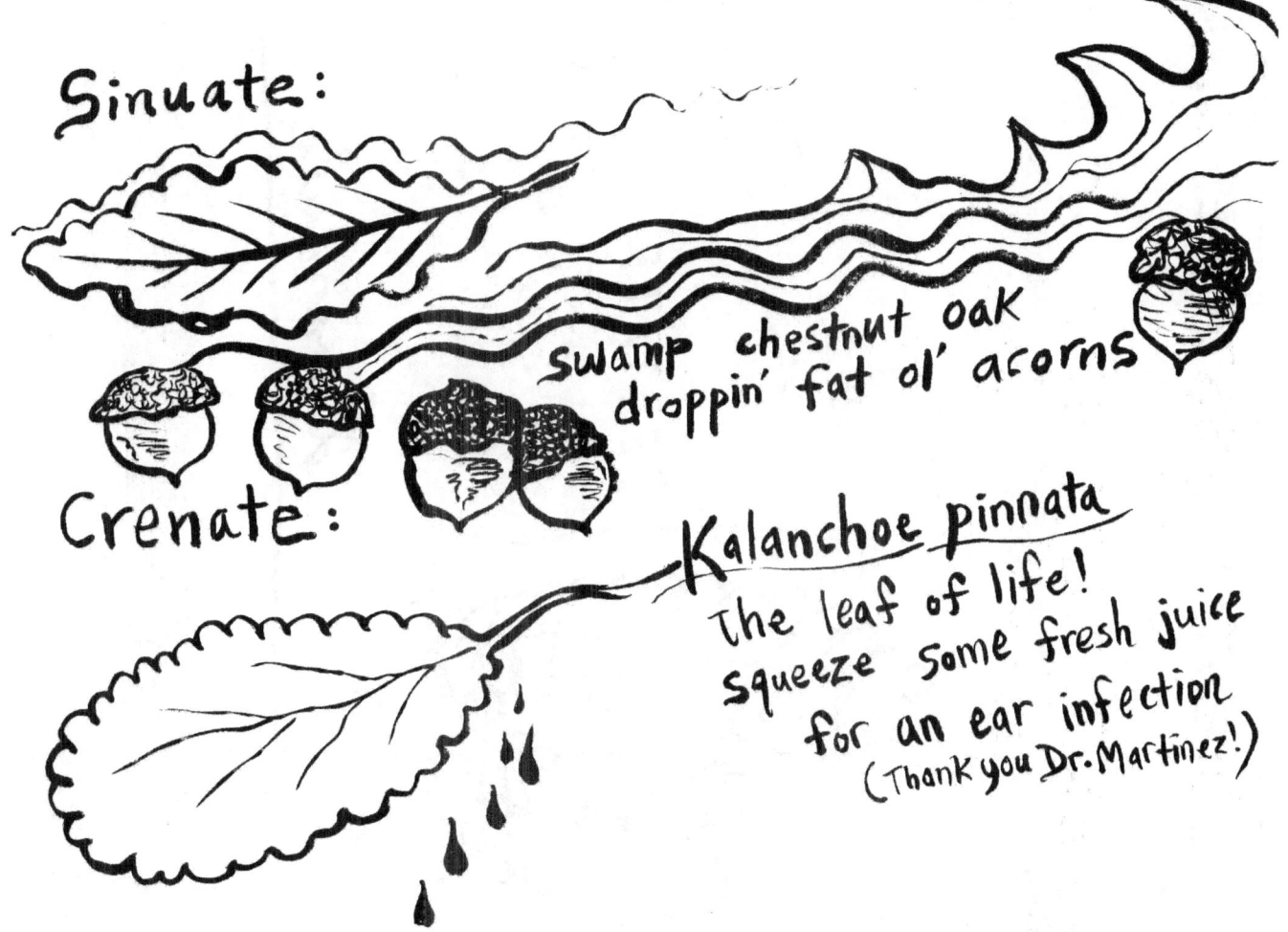

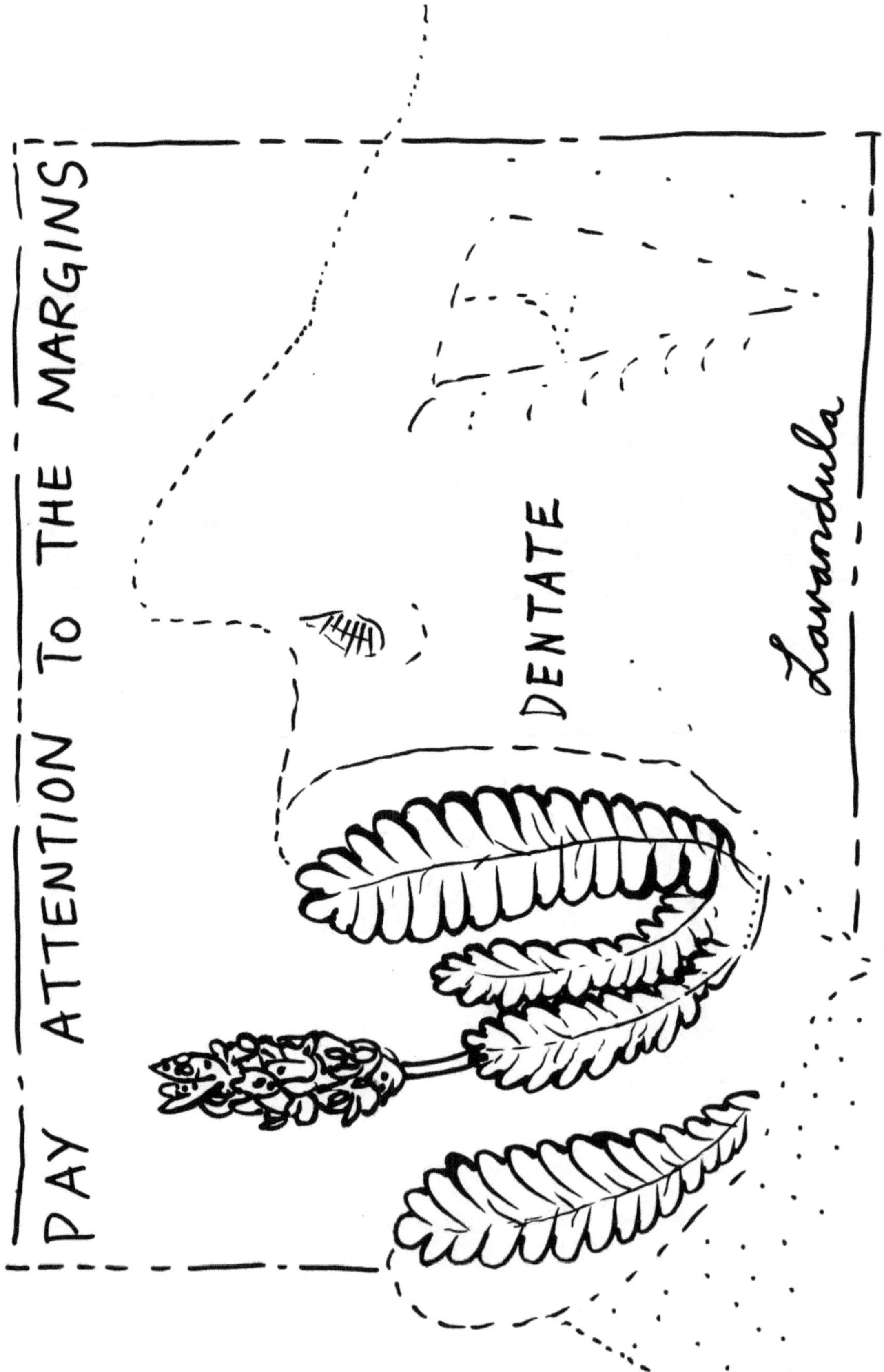

PAY ATTENTION TO THE MARGINS

DENTATE

Lavandula

Folk and butterfly classification

Forest peoples know plants good for snakebite, plants eaten by rodents, or plants to use for fishing in dammed up streams. A palm leaf is used as roof thatching, and cotton as tinder to start a fire. A plant is known for its cross section made by a machete, or by its spiraling growth pattern.

Butterfly mothers search for plants with the right combination of color, smell, and feel. She may fly up and down a ravine, or flitter from lupine patch to lupine patch, finding the perfect plant to lay her eggs on. The survival of her caterpillars depends on the specific plant food choices she makes.

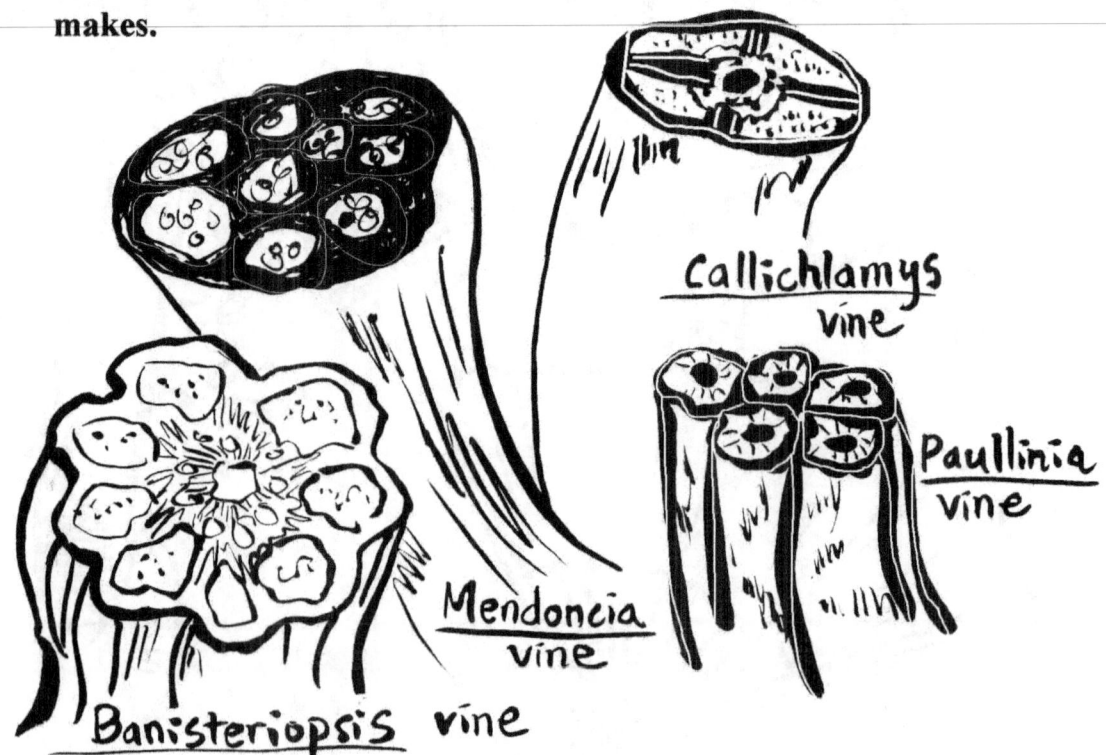

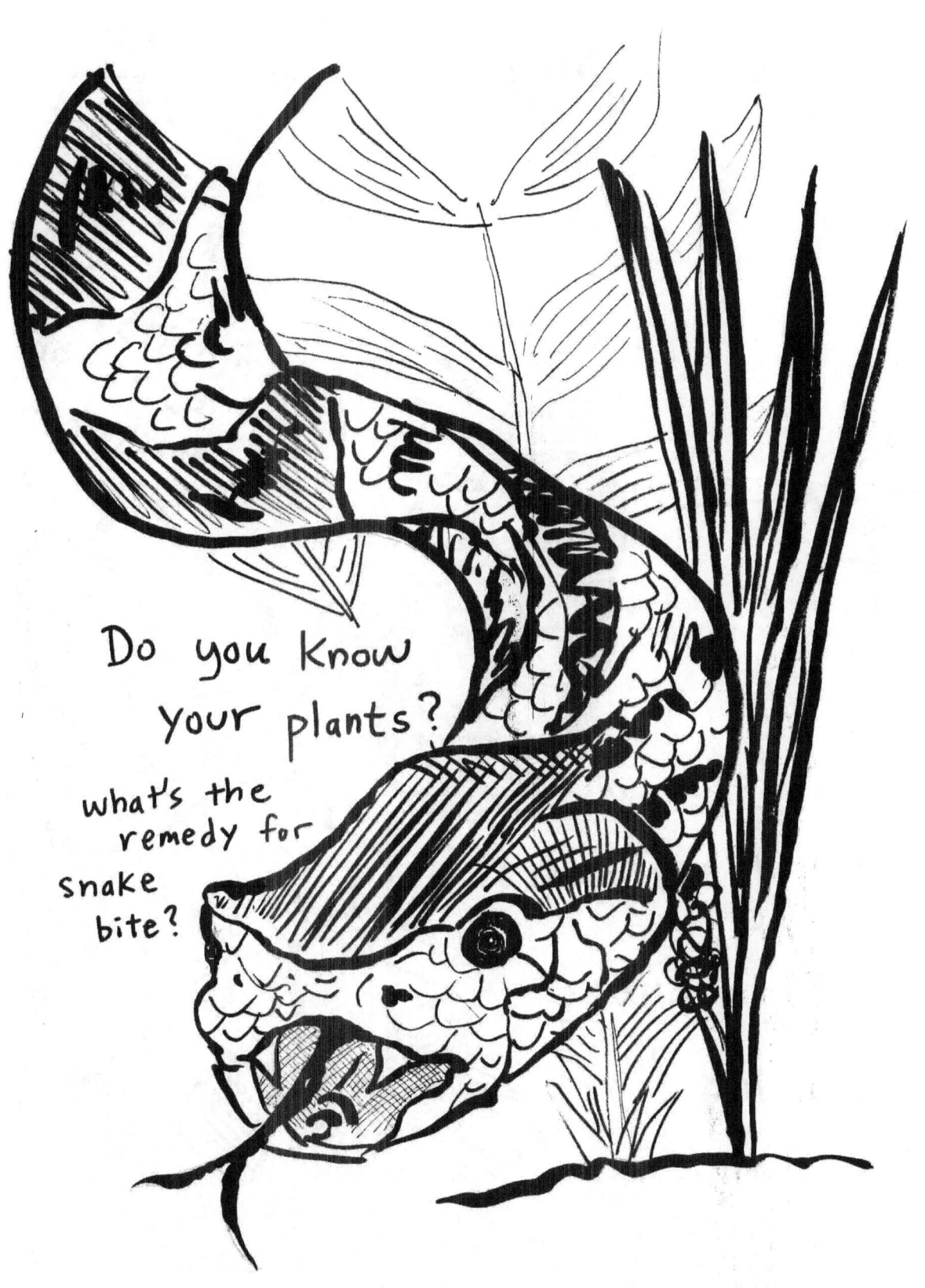

Mission Blue momma looks for lupines
with ant babysitters

Transformation

The world is a charged place, full of buzzing tension and humming with energy. This watery earth is a magnet with a fat metal core; rotating on an axis of charged poles north and south. In storm clouds, positive and negative charges collide and throw down lightning bolts. Electricity zaps out of our bodies and shakes our cells from head to toe.

Plants, like us, are electrical beings living in a dynamic balance with the forces of the universe.

Atoms and molecules

There is a world that we cannot see very well but understand through science experiments and tests. It is the world of atoms – tiny particles of different sizes holding together steady or blasting apart with repulsion. Everything is made up of atoms.

A group of two or more atoms bonded together is a molecule. Molecules zip around real fast when in the GAS form. Boom boom bam bam, bounce up bounce down. As LIQUIDS, molecules cruise the fluid medium and flow in swirling curves. When molecules are SOLIDS, they settle down into a calmer structure and tighter formation. The atomic world is in constant motion and change.

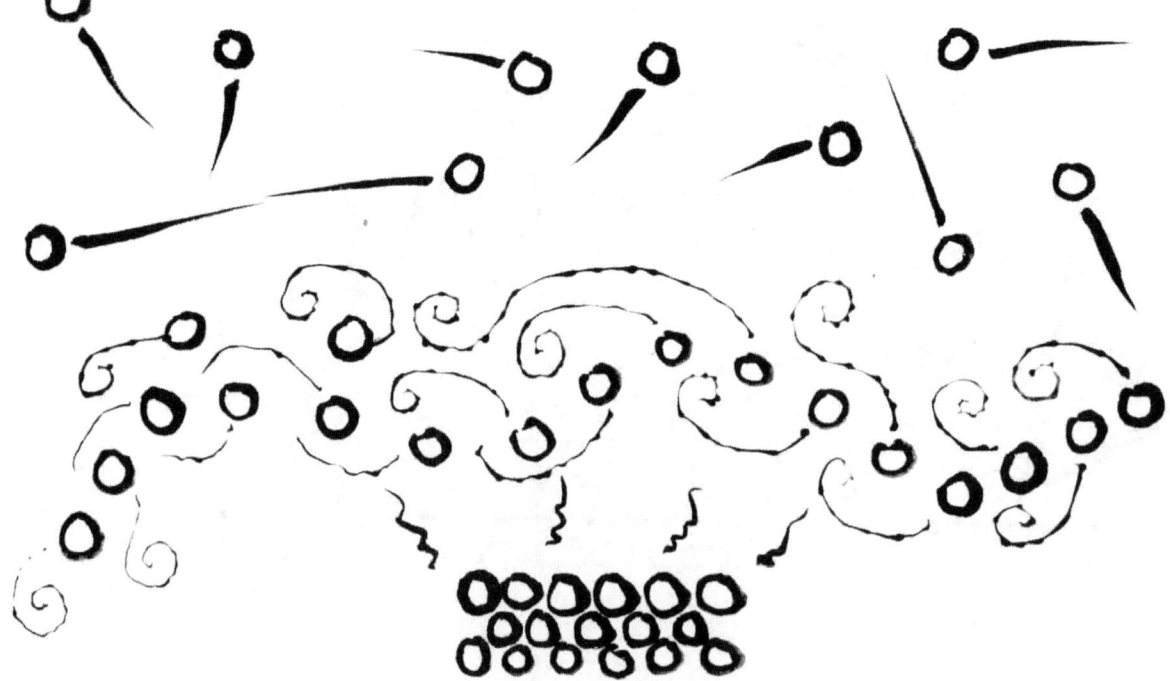

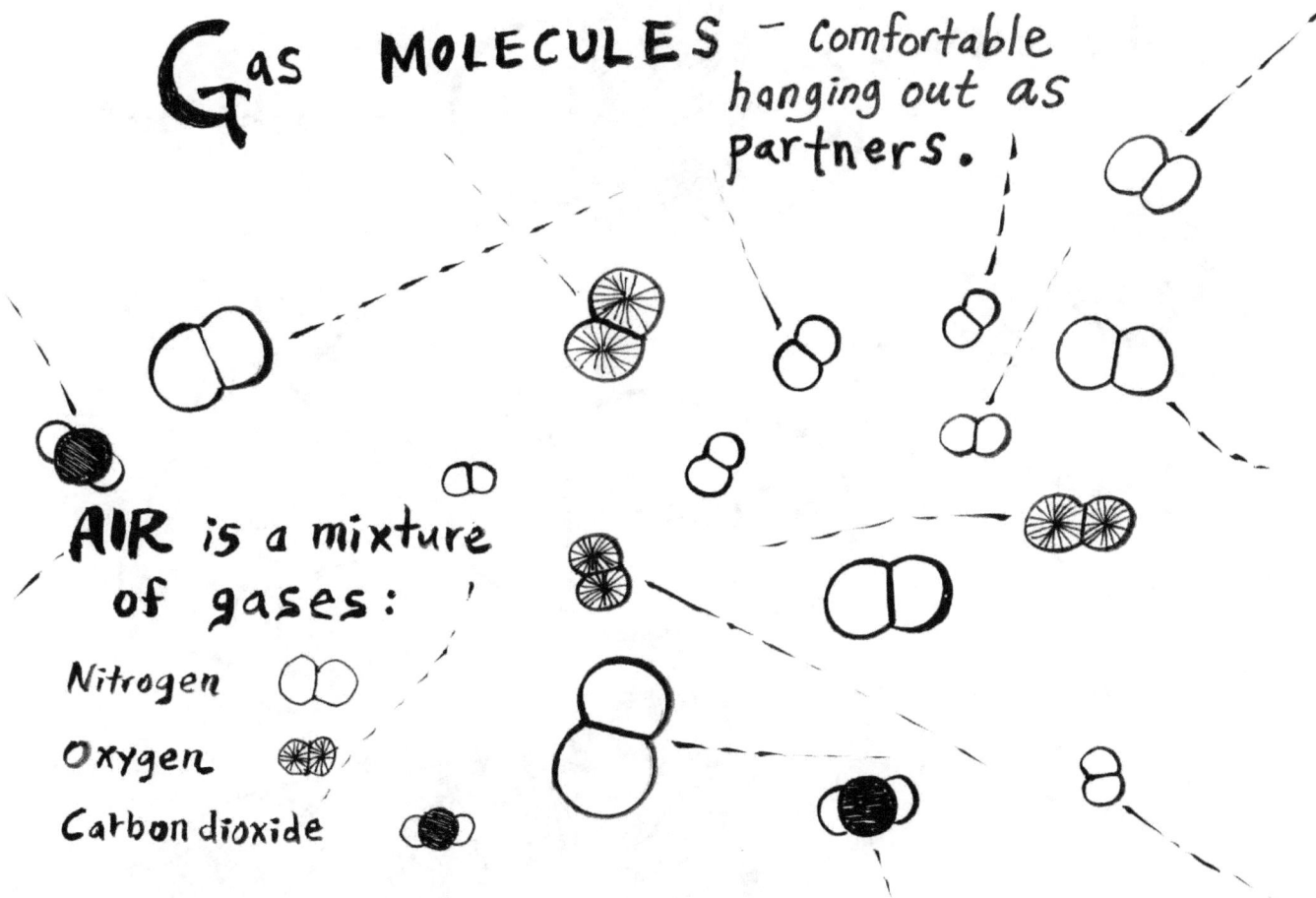

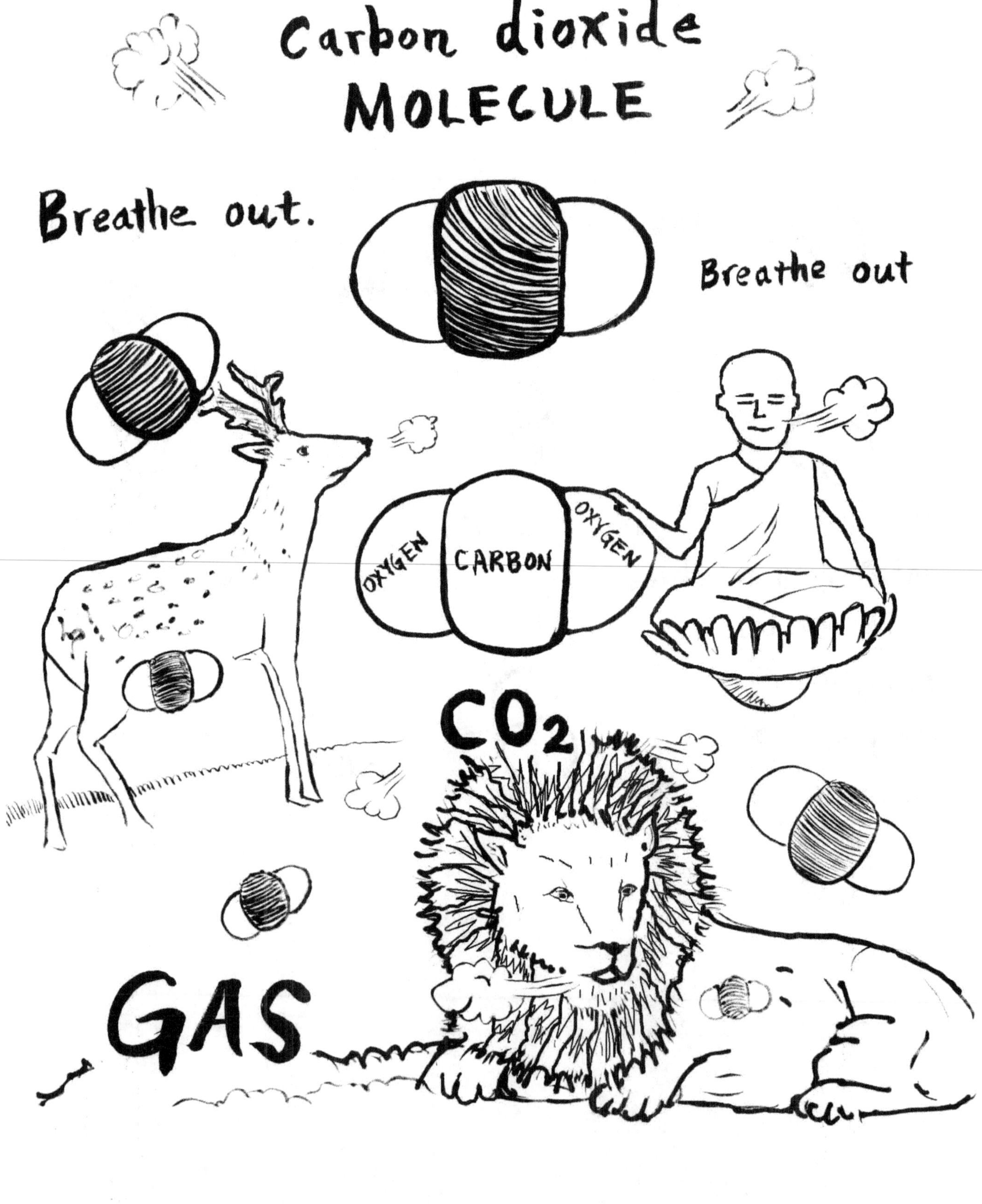
Carbon dioxide
MOLECULE
Breathe out.
Breathe out
OXYGEN
CARBON
OXYGEN
CO2
GAS

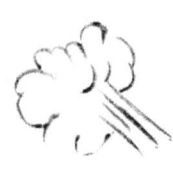

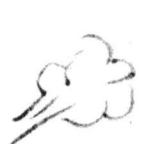

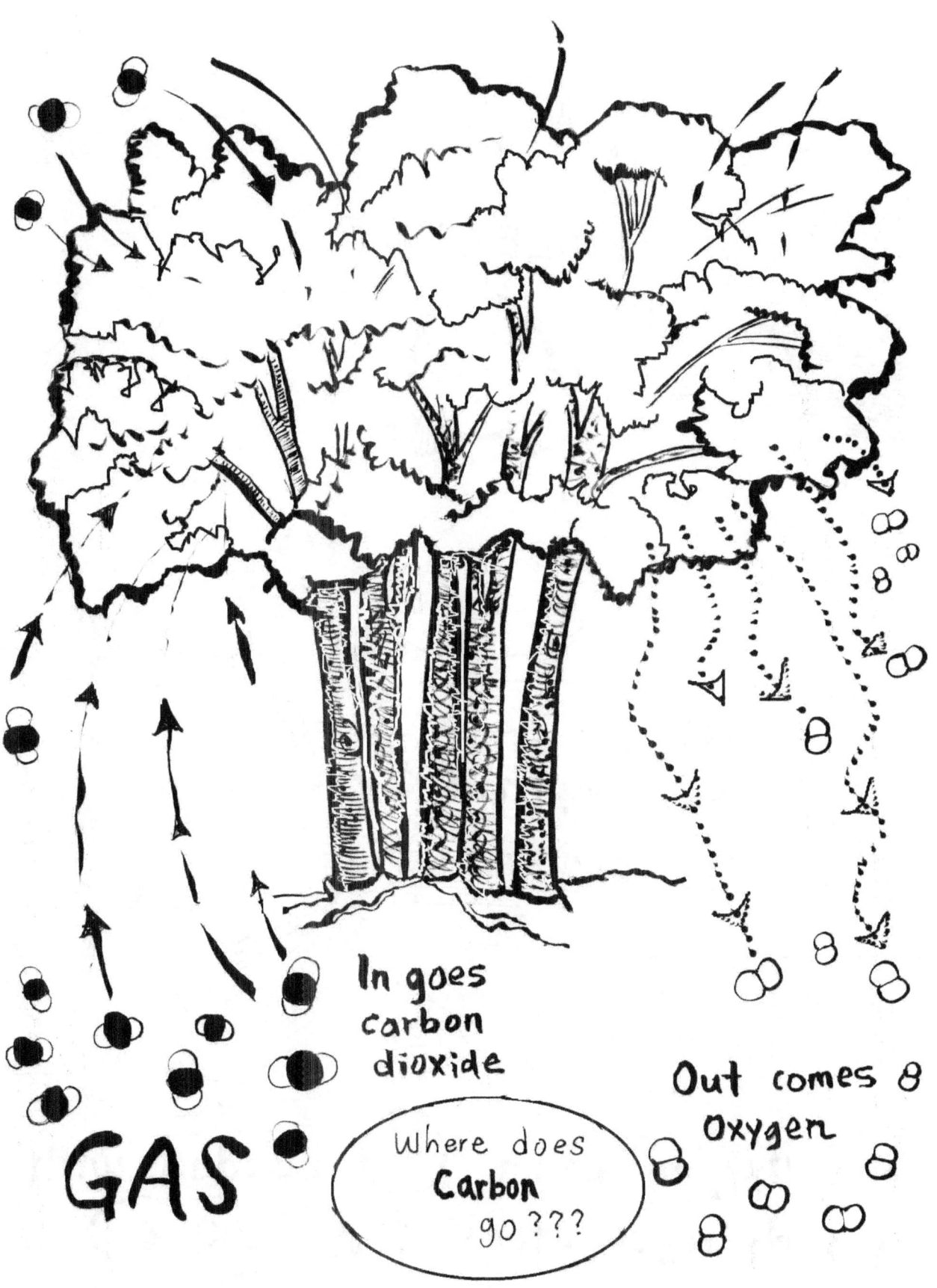

Water molecules hold onto each other tightly

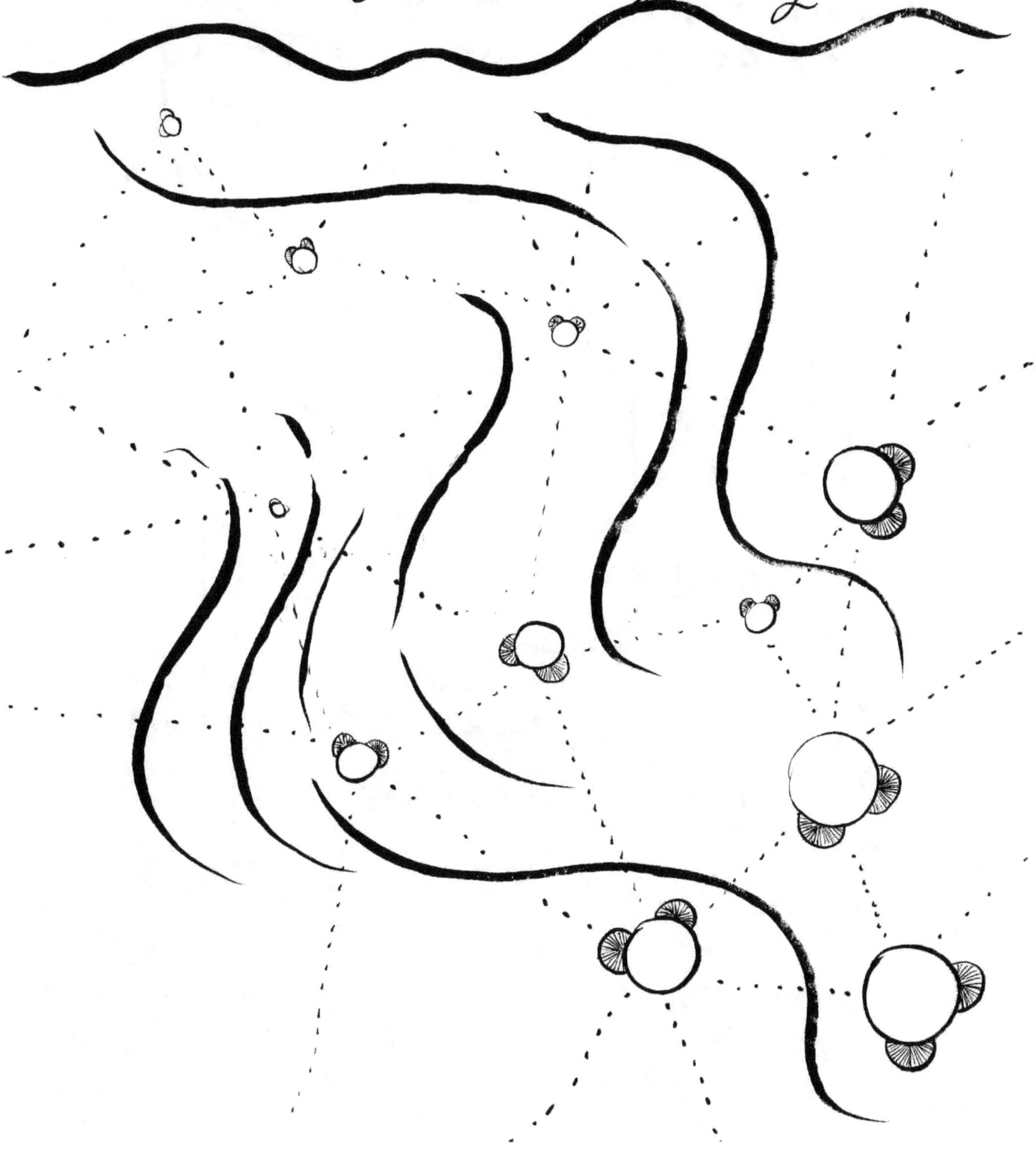

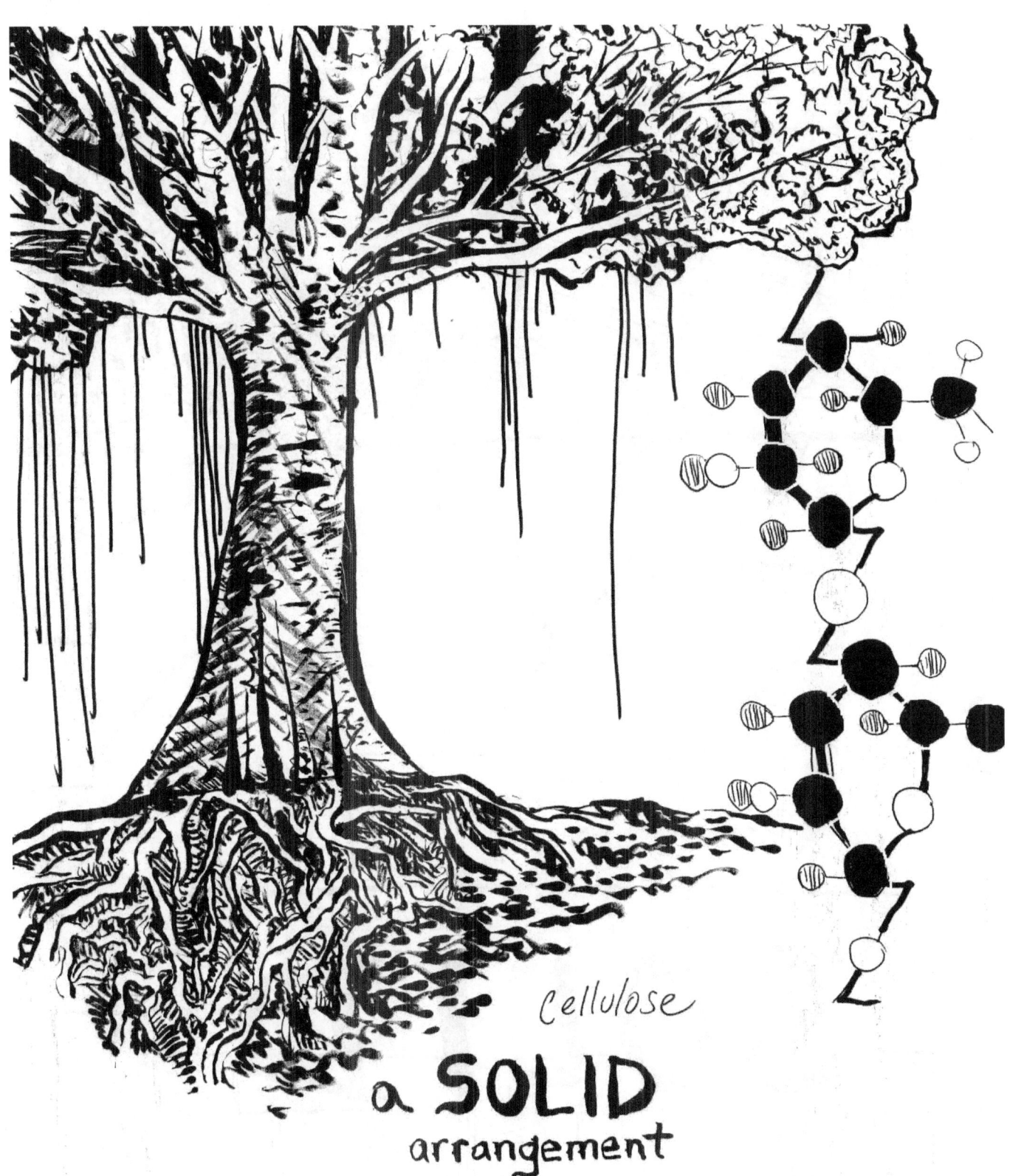

cellulose

a SOLID arrangement

Elements and compounds

An element is a substance, in pure form with nothing else mixed in. It cannot be separated into simpler stuff. Elements make up all *stuff*. Gold, silver, copper, iron, and aluminum are elements, so are oxygen, carbon, calcium, and sulfur.

Many elements of the universe are metals – shiny conductors of electricity. They can be stretched into long wires, or pounded into thin sheets. Some elements are gases that float around and make up our atmosphere. Other elements are multi-colored, brittle, flaky minerals that do not conduct electricity.

Two or more elements together make up a compound. A mixture of definite proportions it is. Water is a compound of hydrogen and oxygen. Clay is a compound of silicon and aluminum. Two or more metals together make up compounds called alloys. Bronze is an alloy of copper and tin. Brass is an alloy of copper and zinc.

In the presence of light, heat, acids, or oxygen, atoms clump together or break apart. Liquids may become gases, solid rocks and metals may dissolve into liquid, metal and acid may join together to form crystals of salt.

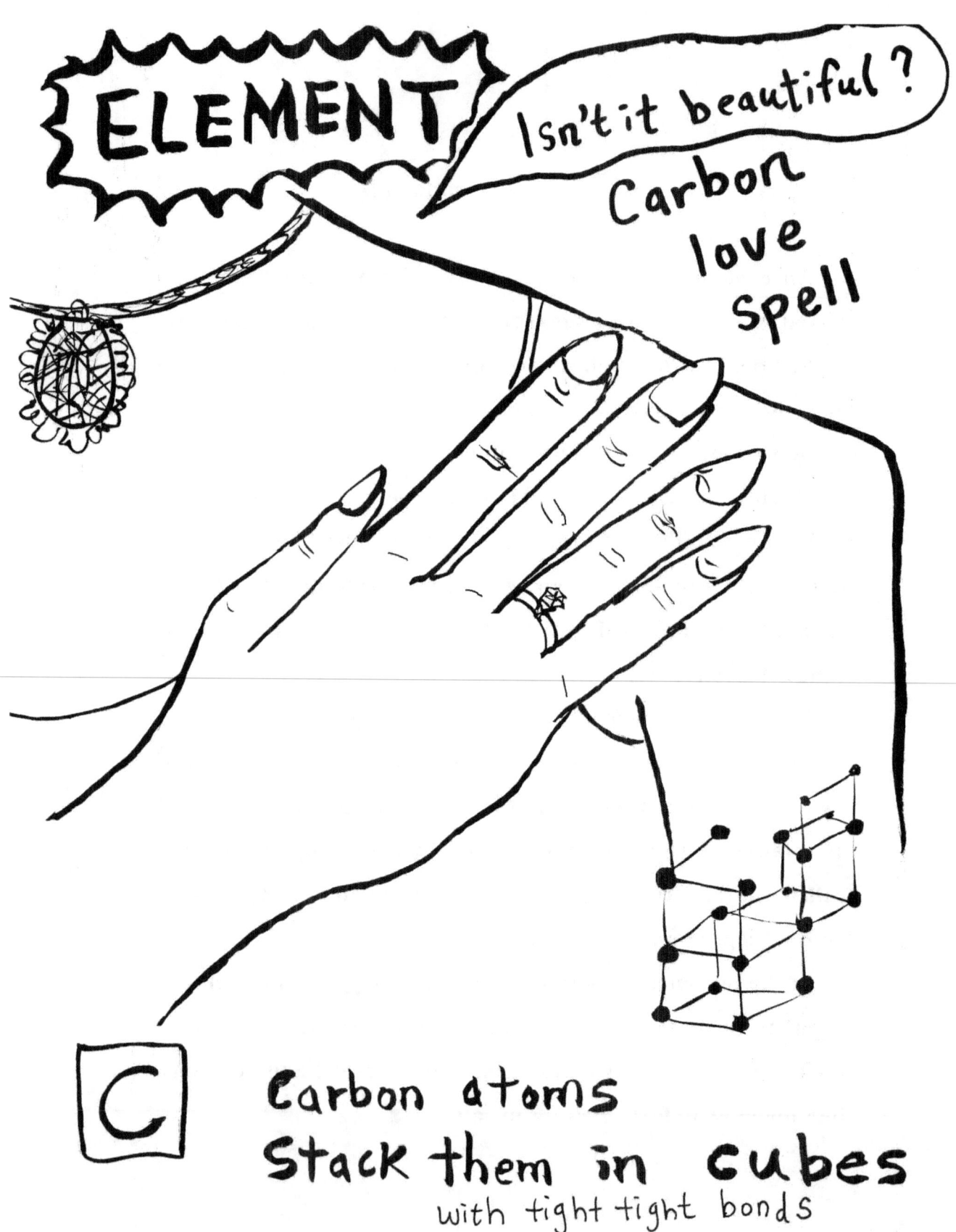

Woody on the outside
carbon on the inside
use me for homework
make a mistake
eraser is at the end

ELEMENT

Carbon as graphite
C
Put my carbon atoms in layers of hexagons

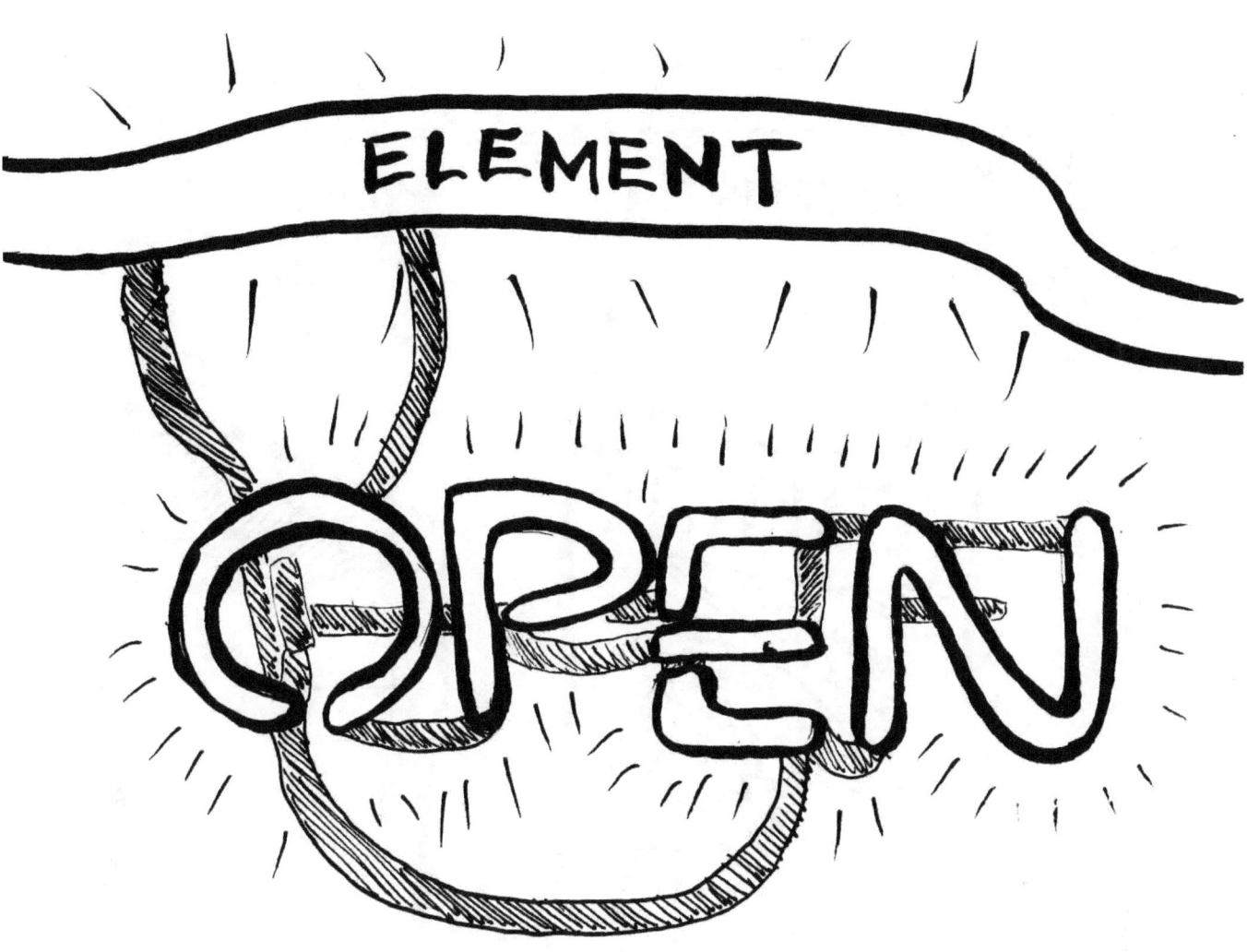

Ammonia

Grow crops   **Clean windows no streaks**

NITROGEN·HYDROGEN·HYDROGEN·HYDROGEN·NITROGE.HYDROGEN·HYDROGEN
HYDROGEN·NITROGEN·HYDROGEN·HYDROGEN·HYDROGEN·NITROGEN·HYDROGEN

The combination of

| N | Nitrogen × 1
| H | Hydrogen × 3 = Ammonia

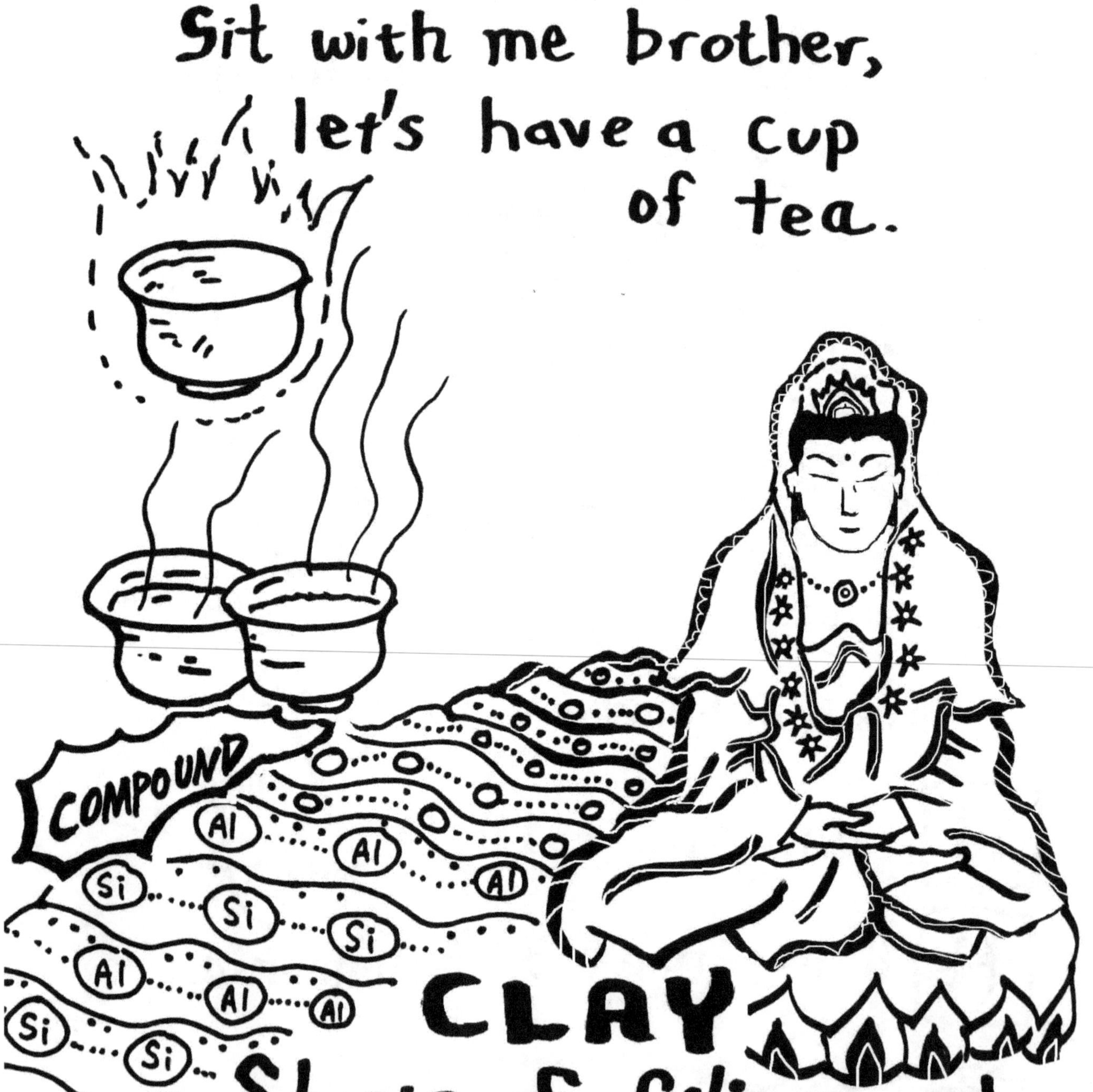

Sit with me brother, let's have a cup of tea.
COMPOUND
Al
Al
Al
Si
Si
Si
Al
Al
Al
Si
Si
CLAY
Sheets of Silicon and Aluminum

Ions

Atoms and molecules become positively or negatively charged as they crash and zip through space. The atoms of some elements are happy sitting by themselves and remain neutral. We call them names like "not reactive". There are atoms that form strong bonds and hard to break structures with others. Then, there are atoms that are always dropping partners and hanging with someone new.

Opposites attract – positive and negatively charged atoms join tight. Same forces repel – positive and positive, negative and negative, push each other away.

A charged atom, or a group of charged atoms, is called an ion. Ions can float in the air, dissolve in a liquid, or bind together as solid masses. In the charged state, atoms go forth to share and forge connections with each other.

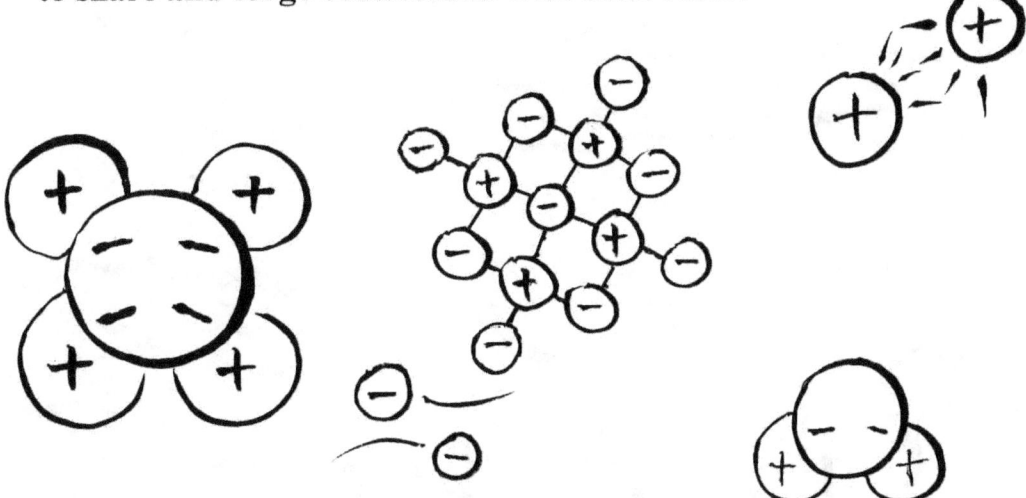

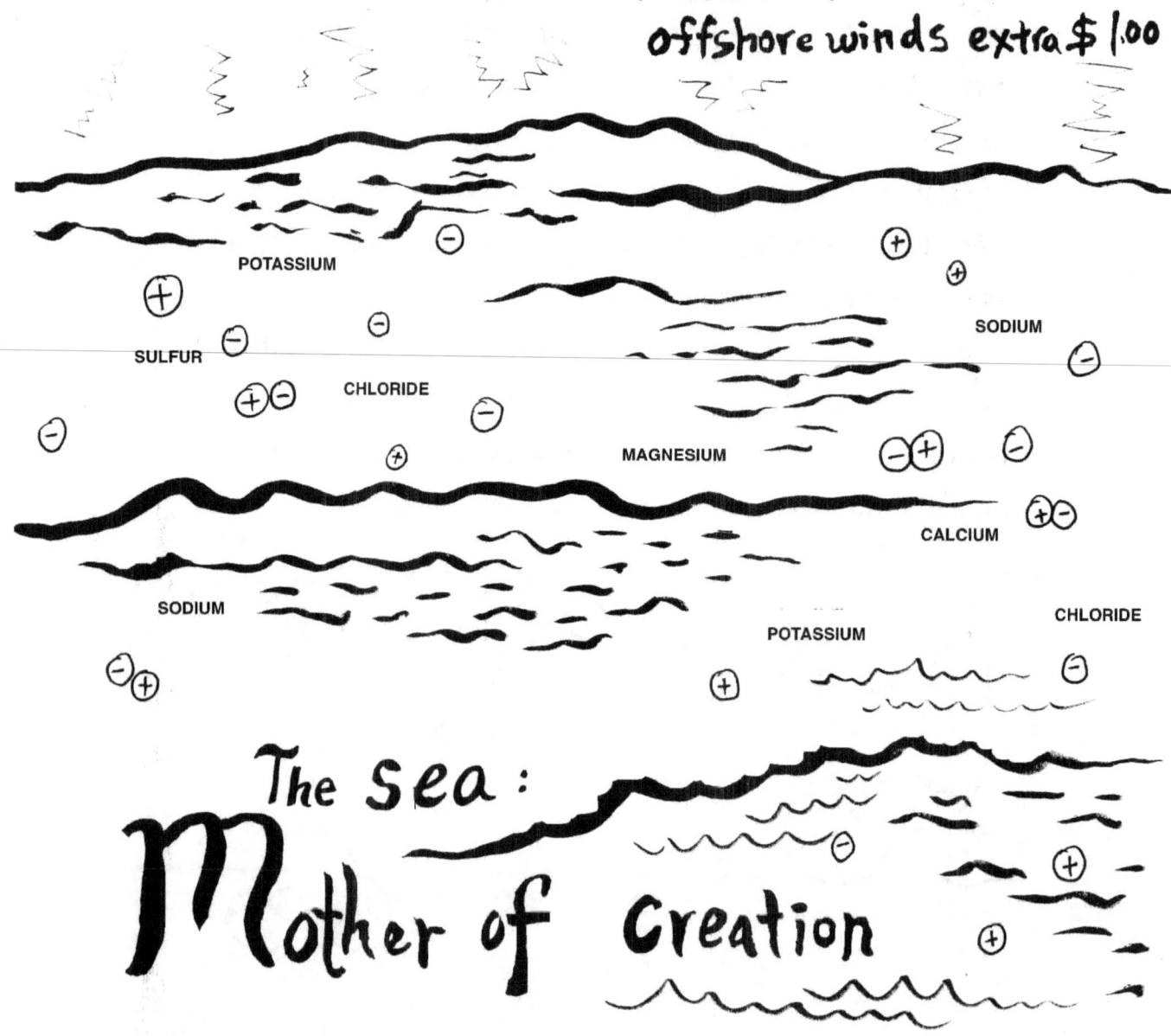

clay particles are markets of ION EXCHANGE

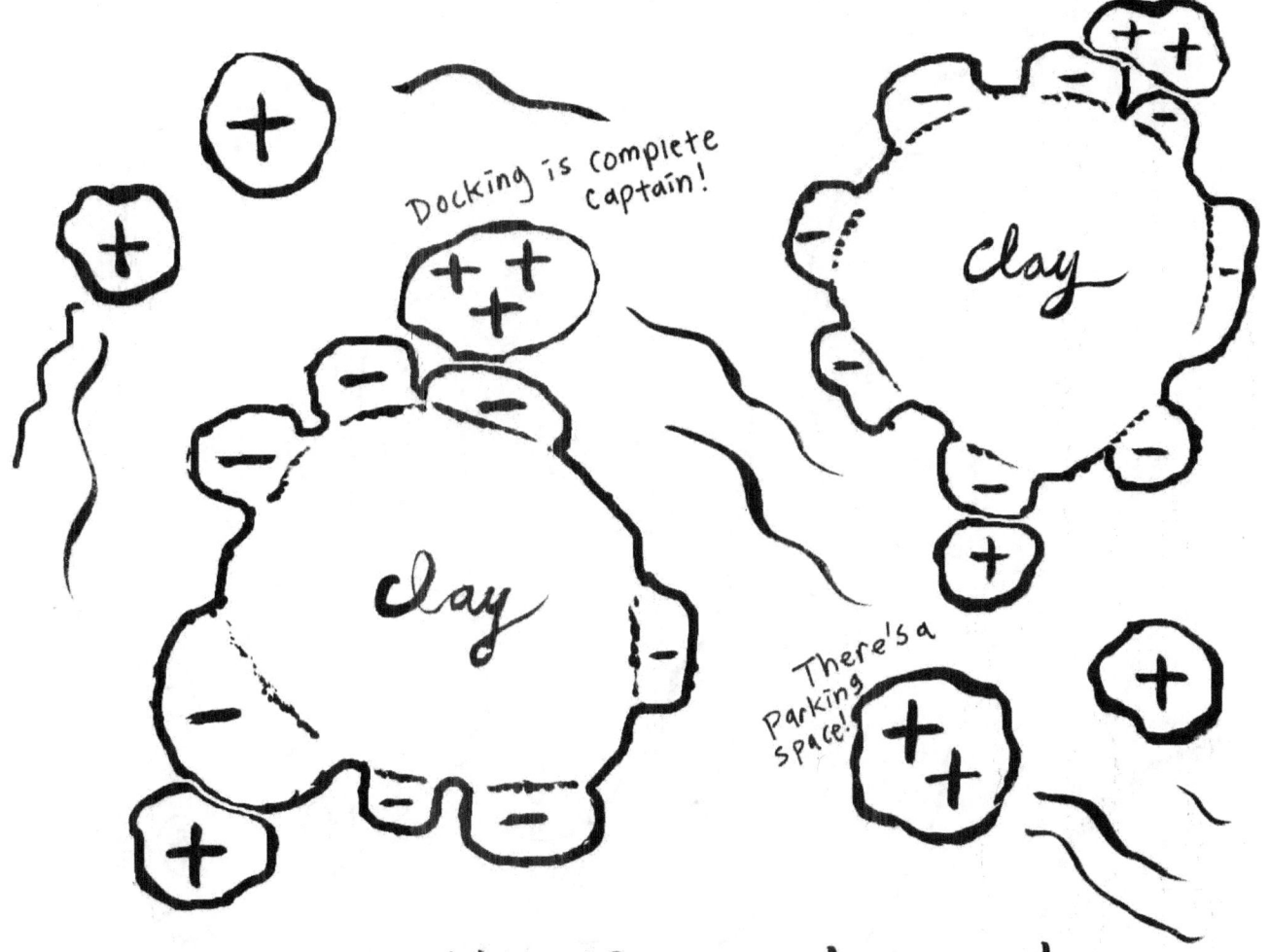

Negative spots on clay attract Positive ions swimming in water

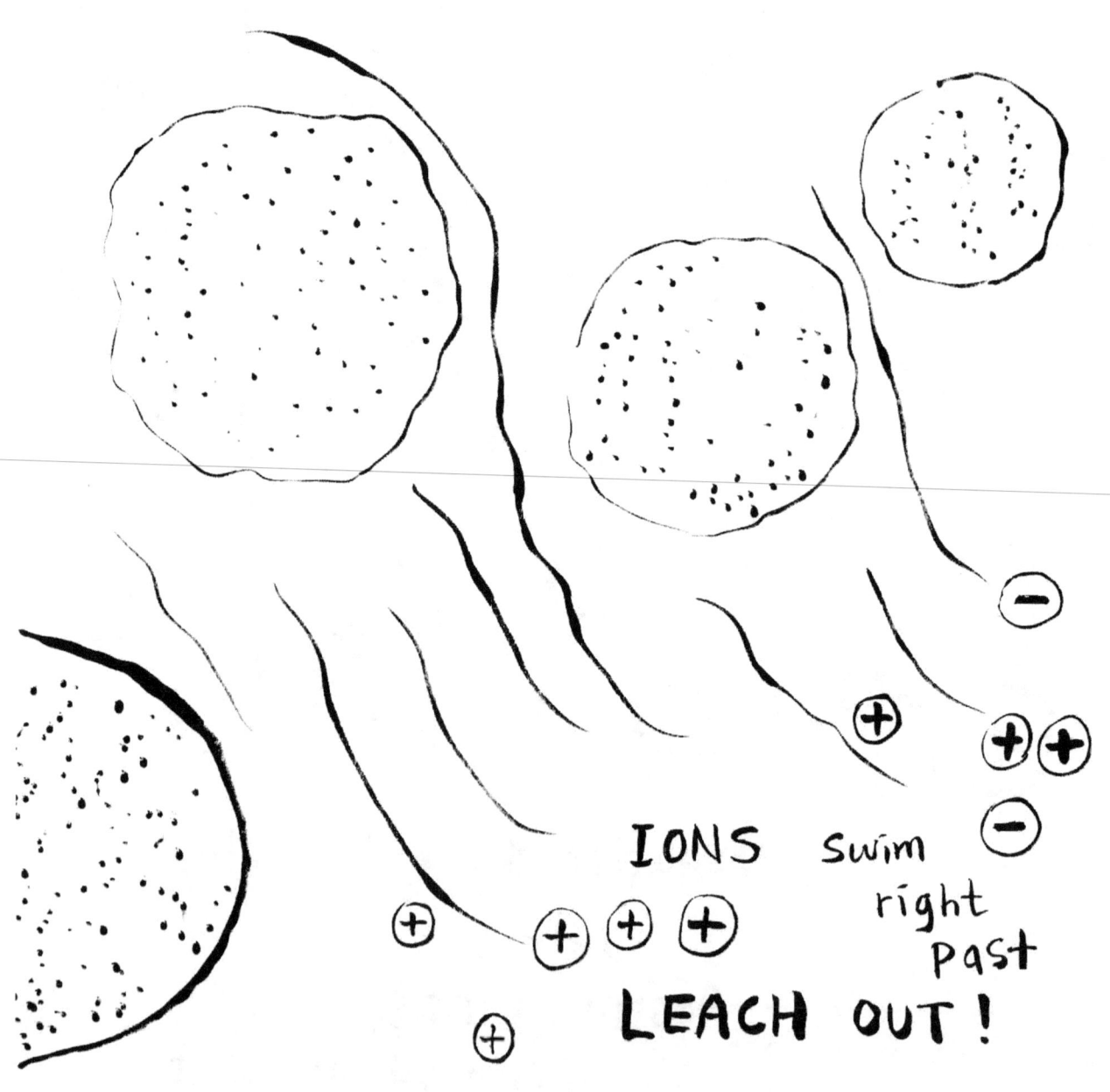

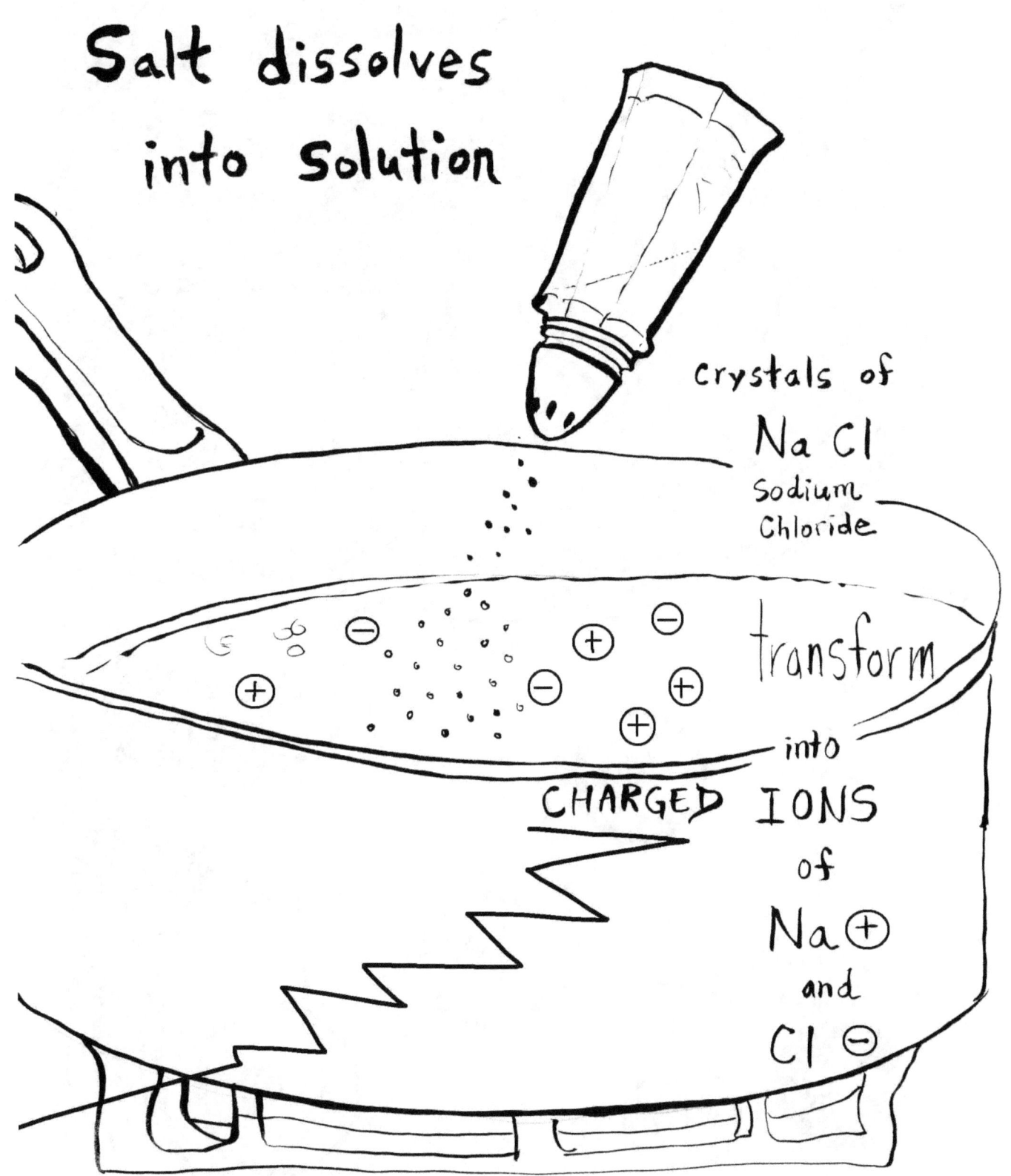

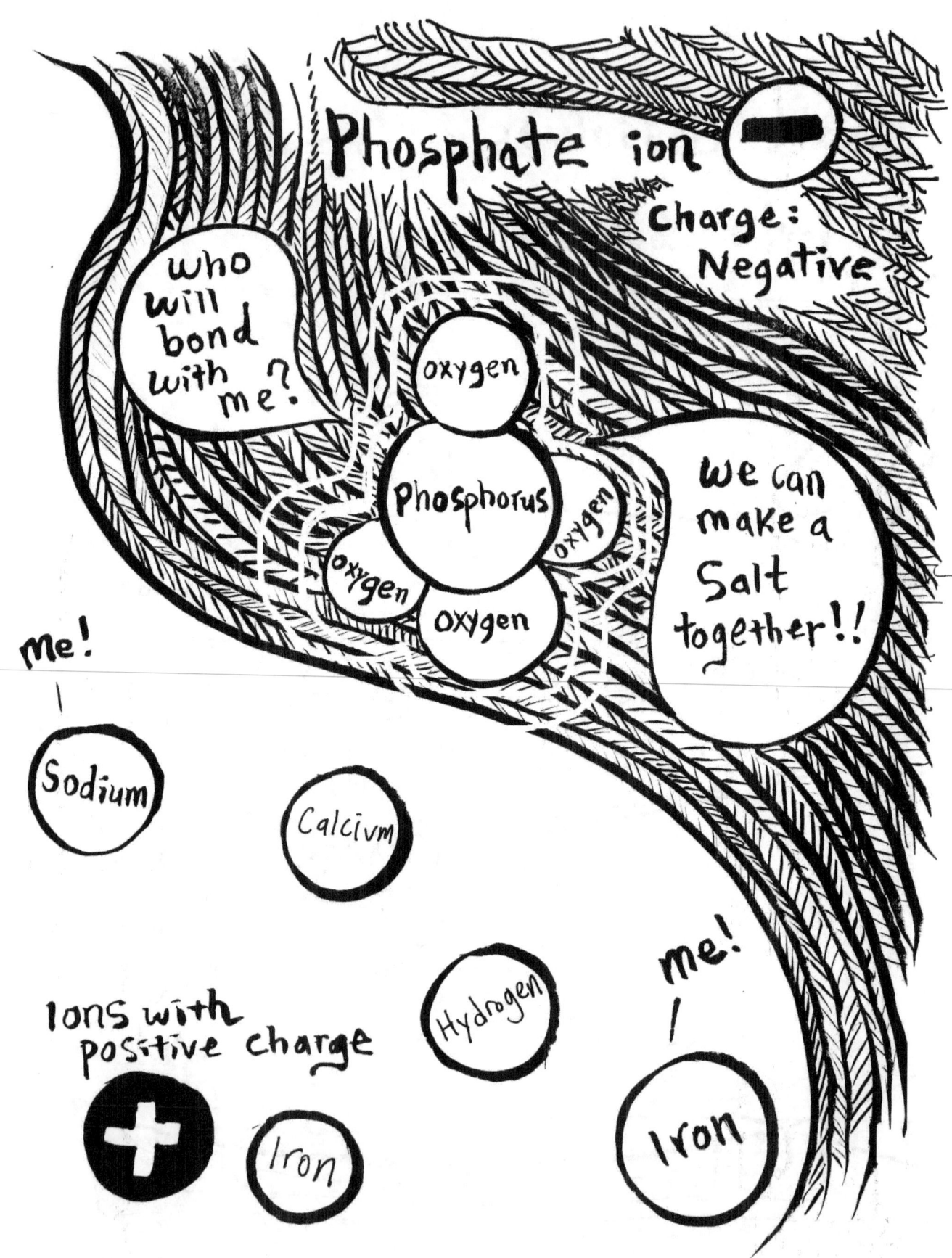

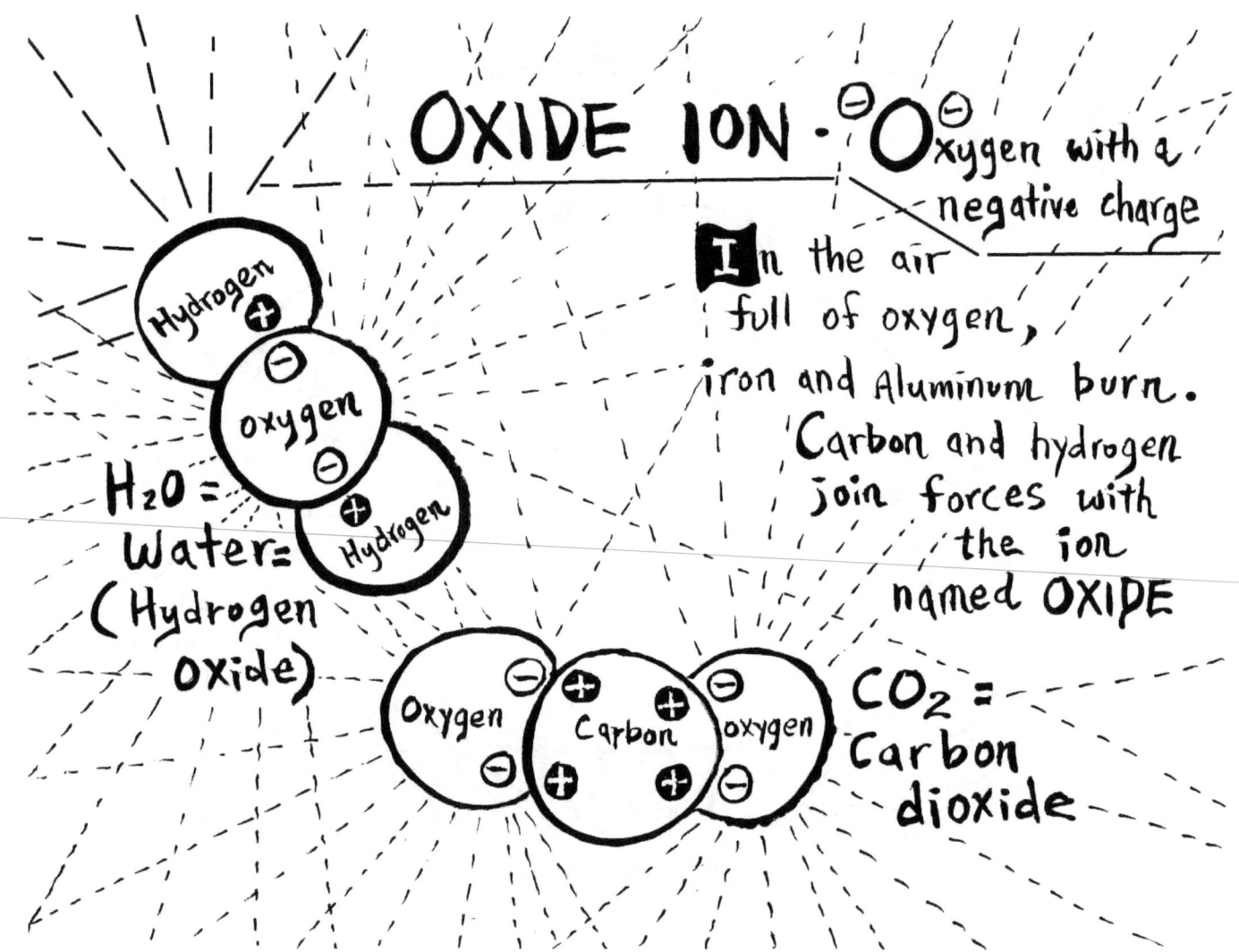

Plant nutrients

Plant parts are made of the air, rocks, metals, water, and the cosmic fire of the sun. These are the basis of life. When you work in the garden or sit down to eat food, you hook into a direct channel with massive and powerful forces that breathe life into our planet. You move with the light of the sun and are shaped by the atoms of the earth. This is communion and sacrifice in action. THANK YOU!

Roots suck up liquid food - they pull up ions, dissolved in water. Other necessary plant elements are grabbed out of the air through the little holes in the leaves and trunks. Too little of a nutrient and the plant may get sick. Too much of a nutrient and the plant may be poisoned.

Plants drink a tea of metals and salts. A salt is a crystalline compound composed of a positive and a negative ion. Some salts dissolve in water (soluble), while others do not. A handful of nutrients are useful for the plant person to know:

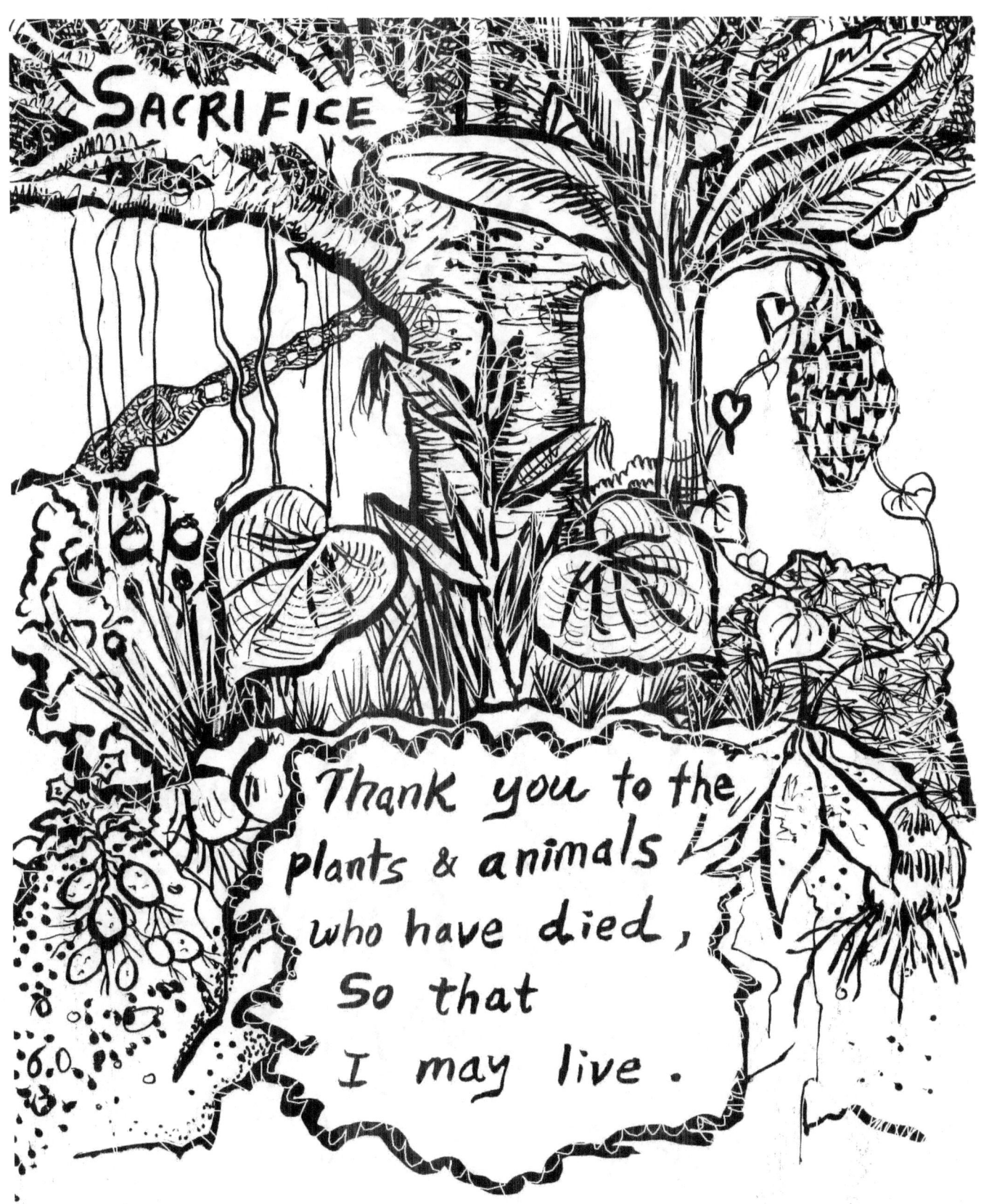

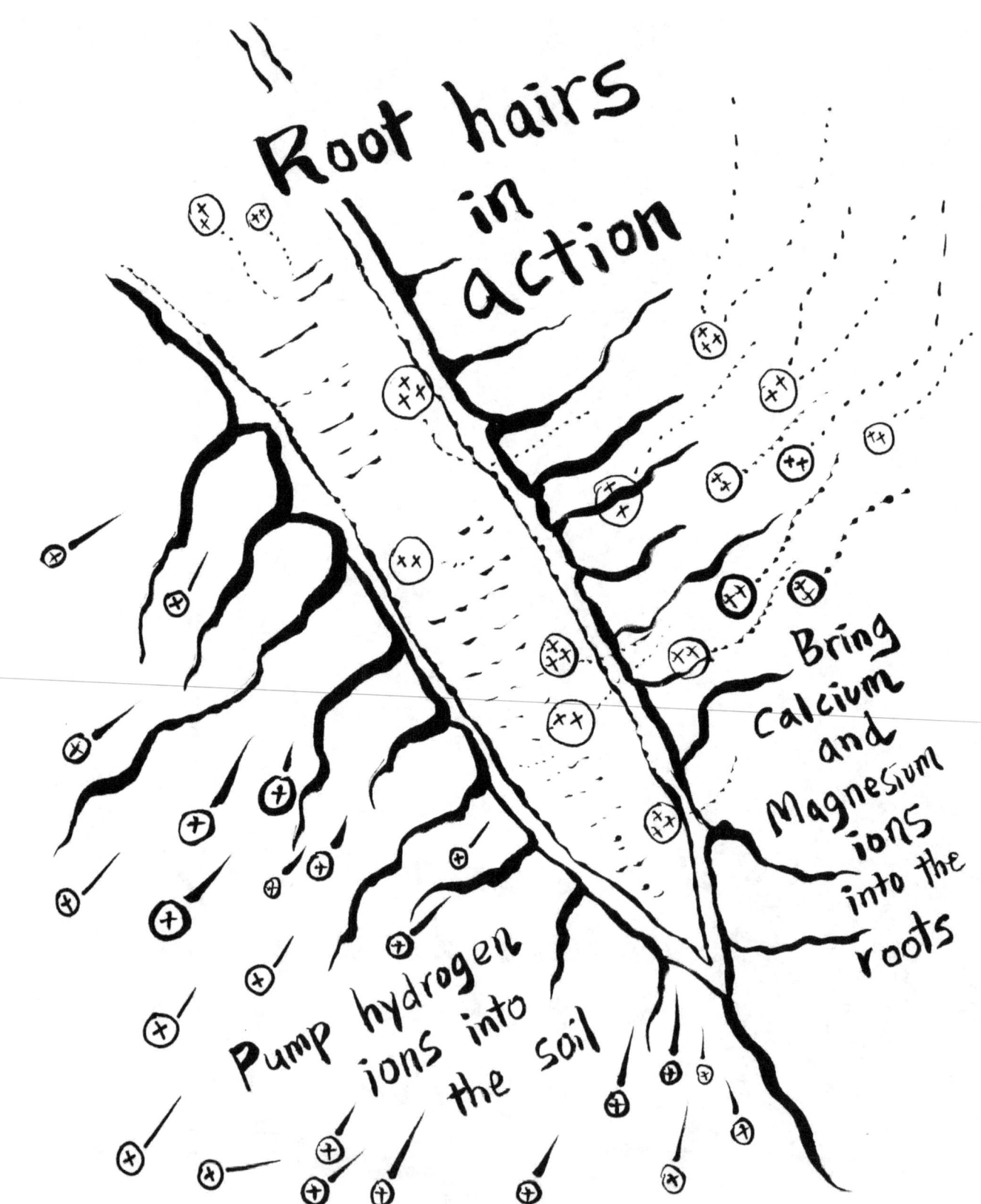

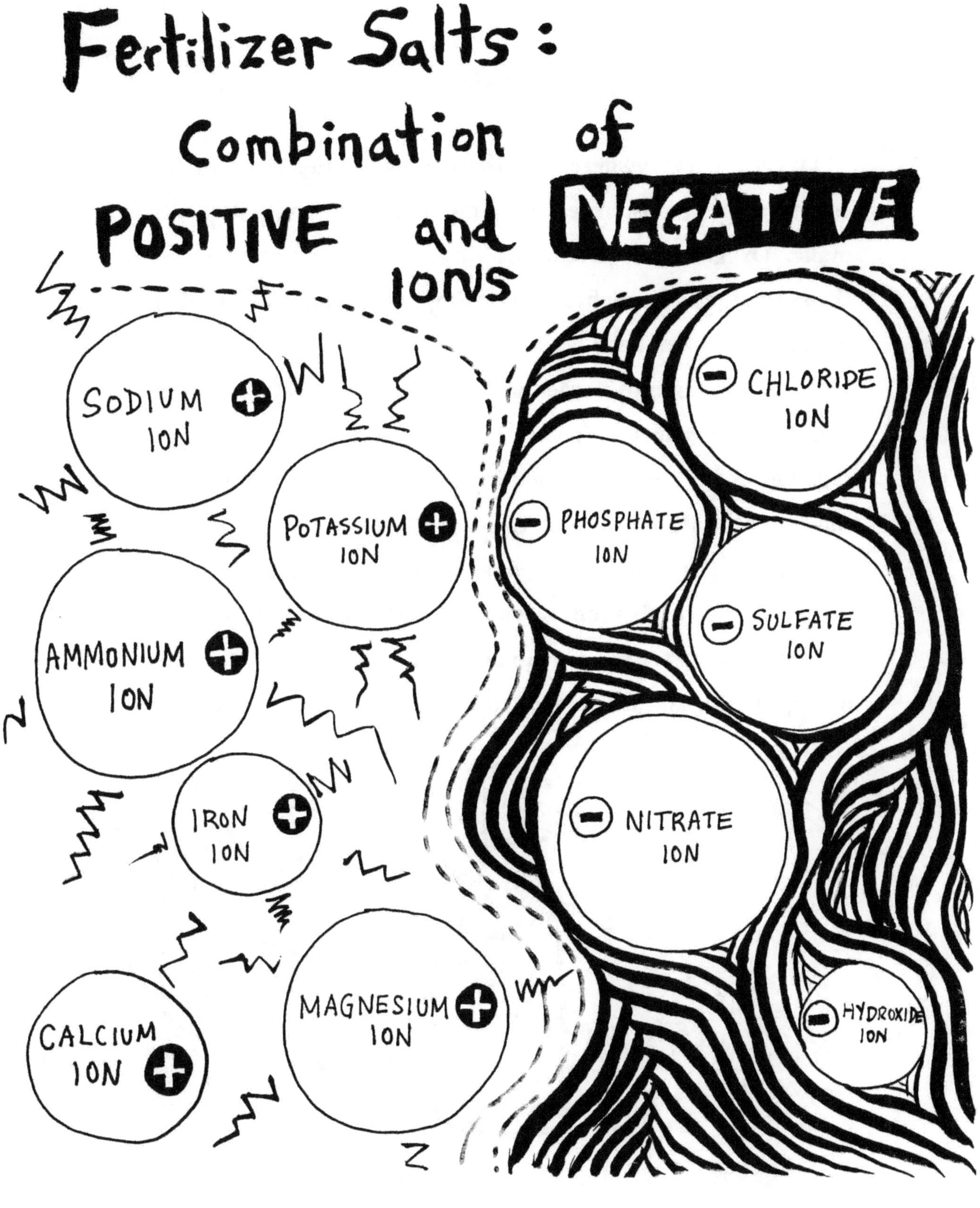

Fertilizer Salts: Combination of POSITIVE and NEGATIVE IONS

- SODIUM ION ⊕
- POTASSIUM ION ⊕
- AMMONIUM ION ⊕
- IRON ION ⊕
- CALCIUM ION ⊕
- MAGNESIUM ION ⊕

- ⊖ CHLORIDE ION
- ⊖ PHOSPHATE ION
- ⊖ SULFATE ION
- ⊖ NITRATE ION
- ⊖ HYDROXIDE ION

Oxygen

Oxygen is everywhere - in the oceans, in the crust of the earth, in the atmosphere. It is the awesome gas that plants make. Oxygen is the part in the air that burns hot and keeps a flame smokin'. Firefighters say " Stop, drop and roll, smother the fire with a blanket." No oxygen, no fire.

Your heart pumps oxygen and blood to your brain, muscles, and all body parts. Red is the color of blood and oxygen together. Check out the blood in your vessels without oxygen, they are blue and going back to get some more.

In plants, oxygen forms a part of all cells. Oxygen is used during plant respiration – when stored sugars are used to generate energy for the growth and repair of plant parts. Take a deep breath and let it go deep into your lungs. That's the stuff!

Hydrogen

To grow and make sugars, a plant needs carbon and hydrogen. Hydrogen comes from the water – H_2O: two hydrogen atoms and one oxygen atom. A thirsty plant cannot make sugars.

Once in a while, water molecules split up and break apart. They become two charged particles called ions. One is H, charge positive. The other is OH, charge negative. The more H ions there are in a liquid, the more acidic it is. Fewer H ions, the liquid is alkaline.

Acidic liquids taste sharp and biting, like the vomit in throw up. Alkaline liquids are also called basic; they taste bitter and dry.

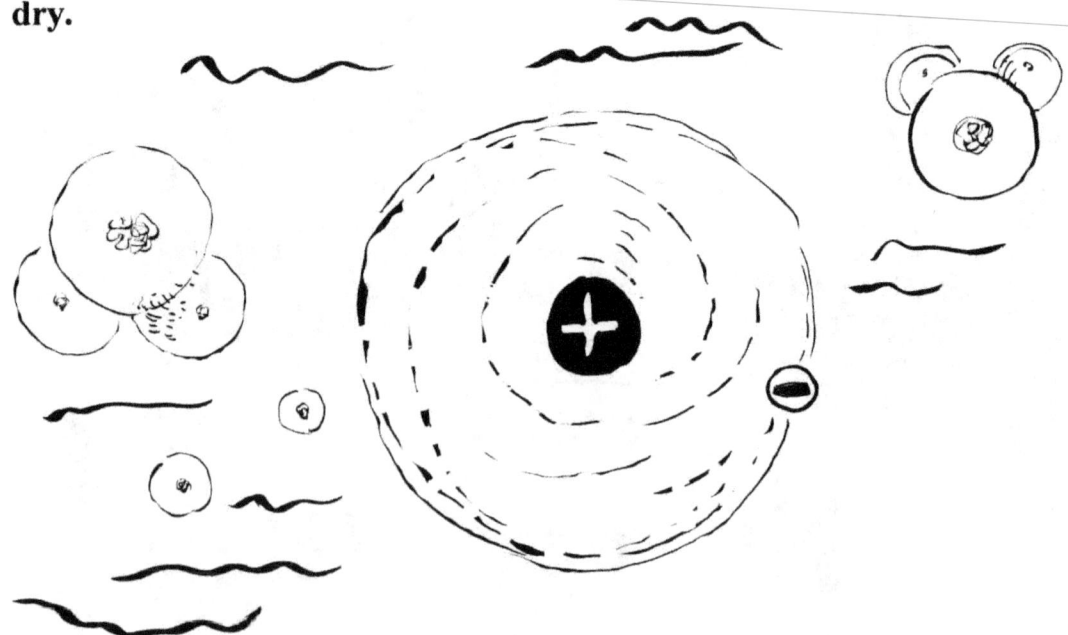

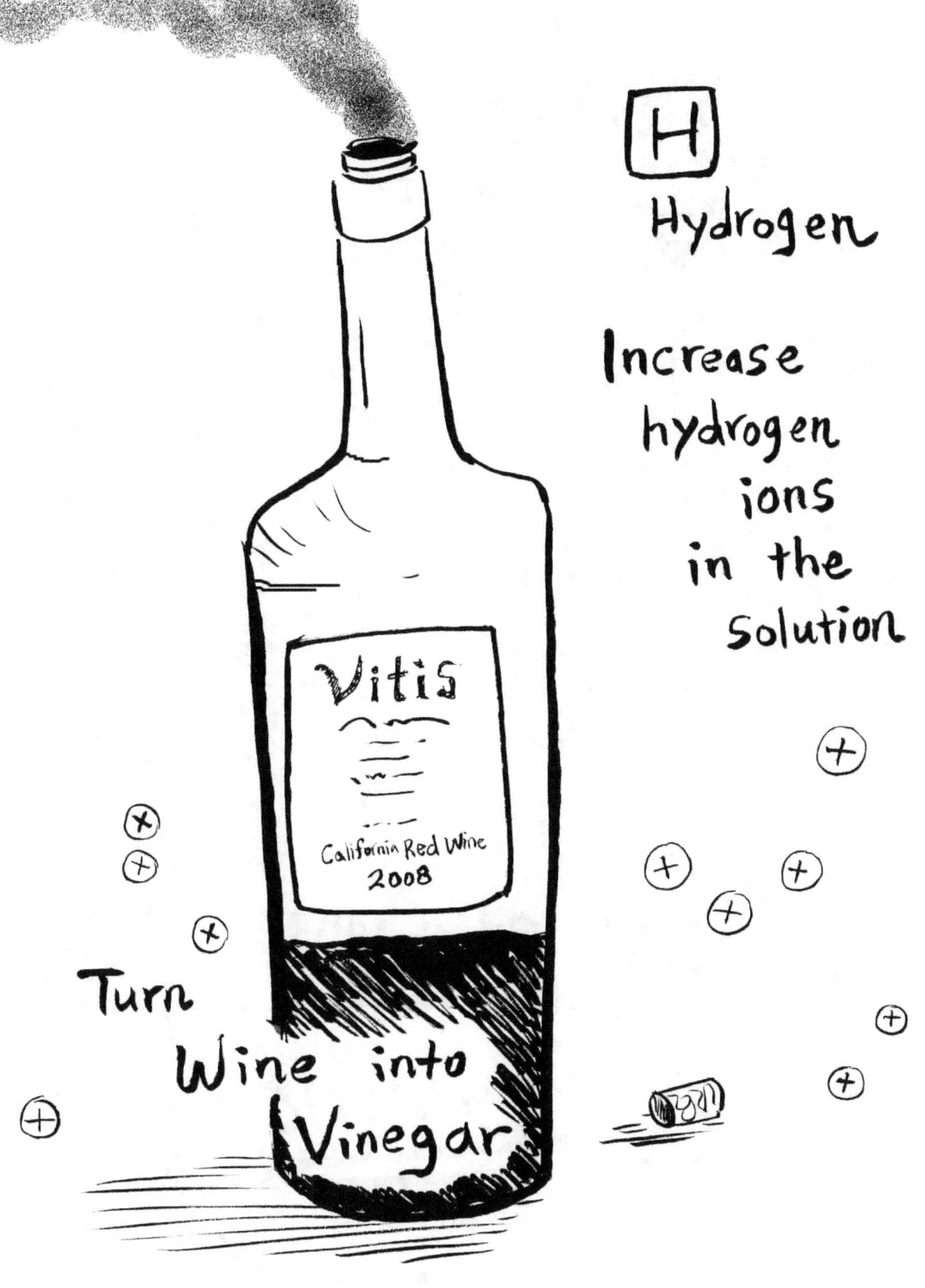

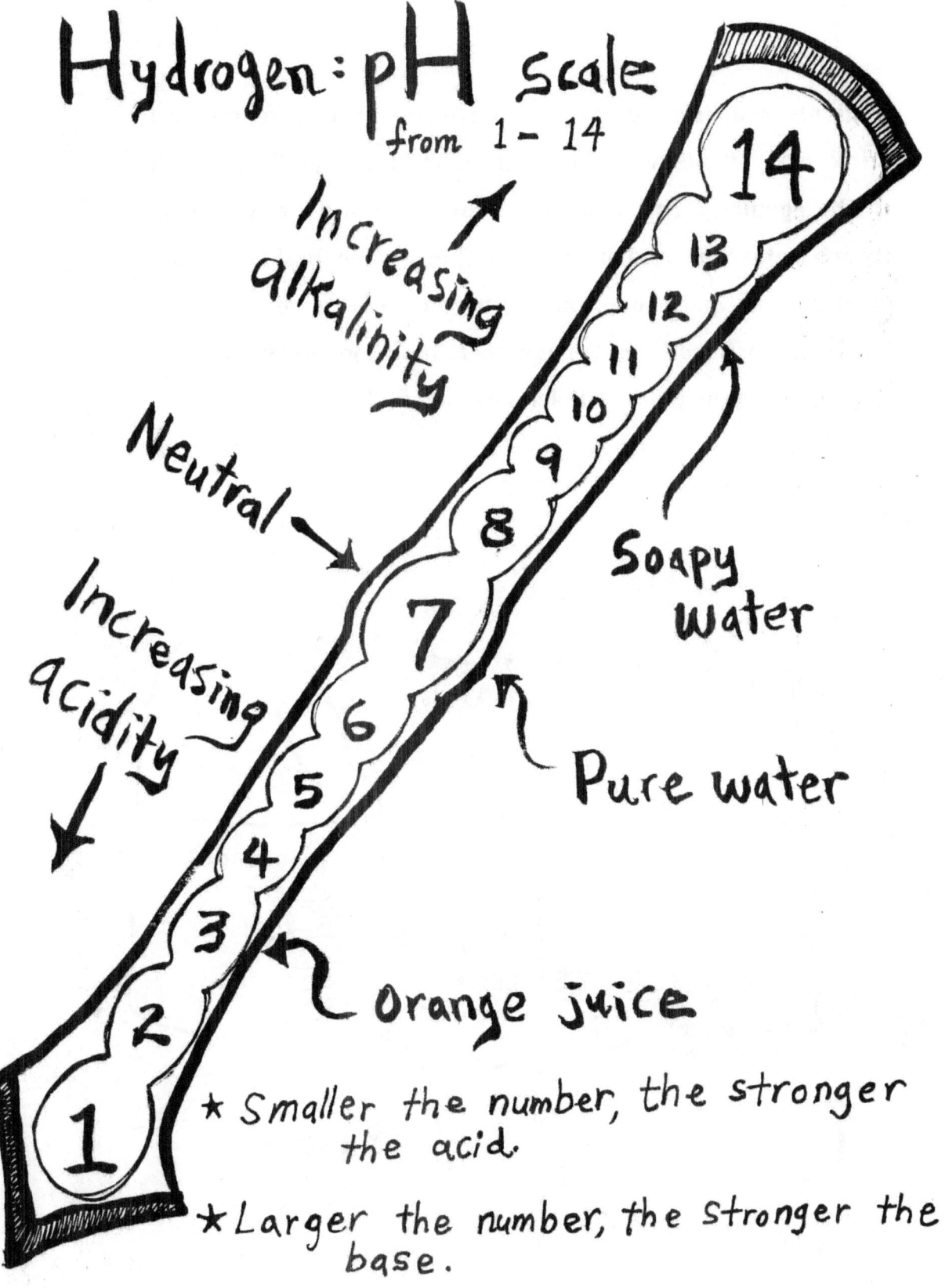

Plants are affected by how basic or acid their mineral drinks are. Plants need the drink to be "just right" to absorb all the goodies. Too acidic, and the plant will be unable to absorb potassium and phosphorus ions. Too basic, and the plant may not get enough nitrogen or iron ions. Worse, very acidic or basic soils may have waaaaaay too much of some elements, and the plants will be poisoned and die!

I am an acid-soil lover. What is my name?

If you don't know: Time to take a class in Plant Identification

Carbon

Plants breathe in carbon dioxide gas from the atmosphere, and store the carbon in leaves, stems, and roots. Carbon dioxide is carbon and oxygen in a ratio of one part carbon to two parts oxygen – CO_2.

Carbon is the backbone around which almost all living beings are created. Plants use carbon to make sugars. These sugar chains grow long, and are packed away as starches in the seeds of wheat and rice, or underground in roots and tubers as potatoes and yams. Carbon makes the cellulose in redwood tree trunks, and the oils in sunflower seeds. Rings of carbon and nitrogen make the proteins in beans and pepperoni.

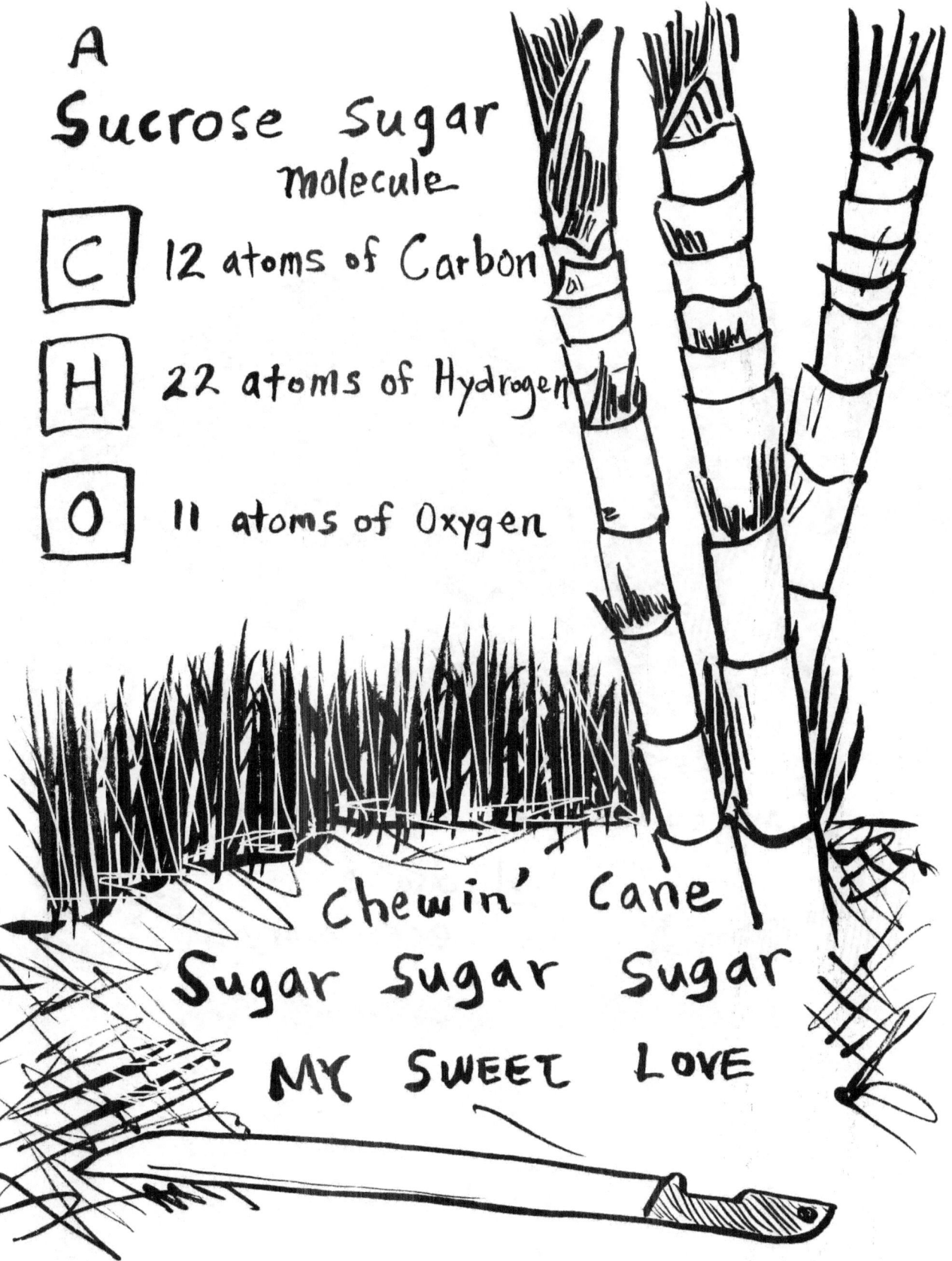

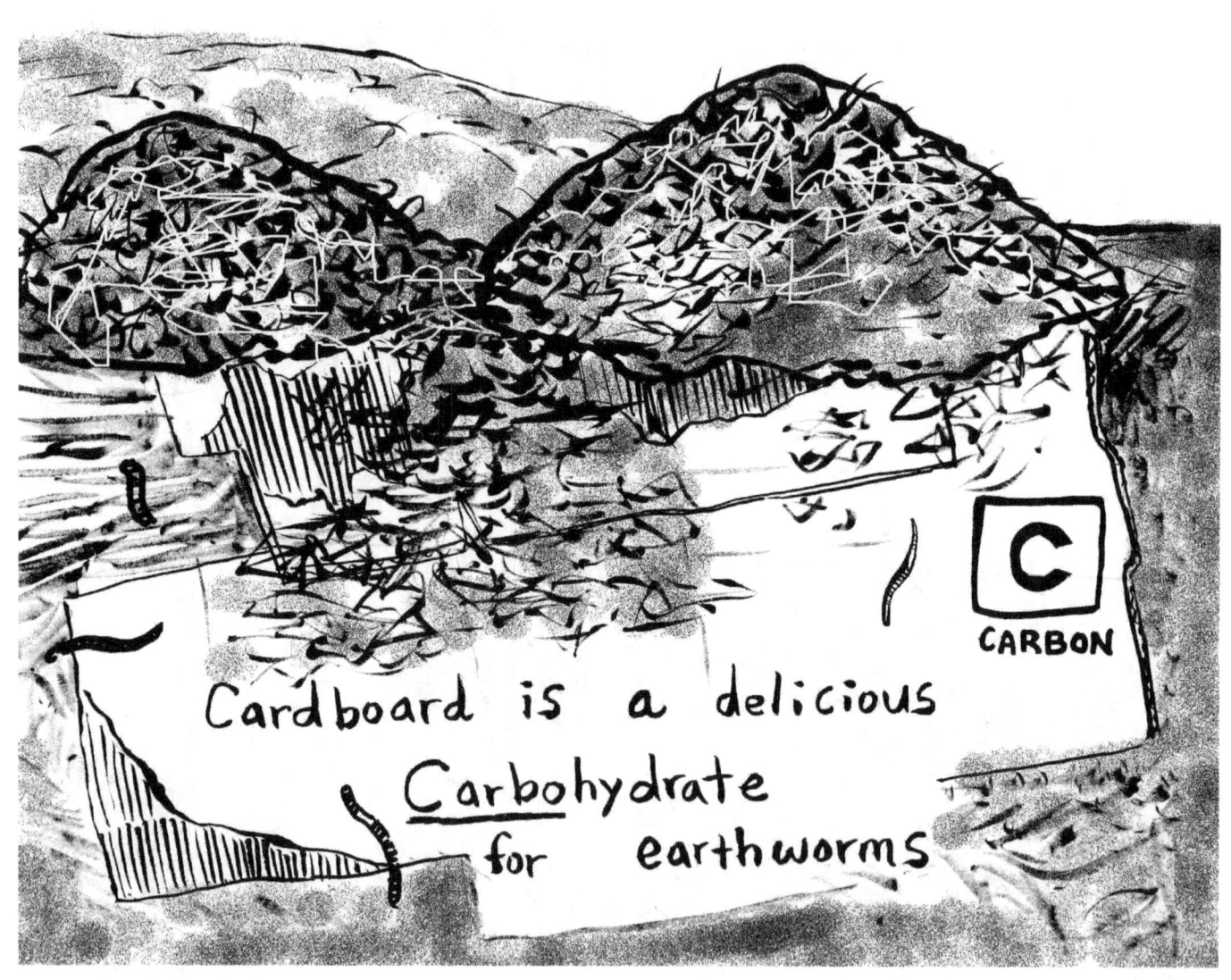

CARBON IS LIFE

Over time, deep layers of dead plants and animals are packed tight, heated, and squashed. They become black oil underground or coal in the mountains. These ancient stores of carbon are mined and piped, then burned to drive engines and turn turbines. The dead give life to our civilization. Carbon not burned up is released back into the sky, to mix with oxygen and other gases.

Cows chewing cud and fermenting the grasses in their stomachs release gas in the form of methane. Burp! Excuse me! Engines in cars and lawn mowers belch excess burn waste into the air through exhaust pipes. After a meal of hard to digest beans, we gas out. A mountain of garbage being eaten by bacteria goes pooot poooot. Stinky!

BPPPPPP....

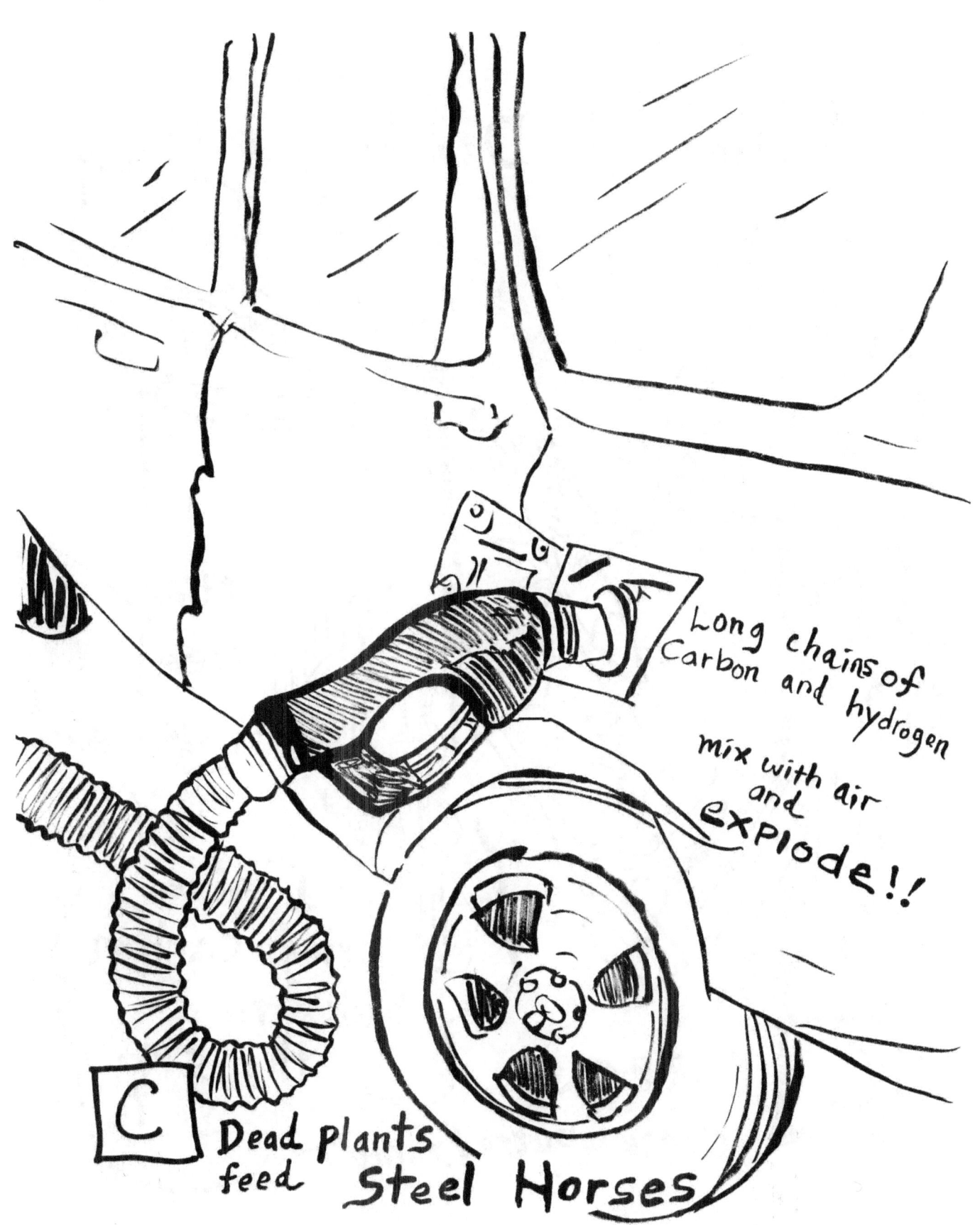

Demons of Death and Decay

Headless Seal on the beach

Rotting tree

C CARBON
Come putrefy me!

I give my carbon back to the sky

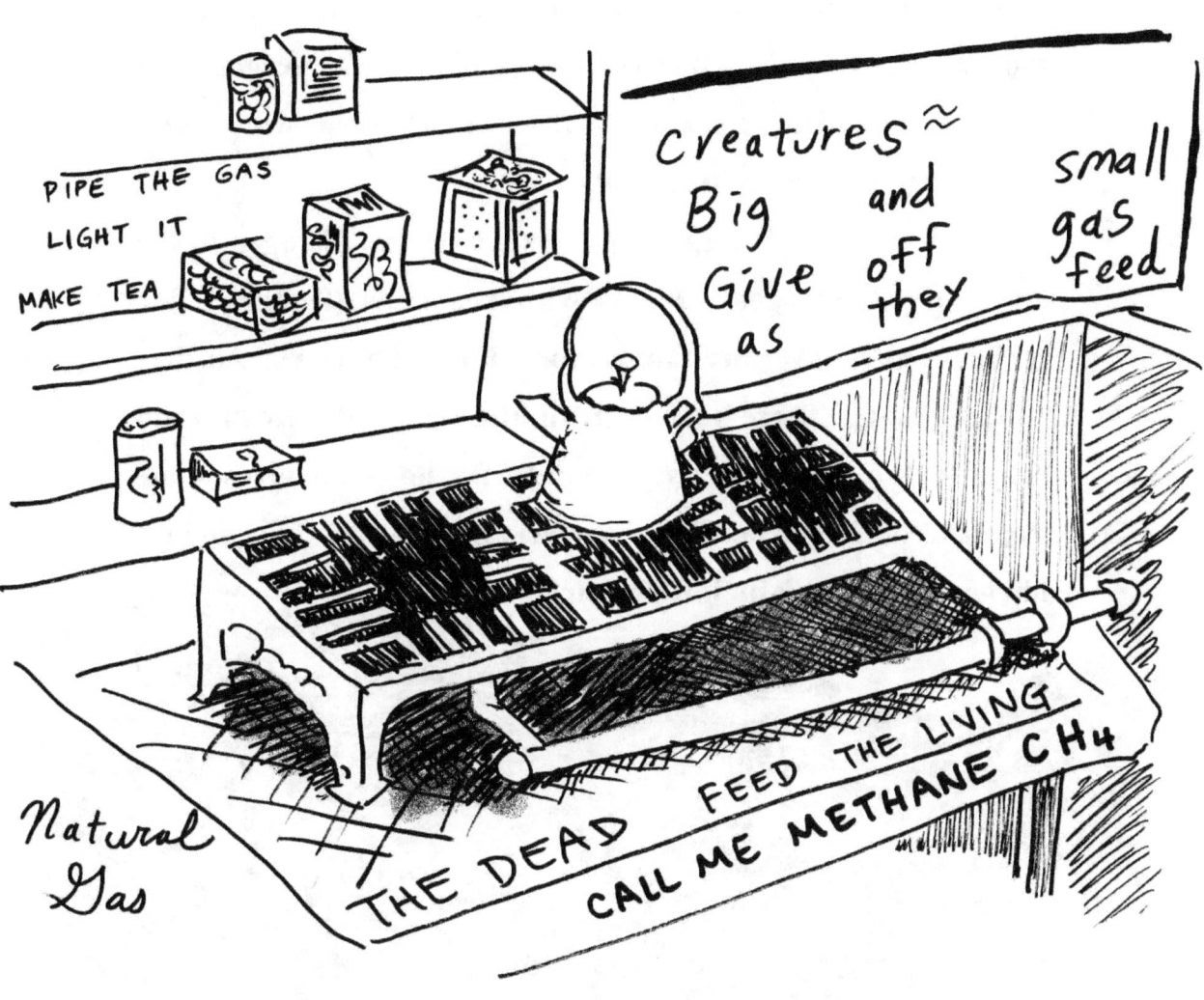

Nitrogen

Nitrogen likes to keep moving, it does not sit still. In the air, nitrogen is a gas that most plants cannot use. We breathe it in all the time, but it doesn't affect us much (It is inert). In the soil, nitrogen forms charged compounds with oxygen and hydrogen, and then tags along with water wherever water goes. Plants suck it up with their roots.

Crack kabooom! Lightning bolts transform nitrogen in the air into soil nitrogen. Plants with pea pods (legumes) like soybeans and clover are famous for a kind of bacteria that live on their roots. These bacteria turn nitrogen in the air into soil nitrogen the plant can use. In return, the plant gives some sugars to the bacteria. Other bacteria change soil nitrogen into nitrogen gas. Back up into the air!

Nitrogen for green leaves
the 'vegetative' growing stage

After this stage, get ready to grow **flowers** and **fruits**. Less **nitrogen**, more **phosphorus** and **potassium**.

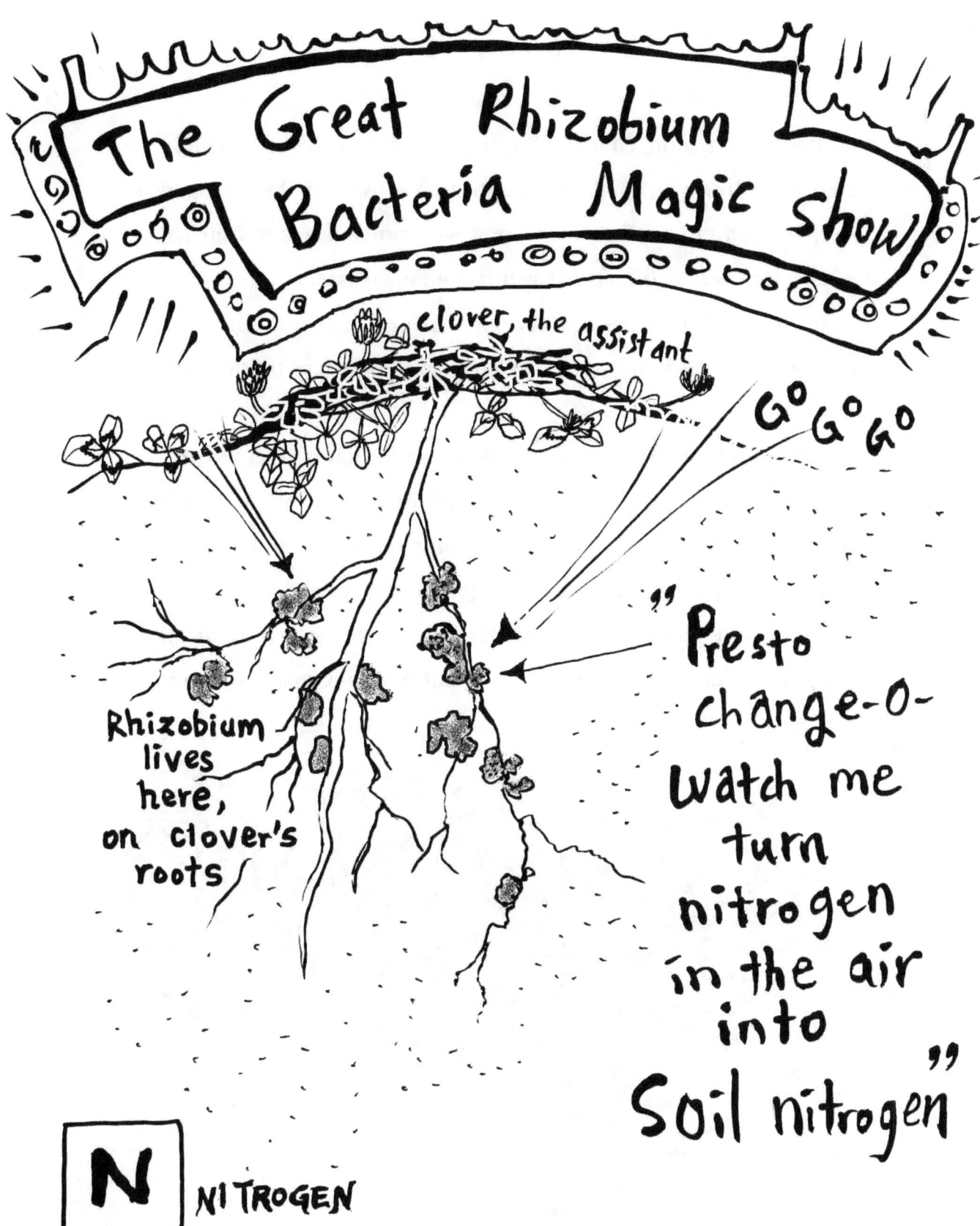

People eat long chains of nitrogen compounds in protein rich foods like meat, fish, and soybeans. Cows eat the nitrogen in the green grass. Extra nitrogen we cannot use is gotten rid of as poop, pee, and farts. It is nitrogenous waste.

Sources of nitrogen for the garden are manures, bat and bird guano (poop and pee together), and fertilizers made from natural gas.

Too much nitrogen can be poisonous to plants and nature. A pile of fertilizer or fresh chicken poop can burn plants brown and dead. Extra nitrogen that plants cannot absorb follows water down the stream or goes underground.

Plants use nitrogen to make green leaves; it is a part of all plant proteins and alkaloids. A plant will not grow without nitrogen.

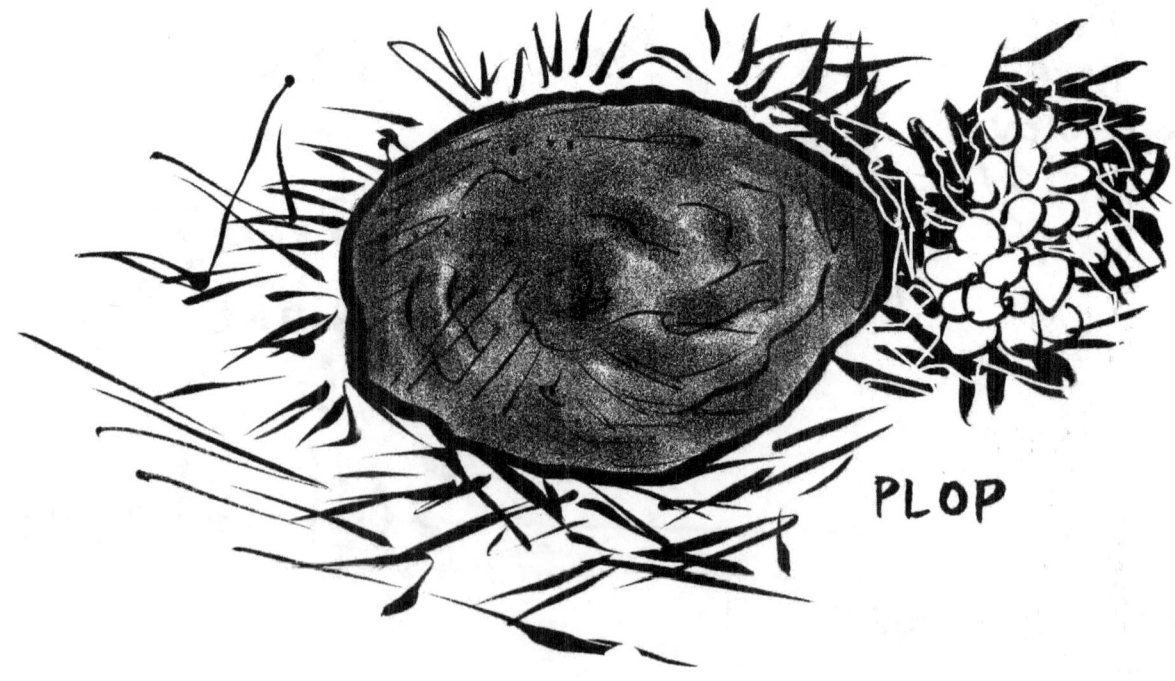

Fish tank water looking cloudy lot of fish poo nitrogenous waste

Ammonia ions

Nitrate ions

Phosphorus

Phosphorus is a mineral of the earth. All living cells have phosphorus; it is an essential element! After urine (pee pee) evaporates, some white salts are left. A good part of that is phosphorus. The hard parts of the skeleton are made of phosphorus, calcium, and oxygen.

Phosphorus is necessary for making flowers, seeds and fruits. Without phosphorus, photosynthesis does not happen.

Potassium

After you burn a pile of wood, potassium is left in the ashes. In its pure form it is a silvery white metal. There is a lot of potassium dissolved in the salty sea.

Potassium is an essential nutrient of all plant cells; it is concentrated in the fruits. It regulates water use in a plant by helping to open and close the pores in leaves and stems. It helps a plant to tolerate hot temperatures and resist disease. Great stuff!

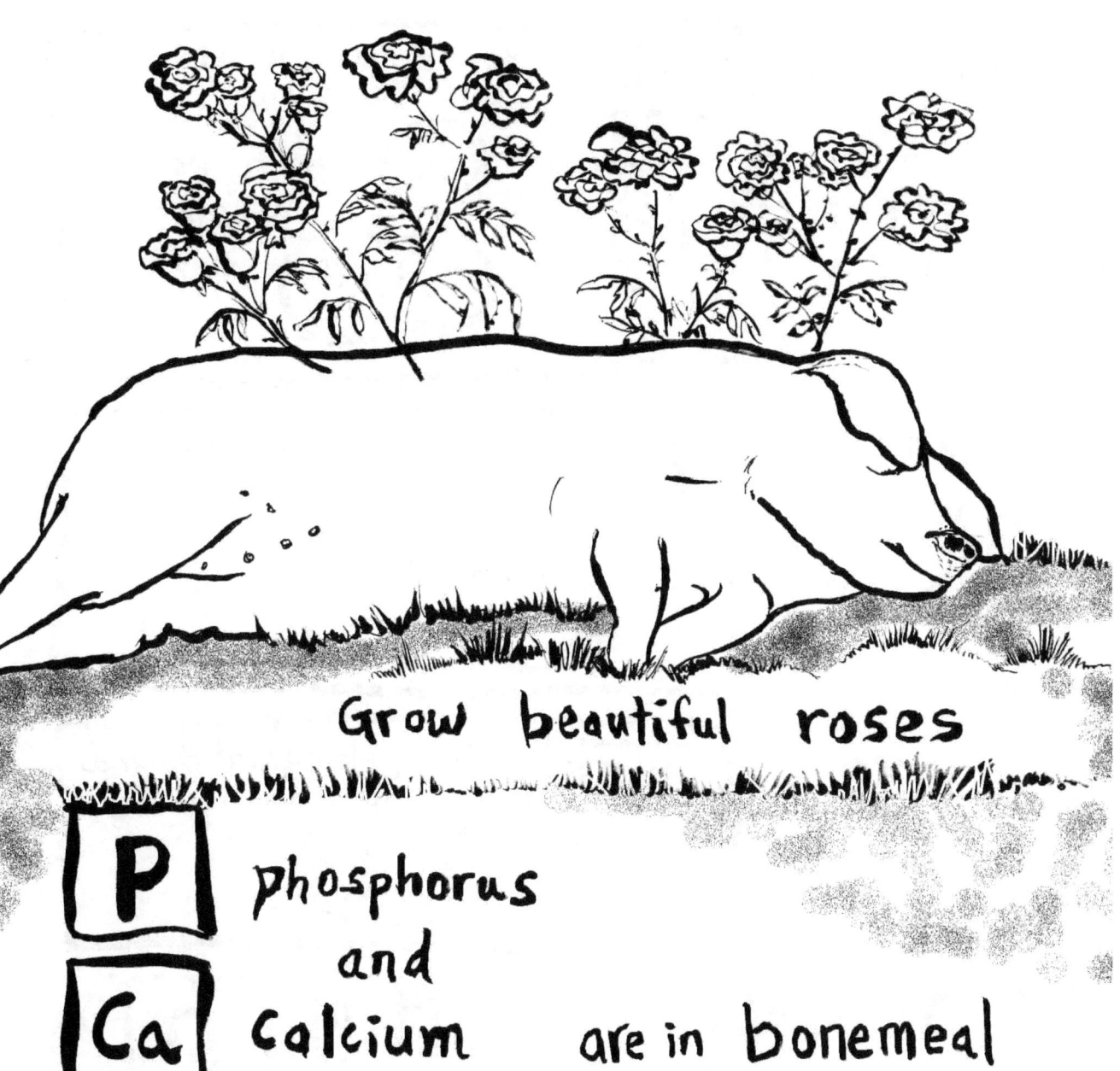

When can phosphorus get sucked up into the plant?

Soil pH is a little alkaline: (>7.3)

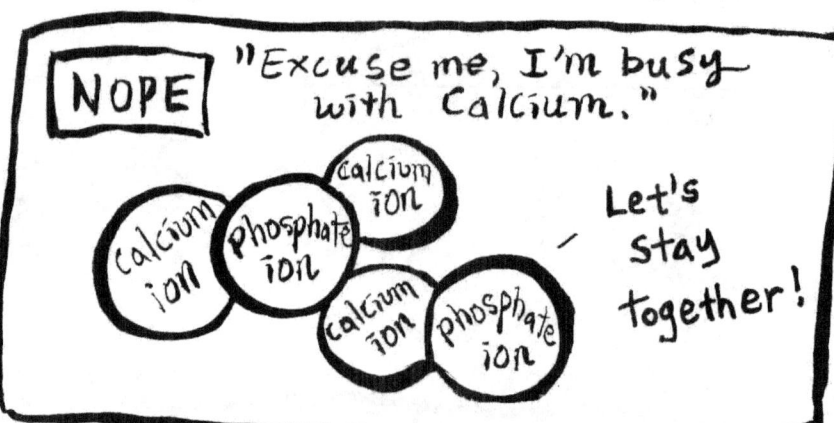

Soil pH is a bit acidic: (<6)

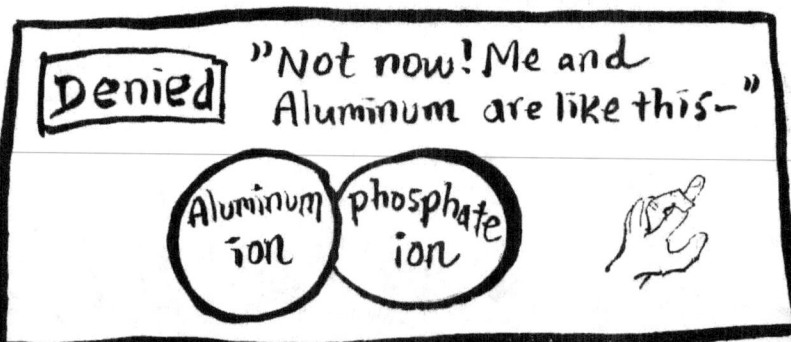

Even more acidic: Soil pH (<5)

IMPORTANCE OF pH IN NUTRIENT ABSORBTION

[P] phosphorus

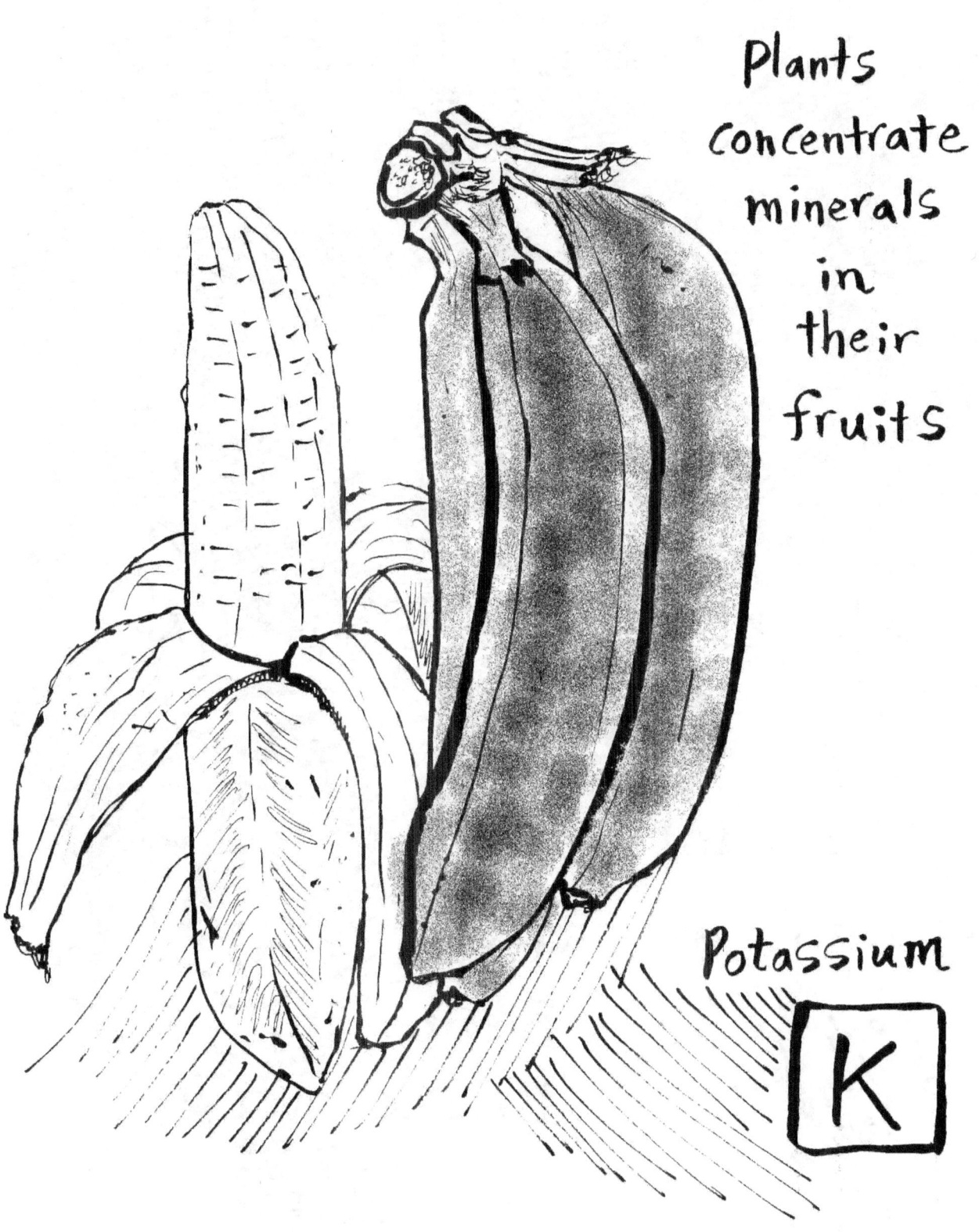

Calcium

Calcium is everywhere. It is in snail and eggs shells, bones and teeth, coral reefs, orange juice, and the gypsum walls of houses. Among the rocks, it is commonly bound to sulfur.

Calcium helps move nutrients in and out of plant cells, and activates enzymes to do work. An enzyme is a protein that gets things happening and moves processes along. Plant use calcium to make the walls of their cells strong.

Sulfur

Sulfur is a bright yellow crystal. In nature, it is often hanging out together with hydrogen and oxygen. It is a part of many plant proteins and vitamins. It is essential in the manufacture of chloroplasts for photosynthesis. Chloroplasts are tiny flat green creatures that capture the sunlight.

When you add sulfur to the soil, it slowly increases the concentration of $H+$ ions and makes the soil more acidic. Sulfur is also a great fungicide – it prevents and controls the fungi that feed on apples, grapes, tomatoes, and more.

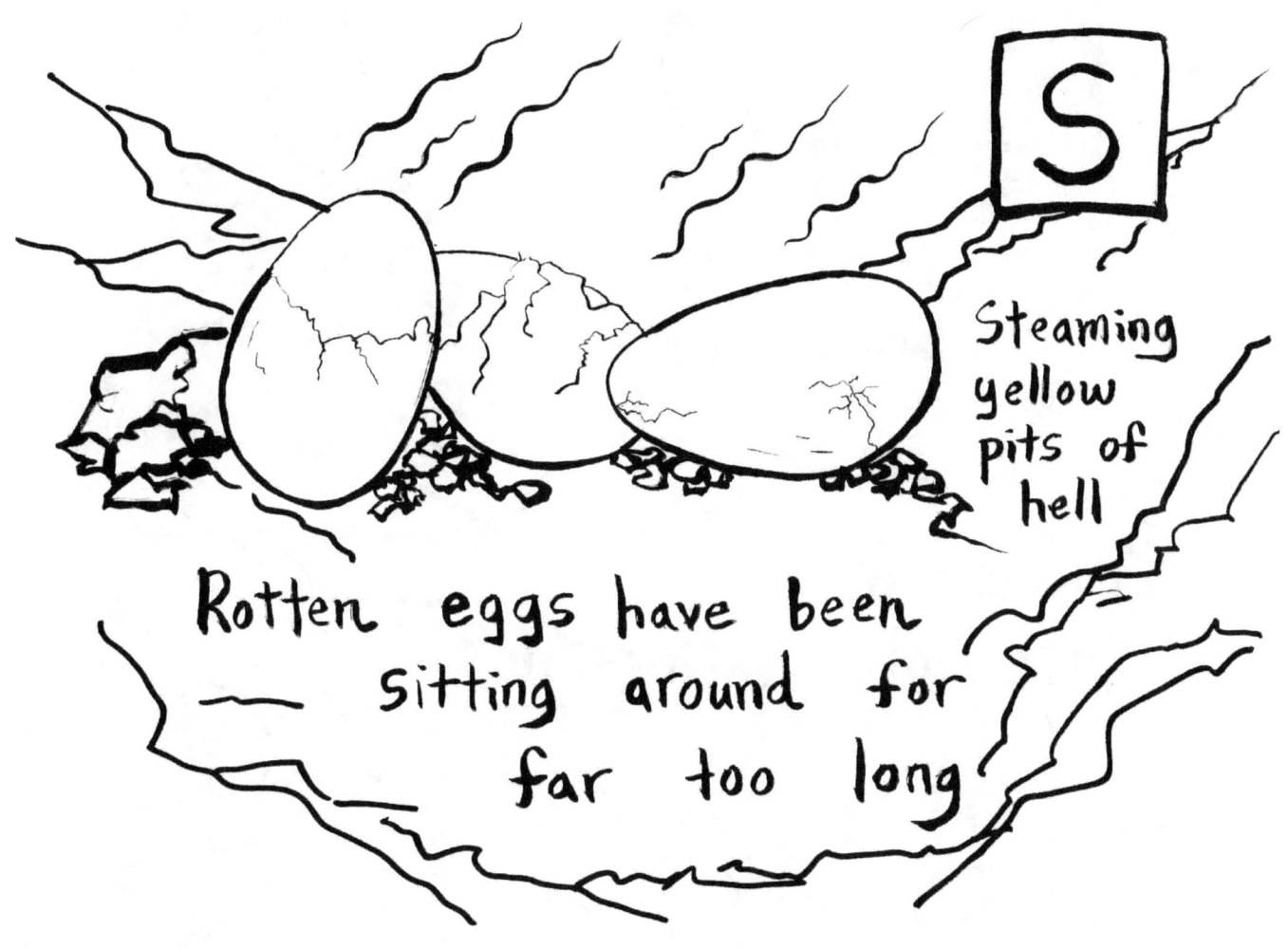

Magnesium

Magnesium is a metal, with an ion that dissolves easily in water. It is at the center of the chlorophyll molecule that drives photosynthesis. Many enzymes in plant cells need magnesium to function. Magnesium helps seeds to germinate, and assists in the formation of fats, sugars, proteins, and vitamins. Green leaves like spinach have plenty of magnesium.

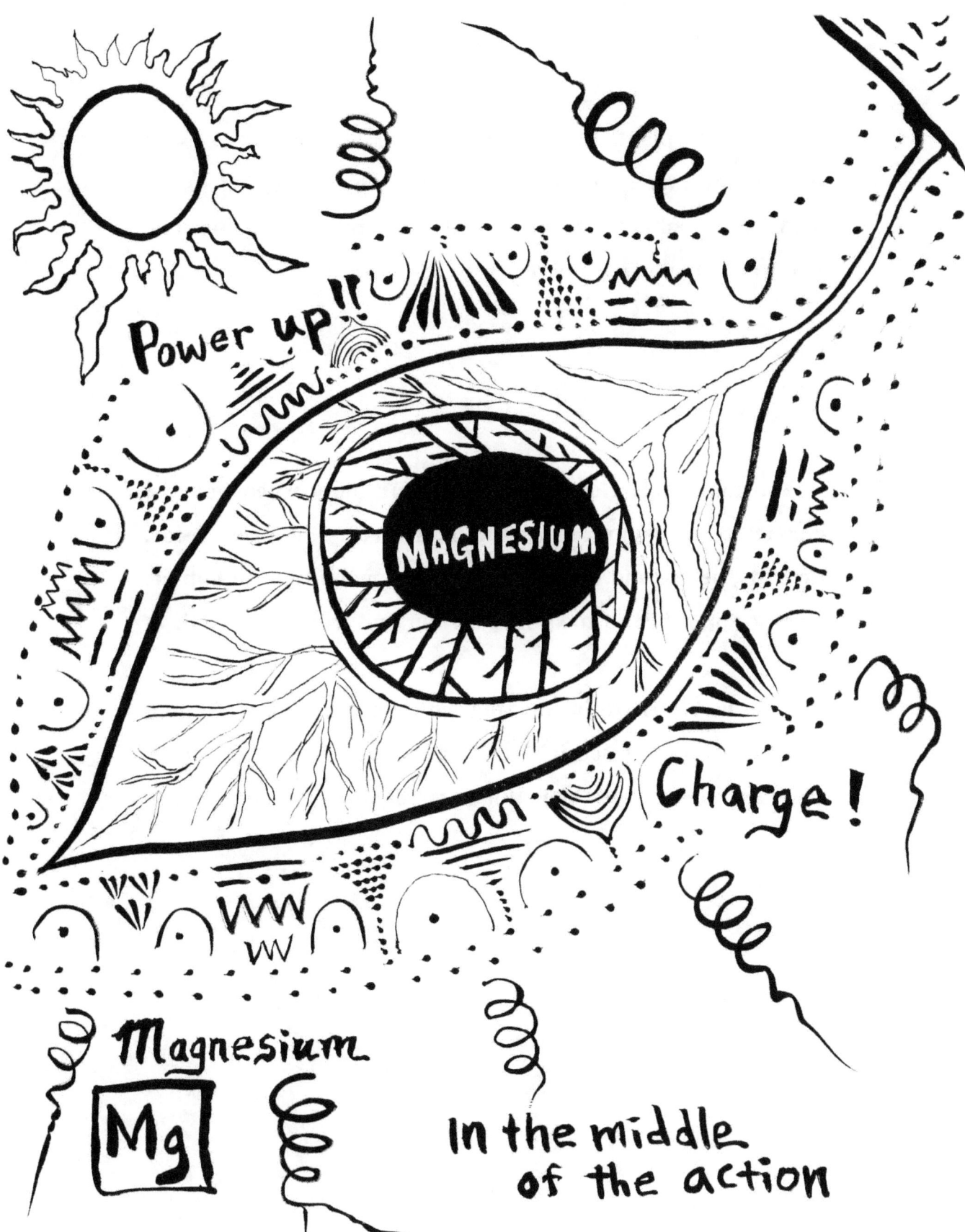

Over time, plants have adapted to live in a diversity of soils all over the earth. In the soil, there are elements that plants need in tiny amounts to grow and make more of themselves. These are called micronutrients. A few of these are:

Zinc

You make this element part of your body when you eat sesame seeds, poppy seeds, pumpkin seeds, sunflower seeds, almonds, beans, and nuts. It is a silvery metal that, in nature, is often found bound to sulfur, carbon and iron as a chunk of rock.

Zinc is required in making chlorophyll and activating enzymes. It is essential in forming and breaking down carbohydrates, and in the making of proteins.

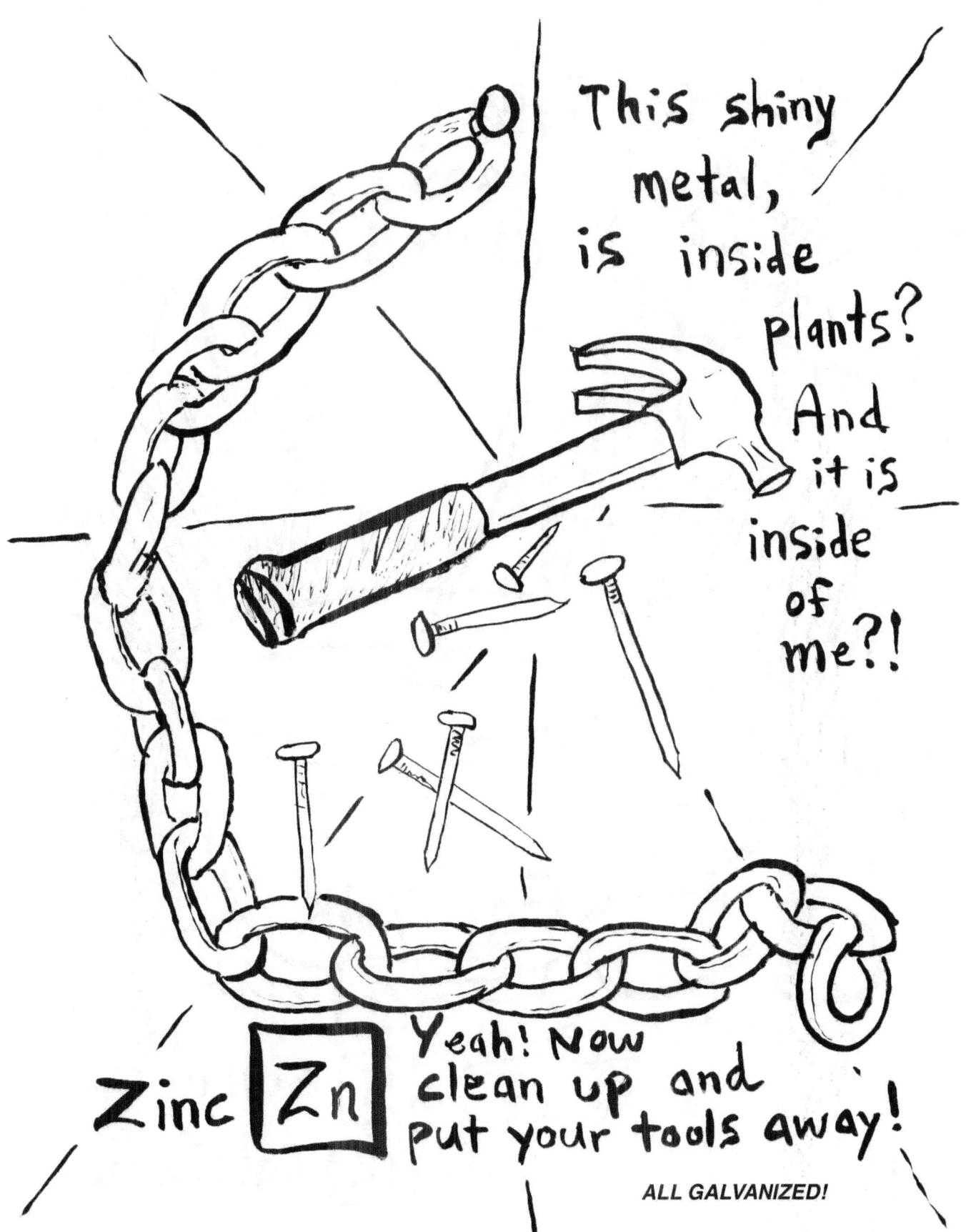

Iron

Iron is a metal found in nuggets of ore carved from the earth. When combined with carbon, iron makes steel. Steel buildings, steel boats, steel planes, steel knives, steel hand pruners. Iron burns slowly in the company of oxygen and water; it gets rusty and breaks apart. There is iron in your red blood cells. If you don't eat enough iron rich foods you may get sick and anemic. Too much iron stored in your body can also be toxic and poisonous.

Iron is necessary to make chlorophyll for photosynthesis. When plants do not have enough iron, it shows in the color of their leaves. It has green veins and yellow leaves, and this occurs to young leaves at the tips. Lack of iron is a problem in soils that are high in pH – soils with few H+ ions.

Copper

Copper is a soft metal useful for making water pipes, pennies, and electric wires. When a shiny copper penny meets oxygen it begins to go black and dull.

Copper is essential in the making of plant cell walls. It is needed for photosynthesis and enzyme functions.

Sodium

Sodium is a soft silver and white metal that dissolves into water. It is found as a compound and not as a free element floating around. Rare on land, it happily dissolves into lakes and oceans. Taste the salty sea!

Sodium cleans. Sodium preserves food, and slows down rot. Soaps can be made with a mixture of sodium and an oil or fat.

In living creatures like plants, sodium helps to maintain the healthy balance of ions in the cells as water sloshes in and sloshes out.

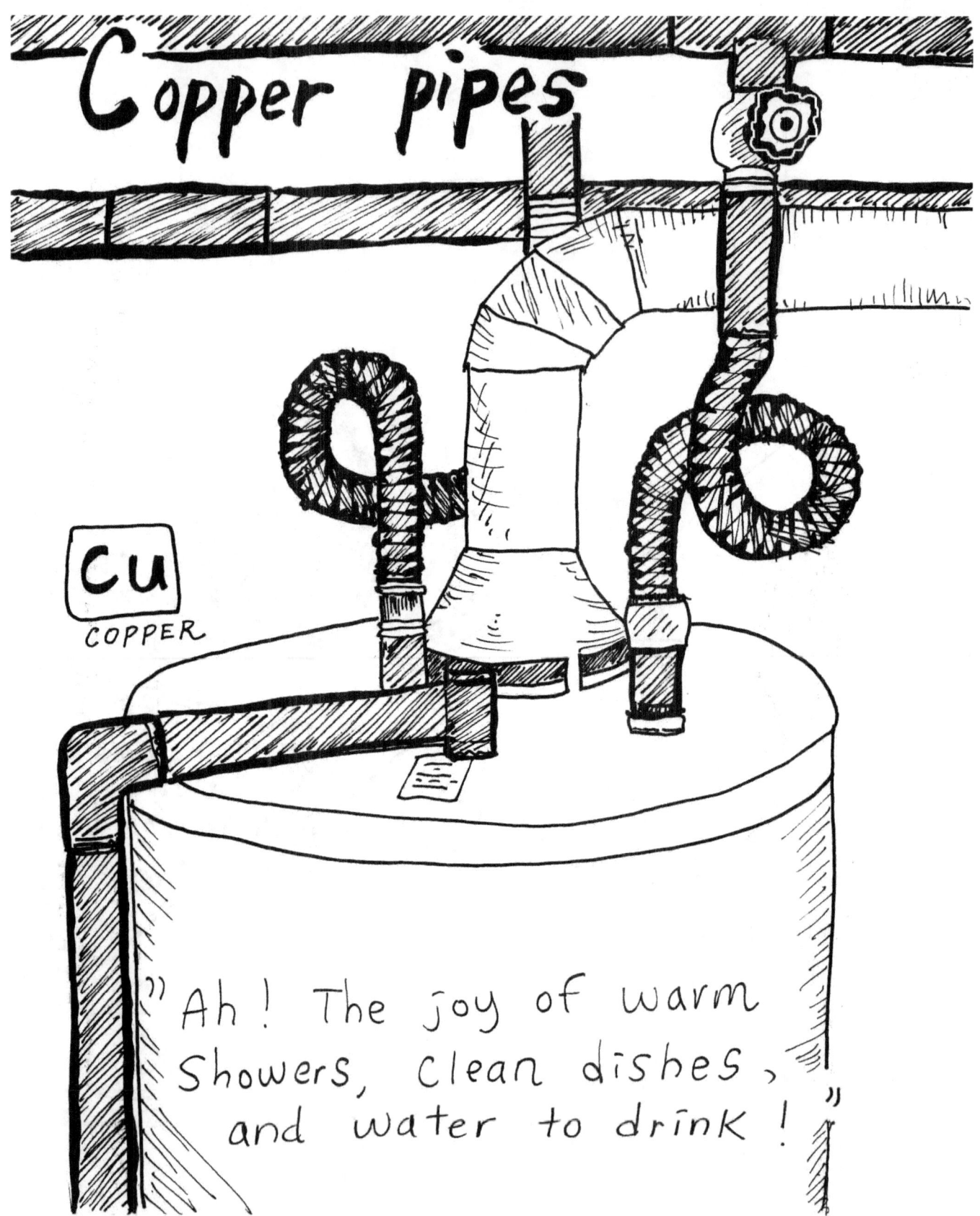

From Italian Dry to Frozen Fish:

- Sodium C14-C16 Olefin sulfonate
- Sodium nitrate
- Sodium nitrite
- Salt
- Tetrasodium etidronate (SOAP)
- Sodium tallowate
- Sodium chloride
- Sodium stearate
- Sodium laureth sulfate (HERBAL LOVE SHAMPOO with Jojoba Rose hips)
- Sodium lauryl sulfate
- Salt (ORGANIC CREAMY PEANUT BUTTER, Made with U.S. Grown)
- Monosodium glutamate
- Disodium inosinate
- Disodium guanylate
- TABLE SALT
- Salt (BUTTER)

味噌 (MISO)

Na Sodium: the element that is everywhere!!!

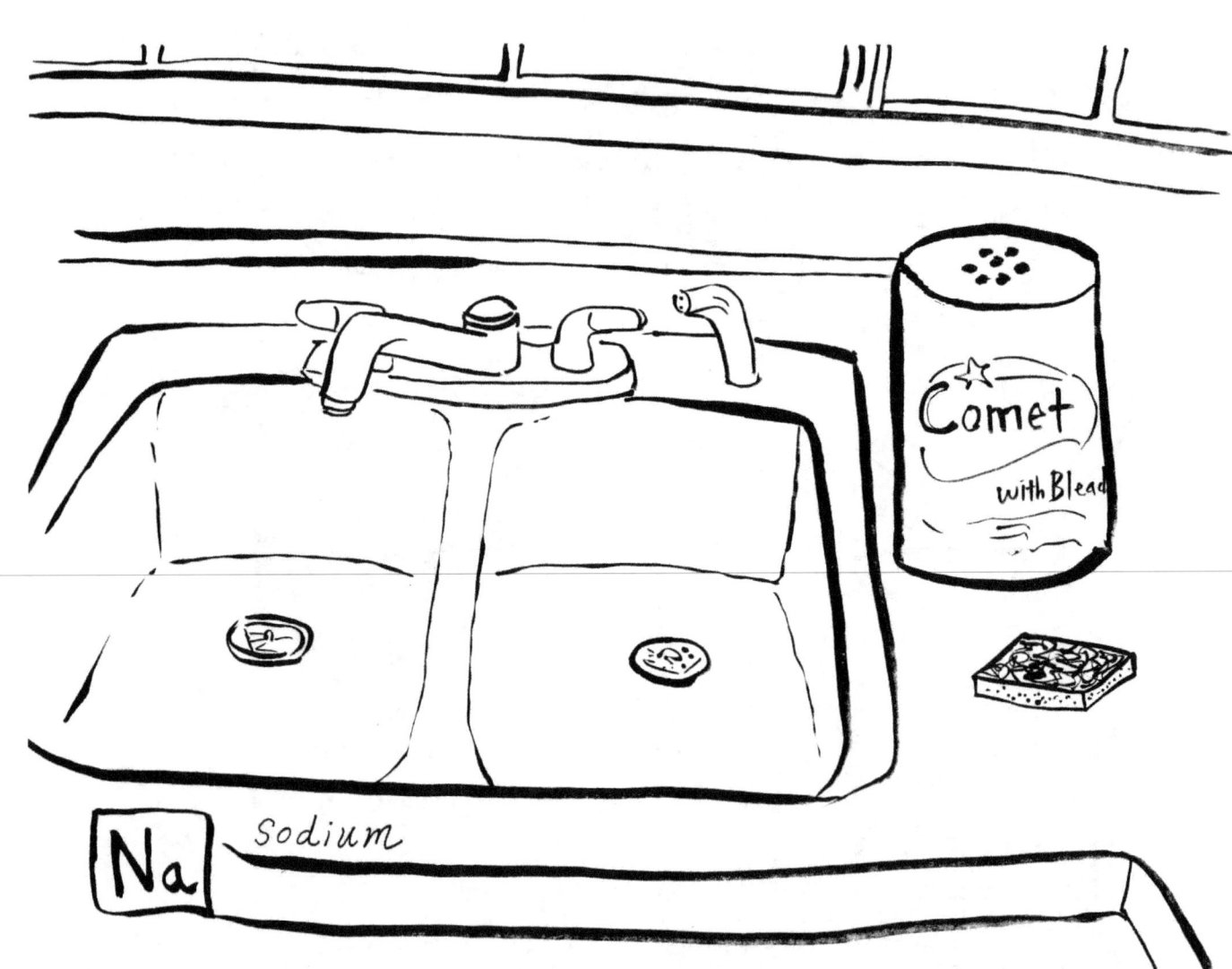

Silicon

Crystals of silicon compounds coat cover the skin of the world. Sand sand sandy beaches are made of silicon and oxygen. Silicon is the glass holding the merlot, and a ceramic pot of rice wine. Silicon makes up the smooth sidewalk of concrete, and carries electric signals inside of computers and stereos.

In plants, silicon makes strong cell walls so that aphids sucking on stems or beetles chewing on leaves have a harder time getting through. Silicon helps a plant survive and resist disease when there is little water, or when the soil is overloaded with heavy metals ions.

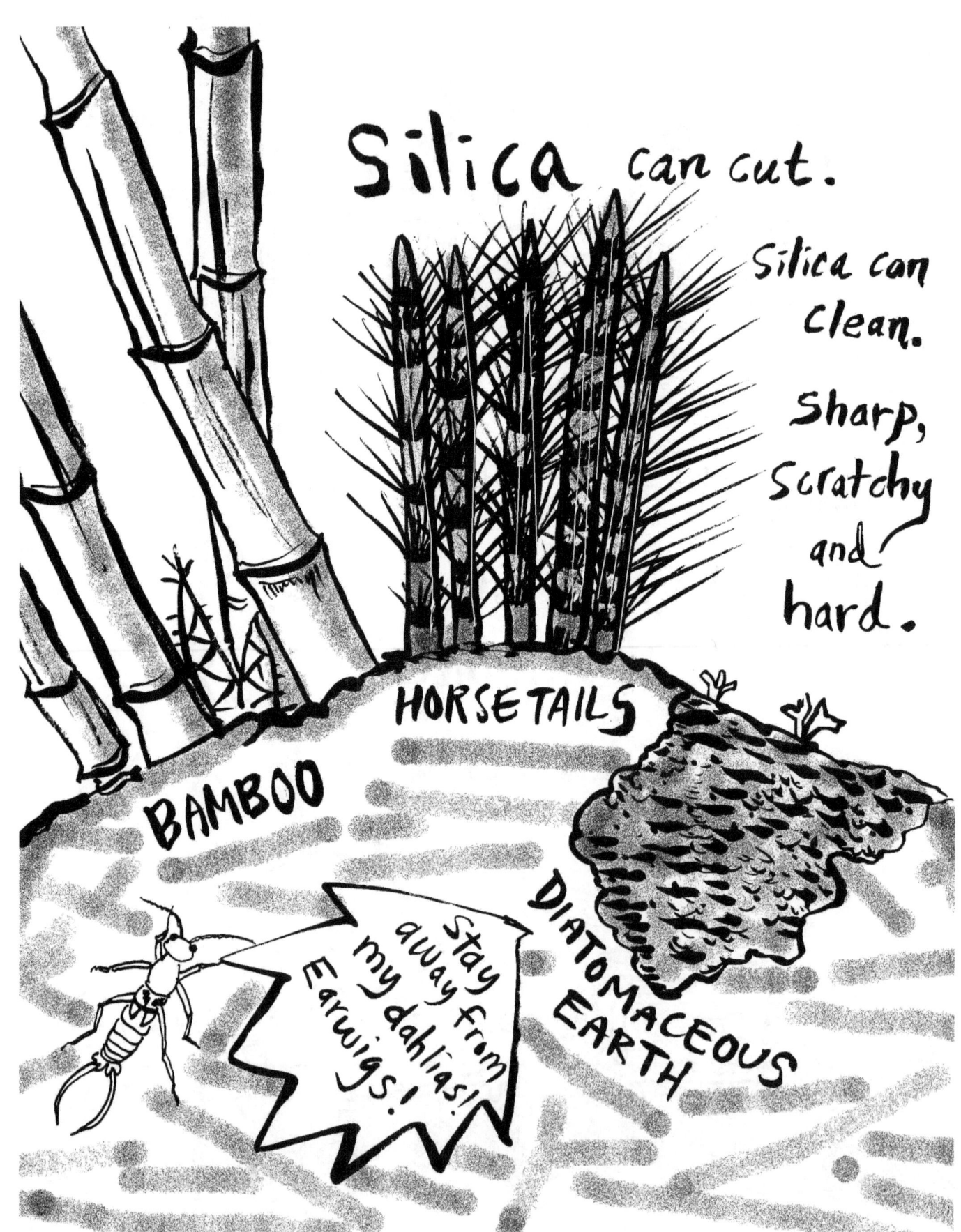

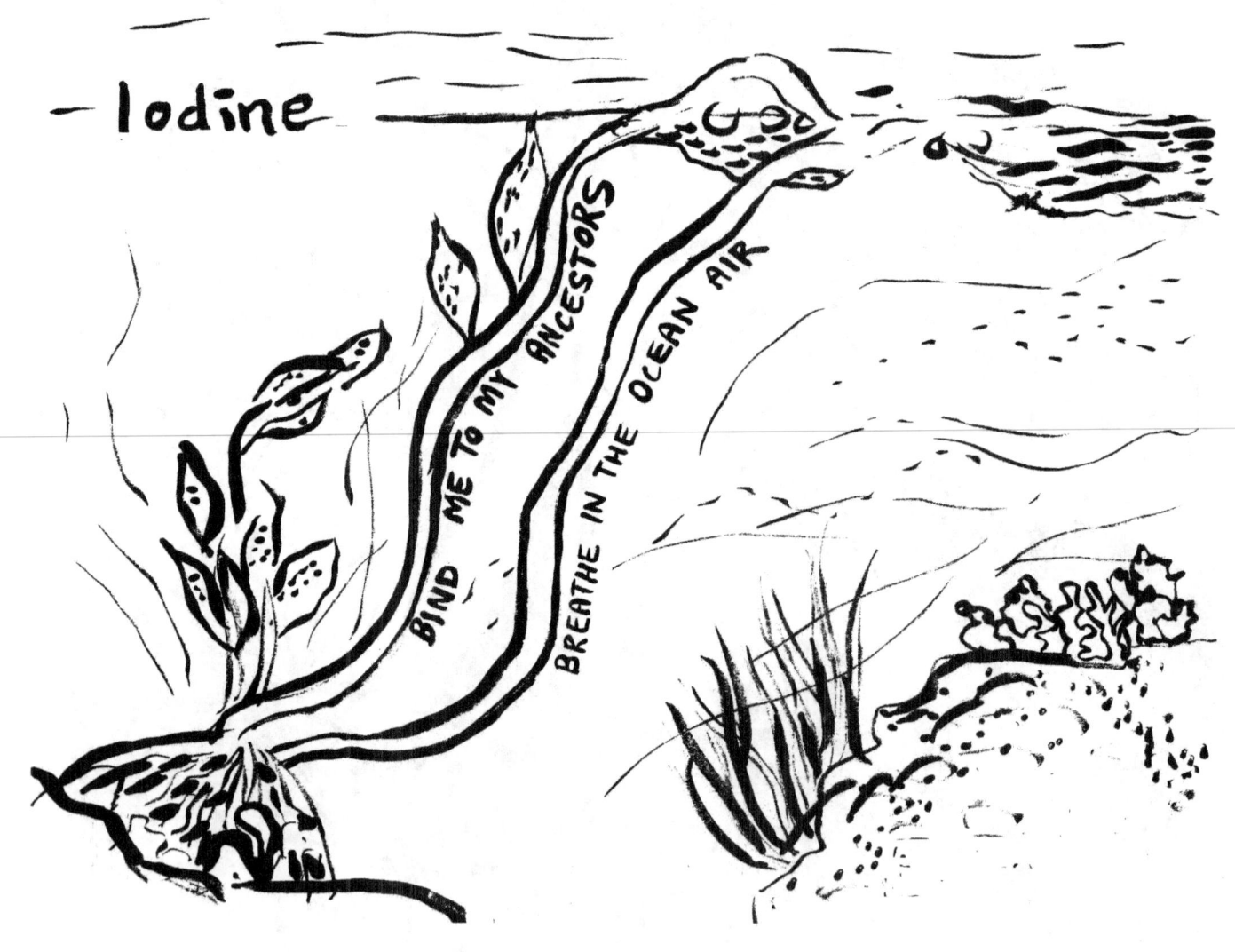

Places to go

The great thing about plants is that they are everywhere. You can begin your studies indoors with houseplants, or by walking out the door. The garden has infinite depth and detail; it is a place that will keep your mind, body, and spirit in good company during time spent on this earth.

Vocabulary words and nature concepts to understand and explore:

PLANT WORLD

Air and wind
Lenticels and stomata; plants as windbreaks; high pressure and low pressure systems; wind formation; indoor air pollution and filters; plant adaptations to windy areas

Water and rain
Condensation and cloud formation; precipitation; transpiration and infiltration; hydroelectricity and turbines; turgor pressure; field capacity and permanent wilting point; irrigation and canals; surface tension; infusions and decoctions

Earth and soil
Soil formation; senescence, decay and decomposition; drainage and erosion; sedimentation; leaching of nutrients; nutrient cycle; soil aeration and compaction; humus and compost formation; liming of soils; loss of topsoil; saturated soil; potting soil ingredients

Fire and light
Fire ecology and burn cycles; solar radiation and thermoregulation; purification and cleansing rituals

FROM ROOTS TO SPORES

Roots
Types: adventitious, aerial, aquatic, lateral, sinker, tap, fibrous

Stems
Resin canals; asexual reproduction; leaf offsets; stem variations: corm, bulb, stolon, tuber, rhizome, pup; succulence; meristems

Wood
Latex vessels; dormant buds; branch collar ridge and compartmentalization

Leaves
Evergreen and deciduous; Crassulacean Acid Metabolism

Growth and repair
Sugars and starch storage; abscission zone; auxin; ethylene gas; amino acids and protein formation; traditional culture food combinations; respiration and photosynthesis

Flowers
Monoecious and dioecious; nectar guides and nectar cups; platform type flowers; staminate and pistillate flowers

Pollination
Wind & water, insect and animal pollination; photoperiod long and short

Fertilization
Fusion of gametes; genetic recombination

Fruit
Types: accessory, aggregate, berry, capsule, caryopsis, cypsela, dehiscent and indehiscent, drupe, fibrous drupe, legume, multiple fruit, nut, pepo, samara, schizocarp, silicle

Seed
Etiolation; phototropism and geotropism; dispersal; scarification and stratification; seed viability over time

Spore
Gametophyte and sporophyte stages; sorus; sporulation

AMONGST FRIENDS AND DECOMPOSERS

Plant parasites
Obligate and facultative parasitism; stem and root parasites; holo- and hemi- parasites

Birds
Predation; migration and flyways

Mammals
Girdling; manual, biological, cultural, and chemical controls

Reptiles and amphibians

Pesticides and permeable skins

Arthropods
Parthenogenesis; Batesian mimicry; beneficial insects; gall formation; herbivory; Integrated Pest Management (IPM); complete and incomplete metamorphosis; stress and pest resistance; chewing and sucking mouthparts

Fungi
Fermentation of sugars; deliquescence; entheogenic and shamanic use; mycorrhizal; saprophytic; parasitic; mutualism and cooperation; mycelium and hyphae

Worms
Soil fertility and worm castings; soil structure and aggregations; vermiculture

Snails and slugs
Heliciculture and escargot; apophallation; hermaphroditism

Bacteria and relatives
Antibiotic resistance; gut flora and human symbionts; binary fission; rhizosphere and nitrogen fixation

Viruses
Vectors for disease; mosaic; variegation

FAMILIES AND TEACHERS

Cone or no cone
Spermatophytes and gametophyte stages

Botany versus horticulture
Plant form, growth habit; edible and ornamental plants; plant life zones

Leafy diversity
Venation; juvenile and adult foliage

Folk and butterfly classification
Oviposition preference; butterfly host plants

TRANSFORMATION

Atoms and molecules
Carbon cycle; hydrogen bonds

Elements and compounds, Ions, Plant nutrients
Cation exchange capacity; fertilizer salts; anions and cations; hydrogen ion pump

Oxygen
Anaerobic conditions; eutrophication, hypoxia in fish, algal blooms; atmosphere of the earth

Hydrogen
Nutrient availability and pH; acid rain; nitrification and fertilizer use; plant root activity; nutrient deficiency and toxicity

Carbon
Sheet mulching; carbon combustion and greenhouse effect; carbon sequestering in oceans and calcium carbonate

Nitrogen
Hydroponics; nitrogen fixing bacteria; ammonification; nitrification; denitrification; oceanic dead zones